EINSTEIN
RELATIVELY SIMPLE
Our Universe Revealed
in Everyday Language

COLLECTION MANAGEMENT

EINSTEIN
RELATIVELY SIMPLE
Our Universe Revealed
in Everyday Language

Ira Mark Egdall

World Scientific

NEW JERSEY · LONDON · SINGAPORE · BEIJING · SHANGHAI · HONG KONG · TAIPEI · CHENNAI

Published by

World Scientific Publishing Co. Pte. Ltd.

5 Toh Tuck Link, Singapore 596224

USA office: 27 Warren Street, Suite 401-402, Hackensack, NJ 07601

UK office: 57 Shelton Street, Covent Garden, London WC2H 9HE

Library of Congress Cataloging-in-Publication Data
Egdall, Ira Mark, author.
 Einstein relatively simple : our universe revealed in everyday language / Ira Mark Egdall.
  pages cm
 Includes bibliographical references and index.
 ISBN 978-9814525589 (hard : alk. paper) -- ISBN 978-9814525596 (pbk)
 1. Einstein, Albert, 1879-1955--Influence. 2. Relativity (Physics) I. Title.
 QC16.E5E25 2013
 530.11--dc23

                                                      2013033953

British Library Cataloguing-in-Publication Data
A catalogue record for this book is available from the British Library.

First published 2014
Reprinted 2014

In-house Editor: Rhaimie Wahap

530.11

Typeset by Stallion Press
Email: enquiries@stallionpress.com

Printed in Singapore by Fuisland Offset Printing (S) Pte Ltd

To the memory of my father,
who taught me to appreciate the wonders of science.

To the memory of my mother,
who taught me to see beauty in the world.

About the Author

IRA MARK EGDALL

Einstein Relatively Simple

Ira Mark Egdall is the author of the eBook *Unsung Heroes of the Universe* and a popular science writer for DecodedScience.com. He is a retired aerospace program manager with an undergraduate degree in physics from Northeastern University. Mark now teaches lay courses in modern physics at Lifelong Learning Institutes at Florida International University, the University of Miami, and Nova Southeastern University. He also gives entertaining talks on Einstein and time travel. When not thinking about physics, Mark spends his time playing with his grandchildren and driving his wife of 45 years crazy.

www.iramarkegdall.com

Prologue

All knowledge begins in wonder.

Aristotle

In June of 1905, former high-school drop-out and lowly patent clerk Albert Einstein published a paper in the German *Annals of Physics* which revolutionized our understanding of space and time. What came to be known as the theory of special relativity predicted a strange new universe where time slows and space shrinks with motion.

In that same journal, Einstein proposed light comes in discreet packets of energy we now call photons. Along with Max Planck's work, this insight sparked the quantum revolution. This in turn set off the greatest technological revolution in human history — enabling the invention of television, transistors, electronic digital computers, cell phones, digital cameras, lasers, the electron microscope, atomic clocks, MRI, sonograms, and many more modern-day devices.

Einstein's follow-up article in September of 1905 proposed that mass and energy are equivalent. His famous equation, $E = mc^2$, came to solve one of the great mysteries of modern science — how the Sun and stars shine. Some four decades later, Einstein's breakthrough ushered in the atomic age.

In December of 1915, Albert Einstein — now Professor of Theoretical Physics at the University of Berlin — surpassed his already staggering accomplishments. In the midst of the turmoil and hardships of World War I, he produced his life's masterpiece: a new theory of gravity. His audacious general theory of relativity revealed a cosmos beyond our wildest imagination. It predicted phenomena so bizarre even Einstein initially doubted their existence — black holes which trap light and stop time, wormholes which form gravitational time machines, the expansion of space itself, and the birth of the universe some 13.8 billion years ago in the ultimate cosmic event: the Big Bang.

Not since Isaac Newton had a single physicist attained such monumental breakthroughs, and no scientist since has matched his breathtaking achievements. In recognition, *TIME* magazine selected Albert Einstein above such luminaries as Franklin Delano Roosevelt and Mohandas Gandhi, as the "Person of the Century" — the single individual with the most significant impact on the 20th century.

Albert Einstein has long since passed from this corporal world. Yet his fame lives on. His discoveries inspire today's generation of physicists — providing stepping stones to a new understanding of the cosmos and perhaps someday a unified theory of all physics. His brilliance, independence of mind, and persistence continue to be an inspiration to us all. He remains the iconic figure of science, whose genius transcends the limits of human understanding.

I wrote *Einstein Relatively Simple* to tell Einstein's story — to hopefully provide the non-expert a clear, step-by-step explanation of how he came to develop both special and general relativity. My goal is a book which is comprehensive, fun to read, and most important, understandable to the lay reader.

With this in mind, the book emphasizes the concepts behind Einstein's theories rather than the mathematics. Analogies and real-life examples serve to illuminate their mind-bending implications. Fanciful stories, from talking particles to alien abductions, offer comic relief while providing a setting for understanding the physics.

I first introduce Einstein the man and then ease into the core tenets of relativity. I feel that understanding the history behind the science — as well as how a scientist thinks — helps us comprehend his theories. The book also cites key historical experiments which confirm predictions of relativity to help the reader accept Einstein's counterintuitive ideas.

Einstein Relatively Simple is based on lay courses in modern physics I teach at Lifelong Learning Institutes at several universities in South Florida.

My students come from all walks of life. Most have no prior background in physics or mathematics.

Can a non-expert really understand Einstein's theories, at least at some level? My teaching experience says yes. After all, you don't have to be an artist to appreciate the beauty of a Michelangelo — you just need to be able to see. You don't need to be a musician to feel the majesty of a Beethoven symphony — you just need to be able to hear. And I believe you do not have to be a trained physicist to appreciate the beauty and grandeur of Einstein's theories — you just need to be able to think.

It is my hope that scientists, engineers, mathematicians, and others in the technology field, as well as educators and undergraduate physics majors (especially those studying relativity for the first time) will also find this book enlightening. The conceptual approach and history of relativity's development presented in *Einstein Relatively Simple* should help crystallize fundamental principles.

Why yet another popular science book on relativity? I have read over 80 popular science books on modern physics, yet have had great difficulty finding a book on relativity which is thorough and at a level my lay students can understand — particularly general relativity. Most popular science books give general relativity short shrift or ignore the subject all together. It is also my hope that *Einstein Relatively Simple* fills this gap in the current literature.

The book is structured on several levels:

- *The text itself* — Explains basic concepts through analogies and stories with minimal to no mathematics.
- *Grey-shaded areas within the text* — Provides high-school level mathematical details. (The reader may skip these grey areas, and still get the core message of each concept.)
- *Appendices* — Expands upon key topics. (Sometimes involves basic calculus.)
- *Endnotes* — Provides additional material for those gluttons for punishment who wish to delve more deeply into the history, physics, and supporting mathematics. (Sometimes involves basic calculus.)

So come explore how an unknown patent clerk came to develop a new theory of time and space, how he came to supplant the illustrious

Isaac Newton with a new theory of gravity. Along the way we will examine the mind of Albert Einstein, who preferred to think in pictures rather than words, follow his thinking, his logic, and his insights.

To quote one of my students; "You'll never look at the universe the same way again!"

Contents

About the Author   vii

Prologue   ix

**PART I   Einstein Discovered: Special Relativity, E = mc²,
            and Spacetime**   **1**

Chapter 1   From Unknown to Revolutionary   3
Chapter 2   The Great Conflict   15
Chapter 3   The Two Postulates   35
Chapter 4   A New Reality   47
Chapter 5   The Shrinking of Time   57
Chapter 6   Simultaneity and the Squeezing of Space   67
Chapter 7   The World's Most Famous Equation   83
Chapter 8   Spacetime   109

**PART II   Einstein Revealed: General Relativity, Gravity,
            and the Cosmos**   **137**

Chapter 9   Einstein's Dream   139
Chapter 10   "The Happiest Thought of My Life"   151
Chapter 11   The Warping of Space and Time   173
Chapter 12   Stitching Spacetime   187
Chapter 13   What is Spacetime Curvature?   195
Chapter 14   Einstein's Masterpiece   215

Chapter 15   The Universe Revealed   231
Chapter 16   In the Beginning   249

Epilogue   269
Appendix A   279
Appendix B   285
Appendix C   291
Appendix D   295
Appendix E   297
Acknowledgements   303
Notes with Sources   305
Figure Credits   359
Also by Ira Mark Egdall   363
Further Reading   365
Index   367

PART I

Einstein Discovered: Special Relativity, $E = mc^2$, and Spacetime

Chapter 1

From Unknown to Revolutionary

The most beautiful thing we can experience is the mysterious.
It is the source of all true art and all science.[1]

Albert Einstein

The year is 1905. Working alone at a Government Issue desk at the Swiss patent office on the corner of Grain Storage and Geneva Lane in Berne, a brash young man with a driving passion for physics is stuck. He has been wrestling with the problem off-and-on for nearly a decade.

His passion has become an obsession. He works on it in every spare moment at the patent office. He discusses the problem with his friend on walks home from work. His thoughts turn to it while in his small apartment with his wife, rocking his new son in his bassinet.

Then one fine day in May it comes to him. "I've completely solved the problem," he tells his friend. "An analysis of the concept of *time* is my solution," he declares over the clip-clop of horse-drawn buggies and rumble of new-fangled motor cars.[2] With this insight, it all falls into place.

In that eureka moment on the streets of Berne, 26-year-old Albert Einstein altered our concept of reality forever. Einstein had begun the "relativity revolution" — a startling new vision on the nature of time and space.

It's Relative!

Einstein's strange new theory came to be called special relativity because it deals with the special case of motion called *uniform* motion.[3] What is

3

uniform motion? An object which travels at a constant speed and in a constant direction is in uniform motion.

Say you are in your car heading north at a speed of 60 miles an hour. As long as you don't speed up or slow down or steer the car in another direction, your car is in uniform motion. (Since, in physics, velocity is defined as both speed and direction, uniform motion is also referred to as traveling at a constant velocity.)

Special relativity, however, said nothing about *non*-uniform motion, where speed or direction does change. Nor did it take into account the effects of gravity. Despite these limitations, Einstein showed the fundamental science accepted for centuries by physicists and lay people alike was wrong. Time and space are not absolute, they are not the same for everyone — they are *relative*.

What does this mean?[4] Let's take a look. Hold on to your hats — this is very strange:

Time is Relative

According to special relativity, *clocks run slower when they move through space.*[5]

Imagine you are attending one of my fascinating physics lectures. Hey, you in the back, wake up! Assume we are both wearing identical super-accurate watches. Say I walk across the front of the classroom at a steady pace — while you remain seated.

Per Einstein, you see my watch running a tiny bit slower than your watch. Why? Because I am moving with respect to you.

Now at the speed I am walking, this slowing of time is a very small effect — less than a billionth of a billionth of a second for each elapsed second. That's why we don't notice it. Nonetheless, it is a real effect.

The slowing of time becomes dramatic at speeds approaching the speed of light. Say I somehow speed by you at 87% the speed of light or about 580 million miles an hour. Because of my tremendous speed, you now see my watch running at only *half the rate* of your watch. That is, for every second that ticks off on your watch, only a half-second ticks off on mine. This is what you see and measure.

The next question is: what do I see? I see the exact opposite — I see your watch running slower than mine! As strange as this sounds, this is exactly what Einstein's theory of special relativity predicts.

Whose point of view is correct? They both are. Time is relative. If your head is beginning to hurt, it means you are beginning to grasp the counter-intuitive ideas of relativity.

Per Einstein's theory, space is also affected by motion:

Space is Relative

Say I now walk across the same room, this time holding up a pen in my hand pointed in my direction of motion. What do you see? You measure the length of my pen as *shortened* — because I am moving with respect to you. Per special relativity, *the length of an object contracts along its direction of motion.*[6]

This effect is also extremely tiny at walking speeds. That is why we don't notice it. But if I were to somehow streak across the room at 87% the speed of light, then you would measure my pen compressed to *half* its length!

What do I see? Again, just the opposite. If you hold up a pen (oriented in the same direction), I measure your pen as shortened by half.

So if I am moving with respect to you, you measure my pen as shortened — and I measure your pen as shortened. Whose point of view is correct? They both are. Space is relative.

Why didn't anyone notice these effects before Einstein? Because, as noted, they only become significant at so-called relativistic speeds — speeds which are an appreciable fraction of the speed of light.

Relativistic Speed

The speed of light is an incredible 670 million miles an hour (approximately). Per Einstein's formula, we would have to travel at hundreds of millions of miles an hour to notice relativity effects. But we don't experience anywhere near these speeds in everyday life. A commercial jet, for instance, travels at some 600 miles an hour relative to the ground, which is only about a millionth the speed of light.

So at everyday speeds, the effects of special relativity are simply too small to notice.[7] But they are still real. As we shall see, all kinds of evidence — from atomic clocks on airplanes, rockets, and satellites to the measured lifetimes of subatomic particles and countless laboratory experiments — have borne out virtually all of Einstein's incredible predictions.

What are we to conclude from over a century of evidence confirming the predictions of relativity? Albert Einstein's strange universe is our universe!

To understand how Einstein came to develop special relativity, how a virtual unknown upstaged the most prominent physicists of his time; we first need to understand a little about the man himself, his early life experiences, his education both formal and informal, and most important — the formation of his character. Let's take a brief look.

The Early Years

Albert Einstein was born on Friday, March 14, 1879 in Ulm, a small city on the banks of the Danube nestled in the German Bundesland of Baden-Württemberg bordering Bavaria. The Einstein family was amongst the 2% of the Ulm population of Jewish ancestry. However, neither parent was particularly religious.

His mother Pauline was the 21-year-old daughter of a well-to-do wholesale grain trader. His father, 32-year-old Hermann, prided himself on being a freethinker.[8] He was, nonetheless, "exceedingly friendly and wise," his son later recalled.[9]

The easygoing Hermann was an electrical engineer who showed "a marked inclination for mathematics".[10] Pauline, on the other hand, was an accomplished pianist noted for a rather strong personality. It appears that Albert got his technical abilities from his father and his extraordinary tenacity from his mother.

Reportedly, Albert did not speak until he was three years old. Then he exhibited an odd habit of whispering to himself. "Every sentence he uttered ... he repeated to himself softly," recalled his younger sister Maja (Fig. 1.1).[11] Because of this, the family maid labeled him "the dopy one."

Einstein's first encounter with science involved a pocket compass his father gave him. How, young Albert wondered, could the compass needle's direction be influenced by an invisible source, by something in empty space? "This experience made a deep and lasting impression on me," Einstein recalled.[12] "Something deeply hidden has to be behind things."

At age ten, his parents enrolled Albert in the prestigious Luitpold Gymnasium in Munich. It practiced a strict, formal, learning by rote method of instruction. Einstein hated it. He was a teacher's nightmare — smart, arrogant, bored, and stubborn, with little respect for authority.[13]

Figure 1.1.   Albert with his Sister Maja.

At age 12, led by what was to become a lifelong desire to find the unity in all things, Albert studied Judaism. He became quite religious for a brief time. But then Max Talmud, a poor Jewish medical student befriended by the family, introduced Albert to popular books in science as well as texts in mathematics and philosophy.[14]

"Through reading (about science), I soon reached the conviction that much in the stories of the Bible could not be true," Albert concluded.[15] "Suspicion against every kind of authority grew out of this experience, an attitude which has never left me."[16]

At age 15, Einstein was expelled by the headmaster of the Gymnasium for disruptions in class and disrespect for teachers.[17] A year later, without completing high school, Albert took entrance exams to a teachers college in Switzerland — the Swiss Federal Polytechnical Institute in Zurich.[18] "Zurich Poly" (later the "ETH") was considered one of the top schools for training mathematics and science teachers in Central Europe.

He failed in French, chemistry, and biology — subjects he did not care to learn — but did very well in mathematics and physics. Based on this, the principal of Zurich Poly arranged for Einstein to attend a small progressive non-denominational school in Aarau, Switzerland for additional instruction. Einstein (Fig. 1.2) then retook the Zurich Poly entrance exams and was accepted in the physics/mathematics program in 1896.

What was Albert's reaction to now being in college? He complained his classes were old-fashioned — they didn't even teach Maxwell's equations, the relatively new theory uniting electricity and magnetism. So the young rebel "played hooky a lot and studied the masters of theoretical physics with a holy zeal at home," as he later put it.[19]

Figure 1.2. Young Albert Einstein.

The only thing that interferes with my learning is my education.[20]

Albert Einstein

Einstein managed to graduate from Zurich Poly with an overall grade of 4.91 out of 6.0, a low B — fifth of the six math/physics students in his class. His "dark and intense Serbian" girlfriend Mileva Maríc, the only female physics student, received the lowest grade.[21] She was not allowed to graduate.

It was now July of 1900, with the 21-year-old college graduate looking for employment.[22] Einstein's impudent classroom behavior came back to haunt him. His physics professor, Heinrich Weber, had written unfavorable references about him. Albert found himself unable to find work and in poor financial straits.

After nearly two years of searching for a job, Einstein's college friend, mathematician Marcel Grossman, came to Einstein's rescue. Marcel's father knew the director of the Swiss patent office. With his help, Einstein landed a reasonably good-paying job as a patent examiner for the Swiss government. Einstein had just what the patent office needed — a physicist who could understand inventions in the growing field of electromagnetism.

I am doing well. I am an honorable federal ink pisser with a regular salary.[23]

Albert Einstein in a letter to a friend

8

So here was the man who was to become the greatest scientist of our age working as a Technical Expert 3rd Class (the lowest rank) reviewing patent applications. The year was 1902 and Einstein was now 23 years old. He worked on physics in every spare moment.

"I enjoyed my work at the office very much because it was uncommonly diversified," Einstein recalled.[24] "I was able to do a full day's work in only two or three hours. The remaining part of the day, I would work out my own ideas. When anyone would come by, I would cram my notes into my desk drawer and pretend to work on my office job."

Later that year, Einstein's father Hermann died. This was "the deepest shock I had ever experienced," Einstein recalled.[25] On his deathbed, Hermann reluctantly gave his consent to the marriage of Albert and his college sweetheart, Mileva Maríc . They were wed in early 1903 — no family members attended the ceremony.

The couple settled into a quiet family life in Berne and had their first son, Hans Albert, the following year. The young father liked to make toys for his boy. Years later his son still remembered a cable car his father made from odds and ends from around the house. "That was one of the nicest toys I had at the time and it worked," Hans recalled.[26] "Out of little string and matchboxes and so on, he could make the most beautiful things."

From 1900 to 1904, Einstein managed to get five physics papers published in the German *Annuls of Physics* (*Annalen der Physik*), Europe's leading physics journal. He wrote two of the manuscripts while working six days a week at the patent office. None were particularly noteworthy. He wrote to his sister, Maja wondering if he would ever make it.

During this period, however, the seeds of great ideas were percolating in young Einstein's mind. His thinking was rooted in the major scientific questions of the time.

Physics in 1900 — The End or the Beginning?

At dawn of the 20th century, physics was for the most part based on the works of three great scientists — Galileo, Newton, and Maxwell. (See Fig. 1.3.) In his treatise of 1638, the brilliant Tuscan scientist Galileo Galilei had established the science of *mechanics* — how forces affect the motion of objects. Among a number of notable achievements, Galileo provided the first formulas for how an object falls to Earth.

Galileo Galilei
(1564–1642)

Isaac Newton
(1643–1727)

James Clerk Maxwell
(1831–1879)

Figure 1.3. The Giants of Classical Physics at the Dawn of the 20th Century.

Some 50 years later, illustrious English genius Isaac Newton extended Galileo's work with ground-breaking theories in mechanics, optics, and universal gravity. Along the way he invented calculus.[27] His *Principia*, published in 1687, is considered the most influential book in the history of physics.

Nearly two centuries later, Scottish physicist James Clerk Maxwell established the third pillar of classical physics. He published his great opus uniting electricity and magnetism in 1864: his theory of *electromagnetism*.

The turn of the century (1900) was a heady time for scientists. First and foremost, there was the outstanding success of Isaac Newton's laws. The predictions of Newton's theories had proved remarkably accurate for over 200 years — from the motion of gases and everyday objects, the paths of the Sun, planets, moons, and comets, to the slightly oblate shape of the Earth and the timing of its tides.

And where Newton's laws did not work, Maxwell's theory took over. Maxwell's equations provided a solid foundation for understanding electricity and magnetism. Its predictive powers proved monumental — revealing light as an electromagnetic wave. By the end of the 19th century, the relationship between heat and energy was also well established, with significant advances in optics, chemistry, and molecular theory as well.

It appeared to some that the foundations of physics had been firmly established for all time. In 1900, physicist William Thomson aka Lord Kelvin reportedly declared: "There is nothing new to be discovered in physics now.[28] All that remains is more and more precise measurement." And when Max Planck, co-founder of quantum mechanics, first considered becoming a physicist, his advisor told him to "switch fields because physics was basically finished."[29]

There were, nonetheless, certain "anomalies" which no theory at the time could explain. In 1887, Heinrich Hertz discovered when you shine ultraviolet light on a metal surface, it loses electrical charge. No one could explain this strange "photoelectric effect". Nine years later, Henri Becquerel discovered that uranium salts emitted a continuous stream of radiation. How this so-called radioactivity worked was a mystery.

Heated objects gave off light only in specific colors, like the red glow of a hot poker.[30] No one knew why. The famous Michelson-Morley experiments failed to find the *ether*, the medium believed to be necessary for the transmission of light. And the orbit of Mercury was a tiny bit off from Newton's predictions.

And most important to our discussion here: No one could explain a stubborn disagreement between Newton's Laws and Maxwell's theory — a fundamental conflict concerning the effects of uniform motion.

Like the initial vibrations of an earthquake, the rumblings of change in the structure of classical physics had begun. Attempts in the early 20th century to uncover what was behind these anomalies would lead to a new set of nature's laws. At once strange and wonderful, these new theories would challenge our most fundamental assumptions about reality itself. They were:

- quantum mechanics.
- special relativity, and
- general relativity.

Quantum mechanics was developed by a number of physicists in the early 20th century, including Einstein. Quantum mechanics is beyond the scope of this book — it requires a book of its own. We discuss some aspects of the theory in the text and notes. Additional information can be found in the suggested reading.

Unlike quantum theory, the two theories of relativity were developed primarily by a single individual, Albert Einstein.

While cutting class and sipping coffee at cafes in Zurich — later in free moments at the patent office in Berne and at home with his wife Mileva and baby Hans Albert — Einstein pondered the physics issues of his day. He revealed the results of his contemplations in what we now call his "Miracle Year."

1905 — The Year of Einstein

In 1905, 26-six-year-old Albert Einstein published three papers in volume 17 of *Annalen der Physik* (Fig. 1.4) which would resolve conflicts in physics that had escaped all other scientists — and provide humanity with a radical new view of reality.[31] Einstein wrote to a friend that he had produced these papers in his spare time. They were:

The Photoelectric Effect — In this seminal paper, Einstein introduced the quantum theory of light to explain the puzzling results of the photoelectric effect. Based on Max Planck's formulation, Einstein made the radical assertion that light behaves like a *particle* as well as a *wave*. Einstein termed his proposition "very revolutionary" and it was.[32] Planck and Einstein's work gave birth to quantum mechanics — the most accurate and strangest theory in the history of physics.

Brownian Motion — Scientists had known for at least a hundred years that microscopic dust particles floating on a water surface continuously jiggle, but no one could explain why. Einstein showed this jiggling is due to the *thermal vibration* of individual water molecules — effectively confirming the existence of atoms and molecules for the first time.

Special Relativity — In this manuscript, Einstein proposed the radical notion that space and time are relative. Biographer Roland Clark called this "one of the most remarkable scientific papers ever written. . . . (it) overturned man's accepted ideas of time and space in a way which was, as *The Times* of London put it, 'an affront to common sense'."[33]

Einstein termed his relativity paper "only a rough draft at this point . . . (which) employs a modification of the theory of space and time."[34] As was typical of Einstein, he vastly understated the significance of his work.

Einstein had no laboratory. He himself did none of the experiments which he referred to in his papers. His only tools were his pencil and paper. He was a true theoretical physicist. His solutions to the photoelectric effect, Brownian motion, and relativity were generated by pure thought.

Einstein's character as well as his extraordinary technical ability played a critical role in these scientific feats. His independence, stubbornness, and rejection of prevailing thinking led to much trouble at school — but were key to his revolutionary breakthroughs.

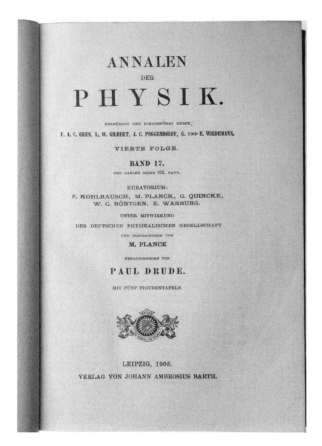

Figure 1.4. Image of first page of *Annalen der Physik* 17, which contains Einstein's famous photoelectric effect, Brownian motion, and special relativity manuscripts.

How did Einstein do it? How did a patent clerk that no one ever heard of discover the relativity of space and time? His path to special relativity began with attempts to understand the physics of Galileo, Newton, and Maxwell — their triumphs and most important, their conflicts.

This is the subject of Chap. 2.

Chapter 2

The Great Conflict

A barque borne fast.

To the mind it may seem
The rushes hurry past.

Every moment thus
From this world we fly,

And it seemeth to us
The world goes by.[1]

Jalāl ad-Dīn Muhammad Rūmī, 13th century Persian poet

Have you ever been in a boat moving steadily down a stream or river? Perhaps you have felt the sensation that you are standing still and the scene along the shore, the water below, and sky above are all moving by you in the opposite direction. Or perhaps you have been in a train sitting idle at the station as the train on the track next to you pulls out. Looking at the other train through the window, you suddenly feel you are moving backwards. At the moment you cannot tell whether your train or the other train is moving.

To better understand this, imagine you are enjoying yourself on a cruise ship on its way to the Caribbean. You decide that between cocktails and stuffing your face, you want to expand your mind. So you sign up for one of my classes on relativity. The lecture is given in an *interior* classroom of the ship.

The ship is presently traveling at a constant speed and in a constant direction, i.e., in *uniform motion*. The sea is particularly calm today. There is nothing to disturb the ship's uniform motion. In addition, there are no windows in this interior classroom, and the entrance and exit doors are closed.

The question is this: Is there any way to determine from inside this interior room whether the ship is moving or standing still?

(You are allowed any measuring devices you can think of to help answer the question. You can do any experiment you choose, as long as you do not receive signals or information from *outside* the room — such as lights, radios, cell phones, etc. The room is effectively sealed from all outside information.)

This is not a trivial question. It haunted the mind of the great Galileo himself. In his *Dialogue* of 1632, he wrote:

> "Shut yourself up with some friends in the main cabin below decks on some large ship, and have with you there some flies, butterflies, and other small flying animals. Have a large bowl of water with some fish in it; hang up a bottle that empties drop by drop into the wide vessel beneath it.
>
> With the ship standing still, observe carefully how the little animals fly with equal speed to all sides of the cabin. The fish swim indifferently in all directions; the drops fall into the vessel beneath; and, in throwing something to your friend, you need throw it no more strongly in one direction than another, the distances being equal; jumping with your feet together, you pass equal spaces in every direction.
>
> When you have observed all these things carefully ... have the ship proceed with any speed you like, so long as the motion is uniform and not fluctuating this way or that. You will discover not the least change in all the effects named, nor could you tell from any of them whether the ship was moving or standing still..."[2] (Underlines are mine.)

In other words, there is no way to determine your (uniform) speed from *inside* a sealed room. (Physicists call this a closed system.) The only way to determine if you are in motion is by observing things outside the room, such as the ship moving relative to the water.

There are, in fact, *two* ways to view the ship's motion: To an observer *on the shore*, the ship is moving. But to an observer *on the ship*, the ship is standing still and the shore is moving by in the opposite direction.

Whose point of view is correct? Both are. Uniform motion is relative. In other words there is no absolute "at-rest".

What Galileo is saying is the laws of physics — which govern the behavior of flying animals, fish in a bowl of water, water dripping from a bottle, a thrown object, and a body jumping up and down — are the *same* from both points of view. This is in essence Galileo's dictum on uniform motion.

*All knowledge of reality starts from experience and ends in it ...
Because Galileo saw this ... he is the father of modern physics; indeed,
of modern science altogether.*[3]

Albert Einstein

Now I'd like you to do a little experiment. Please stand still for a moment and pour a glass of water or other liquid from its container into a cup or glass. The liquid pours straight down with no problem. Surely it is proof that you are not moving. (I do this amazing demonstration in my physics classes, except I usually manage to spill water on myself.)

What would the effect be if you were in a gigantic spaceship large enough to generate Earth-like gravity? Say this spaceship is moving at a constant speed of *67,000 miles an hour* relative to the Sun? Would the water-pouring experiment turn out the same?

Surely wouldn't the water fly out and away as it leaves the bottle? After all, you're moving at 67,000 miles an hour.

Galileo says no.

Why? Because you, the bottle, the water, the cup, and the spaceship all move at the same speed. Since the relative speed between all these objects and you is zero, it is as though you are all standing still. The water will pour out and straight down into the cup, with no problem at all.

Do you still question this conclusion? Well you are in a spaceship traveling at 67,000 miles an hour. It is called planet Earth. Right now, you, the bottle, the water, the cup, and the Earth orbit the Sun at about 67,000 miles an hour.[a]

Our perception of standing still is an illusion, in a sense. Yes, we are standing still relative to the planet Earth. But the Earth spins on its axis and moves in its orbit around the Sun. In addition, we, the Earth, the Sun and everything in our solar system circle the center of the Milky Way galaxy at a speed of about 486,000 miles per hour.

And we and the rest of the Milky Way galaxy in turn move at about 315,000 miles an hour towards our nearest galactic neighbor, the Andromeda galaxy. Finally, we, the Milky Way, and Andromeda move through the universe at 1.2 million miles an hour relative to the radiation left over from the Big Bang (called the Cosmic Microwave Background).

---

[a]To a first approximation, the Earth is in uniform motion. We ignore here the effects of Earth's rotation about its axis and its elliptical orbit around the Sun, as they have a negligible effect on our experiment.

Yet with all this relative motion, from our point of view, we are standing still. This is Galileo's dictum on uniform motion at work.

So uniform motion is relative. It depends on your point of view. Einstein became so ingrained in this way of thinking that, reportedly, while on a train going from Switzerland to Baden-Baden, he asked the conductor, "When does Baden-Baden stop at this train?"[4]

In his *Dialogue* of 1632, Galileo used his dictum on uniform motion to defend Copernicus's radical theory that the Earth is not stationary — it and all the other planets orbit the Sun. People at the time questioned this revolutionary notion.

"How can this be?" they said. "If the Earth moves, why don't we feel it?" Surely the Earth must be at the center standing still, otherwise its motion would cause people and all things not tied down to fly away.

To answer this, Galileo pointed out that all things "at rest" on the planet are actually moving at the same speed with respect to each other and the Earth. Thus we cannot sense any motion (just like on the uniformly moving ship).

> ... *whatever motion comes to be attributed to the Earth must necessarily remain imperceptible to us and as if nonexistent (so long as we look only at terrestrial objects), for as inhabitants of the Earth, we consequently participate in the same motion.*[5]
>
> Galileo, *Dialogue*

The Catholic Church at the time considered the notion that the Earth moves and is not the center of the world as contrary to Holy Scriptures. Galileo was summoned before the dreaded Inquisition. In 1633, seven of ten cardinals found him guilty of suspected heresy.

The now seventy-year-old Galileo was forbidden to neither "hold, defend, nor teach ... said false doctrine".[6] He was put under house arrest for the remainder of his life. And the *Dialogue* was placed on the Index of Prohibited Books — where it remained for nearly 200 years.

It is said that while Galileo acquiesced to the demand that he reject Copernicus, allegedly under his breadth he mumbled, "Yet it moves". Historians argue that Galileo never actually said these words or perhaps said them later to friends, but I love the story anyway.

Two Spaceships Passing in the Night

Imagine you are at the helm of a spaceship in outer space moving along in uniform motion. You see a tiny dot way off in the distance in front of your ship (see Fig. 2.1).

As it approaches, you see an alien spaceship traveling directly towards you. As the ship gets closer, you turn on your on-board radar to measure its speed. Your radar indicates that the alien ship is traveling towards you at a constant speed of 6250 miles per hour.

Soon the ship fills the center of your screen. As the ship goes by, you get a pretty good look at the alien commander. She's kind of cute, except for the two antennae sticking out of the top of her head.

Figure 2.1. Alien Ship Approaching Your Ship in Outer Space.

What does this experience feel like from your point of view? You feel as though you and everything in your spaceship are *stationary* in space and the alien ship is moving towards you.

What does the alien observe from her spaceship? She feels as though *she* is stationary in space. Everything in her spaceship also appears stationary to her. She observes your spaceship coming towards her, and then going by. She feels that you are moving and she is standing still. With her on-board radar, she measures your spaceship's speed as 6250 miles per hour.

In other words, both you and the alien observe *the same thing*. (Except she doesn't think you are so cute.) Whose viewpoint is correct? They both are. Uniform motion is *relative*.

Physicists call these different points of view *reference frames* (or frames of reference).[7] From your ship's reference frame, the alien spaceship is moving. From the alien ship's frame of reference, your spaceship is moving.

Reference frames are a core concept in understanding relativity. We will use the term throughout the book.

Do you see it? An object at rest is undergoing uniform motion. It is at rest in your reference frame, but moving in another observer's frame of reference. This simple relationship was the first puzzle piece in Einstein's path to a theory of relativity.

Galileo's ideas on uniform motion set the stage for the next puzzle piece — Isaac Newton and his Laws of Motion. It began with the concept of inertia.

Newton on Ice

Boston — 1967. It is late in the evening in the dead of winter. I'm driving north on Mass. Ave. approaching the Beacon Street traffic light. The road is treacherous — glare ice. The light turns red. I pump the brakes. The car slides to the right. I steer into the skid. Still sliding. I continue pumping. Still sliding. My hands grip the steering wheel like a vice. Oh, God, this is taking forever. My pale green '57 Chevy glides across the intersection like a rudderless ship, slams into a snow bank, and lurches to a stop.

During those terrifying moments in my careless youth, I experienced what is called *inertia*. What normally holds a car to the road? Friction between the car's tires and the road surface. But on this nearly frictionless icy road, there was virtually nothing to grab the tires and stop the car.

So once it started its slide, the car kept on going at the same speed and in the same direction, i.e., in uniform motion — until an outside force (collision with the snow bank) stopped it. This is inertia at work: an object (my car) continues in uniform motion indefinitely, unless acted upon by an outside force (the snow bank).

This idea of inertia is an ancient one. Chinese philosopher Mozi (ca. 400 BC) said: "The cessation of motion is due to the opposing force.[8] If there is no opposing force, the motion will never stop." The great eleventh century Islamic scientist Ibn al-Haytham had a similar idea: "An object will move perpetually unless an (outside) force causes it to stop or change direction."[9]

Galileo and French scientist/mathematician René Descartes were among the first Europeans to propose the concept of inertia. In fact, Galileo's dictum on uniform motion is based on this concept.

Some 50 years later, Isaac Newton reaffirmed "the idea that the *natural* state of motion is uniform motion."[10] In other words, an object "wants to" go in a straight line at the same speed. And as long as nothing disturbs it, it will.

Out of this came Newton's famous theory of motion. His three simple yet powerful principles defined the science of mechanics — how forces affect physical objects — for over two centuries. They worked so well that they became known as Newton's Laws of Motion. In case you forgot (or never learned them), Newton's three laws of motion are briefly listed here[11]:

(1) *The Law of Inertia*: An object in (uniform) motion stays in (uniform) motion, until acted upon by an outside force.
(2) *The Force Law*: Force equals mass times acceleration ($F = ma$).
(3) *The Force Pairs Law*: For every action, there is an equal and opposite reaction.

Newton's Laws and Galileo's Dictum

Imagine two children playing catch in the back seat of your car. Is the ball toss different when the car is at rest than when the car is in uniform motion? According to Galileo's dictum, there is no difference. Tossing the ball or any activity inside the car works the same (just like inside Galileo's ship). Per Galileo, as long as you receive no information from outside the car, there is no way to tell whether the vehicle is in uniform motion or at rest.

The question is: do Newton's Laws obey Galileo's dictum? Let's apply Newton's Laws to the ball toss. We find Newton's Law's predict the ball behaves the same way whether the car is at rest or in uniform motion. Good — this means Newton's Laws do obey Galileo's dictum.

To demonstrate this mathematically, physicists use the so-called *Galilean transform*.[12] You can think of the Galilean transform as a kind of mathematical vending machine. But instead of putting money in and getting candy out, you: (1) Input the equations for how the ball toss works inside the vehicle at rest, and (2) Get out the equations for how the ball toss works when the vehicle is in uniform motion.

When we put Newton's equations through this exercise, we find we get the same equations out. What does this tell us? It says Newton's Laws are not affected by uniform motion. It also says the physics they represent is the same in both cases. It is mathematical proof that Newton's Laws obey Galileo's dictum.

In more formal language, the Galilean transform gives us a formula to go from one uniformly moving reference frame to another. And it shows that Newton's laws are *the same* in all uniformly moving reference frames.[13] (For more on the Galilean transform, see Appendix A.)

Galileo's dictum on uniform motion and Newton's Laws of Motion apply to the field of physics called *mechanics*. As noted, this describes how forces affect physical objects. The great question in the 1800s was whether these principles and laws also apply to electricity and magnetism. This in turn set the stage for the last puzzle piece in Einstein's relativity quest.

Electricity and Magnetism — Two Sides of the Same Coin?

While getting ready to give an evening lecture, in 1820 Danish scientist Hans Christian Ørsted set up an experiment on electricity. He placed a magnetic compass on the setup, hoping to test the long-suspected relationship between electricity and magnetism.

Students began filing into the lecture hall. Ørsted decided to try his experiment for the first time in front of the class. He turned on the power from a battery. An electric current began flowing through the wire as expected. Then he saw it. The magnetic needle began to jiggle ever so slightly (see Fig. 2.2).

What made the compass needle jiggle?[14] The current flowing in the wire had produced a magnetic field. After all, a magnetic compass needle

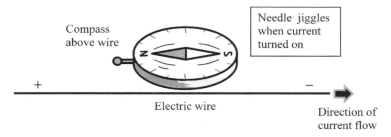

Figure 2.2.   The Ørsted Experiment. *Electric current in wire creates a magnetic field around it, causing needle of compass above it to jiggle.*

is sensitive to magnetic fields — the Earth's magnetic field is what makes it point north in the first place. The current in the wire produced its own (relatively weak) magnetic field — causing the needle to jiggle.

Ørsted's little demonstration definitively showed for the first time that "moving electricity produces magnetism."[15] However, due to the feebleness of the effect, the student audience did not realize the significance of what they had just witnessed.

Ørsted's discovery is the basis for modern electric motors. For example, turning on your ceiling fan causes a *current* to flow in wires inside the fan. This produces a magnetic field, just as in Ørsted's experiment. Electro-magnets inside the fan then rotate in response — in turn, causing fan blades to rotate. Electric motors inside washing machines, clothes dryers, hair dryers, vacuum cleaners etc., all operate on the same principle.

In 1831, English experimenter extraordinaire Michael Faraday, the "self-taught son of a blacksmith," demonstrated the opposite effect.[16] He showed that if you move a magnet around a wire, it generates an electrical current in the wire.

Faraday had converted mechanical energy (the rotation of the magnet) into electrical energy (current flow). This phenomenon is called *electromagnetic induction*. Today's power plants, automobile generators/alternators, portable generators, etc., all use a version of Faraday's discovery to generate electric power.

To summarize, from the experiments of Ørsted and Faraday, scientists knew an electrical current produces a magnetic field — and, conversely, a moving magnet produces an electric current. Now all that was needed was a theory which provided the mathematical underpinnings for these phenomena.

At first, physicists turned to what they knew — Newton's Laws of Motion. Newtonian physics was such a triumph that scientists hoped it would explain all physical phenomena. But when physicists attempted to explain electricity and magnetism in terms of Newton's Laws, they soon ran into trouble.

For one thing, Newton's force law ($F = ma$) applies to objects in *constant contact*. You make an object accelerate by pushing on it. But as soon as you are *no longer in* contact with that object, it stops accelerating — it now moves in uniform motion (assuming no outside force). Newton's third law (forces come in pairs) also applies only to objects in constant contact.

But electricity and magnetism exert forces without being in contact. These forces are in fact transmitted through space. We see this when the Earth's magnetic field causes a compass needle to align with magnetic north. (This is the same invisible "action at a distance" Albert Einstein found so mysterious as a child.)

In another example, take two ordinary bar magnets (like the ones used to hold photos on a refrigerator) and place them far apart on a table. Then slowly move just one of them towards the other. Aha! The second magnet begins to move when the first one gets close enough, but before they are in contact.

We experience the same "action at a distance" effect with electricity. Rub your feet against a carpet. You are actually rubbing off some of the electrons from molecules and atoms on the carpet onto your body. With these extra electrons, you have a net negative electric charge. Now slowly move your finger close to a metal object. Again you feel the shock of this "static electricity" before you make contact with the object. The electrical force has traveled through space from your finger to the object.

In summary, Newton's second and third laws of motion require direct contact.[b] But electric and magnetic forces transmit through space. Objects do not need to be in direct contact to be affected by electricity and magnetism.

---

[b]Unlike Newton's Laws of Motion, his Law of Gravitation assumes action at a distance, as we discuss in Chap. 9.

After many struggles and false-starts, by the mid 1800s physicists had established some *new* laws for electricity and magnetism. This pioneering science was mostly the work of Hans Christian Ørsted, Charles de Coulomb, André-Marie Ampère, and especially Michael Faraday.

The collection of equations they had so painstakingly developed worked quite well, but they represented a disparate group of separate theories. In addition, they failed a key principle — they did not obey the law of conservation of electric charge.

Maxwell's Breakthrough

It is a glorious feeling to recognize the unification of complex phenomena that appear to direct sense experience as completely separate things.[17]

Albert Einstein

Theoretical physicist James Clerk Maxwell was born in 1831 in Edinburgh, Scotland. Like Newton, he was a brilliant mathematician. Like Einstein, he showed an early love for geometry. And like both, he engaged in extensive self-study during his undergraduate years at the University of Edinburgh.

Maxwell's prodigious accomplishments included advances in optics, color photography, kinetic theory, thermodynamics, and the mathematics of control theory. But the work for which Maxwell is most highly regarded is his great opus on electricity and magnetism published in 1864. Here, his extraordinary mathematical prowess set him apart from his contemporaries.

His masterpiece united all separate theories and experimental evidence in electricity and magnetism into a single comprehensive construct. It was "the crowning achievement of 19th century physics."[18] Curiously, James Clerk Maxwell died in 1879, the same year Albert Einstein was born.

What was so special about Maxwell's theory?[19] It showed electricity and magnetism are actually part of a single phenomenon — *electromagnetism*. His mathematics also confirmed what Ørsted and Faraday had shown experimentally — changing electric fields produce magnetic fields, and changing magnetic fields produce electric fields. And his equations obeyed the principle of conservation of charge.

25

Does this really mean that electricity and magnetism are part of the same phenomenon? Yes. Consider again those simple magnets we use to stick photos on our refrigerators. Where do they get their magnetism from?

Maxwell's Equations tell us that a moving electric field produces a magnetic field. Is there a moving electric charge inside these magnets? Absolutely. Within the atoms of these magnets are electrically-charged electrons. Their motion is what produces the magnetic fields of everyday magnets.[20]

But Maxwell is not done with us — not by a long shot. When he studied his equations, he realized there is an intimate relationship between electric and magnetic fields: one produces the other.

Maxwell reasoned — since a changing magnetic field generates an electric field and a changing electric field generates a magnetic field — perhaps they can feed off each other. In other words, the first creates the second which in turn creates the first and so on. Together they form a "cyclical motion," resulting in a "moving train of electric and magnetic fields" which continuously produce each other.[21]

What is the result? A never-ending *wave* of electric and magnetic fields — an electromagnetic field which propagates through space. Maxwell predicted the existence of electromagnetic radiation!

How do we create an electromagnetic wave? By taking a particle which has electric charge and accelerating it. For example, move an electron up and down. Since an electron is an electrically charged particle, this up-and-down motion creates a changing electric field. And this changing electric field creates a magnetic field. And so on. So by moving the electron up and down, we get a "self-perpetuating" set of electrical and magnetic fields, or electromagnetic (EM) radiation.[22]

To see what EM radiation looks like, take a look at Fig. 2.3.[23] The constantly changing electric field produces a changing magnetic field and vice versa. The key word here is *changing*. If either field is not changing then there is no resultant wave, no EM radiation. As we shall see, this is a crucial point in Einstein's path to special relativity.

Maxwell wondered at what speed these EM waves traveled.[24] We can imagine him calculating the value from his equations. He wrote down the number and recognized it immediately. To his delight, the value he arrived at was a little less than 300 million meters per second or about 670 million miles per hour. This is the *speed of light*!

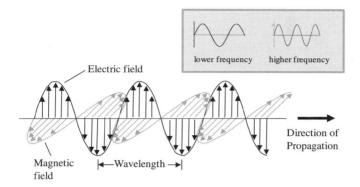

Figure 2.3. The Electromagnetic Wave. *Its electric field runs perpendicular to its magnetic field. The wave pattern moves to the right over time.*

(By Maxwell's time, the speed of light was known to within an accuracy of a few percent.)

In one of the most serendipitous discoveries in science, Maxwell realized this combination of electrical and magnetic waves travels at the same speed as light does! Faraday's suspicions had been correct — light is EM radiation. They are one and the same. This mysterious entity we call light is in fact a continuously changing wave of electric and magnetic fields. Maxwell had discovered another aspect of nature never before known to man!

Studying on his own, Albert Einstein was greatly impressed by Maxwell's unification of electricity, magnetism, and light into a single theory. "Maxwell's theory was the most fascinating theory at the time I was a student," Einstein later wrote.[25] Inspired by Maxwell, the unification of disparate theories into a single, coherent structure was to become Einstein's life work.

> *The incorporation of (light) into the theory of electromagnetism represents one of the greatest triumphs in the striving toward unification of the foundations of physics.*[26]
>
> Albert Einstein

Let There Be Light

Is this EM radiation the same light we see with our eyes? Yes. So-called visible light is just a particular frequency range of EM radiation. Just like our hearing is restricted to a certain frequency range of sound, our eyesight is also restricted to a certain narrow frequency range of light, of EM radiation. The rainbow of colors we see as red, orange, yellow, green, blue, and violet are simply different frequencies of this EM radiation band (see Fig. 2.4).[27]

From long waves which vibrate at as little as a few times per second to gamma rays which can vibrate in excess of a trillion trillion times every second, and everything in between — radio waves, microwaves, infrared, visible, ultraviolet, and X-rays — all electromagnetic radiation is light.

Although these different forms of light exhibit dramatically different physical effects, the *only* characteristic which sets them apart is their particular frequencies. So "light" and "EM radiation" are different words for the same phenomenon. And all EM waves travel at the speed of light in a vacuum, regardless of their frequency.

Based on Max Planck's equation, Einstein proposed the higher the frequency of light, the higher its energy. For example, X-rays are high frequency EM radiation. Their corresponding high energy enables them to transmit through the soft tissue in our bodies (but not through bone).

In 1887, Heinrich Hertz demonstrated the propagation of electromagnetic (EM) waves experimentally. Then in December of 1901, Guglielmo Marconi transmitted EM radio waves from Cornwall, England into the air and across the Atlantic Ocean to a receiver at St. John, Newfoundland. The Communication Age was born.

Today, EM radiation is the principle behind all wireless communication. Radio stations, television stations, cell phones, portable land line phones, satellites, space vehicles, electronic car keys, garage door openers, and other remote control devices all transmit information via EM

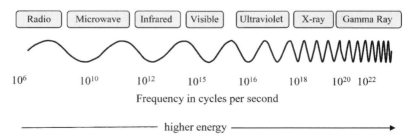

Figure 2.4. The Electromagnetic Spectrum. *EM radiation comes in different frequencies and wavelengths, but it is all light.*

radiation. They may use different frequencies, but all bear witness to Maxwell's grand vision.

Troubles with Maxwell

Despite the great success of Maxwell's Equations — for all they revealed about the nature of electricity, magnetism, and light — there were problems, serious issues which puzzled physicists for decades:

Trouble #1: Galileo's Dictum

We learned earlier that Newton's Laws are *not* affected by uniform motion. All phenomena described by Newton's Laws behave exactly the same inside a uniformly moving vehicle as they do inside a stationary one. Thus Newton's Laws and the equations which represent these laws obey Galileo's dictum on uniform motion.

But Maxwell's Equations — ah, that's another story. Physicists in the late 19th century found Maxwell's Equations *do not* obey Galileo's dictum. They are affected by uniform motion.

How did they determine this? They put Maxwell's Equations through the Galilean transform, and got a different set of equations out.

Does this say the laws of physics for electricity, magnetism, and light are different inside a uniformly moving vehicle than inside the same vehicle when it is at rest? Yes. But this means if we perform an experiment with electricity, magnetism, or light, we could tell inside a closed vehicle whether it is at rest or in uniform motion. This violates Galileo's dictum!

But wait a minute. Our own experience tells us something different. For instance, your battery-powered laptop computer works the same — whether stationary on the ground or in an airplane traveling at some 600 miles an hour — as thankfully do all electromagnetic devices on the airplane.

How about the microwave oven inside your Recreation Vehicle (RV)?[28] It heats up a cup of tea in the same way, whether your RV is parked in your driveway or going at 60 miles an hour down a smooth highway. So our every day experience tells us that electromagnetic phenomena are not affected by uniform motion.

However, physicists in the late 1800s were not so sure. After all, electromagnetism was still a relatively new science. Experience with its behavior was much more limited than it is today. Either electromagnetism *is* affected by uniform motion, they thought, or Maxwell's great theory needs modification.

This brings up yet another question. Let's say, as Maxwell's mathematics seemed to imply, electromagnetism does act differently for things at rest than for things in uniform motion. OK, but what do we define as "at rest"?

Is the laboratory in which the experiments are conducted at rest relative to the Earth? Yes, you say. But the Earth moves around the Sun. And the Sun moves around the center of the Milky Way Galaxy, etc. You get the picture? Since everything in our universe is moving relative to something else, where do we establish as that *special* place which is at rest, the place that is stationary everywhere in the cosmos?

Is there no place in the universe we can define as "at rest"?

If you find this confusing, so did physicists at the dawn of the 20th century. This brings up our second issue with Maxwell's theory — the *ether*.

Trouble #2 — the Ether

Physicists in the late 19th century knew that sound waves always propagate through some kind of medium, such as air. For example no sound can be transmitted through the vacuum of outer space. Why? Because there is no medium to carry the sound.

So, they figured, the same idea must also apply to light waves — they must move through some kind of medium. This mysterious light transmitting medium was dubbed an exotic name: the luminiferous ether. The prevailing belief was that this ether is a kind of transparent "background" material which permeates the entire universe.

The ether theory,[29] unsubstantiated by any empirical evidence, soon took on a life of its own — gaining virtually universal acceptance. All that was needed was to perform some kind of test which would show this ether actually exists.

In 1887, American physicists Albert Michelson and Edward Morley performed a set of famous experiments in attempts to detect the ether.[30] They sent two beams of light in perpendicular directions and returned them to the same starting point. (Here the ether was assumed to be at rest relative to the Sun.)

One beam of light was sent in the direction of Earth's motion, directly into the ether which supposedly fills up all space. The other was sent perpendicular to Earth's motion. They expected that the two beams would travel at different speeds.

Why? Because the beam heading into the ether and returning would be slowed more by the ether "headwind" than the beam traveling perpendicular to it. To see this, let's look at it from two points of view:

From the ether's point of view (the ether reference frame) — The Earth moves through the ether as our planet orbits the Sun.

From the Earth's point of view (the Earth reference frame) — The Earth is standing still and the ether moves in the opposite direction. Thus from the Earth's point of view, there is a constant headwind of ether. (Just like when drive your car through still air — if you stick your hand out the window you feel a headwind.)

So if the speed of light is relative to the ether, then a light beam heading directly into the ether and back should be slowed more than one heading perpendicular to it.

Michelson later explained the expected results of the experiment to his children.[31] He compared the two perpendicular light beams in his experiment to swimmers racing on a river. "Two beams of light race against each other," he told his daughter, "one struggling upstream and back, while the other, covering the same distance, just crosses (perpendicular to the current) and returns. The second (crossing) swimmer will always win, if there is any current in the river."

Meticulous testing by Michelson and Morley however, showed that the two perpendicular light beams traveled at the same speed no matter what direction they went in. They repeated the experiment. They placed the entire experimental apparatus on a platform and rotated it to different orientations. They waited six months and repeated the experiment when the Earth moved in the opposite direction relative to the Sun. But no matter what they did — the two beams always travelled at the same speed.

This was a great puzzle. The ether theory was so ingrained in the thinking of the time that scientists continued to believe in it, despite this evidence to the contrary.

Perhaps, they thought, there was something they didn't understand about the experiment.

Constant Light Speed?

Giving up the notion of the ether was a very difficult proposition. Why? For one thing, Maxwell's equations said that light *always travels at the same immutable speed*, the speed of light. In other words, the speed of light is constant. OK, so light always travels at the same speed. But at the same speed relative to what?

Does light always travel at the same speed relative to the source of that light? For example, does the light from a light bulb always travel at the speed of light relative to the light bulb? Or does light travel at the same speed relative to the Earth?

Why Earth in particular — maybe it's relative to the Sun? Or the Milky Way galaxy? Oh, boy. Here we go again. Understandably, there was confusion amongst physicists as to how to interpret the prediction from Maxwell's equations that the speed of light is constant.

Some physicists proposed that light moved at a constant speed relative to the ether, and this ether was at rest throughout the universe. So this stationary luminiferous ether constituted a *special* reference frame — an absolute frame of reference at rest everywhere in the cosmos. This seemed to be the most sensible answer at the time (except that the Michelson–Morley experiment failed to detect this ether.)

And what exactly was this so-called ether made of? Good question. The composition of this ether was one of the most important issues in physics at the end of the 19th century. During a 1900 presidential address of the British Association of the Advancement of Science, physicist Joseph Larmor posed a question — was the ether "merely an impalpable material atmosphere for the transference of energy by radiation" or "the very essence of all physical actions?"[32] In other words, Larmor questioned the nature of the ether, but not its existence.[33]

A Patent Clerk's Dilemma

Einstein, sheltered in his patent office, was not aware of all that was going on in the field of physics at the time, but he was deeply aware of the conflict between Newton and Maxwell. He knew Newton's equations obeyed Galileo's dictum on uniform motion and Maxwell's equations did not.

Einstein was also aware that physicists continued to assert the existence of a universal medium through which electromagnetic waves (light) propagate, despite the fact that the Michelson–Morley experiments failed to find evidence for this ether.

These issues troubled many physicists at the time, but no one more than the obscure patent clerk. Einstein was deeply disturbed by the dichotomy between Newton and Maxwell — the fact that the two great theories of physics differ with respect to such a fundamental principle as Galileo's dictum. He found this apparent contradiction abhorrent, generating "a state of psychic tension in me ... (over) seven long years of vain searching," as Einstein later put it.[34]

As is common in all walks of life, the older established physicists were set in their ways — they could not give up the concept of the ether. What the world needed was a young scientist who possessed the independence of thought to challenge the experts.

So it was that in 1905, 26-year-old Albert Einstein resolved the great conflict between Newton and Maxwell and settled the ether issue. This monumental breakthrough required Einstein's unique ability to let go of deeply held assumptions — as well as the courage to accept the bizarre implications of his new theory on the nature of space and time. How Einstein managed to do this is the subject of the next chapter.

Chapter 3

The Two Postulates

Each principle (postulate) by itself is harmless, yet taken together form an explosive mixture destined to rock the very foundations of science.[1]

Banesh Hoffman (Einstein collaborator in later years)

After yet another business failure, in 1894 Einstein's father moved his family to Pavia, Italy — where a wealthy uncle had agreed to finance an electrochemical factory.[2] Albert was left behind at the home of a distant relative to complete his studies at the Gymnasium. He had three years to go, a very long time for a 15-year-old (Fig. 3.1).

Spiraling towards depression, Albert wanted to leave school and follow his family to Italy.[3] Hearing of this, the principal of the Gymnasium reportedly took his revenge. He formally expelled Einstein for disruptions

Figure 3.1.   Albert Einstein — Age 14.

in class and disrespect for teachers (as noted earlier). Albert then hopped a train across the Alps to Italy. Arriving in Pavia, the high-school drop-out announced to his startled parents that he was never going back to Germany.

Einstein looked back at his time in Italy as a very happy one. Away from the suffocating rigidity of his Munich school, he enjoyed the spirited people and atmosphere of freedom. Young Albert was able to relax and follow his daydreams.

One day, riding his bicycle in the bucolic Italian countryside, the now 16-year-old asked a curious question — one that would rock the very foundations of classical physics: *What would the world look like if I were sitting on a beam of light?*[4]

As we shall see, the implications of this deceptively-simple query are profound.

Riding on a Wave

Imagine Surfer Sally on her surfboard riding an ocean wave. She and her surfboard are moving at the same speed as the wave. So from Sally's point of view — her reference frame — she and the wave are at rest.

Say a motor-boat is cruising alongside Sally at the exact same speed. What does a camera mounted on the motor-boat record? It sees Sally, her surfboard, and the wave standing still. Thus the camera and Sally see a *stationary* water wave in space. (See Fig. 3.2.)

The question is — does this simple analogy also apply to light?

Young Albert Einstein imagined moving at the same speed as light. He reasoned that if he did, he could travel alongside a light beam. And per Galileo's dictum — just like Surfer Sally sees the ocean wave at rest — he would see a light wave *standing still* in space.

Figure 3.2. Surfer Sally and Wave. *As seen from boat going at same speed, she and the wave are standing still.*

But according to Maxwell's equations, this is impossible. Why? Because of how a light wave is sustained.

As noted, an electromagnetic (light) wave keeps itself going by its changing electric part moving forward and so instantly "powering up" the magnetic part. The changing magnetic part in turn moves forward and produces a "further surge of electricity."[5] And the cycle repeats.

Thus light is a continuously vibrating electromagnetic wave. The key word here is *continuously*. Per Maxwell, a light wave *must move to exist*. Simply put, "light cannot be made to stand still."[6] If a light beam is stationary, according to Maxwell there is no electromagnetic wave — there is no light.

So, Einstein asks, what happens if I travel at the speed of light alongside a beam of light? It will now appear to be standing still to me, won't it? So what will I see? Does the light beam cease to exist for me, but still exist for everyone else? If so, how can that be?

> *After ten years of reflection, such a principle resulted from the paradox upon which I had already hit at the age of 16: If I pursue a beam of light with the velocity (of light), I should observe such a beam as a spatially oscillating electromagnetic field at rest. However, there seems to be no such thing . . .[7]*
>
> Albert Einstein

This vision haunted Albert Einstein for ten years, bringing him "to the point of despair," as he later put it.[8] Then in 1905, he arrived at a startling conclusion — one that resolved the conundrum but had revolutionary implications.

What was Einstein's deduction? You can never catch up to a light beam! No matter how fast you travel, it still goes at the same speed relative to you.

You see, since you can never catch up to a beam of light, its speed relative to you must always be the same — no matter what your speed. So a light beam's speed is completely independent of how fast you are moving!

Per Einstein's construct, you always measure the speed of light (in a vacuum) as exactly the same value, c — approximately 670 million miles an hour — no matter what your uniform motion. (Physicists use the symbol "c" to represent the speed of light, which is more precisely 670,616,629 miles per hour.)

You Can't Catch Up to a Light Beam

Wait a second. Per Newtonian physics (and our common sense), you can in principle catch up to any speeding object. Imagine Officer Krupke in his patrol car chasing a getaway car from a recent bank robbery. Say the getaway car is traveling at a speed of 100 miles an hour relative to the road, and Krupke's police car is traveling at 80 miles an hour relative to the road.

From Officer Krupke's point of view in his speeding car, the getaway car is going only 100 minus 80 or **20** miles an hour relative to him. In principle, all Krupke needs to do to catch the thief is go fast enough.

Now imagine Krupke chasing a beam of light in his super-rocket car. Say he is traveling at 80% the speed of light. You would expect that relative to Krupke, the light beam is traveling at only 100%–80% or **20%** the speed of light. Right?

Not according to Einstein. The light beam still travels at **100%** the speed of light relative to Krupke.

No matter what speed Krupke travels at, he measures the light beam moving at full speed. The speed of the light beam is totally independent of Krupke's motion. It always goes at full speed c (in a vacuum) relative to him and relative to everyone else. This is Einstein's wild conclusion.

In other words, light *always* travels at the same speed for all observers in uniform motion. Einstein called this principle the "light postulate". And from this principle, he resolved one of 19th century science's greatest mysteries: the failure of the Michelson–Morley experiments to find the so-called ether.[9]

The Light Postulate and the Ether

In 1905, Einstein simply abandoned the concept of the ether — the medium believed to be required for the transmission of light. Ever the empiricist he concluded: if there is no evidence for the ether wind, then it simply doesn't exist. This explained *why* Michelson–Morley couldn't find the ether — light does not need a medium in which to propagate. There is no ether!

> ... the unsuccessful attempts to discover any motion of the earth relative to the "light medium" suggest that the phenomena of electrodynamics as well as of mechanics possess no properties corresponding to the idea of absolute rest.[10]

Albert Einstein in his 1905 paper on relativity

And, Einstein pointed out, since there is no ether, there is no *special* reference frame. Thus there is no place of absolute rest — everything in the universe is moving with respect to everything else.

But with no ether, what is light moving at a constant speed relative to? Einstein's answer — relative to anything and everything. In more formal terms, Einstein's "light postulate" says the *speed of light is the same for all uniformly moving reference frames.*

In other words, the speed of light is absolute — it is always the same value. No matter what speed you go at relative to the source of a beam of light, the light always travels at the same speed relative to you.

You mean I can go directly towards a beam of light at any speed, and it will still come towards me at the same speed, c? Yes. Even if I travel at nearly the speed of light? Yes. What if I move away from the light beam at any speed — would it still travel towards me at the same speed, c? Even if I move away at nearly the speed of light? Yes and yes!

So the light postulate can also be stated as: *the speed of light is always the same, independent of the speed of the source of the light.*

Now let's "invert the situation." Let's look at this from a car's point of view.[11] From the car's frame of reference, its headlights are standing still and *you* are moving towards them. But you, the observer, still measure the speed of light as c. So we can restate Einstein's light postulate as: *the speed of light is the same, independent of the speed of the observer.*

This astounding postulate tells us that the speed of light is always the same, no matter how fast or in what direction you move. It is the same no matter how fast or in what direction the source of that light moves. As outlandish as this may sound, as much as it may violate our common sense — this is exactly what Einstein proposed in 1905.

Per special relativity, no matter what speed you or anyone else moves at — the speed of light (in a vacuum) is always the same.

Is this what we measure? Imagine a super-rocket in outer space with its nose light on. (See Fig. 3.3(a).) Say you are also in outer space holding a device which measures the speed of light. Initially, the rocket is at rest with respect to you. As expected, your device measures the speed of the light beam from the rocket's nose to be c or about 670 million miles an hour.

Now say this super-rocket approaches you at 100 million miles an hour (as in Fig. 3.3(b)). What does your device now measure for the speed of that beam of light?

Newton would say about 670 million *plus* 100 million or about **770** million miles an hour.

39

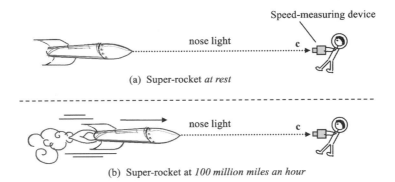

Figure 3.3. **Einstein's Light Postulate.** *You always measure the same speed for light, c or about 670 million miles an hour (in a vacuum), no matter what the speed of the light source.*

But per Einstein, you measure the same speed c or about **670** million miles an hour. The speed of the rocket has no effect on the speed at which its light beam approaches you.

Do you see it? No matter what the speed of the source of the light beam — and conversely no matter what your speed — light always measures as travelling at the *same* speed: c.

In 1905, Einstein made a compelling theoretical case for the constancy of the speed of light — but physicists remained skeptical. After all, this proposition turned prevailing thinking on its head. As good scientists, they asked "Where is the proof of this bold assertion — are there any measurements which show that the speed of light is truly independent of the speed of its source?"

At the time of Einstein's landmark special relativity paper, no such proof existed. The brash 26-year-old, however, had great confidence in his light postulate and its implications. An analysis of stars would soon validate this self-assurance.

Star Dance

The first confirmation of Einstein's light postulate came in 1913 with the famous de Sitter binary star analysis. A "binary" star is a system of two stars orbiting their common center of mass. At least half the stars we see in the sky are binary stars. (We see a single star because our eyes do not have the resolution to resolve the two images — but astronomical telescopes do.)

Dutch astronomer Willem de Sitter studied telescopic images of a number of double star systems. For stars which happen to orbit each other in-plane with the Earth, we see one star come towards us as the other moves away (as shown in Fig. 3.4).

Let's look at two possibilities:

Einstein is wrong — A star's motion *does* affect the speed of its light.

If Einstein is wrong, and the speed of the starlight *is* affected by motion of its source, we should see some very strange effects. Here's the key point: we do not "see" an object until its light reaches our eyes. So if a star's motion affects the speed of its light, this will affect when we see each star. Thus as we see it, the timing of the two binary stars would appear to be off as they orbit each other.

For example when one star is at the top of its orbit — it is heading towards us (again see Fig. 3.4). If Newton is correct, this star's motion will add to the speed of its light. As a result, light from the top star travels towards us faster than c. Thus we would see the top star sooner than we should.

The star at the bottom of the orbit moves away from us, so its motion would subtract from the speed of its light. So the light from the bottom star would travel slower than c. If this is true, we would see this star later than we should.

As a result, the two stars would appear to be out-of-sync with each other. Their relative positions and the timing of their orbits would look irregular.

Now the second possibility:

Einstein is right — A star's motion *does not* affect the speed of its light.

In this case, each star's light reaches us at the same time, no matter what their motion in their binary orbit. As a result, the separation between the two stars always appears as expected. So we see a nice, orderly, symmetric pattern of star motion through our telescope.

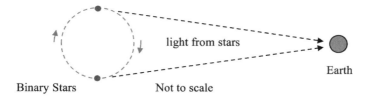

Figure 3.4. De Sitter Star Experiment. *Binary stars orbiting each other in plane with Earth. In this example, the top star moves towards Earth as the bottom star moves away from Earth.*

41

What did de Sitter see?[12] His study of telescopic observations showed *well-behaved* binary orbits, just as Einstein's light postulate predicts. De Sitter saw no apparent irregularities in the motion of binary stars, no asymmetries. Supported by mathematical analysis, he concluded Einstein was right — the speed of light is indeed independent of the speed of its source.

Numerous tests since have confirmed Einstein's light postulate. For instance, in 1964 physicists at the CERN particle research facilities conducted experiments with neutral pions — subatomic particles which emit random bursts of light (at speed *c*).[13] They accelerated these pions to speeds of **0.99975c** (relative to the laboratory), then measured the speed of the light they emitted.

Newtonian physics predicts the pion speed and light speed would add, giving a net light speed relative to the laboratory of **1.99975c**. But CERN physicists measured a value of just *c*. As Einstein's light postulate predicts, the motion of the source of the light (the pions) had no effect on the light's speed.

And in 1977, MIT physicist Kenneth Brecher performed a vastly more accurate version of the de Sitter star experiment with X-ray pulsars (neutron stars orbiting with regular stars).[14] These tests verified Einstein's light postulate to one part in a billion!

So Einstein's counter-intuitive light postulate is true — the speed of light (in a vacuum) is always the same. It is independent of the speed of its source, or the speed of the observer. Reality is stranger than we can imagine.

Einstein's light postulate is of immense significance. It is the physical principle behind special relativity — from it Einstein derived all his predictions, beginning with a new transform for uniform motion.

Light Reveals a New Transform

In Chap. 2, we learned the *Galilean transform* represents Galileo's dictum on uniform motion mathematically. At least this is what everyone thought until Einstein. In his June 1905 relativity paper, the young upstart showed that his light postulate leads to a *new* transform formula for uniform motion.

What is so special about Einstein's new formula? When applied to Maxwell's electromagnetic theory, Maxwell's equations remain unchanged. Einstein's new uniform motion formula leaves Maxwell's electromagnetic equations intact!

A great breakthrough? Yes and no. You see, unbeknownst to Einstein, he was not the first to come up with this new formula.

The Lorentz transform

At the dawn of the 20th century, Dutch physicist Hendrik Lorentz (and independently Irish physicist George Fitzgerald and others) tried to explain the failure of Michelson–Morley to find the ether. Lorentz proposed the "ether wind" somehow compressed all atoms in its path. This in turn shortened the rulers (meter sticks) used in the experiment.

Lorentz theorized that the light beam traveling into the ether had slowed down, but the shortened meter sticks gave false readings. So the slower light speed was compensated for by the shortened rulers. Thus the light beam did slow down in the direction of the ether, but appeared to have the same speed.

Sound far-fetched? Lorentz thought so too, but it was the best he could come up with.[15]

Even though the Lorentz–Fitzgerald physical interpretation was incorrect, their work was of great value.[16] In calculating the supposed amount of compression due to the ether, they generated a set of equations which were later expanded by Lorentz and became known as the *Lorentz transform*.

Remember, a transform works like a machine. You put an equation in the machine and it spits out a new "transformed" equation. It gives physicists a mathematical way to see how an equation changes when it is "transformed" from inside a vehicle *at rest* (stationary reference frame) to inside the same vehicle when it is *in uniform motion* (moving reference frame).

Lorentz (and others) showed that when you apply the Lorentz transform to Maxwell's equations, the laws of electromagnetism remain unchanged. In other words, when you put Maxwell's Equation through the Lorentz transform, they come out as the *same* equations.

More formally, the Lorentz transform makes Maxwell's equations "invariant" with respect to uniform motion. (Invariant is a fancy mathematical term meaning "does not vary" or "does not change".)

Wonderful. The Lorentz transform did the trick mathematically. Ah, but no one understood what it meant physically — until Einstein.

When he wrote his 1905 relativity paper, Einstein was not yet familiar with the work of Lorentz and Fitzgerald. This was due to his isolation working six days a week at the patent office. He had virtually no contact with other physicists, and libraries were closed by the time he got off work.

So in his 1905 manuscript, Einstein independently derived the same transform formula from his light postulate. However, since Lorentz had developed it first, it is known as the "Lorentz transform" or sometimes the "Lorentz-Einstein transform". We will use the former name here for brevity. (For mathematical details on the Lorentz transform, see Appendix A.)

Einstein proposed this so-called Lorentz transform as a new formula to go from a vehicle at rest to a vehicle in uniform motion. And, as noted, if you apply the Lorentz transform to Maxwell's equations, you get a new set of equations — which (after some algebraic manipulations) are identical to Maxwell's original equations. What does this tell us? Maxwell's equations are unaffected by uniform motion.

What does this mean physically? Since the transformed equations are the same as Maxwell's original equations, it tells us electromagnetic phenomena are not affected by uniform motion. It says Maxwell's equations do obey Galileo's dictum on uniform motion. Hallelujah!

So Maxwell's equations, like Newton's Laws, obey Galileo's dictum after all. This was powerful knowledge in the hands of Einstein. Based on this, he proposed a second core principle in 1905 — one for which he held a deep personal conviction — the universality of the laws of physics. He called it the "relativity postulate".

The Relativity Postulate[17]

Imagine two identical scientific laboratories able to perform any type of experiment known to man. The first laboratory is inside a *stationary building* with no windows or open doors. There are also no phones, radios, TV's etc. inside this laboratory. Once inside the laboratory, there is no way to receive any signal or information of any kind from the outside world.

The second laboratory is also isolated in the same way. But it is inside a vibration-isolated tractor-trailer truck traveling on a smooth road *in uniform motion* — say at 50 miles per hour heading due north. In relativity terms, the two laboratories, the two closed systems, constitute two reference frames moving uniformly relative to each other.

Einstein proposed that any and all experiments performed within the so-called *stationary* laboratory would get the same results as identical experiments done solely within the uniformly moving laboratory. In other words, the behavior of all physical phenomena is unaffected by uniform motion. This is the essence of Einstein's relativity postulate:

The laws of physics are the same for all (uniformly moving) frames of reference.

Once you are inside one of the closed laboratories, any test you do or observation you make comes out the same as in the other closed laboratory. There is no way to tell whether your laboratory is moving uniformly or at rest.

At first glance, this appears to simply be Galileo's dictum on uniform motion. After all, isn't being inside a uniformly moving laboratory just like being inside the hold of Galileo's uniformly moving ship? It is. But we must remember, when Galileo proposed his dictum in 1632 it applied only to the known science of mechanics. Now in 1905, Einstein says Galileo's dictum also applies to the new science of electromagnetism.

To represent this idea mathematically, Einstein took a radical step which was to have far-reaching consequences. He dropped the Galilean transform and declared the Lorentz transform applies to both Newton's Laws and to Maxwell's equations. In other words, the Lorentz transform replaces the Galilean transform and applies to all mechanical as well as all electromagnetic phenomena in uniform motion.

This approach resolved the great conflict between Newton's Laws and Maxwell's theory regarding Galileo's dictum. But there was a price. Newton's Laws of Motion had to be modified.

Do you see the irony here? Physicists at the time probed Maxwell's equations — trying to find a way to make them independent of uniform motion, just like Newton's. But Einstein says Maxwell's equations *are* independent of uniform motion, as long as you use the Lorentz transform to represent that motion.

However, per Einstein, the great Newton's venerated Laws of Motion are incorrect — they are just an approximation for speeds much slower than the speed of light. To accurately represent how things really work, we must abandon Newtonian principles and accept that time and space are relative. We must use *"relativistically modified"* Laws of Motion to reflect reality. (More on this in later chapters.)

Then our audacious patent clerk goes even further. In a bold leap characteristic of Einstein, he declares that his relativity postulate applies not just to mechanics and electromagnetism, but to all physical phenomena. What is Einstein's basis for this colossal generalization? Pure intuition. His relativity postulate, what he calls the Principle of Relativity,[18] effectively says that:

> *There is no way, using everyday objects or electricity, magnetism, light, or __any other__ physical phenomenon, to detect (in a closed system) whether one is in uniform motion or at rest.*

In essence, Einstein's relativity postulate is Galileo's dictum applied to *all* physical phenomena in the universe. It tells us that one must always state her or his speed relative to something else — there is no "at rest" frame of reference. It says that *all* the laws of physics are the same within every uniformly moving frame of reference. In effect, Einstein elevates Galileo's dictum to a universal, cosmic law.

In summary, Einstein based his new theory of special relativity on two postulates.[19] The Light Postulate says the speed of light is unaffected by the speed of its source or by the speed of the observer. The Relativity Postulate proposes that all the laws (and equations) of physics are the same for all uniformly moving reference frames — they are unaffected by uniform motion.

And the mathematics of the Lorentz transform provides the formula to go from one uniformly moving reference frame to another.

Profound Implications

At the turn of the century (1900s), the conflict between Newton's Laws and Maxwell's equations was well known to physicists. The solution was staring them all in the face.[20] Several physicists — especially Lorentz and French physicist Henri Poincaré — went part of the way.[21] But only Albert Einstein made the full jump to special relativity.[22]

Why? Because resolving this conflict required the letting go of long-held, cherished assumptions: (1) the ether is required for the transmission of light, and (2) time and space are absolute. Only Albert Einstein had the vision and the courage to break from these deeply entrenched beliefs.

Based on his two postulates, Einstein proposed that time and space are relative — these fundamental entities change with relative motion. We explore this strange new reality in the next chapter.

Chapter 4

A New Reality

To his contemporaries, the Lorentz transform was an interesting
mathematical tool — to Einstein it was "a revelation about nature itself."[1]

Roland C. Clark

Einstein had a genius for seeing what others could not. Experiments could not find the ether supposedly required for the transmission of electromagnetic waves. Maxwell's equations did not obey Galileo's dictum. Lorentz (and others) proposed a new transform. This new recipe made Maxwell's equations mathematically independent of uniform motion — but no one understood its physical significance.

Virtually out of nowhere, Einstein solved these riddles. He proposed (1) there is no ether, and (2) light always travels at a constant speed. And oh by the way, you can throw out everything you thought you knew about time and space — they are relative. And the Lorentz transform tells us how much time and space change with relative motion. Thus began the relativity revolution.

What the Lorentz Transform Really Means

Crash is a famous race car driver specializing in land speed records.[2] His pit boss Steady Eddie is a technical wiz when it comes to engine design and build. He also has a keen interest in physics. One day Eddie reads about Einstein's theory of special relativity — how motion affects time and space. He tells Crash about Einstein's predictions, but Crash doesn't believe him. "You're pretty smart, but this sounds crazy," he says. They both agree to do an experiment. So they take their new turbojet-powered race car out to a long, straight test track in the Black Rock Desert in northern Nevada.

Crash gets in the race car, revs it up, and accelerates. When he reaches a constant ground-speed of 600 miles an hour, Crash zooms across a mile-long strip. From the sidelines, Steady Eddie measures the time interval it takes the race car to cross the strip from start to finish. His stopwatch reads **6 seconds**. (This, of course, is just the time interval expected for a car traveling at 600 miles an hour for one mile.)

Mathematically this is:

$$distance = speed \times time$$

So

$$time = distance/speed$$
$$= 1 \text{ mile}/(600 \text{ miles/one hour})$$
$$= 1 \text{ mile} \times (1 \text{ hour}/600 \text{ miles})$$
$$= 1 \text{ mile} \times (1 \text{ hour}/600 \text{ miles}) \times (3600 \text{ seconds}/1 \text{ hour})$$
$$= (3600/600) \text{ seconds}$$
$$= \textbf{6 seconds}$$

Now the question is, what time interval does *Crash* in the race car measure with his stopwatch? Einstein tells us that time inside Crash's speeding race car runs *slower* due to the car's motion. This is called *time dilation*.

According to the Lorentz transform, Crash in the race car measures a time interval to cross the drag strip of **5.999999999998 seconds**. (We assume here that the stopwatches have extraordinary accuracy and precision.) This is a smaller time interval than Steady Eddie measures.

"OK, you were right," says Crash, "but the effect is miniscule."

"Ya," says Eddie, "It is because the race car's speed of 600 miles per hour is less than a millionth the speed of light." (Recall the speed of light is approximately 670 million miles an hour.)

Again, this is why we don't notice time dilation in our everyday activities — our speeds are way too slow. The greatest speeds we experience relative to the Earth are on commercial jet airplanes, which cruise at under 600 miles an hour (unless you are a fighter pilot or astronaut).

But time dilation is still real and cannot be dismissed. It is a fundamental property of nature, and leads to a profound shift in our understanding of the universe.

Crash and Eddie decide to look at the *length* of the race car under the same conditions. Just before the race, they measured the race car's length at rest as **28 feet** from end to end.

During the race, steady Eddy on the sidelines makes his own measurement of the race car as it speeds by. He uses his stopwatch to record the time when the front of the race car passes him — and then records the time when the back of the race car passes him. He knows that distance can be computed as speed divided by the time interval. Using his stopwatch measurements and this relationship, what does Eddie calculate for the length of the moving race car?

Steady Eddy measures the moving car's length as **27.999999999989 feet**, as predicted by the Lorentz transform. This shortening of the measured length due to relative motion is called *length contraction*.

"But again the change is miniscule," Crash says.

"I know. It is also because the race car's speed is so small compared to the speed of light," Eddie responds. "But you have to admit that Einstein was right. Both the time interval and length do change due to the race car's motion."

At Relativistic Speeds

Now what would the effect be at speeds which are a substantial fraction of the speed of light? Let's suppose that the race car could travel at the incredible speed of 580 million miles per hour or 87% the speed of light. So what do Crash and Eddie measure for the time interval and length of the race car? Let's take a look.

Imagine Crash buckling himself into his new super-rocket race car. He fires the rocket motors, and finds himself hurling along at a uniform velocity of 87% the speed of light. Of course, now the distance has to be much longer to accommodate the car's much greater speed. Assume the new distance is at just the right length, so that Eddie still measures a time interval from start to finish of **6 seconds**.

But at this extreme speed, what does Crash measure? Crash in the rocket-car looks at his stop watch at the end of his run, and sees a reading of only **3 seconds**. This is only half the time interval measured by Steady Eddy.

Then Steady Eddy, using his stopwatch and the race car's speed of $0.87c$ calculates the moving race car's length. He gets a value of a mere **14 feet**! To Eddie, the race car has contracted to half its length. (See Fig. 4.1.)

At Rest

V = 0.87c

28 feet long

14 feet long

Figure 4.1. Length Contraction. *Race car is shortened in direction of motion.*

The Lorentz transform tells us that once speed becomes a significant fraction of the speed of light, the changes in the time interval and distance due to relative motion become dramatic.

At the everyday speeds we experience, Newton's Laws of Motion are an excellent approximation. But for speeds approaching the speed of light, Einstein rules.

The Lorentz Transform

How did we calculate the values for time and distance in the Crash/ Steady Eddie story? Again, from the Lorentz transform. And at the heart of the Lorentz transform is a simple formula which tells us how much time and space change with motion — called the *Lorentz Factor.* Let's see how it works:

From Eddie's point of view (reference frame), Crash's time in the moving race car is running slower than his. How much slower? This is determined by the relative speed of the race car and the Lorentz Factor. For Crash's speed of 87% the speed of light, the Lorentz Factor is 0.5.

The formula for the Lorentz Factor, F is[3]:

Lorentz Factor = square root of (one minus the velocity squared)
$$F = sqrt\ (1 - v^2)$$

The symbol v stands for the relative velocity as a *fraction* of the speed of light.

The square root is abbreviated as "*sqrt*". The square of a number is the number multiplied by itself. For example, the square of 2 is 2 times 2 which equals 4. The square of 3 is 3 times 3 which equals 9. The square root of a number is simply the value that, when squared, gives the original number. For example, the square root of 4 is 2. And the square root of 9 is 3.

So if you are moving at 87% the speed of light relative to me, v equals 0.87. For a velocity $v = 87\%$ the speed of light, the Lorentz Factor, F is:

$$F = sqrt\ (1 - v^2)$$
$$= sqrt\ (1 - (0.87)^2)$$
$$= sqrt\ (1 - 0.75)$$
$$= sqrt\ (0.25)$$
$$= 0.5$$

Thus Crash's time runs at 0.5 or 50% slower than Steady Eddie's. We said that Eddie measures a time of 6 seconds. So Crash in the speeding rocket-car measures a time interval to cross the one-mile track of 6 times 0.5 or 3 seconds. Time is relative.

Now let's look at length contraction. Here the distance between two points in space is measured (in the direction of motion) as different values by Crash and Eddie. The difference is again determined by the amount of relative motion and the Lorentz Factor.

The same Lorentz Factor for time dilation applies for length contraction. So for Crash's speed of 87% the speed of light, the Lorentz Factor is the same 0.5 or 50%. Steady Eddie measures the speeding race car to be 50% or half the length it was when at rest. Recall the car measured *28 feet* long when stationary. With the car moving at 87% the speed of light, Eddie measures its length to be only half or *14 feet long* (as previously shown in Fig. 4.1). Space is relative.

(Einstein's time dilation and length contraction formulas and how they are derived from the Lorentz transform are given in Appendix A.)

If you are confused, incredulous, doubtful at the notion that time runs differently for people in relative motion, or that the distance between two points in space somehow changes with relative motion; you are not alone. Physicists at the time Einstein published his theory of special relativity had similar reactions. Our experience, our so-called common sense is of no help here. These changes in space and time are so very small that they go unnoticed at our everyday speeds. But as Einstein himself wryly noted, "common sense is the collection of prejudices acquired by age 18."[4]

Through the Lorentz transform, Einstein also discovered how we commonly *add* one speed to the other is also incorrect. This method based on Newtonian physics (and common sense) does not reflect reality.

Einstein once again turns the world upside-down and tells us speeds do not simply add — they combine in a way which never exceeds the speed of light.

How Speeds Really Combine

As of this writing, Jan Železný of the Czech Republic holds the world's record for the javelin throw — a distance of some 107.7 yards (98.48 meters).[5] Like all javelin throwers, Jan runs as fast as he can up to the start line, then throws his javelin. Why? Because his running speed increases the speed of the javelin throw. And, of course, the faster he throws the javelin, the greater the distance it travels.

For the sake of argument, imagine Jan standing still at the start line (Fig. 4.2(a)). Here he throws his javelin using *arm speed* alone. Say his arm speed gives the javelin a speed of 60 miles an hour.

Then Jan runs to the start line, and releases the javelin while still running. (See Fig. 4.2(b).) Say he is running at 20 miles an hour. So we would expect that the javelin now travels at the arm speed of 60 miles an hour *plus* a running speed of 20 miles an hour — for a combined speed of 60 plus 20 or **80** miles an hour.

Now imagine Jan is standing still holding a laser in his hand. You are way over on the other side of the track. You intend to measure the speed of the laser beam as it comes towards you. Jan, standing still, turns on the laser. As expected, neglecting air effects you measure the speed of the laser beam as the speed of light, *c* (about 670 million miles an hour).

(a) Stationary Javelin Thrower   (b) Running Javelin Thrower

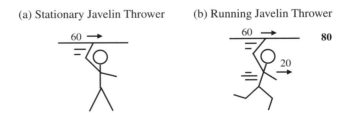

Figure 4.2. Javelin Thrower. *(a) Arm speed alone gives javelin speed of 60 miles per hour. (b) Arm speed of 60 plus running speed of 20 gives javelin speed of 80 miles an hour. (All speeds relative to ground.)*

Now Jan does something very strange. He straps a powerful jetpack on his back. Then, holding the laser, he yells "Cowabunga!" fires the jetpack rockets and flies towards you at 100 million miles an hour! (This is shown in Fig. 4.3.)

So at what speed does Jan's laser beam now approach you? Isaac Newton would say that the two speeds simply add. This would mean that the laser beam is now traveling towards you at about 670 million plus 100 million or 770 million miles an hour. But, Einstein says, this is wrong. For one thing it violates the light postulate. And it is faster than the speed of light, also a no-no according to special relativity.

Per the light postulate, the light beam approaches you at the *same* speed — the speed of light c or about 670 million miles per hour. In fact you would measure the same speed for the laser beam, no matter what speed Jan and the laser are traveling at. Per Einstein's light postulate, the speed of the laser *beam* is independent of the speed of the laser (its source).

Now you may be asking — why do speeds simply add for the running javelin throw but don't add for the jetting laser? Einstein was troubled by this same question. "The constancy of the velocity of light is not consistent with (Newton's) law of the addition of velocities," he stated.[6] "(As a result) I had to spend almost a year in fruitless thoughts."

Then it suddenly came to him — Newton's simple adding of velocities is based on the assumption that time is absolute. But, per Einstein, time is relative: it goes by at different rates depending on relative motion. Based on this idea and the mathematics of the Lorentz transform, Einstein came up with a new relativistic equation for combining speeds — one that works for the javelin and the laser (and all other objects).

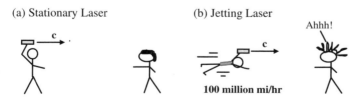

(a) Stationary Laser   (b) Jetting Laser

Ahhh!

c

c

100 million mi/hr

Figure 4.3.   Laser Holder. *(a) Observer measures stationary laser beam's speed as c. (b) Observer still measures speed of beam from jetting laser as c.*

Einstein tells us we first add the two speeds ala Newton (with speeds again as a fraction of the speed of light). But we then must divide this sum by a "special quantity" — one plus the product of the two speeds. Where did this special quantity come from? From the Lorentz transform. (The derivation of Einstein's speed-combining equation from the Lorentz transform is also given in Appendix A.)

To see how Einstein's approach differs from Newton's, let's look at some examples:

Small Speeds — For small speeds relative to the speed of light, simply adding per Newton is an excellent approximation. Recall Jan's javelin traveled at **60** miles an hour due to arm speed. If he then ran at **20** miles an hour, per Newton the javelin's resultant speed is simply 60 plus 20 or **80** miles an hour. However, Einstein says you have to convert the two speeds to a percentage of the speed of light, add them and then divide the sum by his special quantity — one plus the product of the two speeds. This gives a resultant value of **79.999 999 999 999 8** miles an hour.[7]

Newton's simple addition gives results extremely close to Einstein's, even at speeds of hundreds of thousands of miles an hour. This is why we don't notice Einstein's correction in everyday life.

Appreciable Speeds — For speeds in the millions of miles an hour — those which are a significant fraction of the speed of speed of light — Newton's method simply won't do. For example, Newton says that speeds of **0.8c** (80% the speed of light) and **0.9c** (90% the speed of light) simply add to give a combined speed of **1.7c**.

But this is faster than the speed of light! Einstein again says to divide the sum by his special quantity — giving a combined speed of only **0.988c**. This is a big number but still less than the speed of light. In fact, per Einstein's method, combining *any* two speeds smaller than c always gives a resultant speed smaller than c.

Speed c — What if we combine two speeds where one or both of them are *equal to* the speed of light c? Per Einstein's formula, the combination always comes out equal to c. For example, let's combine speeds of **0.9c** and **c**. What is the result? Newton would say **1.9c**. But Einstein's formula gives a combined speed of just c. (See below for details.)

For two initial speeds, $v_1 = 0.9$ and $v_2 = 1.0$, the combined speed V is:

Newton's Speed Combining Formula
$$V = v_1 + v_2$$
$$= 0.9 + 1.0$$
$$= 1.9$$

Einstein's Speed Combining Formula

$$V = \frac{v_1 + v_2}{1 + v_1 v_2}$$

$$= \frac{0.9 + 1.0}{1 + (0.9)(1.0)}$$

$$= \frac{1.9}{1 + 0.9}$$

$$= \frac{1.9}{1.9}$$

$= 1.0$ which is 100% the speed of light or c

With Einstein's formula, there is no way to combine two speeds and get a resultant speed greater than the speed of light. Einstein's clever formula limits *all* combined speeds to no more than the speed of light, c!

Why all this stuff on how to combine speeds? Because it reveals something unexpected about nature — according to special relativity, *nothing (no signal) can travel faster than the speed of light through space.* For the first time in the history of science, a theory proposes a natural speed limit for all things in the universe. (See Fig. 4.4.)

Figure 4.4. **Nothing Can Go Through Space Faster than the Speed of Light.**

Time is relative. Space is relative. And speeds do not simply add as Newton proposed, but combine *relativistically* — their combination never exceeding the speed of light.[8] These were considered strange ideas in 1905 to say the least. But in the over 100 years since Einstein's seminal manuscript, an abundance of experiments, tests, and observations have again and again validated the principles and mathematics of special relativity to extraordinary accuracy. They have become accepted science and vital elements of modern technology.

The Next Chapter

Perhaps the most captivating and puzzling aspect of special relativity and the most difficult to accept is the notion that time is relative. Einstein's proposition that time does *not* go by at the same rate for everyone everywhere challenges our basic beliefs about reality itself.

We trace the steps Einstein took to this remarkable insight in the next chapter. On our journey, we examine some of the same issues that perplexed Einstein and follow the same path of logic he took towards their resolution. Perhaps we can, if just for a moment, think a little like Einstein, and begin to comprehend the magnitude of his vision.

Chapter 5

The Shrinking of Time

Was this not revolution indeed? It is probably the
greatest mutation ever in the history of human thought.[1]

Jean Ullmo

When we say that time is relative, we mean that *all* aspects of time are relative. Imagine again a spaceship speeding away from the Earth at 87% the speed of light. According to the Lorentz Factor, clocks on the spaceship run at just about half the rate of clocks on the Earth.

Our intrepid astronauts inside the spaceship age at half the rate of people back on Earth. Everything else being equal, the microbes on-board the ship live twice as long as identical microbes do back on Earth. All physical characteristics which are a function of time are similarly affected. Clocks running at different rates are merely one manifestation of the relativity of time.

To see how time dilation comes about, we present Einstein's famous light-clock thought experiment in this chapter. We then show how Einstein's light and relativity postulates lead directly to the shrinking of time. Finally, we summarize key real-world experiments which confirm that time is indeed relative.

Light-Clocks and the Shrinking of Time

In Chap. 3, we saw that our so-called intuition is wrong. Per Einstein (Fig. 5.1), the speed of light is the same for all observers. What is the impact of this most startling realization? As we shall see, it is nothing short of revolutionary, affecting the very nature of *time* itself.

Figure 5.1.   Einstein at the Patent Office.

Here we invoke Einstein's famous "light-clock". It is totally impractical but based on sound principles of physics. The great physicist often used such thought experiments to explain his ideas.

A light clock is shown in Fig. 5.2. It shows a single particle of light, a single photon for simplicity (per Brian Greene's *The Elegant Universe*).[2] Our light clock contains two parallel mirrors, and a photon bouncing between them.

The photon continuously travels from the bottom mirror to the top mirror and back at the speed of light. Let's imagine when the photon hits the top mirror a "tick" is sounded through a speaker. When the photon arrives at the bottom mirror, a "tock" is sounded. Thus, as the photon bounces back and forth between the two mirrors, we hear a "tick-tock-tick-tock-tick-tock ..." just like in an old-fashioned analog clock.

Now imagine there are *two* identical light-clocks. The first clock is at rest relative to you. But the second is moving from your left to your right at a constant speed. This is shown in Fig. 5.3.

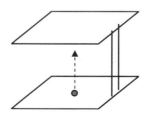

Figure 5.2.   The Light-Clock. *Two parallel mirrors with a photon bouncing between them.*

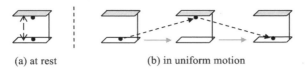

Figure 5.3.   Stationary Light-Clock and Moving Light-Clock. *(a) Light clock at rest: photon traveling up and down, (b) Light clock in uniform motion: photon travels longer <u>diagonal</u> path but at same speed. Longer path means longer time — moving clock runs slower than clock at rest!*

Look at the two clocks. From *your* point of view, the first clock is at rest, so you see the photon in this stationary clock going straight up and down. But the photon in the moving clock travels a *diagonal* path.

So the photon in the moving clock has to travel a longer distance to go between the two mirrors.

Now, and this is the key point, both photons are moving at the same speed, *c*. Why? Because, per the light postulate, the speed of each photon is unaffected by the moving clock's motion. All photons travel at speed *c*.

But the photon in the moving clock has to travel a longer diagonal path between the two mirrors — and a longer path at the same speed means a *longer time!*

So what do you hear from the two clocks? The stationary clock (the one at rest with respect to you) goes "tick-tock-tick-tock-tick-tock ..." But the moving clock goes "tick ... tock ... tick ... tock ... tick ... tock ...: Why? Because to you, time on the moving clock runs more slowly. To you, time itself has slowed down due to the relative motion of the moving clock through space.

The Light Postulate is what Makes Time Relative

The photon on the moving clock is traveling at the same speed as the photon on the stationary clock. So the photon on the moving clock *must* take longer to travel its longer diagonal path. Thus time goes by more slowly on the moving clock relative to the stationary clock. Therefore, as Einstein realized, the light postulate leads directly to time dilation — clocks run slower when they move.

Clock Moves at Faster Speed

What if the moving clock goes by you (from left to right) at a faster speed? As the moving clock's horizontal speed increases, the distance the photon must travel between the two mirrors also increases. This diagonal path becomes longer and longer.

This results in an even slower time between ticks of the clock. Thus time slows down more and more as the clock's horizontal motion increases with respect to you.

In fact, if we use high school plane geometry (Euclidean geometry and the Pythagorean Theorem), we can calculate the relationship between the horizontal speed of the moving clock and the slowing of its time. When we do this, lo and behold, we get the Lorentz transform equation for time dilation![3] (See endnote for derivation.)

From a New Perspective

Now say you are somehow sitting on top of the "moving" clock. What do you see? From your new frame of reference, you and the "moving" clock are standing still. And the other clock — the former "stationary" clock — is now moving by you in the opposite direction.

So you now see the photon in your "moving" clock — the clock you are sitting on — traveling straight up and down. You look over at the "stationary" clock and see that photon traversing a zigzag diagonal path. Thus from your new point of view, time on the clock you are sitting on is running normally, but time on the "stationary" clock over there is running more slowly.

So you on the "moving" clock see the exact opposite of what someone sitting on the "stationary" clock would see. Whose point of view is correct? Both are. Time is relative.

This notion of time being relative may be difficult to accept, to say the least. In trying to grasp this aspect of reality, you may find yourself fighting your own intuition. But the relativity of time is no illusion. How do we know? Let's look at the evidence.

It is Raining Muons[4]

I found it surprising when I learned the first unambiguous test of time dilation was not performed until 1941 — 36 years after Einstein first proposed it. The experiment was performed by Bruno Rossi and David Hall of the University of Chicago at Echo Lake in Colorado. A similar experiment was performed in 1963 by David Frisch and James H. Smith of MIT.[5]

These famous experiments involved the detection of exotic particles called *muons*.

What are muons? They are a heavy version of electrons. Muons have the same properties as electrons (such as an electric charge of −1) except muons weigh some 200 times more than electrons.

Because of their heavy mass, muons are highly unstable. On average, they exist for only a few microseconds before they spontaneously transform into lighter particles. (A muon usually transforms into an electron and other subatomic particles called neutrinos.)

Let's imagine we had a jar of freshly minted muons in our laboratory. After a few millionths of a second, we would find that nearly all of the muons are gone. They have transformed into lighter particles. Physicists call this transformation process "particle decay".[6]

As of this moment, a rain of muons is pouring down on us from Earth's upper atmosphere. How are they produced? Cosmic rays from outer space (mostly atomic nuclear particles called protons from the Sun) strike air molecules high in our atmosphere.[7] These collisions produce muons, many of which reach all the way down to the surface of the Earth.

The problem is: most muons don't exist long enough to survive the long trip from the upper atmosphere to the Earth's surface. Yet scientists detect an enormous number of muons even at sea level. What is the answer to this puzzle?

Let's look at the data from the 1963 Frisch/Smith experiment.[8] They placed a muon detector near the top of Mount Washington in New Hampshire and counted the number of muons detected per hour. They then moved their equipment to Cambridge, Massachusetts to get muon rates at sea level.

Frisch and Smith compared the muons rates recorded on Mount Washington with rates at sea level to see how many muons (on average) survived the trip. This is depicted schematically in Fig. 5.4.

To understand what happens to our muons, we need to consider their "half-life". The so-called half-life of a particle is the time it takes for half the particles to transform (decay) into other particles. Muons, for example, have a half-life of 1.5 microseconds (1.5 millionths of a second).

So if we had 100 freshly created muons in a jar, only about 50 would still exist after 1.5 microseconds. Now if we wait another 1.5 microseconds, there will only be about 25 muons left, and so on. In other words, the muon population is cut in half every 1.5 microseconds.

61

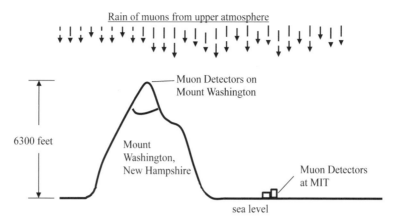

Figure 5.4. **Differences in Muon Count between Mount Washington and at Sea Level Confirm Special Relativity.**

In the Frisch/Smith muon experiment, they counted a rate of about **570** muons per hour near the top of Mount Washington. Calculations based on muon speed (0.994c) and their half-life predicted readings at sea level should be about **36** muons per hour. This says on average most muons simply do not exist long enough to survive the 6300 foot trip from Mount Washington to sea level, even at speeds of 0.994c.

What did scientists actually record at sea level? A rate of about **412** muons per hour! This is over 11 times the expected rate. How did so many muons "stay alive" long enough to reach the ground?

The answer, as you may have suspected, is time dilation. To understand this, imagine that muons have tiny clocks traveling along side them. Einstein tells us that these "muon clocks" are ticking at a slower rate than those on the ground.

Why? Because the muons are moving at 0.994c (relative to the ground).[9] From the muons perspective (their frame of reference), much less time has passed. Time itself has slowed due to the motion of the speedy muons. Therefore the muons have a longer time to exist before they transform (decay) into lighter particles.

Special relativity predicted roughly 428 muons per hour at sea level — in admirable agreement with Frisch/Smith measurements of about 412 muons per hour. The experiment was successful (as was the earlier Rossi/Hall experiment.) Both showed that time dilation is real.

Later tests confirmed these conclusions. In 1966, physicists used the controlled laboratory environment at CERN — the world's largest particle accelerator facilities — to make highly accurate measurements of time dilation.[10] Muons traveling at 99.7% the speed of light showed a 12 × increase in their lifetimes. This agreed with special relativity predictions to an accuracy of 2%.

In 1985, a team led by Matti Kaivola of the Helsinki University of Technology, Finland used high speed neon atoms to measure the effects of time dilation.[11] Measurements agreed with Einstein's predictions to an incredible 40 parts per million. Experiments at Colorado State University in 1992 extended this to an accuracy of less than three parts per million.[12] In 2005, lithium ions tests at the Max Planck Institute for Nuclear Physics in Heidelberg produced the greatest accuracy yet — agreement with special relativity to two parts per ten billion.[13]

Rocket Time

OK, so time dilation is real. We see its effects in decay rates of muons in our atmosphere, in particle accelerators deep beneath the Earth, in atomic clocks on airplanes and rockets (see Chap. 11), and in sophisticated laboratory experiments.

In fact, no experiment, observations, or measurements performed to date has failed to confirm Einstein's time dilation predictions. As counter-intuitive at it may seem, Einstein was right. Time does slow down with motion.

To get an appreciation of the range of extremes of this effect, let's imagine our friend Crash has left the Earth in a rocket ship capable of speeds approaching that of light. Crash brings a clock with him which emits a short "beep" in the form of a radio signal. It beeps on the hour, every hour.

His pal Steady Eddie is back on Earth with a radio receiver and his own clock. Eddie records the periodic beeps he receives from Crash's rocket and compares them to his Earth clock.

Now Eddie has to take into account that as Crash travels, his radio signals have to travel longer distances as the rocket moves away from the Earth. So Eddie has a computer program which takes the rocket's distance from Earth into account. This way, Eddie can determine what the time interval is between the rocket's radio signals, independent of distance.

(For simplicity, we ignore the effect of the so-called Doppler Effect on the time interval as seen by Eddie on the Earth.)

If Newton were to learn of this experiment, he would predict that, once we adjust for the distance, the signals from the rocket will be received on the Earth on the hour every hour. Why? Because in Newtonian physics, time is absolute — there is no time dilation.

But Einstein predicts that the rocket's motion will affect the timing of those signals, as seen from Earth. The amount is determined by the Lorentz Factor, $F = sqrt\ (1 - v^2)$.

Per special relativity, time on the rocket is running slower than time on Earth, Crash on the rocket thinks his time is running normally. But to Eddie on Earth, everything in the rocket appears to be going in slow motion. Thus what Crash sees as a time interval of an hour on the rocket appears to be a *longer* time interval to Eddie on Earth.

So if Eddie records the time interval between rocket signals, what will he see? He will observe longer time intervals between beeps than Crash does. And the faster Crash's rocket goes, the longer the time interval between signals as recorded by Eddie on the Earth. (This is summarized in Table 5.1.)[14]

Let's look at some examples:

At Everyday Speeds — Say Crash sets the rocket to a leisurely uniform speed of only 670 miles per hour relative to Earth. This again is roughly the cruising speed of commercial jet airplanes. Crash is now traveling at about a millionth the speed of light relative to Eddie on the Earth.

Table 5.1. Time Interval of One Hour on Rocket Dilates to *Longer* Time Interval on Earth.

Rocket Speed in Miles per Hour	Rocket Speed, v as Fraction of Speed of Light	Reciprocal Lorentz Factor, $1/F = 1/sqrt\ (1 - v^2)$	Time Interval as Recorded on Earth (hr: min: sec)
670 mph	0.000001	1.0000000000005	1:00:00
16,000,000	0.024	1.000285	1:00:01
168,000,000	0.25	1.0329	1:01:59
336,000,000	0.5	1.1555	1:09:20
503,000,000	0.75	1.5120	1:30:43
604,000,000	0.9	2.301	2:18:05
670,610,000	0.99999	225	224:54

Here the reciprocal Lorentz Factor is only 1.000 000 000 000 5. Thus for one hour on Crash's rocket clock, Eddie's earth clock shows a reading of 1 hour 00 minutes and 00 seconds. At this rocket speed, the time dilation effect is too small to show up on Eddie's earth clock readout.

At Relativistic Speeds — As the rocket moves to higher and higher speeds, the reciprocal Lorentz Factor increases dramatically. If Crash's rocket was somehow able to travel at 99.999% the speed of light, the reciprocal Lorentz Factor would be about a whopping 225.

This means that a time interval of one hour on the rocket records as 225 hours on Earth! At this speed, Crash and everything in the rocket ship are aging 225 times slower than all things on Earth. (Go fast to stay young!)

At the Speed of Light — Imagine the rocket's speed approaching the speed of light. In this scenario, the Earth time interval (corresponding to one hour of rocket time) approaches *infinity*. But here Crash observes nothing strange or different about time on his ship. Time continues to pass as usual from his point of view — no matter what his uniform velocity. It has to be this way because of Galileo's dictum/Einstein's relativity postulate. Since the rocket is traveling in uniform motion, there is no way *internally* for Crash to detect whether he is moving or at rest.

The rocket cannot actually reach the speed of light. Per special relativity, this is impossible. Why? Well for one thing, it takes an infinite amount of energy for an object *with mass* to achieve the speed of light (as we shall see in Chap. 7). But a massless particle like a photon can and does travel at the speed of light.

OK, so what happens for a photon traveling *at* the speed of light? Here the reciprocal Lorenz Factor is infinite. This implies that to a photon, all events occur *at the same time*! Thus a photon experiences no aging. The hands on a photon's "clock" stand still. From its point of view, time is frozen.

What about a photon and length contraction? Consider a photon emitted by the Sun traveling to the Earth. From our point of view on Earth, the approximately 93 million mile trip takes about 8.3 minutes. From the photon's point of view, it is standing still, and the Earth is traveling towards it at the speed of light.

This length contraction at the speed of light reduces the distance from Earth to the Sun to *zero*. To the photon, the trip from the Sun to the Earth happens instantly.

So from the photon's point of view, it gets from the Sun to Jupiter instantaneously, to the star Alpha Centauri instantaneously — it gets everywhere instantaneously.[15] Everything in front of it is compressed to zero distance away. This is the power of time dilation and length contraction at the speed of light.

Next Chapter

In his 1905 relativity manuscript, Albert Einstein presented a simple thought experiment with profound implications. Imagine you are at a train station when the 7 pm metro liner arrives exactly on schedule. What do you observe at that very instant? You see the small hand of the train station clock pointing to the number 7 at the exact moment the train arrives. Thus the time of 7 o'clock as seen on the station clock is simultaneous with the train's arrival. They are two simultaneous events.

Einstein brilliantly pointed out what this means — *simultaneous events actually define time itself.*[16] He then showed that two events happening at the same time for you *do not* necessarily happen at the same time for me (if we are in relative motion). Therefore, he explained, if simultaneity is relative, then *any* measurement of time must also be relative.

From this premise, Einstein went on to show that not only is time relative, but space is as well. The mind-boggling concepts of the *relativity of simultaneity* and *length contraction* are the subjects of the next chapter.

Chapter 6

Simultaneity and the Squeezing of Space

The distinction between past, present, and
future is only an illusion, even if a stubborn one.[1]

Albert Einstein

In his 1905 paper on special relativity,[2] Albert Einstein made a prediction that has been called "one of the deepest insights into the nature of reality ever discovered."[3] He stated that events happening at the same time for you may not happen at the same time for me.

For example, imagine you are on a single train car traveling in uniform motion. You observe two flash bulbs going off at the exact same time — one at the rear of the train car and one at the front. I am standing on an embankment outside the train watching it go by.

Will I also see both flashbulbs go off at the exact same time? No. According to Einstein, I will see the two flashes at different times. What is simultaneous to you is not simultaneous to me. In other words, "there is no universal definition of time and simultaneity."[4]

Another one of our most deeply held assumptions about reality is turned on its head. And as we shall see, this extraordinary, hard-to-believe phenomenon is a direct result of Einstein's two postulates.

The Relativity of Simultaneity

Two events are called *simultaneous* if they occur at the same time. Newtonian physics tells us that what is seen as simultaneous by one observer is seen as simultaneous to all observers in the universe. Simple and obvious. Einstein, however, informs us that the simultaneity of events is affected by relative motion.

In my opinion, physicist Brian Greene gives the clearest and simplest explanation of this so-called "relativity of simultaneity" in his book *The Elegant Universe*.[5] Imagine two neighboring countries — Forwardland and Backwardland — are perpetually at war with each other. After long years of negotiation, the presidents of the two countries finally agree to sign a peace treaty.

In order to assure their respective citizens of total fairness, both presidents agree to sign copies of the treaty at the same time. They arrange to sit at opposite ends of a long table, with a light bulb placed at its exact center. Each is to sign when they see the light turned on. Since they are both equidistant from the light bulb, they expect to receive its light at the same time. Thus they will sign simultaneously.

The two presidents also agree to hold the signing ceremony on a special vehicle fitted with glass sides. The vehicle is to be driven on a straight road bordering the two countries, so citizens on both sides can witness the signing. The international press is invited to record the signing ceremony. They place cameras on the vehicle and on the side of the road.

All is ready. The vehicle proceeds down the straight border road at a uniform speed. The two presidents sit with pen in hand. The light at the center of the table is turned on. Both presidents see the light, bend and sign the treaty.

The dignitaries on the vehicle see the Forwardland and Backwardland presidents sign at the same time. Cheers break out inside the moving vehicle. Congratulations and handshakes are given all around.

However along the road, riots break out. People of Backwardland claim they saw the Forwardland president sign the peace treaty slightly *before* their president signed. Press and camera crew stationed on the ground agree.

Later that day, members of the press meet at a nearby studio to try and sort out what happened. They compare the video recordings from cameras on the vehicle to recordings from cameras on the ground. Sure enough, cameras that were on the vehicle show both presidents signing at the same time.

But cameras on the ground show that the Forwardland president signed slightly before the Backwardland president. Everyone is incredulous. How could this happen?

To figure this out, let's look at the signing from both points of view — observers in the moving vehicle (vehicle frame of reference) and observers by the roadside (roadside frame of reference).

Vehicle reference frame — Einstein's relativity postulate tells us that from the point of view of people on the uniformly moving vehicle, they and everything inside the vehicle are *standing still*. Figure 6.1 shows this view, with the two presidents sitting at opposite ends of the table. The president of Forwardland, Felicia Farkward is facing forward — we'll call her *F*. The president of Backwardland, Borat Badanov, is facing backward — we'll call him *B*.

The light bulb is turned on. The light beam from the bulb travels at the same speed *c* in all directions. Since both presidents are the same distance from the light bulb, the light beam reaches them at the same time. The two presidents thus see the light beam at the same time and sign the treaty simultaneously.

Roadside Reference frame — To observers on the roadside, the light bulb flashes as the vehicle moves uniformly to the right. Thus the Forwardland president (*F*) moves towards the light, so the beam has a shorter distance to get to her. The Backwardland president (*B*) moves away from the light, so the beam has a longer distance to get to him. (This is shown in Fig. 6.2.)

Now this is key — per Einstein's light postulate the speed of light is unaffected by the speed of the vehicle. So both beams travel at the same speed, *c*. And since the light has to travel at the same speed but a shorter distance to get to *F*, it reaches *F* first. Therefore *F* signs before *B*. In the roadside frame of reference the signings are *not simultaneous*.

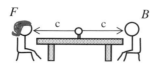

Figure 6.1. Vehicle Frame. *Light reaches both presidents at same time.*

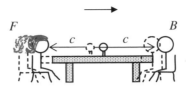

Figure 6.2. Roadside Frame. *Distance from bulb to F shorter; light reaches F first.*

Is this really so? Let's look at what the cameras saw. Figure 6.3 shows what cameras inside the vehicle recorded. (The light beam track has been added for clarity.) The dignitaries, press, and cameras inside the vehicle observed the following sequence: (1) the light turns on, (2) the light spreads uniformly in all directions, (3) the light beam reaches both presidents at the same time, and (4) both presidents sign at the same time. The signings are simultaneous.

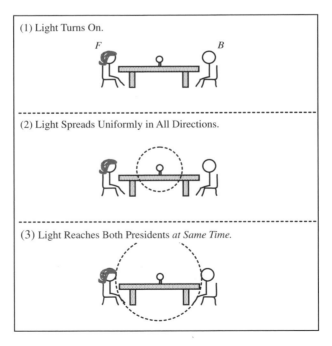

Figure 6.3. View from INSIDE VEHICLE. *Both presidents see light at same time, so sign simultaneously. (See animation on relativity of simultaneity in marksmodernphysics.com)*

70

Figure 6.4 shows what cameras on the roadside recorded. Because of the constancy of the speed of light and the relative motion of the vehicle, this sequence is quite different: (1) the light turns on, (2) the light beam again spreads uniformly in all directions (its speed is unaffected by the vehicle's motion), (3) since *F* is moving towards the light and *B* is moving away from the light, it reaches *F* first, and (4) *F* signs the peace treaty before *B*. The signings are not simultaneous.

Summary

The treaty signings are simultaneous to observers sitting on the train, but not simultaneous to observers standing on the ground. *Simultaneity is relative*. Observers in relative motion do not agree on which events occur at the same time. Newton's notion of absolute time is destroyed! There is no universal clock.

All this follows from Einstein's two postulates: the speed of light is independent of the speed of its source, and uniform motion is relative.[6]

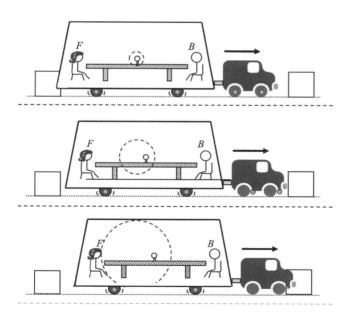

Figure 6.4. Sequential View from SIDE OF ROAD. *F sees light before B, so signs first (not drawn to scale). (See animation on relativity of simultaneity in marksmodernphysics.com)*

Now what if one of the people watching the signing ceremony from the roadside decides to run alongside the vehicle? Let's assume this person is able to run fast enough to match the speed of the presidential vehicle. (He would then be in the same reference frame as the vehicle.) This observer would see both presidents signing at the *same* time, just as observers inside the vehicle do.

It is curious that observers who are standing alongside the road see the Forwardland president sign first, but an observer moving alongside the road at the same speed as the vehicle sees them sign at the exact same time. So it is *relative motion* which determines whether observers see the same two events as simultaneous or not.

For two observers who are stationary with respect to each other, if one sees the two events as simultaneous, then the other observer will as well. However, if there *is* relative motion between two observers, if two events appear simultaneously to one observer, the events may not occur at the same time for the other observer.

Whose point of view is correct? They both are. Simultaneity is relative.

Like the relativity of time and space, the relativity of simultaneity is an extremely small effect at everyday speeds. Of course, it must be. Otherwise, it would have been noticed long before Einstein.

What if Galileo and Newton heard this story? They would agree with Einstein's conclusion that observers on the vehicle see the signings occur at the same time. But they would argue that observers on the roadside would also see simultaneous signings. Why? Because they believed the light's speed would be affected by the speed of the vehicle.

Under their scenario, to observers on the roadside the speed of the light moving in the backwards direction would be slowed by the vehicle's motion in the opposite direction. And the speed of the light moving in the forward direction would increase due to the vehicle's motion in the same forward direction.

So the slower backwards beam would make up for the shorter distance to F. And the faster forward beam would make up for the longer distance to B. The net result: F and B would see the light at the same time.

But Einstein knew something Galileo and Newton did not. The speed of light is absolute — it is not affected by the vehicle's motion. Thus the light spreads out uniformly in all directions. So F sees the light before

B — and signs first. Relativity of simultaneity is a direct consequence of Einstein's light postulate.[7]

These different views of simultaneity for observers in relative motion led Einstein to another profound insight regarding the nature of time. It concerns how we define "now" and "past, present, and future".

Tense and Pretense

> Experience of the now means something special for man, something essentially different from past to future. But this important difference does not occur within physics . . . A matter of painful but inevitable resignation.[8]
>
> Albert Einstein

Let's define *now* as the moment the two presidents signed the treaty. All the dignitaries and press on the vehicle would agree with this definition. But what about the people on the side of the road? What is their "now"? They saw the Forwardland president sign earlier, so we could call this their past. They saw the Backwardland president sign later, so we could call this their future.

Now for the people on the ground is different than now for those on the train. The relativity of simultaneity muddles our notion of tense.

Let's look at this a little more carefully:

On the Vehicle — Let's define "now" or the present as the exact moment when the two presidents sign simultaneously. So in this frame of reference the past is when the two presidents are waiting for the light to reach them, or before they both sign. The future is after both presidents have signed the treaty together.

On the Roadside — What are past, present, and future for observers on the ground? We can't choose the same "now" as for the people on the vehicle, because people on the ground saw the two presidents sign at different times. So we are forced to choose a different "now". *Now is relative!* So let's choose "now" for people on the ground to be the midpoint in time between F signing and B signing. In this case, F signed in the past, and B signed in the future.

So past, present, and future are different for people on the ground than they are for the people on the train! This is summarized in Table 6.1.

This brings up the question: what exactly do we *mean* by "now"? Now to me may not be the same now for another observer. Because time and space are relative, two observers in relative motion have "different

Table 6.1.   Past, Present, and Future are Relative! *They are different for observers in relative motion. (Midpoint is the time midway between F signing and B signing.)*

Reference Frame	Past	Present	Future
On moving vehicle	Before both sign	Both sign	After both sign
On ground	F signs	Midpoint	B signs

conceptions of what exists at any given moment, and hence different conception of reality," explains Brian Greene.[9] In other words, given relative motion between you and other observers — your past is some other observer's present,[10] and something that is in the undecided future to you has already happened to yet another observer.

Whose point of view is the right one? No observer's notion of "now" is any more valid than any others. They are all valid. *Tense is relative.*

So time is relative and simultaneity is relative. Einstein's third leg of his relativity construct is that space is relative as well. Like time, this so-called length contraction manifests itself in a measurement — the distance between two points in space.

The Shrinking of Space

Einstein tells us we should not think about the length of an object as a fact. Length, rather, is a "relationship between the object and the measurer."[11] Like time, the measurement of length depends upon the relative motion between the object and the observer.

To get a quantitative feel for length contraction, imagine our fearless race car driver Crash is again in outer space on a rocket capable of relativistic speeds. Only this time Eddie's measurements from Earth involve the shrinking of space, not time.

Crash's rocket is huge. Measured at rest, it extends some 100 yards from end-to-end — the length of a football field (This is nearly the size of the Saturn V rocket which launched astronauts to the Moon.) Standing upright on the launch pad, Crash's rocket is about as high as a 25-story building.

Crash makes multiple passes by the Earth at different uniform speeds. Steady Eddie is again on the Earth, observing the rocket with a high-powered telescope. What does he measure for the rocket's length? Steady Eddie on the Earth finds that the length of the rocket varies with its speed. In fact, from Eddie's point of view the faster the rocket goes by, the smaller is its length — the predicted amount determined by the Lorentz Factor, $F = sqrt\,(1 - v^2)$ This is summarized in Table 6.2.[12]

Let's look at this in more detail.

Everyday Speeds — In Crash's first pass, he is cruising along at roughly commercial airplane speed of 670 miles per hour. This is approximately one-millionth the speed of light. Length contraction at this speed is so small it doesn't show up on Eddie's measuring device. (Thus length contraction goes unnoticed in everyday life.)

Relativistic Speeds — As the rocket's speed increases, the effect becomes more and more pronounced. At half the speed of light, Eddie measures a rocket length of only 86.5 yards. At $0.99999c$, the 100 yard long rocket contracts to a mere 0.44 yards. To Eddie, the football-field size rocket is now only about 16 inches long!

But to Crash in the rocket, all is normal. Remember that Crash is in uniform motion — so to him the rocket and everything inside is at rest. From his point of view, there is no "shrinking of space" inside the rocket.

Physicists have imagined all kinds of tricks with Einstein's length contraction. A famous example is the so-called "pole-barn paradox". Let's take a look at this amusing and instructive thought-experiment.

Table 6.2. Rocket Length of 100 Yards Contracted due to Relative Speed.

Rocket Speed in Miles per Hour	Rocket Speed, v as Fraction of the Speed of Light	Lorentz Factor, $F = sqrt(1-v^2)$	100 yards Contracts to
670	0.000001	0.9999999999995	100 yards
16,000,000	0.024	0.9997	99.97
168,000,000	0.25	0.968	96.8
336,000,000	0.5	0.865	86.5
503,000,000	0.75	0.661	66.1
604,000,000	0.9	0.435	43.5
670,610,000	0.99999	0.0044	0.44

Simultaneous Pole Squeeze

It is the year 2323, Daredevil Dave XII, the great-great-great-great-great-great-great-great-great grandson of the famed motorcycle stuntman will perform an amazing demonstration of Einstein's length contraction. Dave plans to show a world-wide audience how to fit an 18-foot pole into a 10-foot barn.[13]

If Dave is at rest with respect to the barn, there is, of course, no way to fit the pole into the barn. The pole is almost twice the length of the barn, as shown in Fig. 6.5. But at high enough speed, according to Einstein the pole should contract and fit inside the barn. At least that's the idea.

So Dave straps a jet-pack on his back, and sets the controls to a speed of 0.866c. Again this is about 580 million miles an hour. He then straps the 18-foot pole to his mighty arm, fires the jetpack, and finds himself hurled headlong towards the 10-foot long barn.

Both the front and rear barn doors are open. But Dave's assistants plan to quickly shut both doors when the pole is fully inside the barn, thus proving that the pole is indeed inside the barn. They will then immediately open the rear door to let Dave and the pole out. (Very quickly!)

Barn Frame of Reference — From the barn's point of view, the pole is now speeding towards it at 0.866c. As we saw in Chap. 4, the Lorentz Factor for this speed is 0.5. So a relative speed of $v = 0.866c$ produces a length contraction of 50%. Thus the barn sees the approaching 18-foot pole contracted to 9 feet long. At this speed the 9-foot contracted pole does fit inside the 10-foot barn. (This is shown on Fig. 6.6(a).)

Is it really that simple? Well, not quite. We have to look at this crazy stunt from the pole's reference frame as well.

Pole Reference Frame — From the pole's point of view, it is stationary and the barn is moving towards it at 0.866c (See Fig. 6.6(b).) So from the

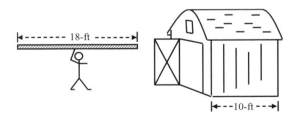

Figure 6.5.   Daredevil Dave, Pole, and Barn at Rest.

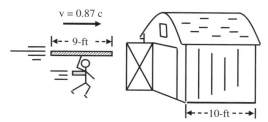

(a) **Barn Reference Frame.** *Moving pole contracts to 9-feet and fits inside barn!*

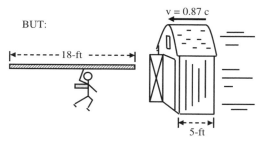

(b) **Pole Reference Frame.** *Moving barn contracts to 5 feet, so pole can't fit inside barn???*

Figure 6.6. Pole/Barn Paradox. *View from both reference frames.*

pole's perspective, the barn has contracted from 10 feet long to 5 feet long. And remember in this reference frame the pole is at rest. So it remains 18 feet long.

So now we have an issue: How can an 18-foot pole fit into a 5-foot barn?

From the barn's reference frame, the pole fits. From the pole's reference frame, it doesn't. In particular, how do Dave's assistants manage to close both the front and rear doors of the barn with the pole contained inside it?

Have we arrived at a contradiction to special relativity? Have we finally tripped up the elusive Dr. Einstein? Nope. Einstein manages to escape as usual:

Barn Reference Frame Again — Figure 6.7 shows a bird's-eye view of the sequence of events from the barn's frame of reference. Here the stationary barn is 10 feet long and the speeding pole is contracted to half its length or 9 feet long.

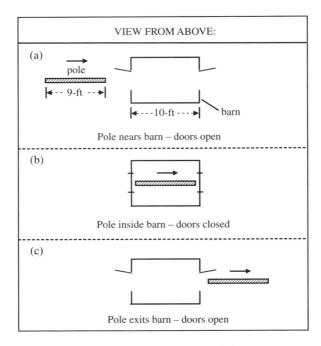

VIEW FROM ABOVE:

(a)
pole
|◄-- 9-ft --►|
|◄---10-ft---►| barn

Pole nears barn – doors open

(b)

Pole inside barn – doors closed

(c)

Pole exits barn – doors open

Figure 6.7. Barn Reference Frame: *Pole-barn sequence.*

An observer on the barn sees: (a) The moving pole approaching the stationary barn at 0.866c — both the front and rear barn doors are open, (b) the pole now fully inside the barn. The assistants close both barn doors *at the same time*, and (c) the assistants open both barn doors, and the pole proceeds to exit the barn. Notice that the front and rear barn doors are closed simultaneously. This is key.

Pole Reference Frame Again

Now let's look at a bird's eye view of the sequence of events from the pole's frame of reference. (See Fig. 6.8.) In this case the stationary pole is a full 18 feet long, but the barn is contracted to half its length or only 5-feet long.

The pole (and Daredevil Dave) sees the following: (1) The barn nears the pole; both barn doors are open, (2) an assistant closes the rear door as the right side of the pole is encompassed by the barn, (3) an assistant

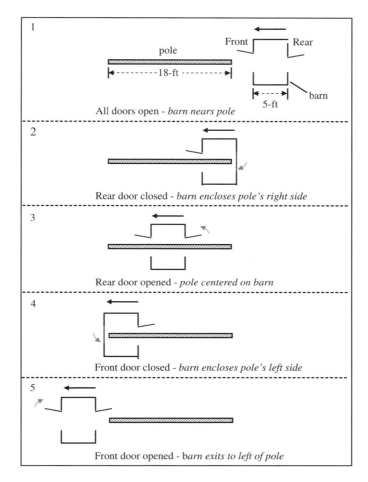

1

pole

Front ⌐ Rear

|◄-------- 18-ft --------►|

5-ft

barn

All doors open - *barn nears pole*

2

Rear door closed - *barn encloses pole's right side*

3

Rear door opened - *pole centered on barn*

4

Front door closed - *barn encloses pole's left side*

5

Front door opened - b*arn exits to left of pole*

Figure 6.8. Pole Reference Frame: *Pole-barn sequence.*

opens the rear door as the barn is now centered on the pole, (4) an assistant closes the front door as the barn contains the left side of the pole, and (5) the barn exits to the left as an assistant opens the front door.

Say what? Didn't we just say in a previous paragraph that the front and rear barn doors were closed at the same time? Now we are saying that the assistants closed the rear door first, and then they closed the front door. Which point of view is correct? They both are — simultaneity is relative.

Just like in the presidential signing ceremony, events that happen at the same time in one reference frame do not necessarily happen simultaneously in another reference frame. So the doors are closed and reopened at the same time in the barn reference frame — but at different times in the pole reference frame.

Do you see it? From the point of view of the barn, the front and rear doors are closed and reopened when the pole is fully inside the barn — simultaneously. But from the point of view of the pole, first the rear door is closed and reopened and then, after the barn passes over the pole, the front door is closed and reopened — not at the same time!

Once again, our oh so clever Albert Einstein is victorious. That a solitary young man with virtually no contact with physicists of his day could have thought up such a profound and all encompassing theory as special relativity is nothing short of astounding.

Yes, Lorentz and Fitzgerald come up with some of the mathematics, and both they and French physicist Henri Poincaré had suggested some of the ideas of special relativity, but only Einstein made the full leap. He alone was able to cast off the shackles of Newtonian physics with, as physicist Kip Thorne put it, "a clarity of thought that others could not match."[14] We are awed by Einstein's fearlessness and humbled by his genius.

Perhaps you are still doubtful. Maybe you are asking how space itself can contract? And for that matter, how can time shrink? Einstein thought deeply about the physical implication of his theory. He found his answer in the strict empirical view that reality is only what we *measure*.

What are "Time" and "Space"?

It might appear possible to overcome all the difficulties attending the definition of "time" by substituting "the position of the small hand of my watch" for "time".[15]

Albert Einstein

While working at the patent office, Albert Einstein began to meet periodically with Maurice Solovine, a philosophy student at the University of Bern, as well as Conrad Habicht, a former math student at Zurich Poly. They had responded to an ad placed by Einstein in 1901 to tutor students in mathematics and physics, and soon became lifelong friends. The trio had lively discussions and reading on the classics, science, and philosophy. Mocking pompous formal scholarly societies of the period, they called themselves the "Olympia Academy".[16] (See Fig. 6.9.)

Amongst the books they read were works by 18th century Scottish empiricist David Hume, and 19th century Austrian physicist/philosopher Ernst Mach. Hume said time itself has no *"absolute* existence . . . independent of observable objects (e.g. clocks) whose movements permit us to define time."[17] (Italics are mine.)

Mach wrote a "scathing criticism" of Newton's absolute time and absolute space, because they are concepts which cannot be measured. From these works and others, Einstein acquired a philosophy of science which profoundly influenced his development of relativity.

Einstein came to embrace the notion that nothing exists beyond what we observe, what we can measure. The young patent clerk defined *time* as simply "what you read on a clock" — and *space* as simply "the distance you measure between two points." The notion of time and space as anything beyond these "operational" definitions were, according to Einstein, simply the creation of the human mind.[18]

In other words, time is relative — how fast it passes depends on the motion of the observer. This is measurable. However, the concept of time we hold in our minds is merely an abstraction.

Einstein applied a similar view to "space". What exactly is space? This seemingly simple question has puzzled philosophers and scientists since ancient times.

We are conditioned to think of space as immutable, as rigid. After all, if I measure the distance between two points in space with great care,

Figure 6.9. The "Olympia Academy". *Albert Einstein with friends Habicht (left) and Solovine (center), ca. 1903.*

using exquisitely accurate instruments, I expect that my readings are reliable and repeatable. It is most reasonable to assume that, given you use equivalent measuring instruments and the same diligence, you would measure the same value for this distance as I do (or extremely close to it).

However, as modern physics teaches us again and again, we must be careful what we assume. Our experience, our very intuition is often an unreliable guide to reality. So it is with space.

In 1905, Einstein proposed that *the distance* between the same two points in space is *not* the same for all observers. Like the time interval, this "space interval" is relative. To a moving observer, the distance between two points in space contracts along the direction of motion.

But how can space contract? And how can the apparently *same* space contract differently for a number of observers in different amounts of relative motion? Here Einstein is saying there is no "space" per se — only the distance between two points. The distance between the two points is measurable, albeit differently by the two observers. But "space" itself is again a mere abstraction.

Einstein tells us we must think of time and space as only the position on a clock and markings on a ruler.

> Space and time are orders of things, and not things.[19]
>
> Gottfried Leibniz

Einstein was to later develop a much broader view of space and time — first in considering the spacetime physics of his mathematics teacher, Hermann Minkowski, and then in his development of general relativity. (We discuss this further in Chap. 8 and Part II of this book.)

The Next Chapter

Young Albert is not done with us yet. In the next chapter, we learn how the relativity of time and space leads to a completely new paradigm for mass and energy — and the most famous equation of all time, $E = mc^2$.

Chapter 7

The World's Most Famous Equation

$E = mc^2$ is the secret of the stars. It is the cosmic engine that drives
the entire universe ... It's the reason why the stars shine,
and why the sun lights up the Earth.[1]

Michio Kaku

The summer of 1905 was a particularly memorable one for Albert
Einstein. He had submitted his three seminal papers to the highly
regarded German physics journal *Annalen der Physik* by June. Still working at the Bern patent office and isolated from the physics community,
he found himself pondering how special relativity might relate to
energy. In September of 1905, he published the results of his contemplations in the same journal. This remarkable three-page supplement has
been called "perhaps the most profound afterthought in the history of
science."[2]

In this short manuscript, Einstein used Maxwell's theory of electromagnetism and the postulates of special relativity to derive a new equation. Einstein presented the equation in the form, $m = E / c^2$. It wasn't until
a later paper that he wrote it in its popular form, $E = mc^2$. What does this
equation mean? It means that energy and mass are *equivalent*, that energy,
like mass, has inertia. Thus energy, like mass has weight!

The argument is amusing and attractive; but I can't tell whether
the Lord isn't laughing about it and playing a trick on me.[3]

Albert Einstein in letter to a friend

When I first read about $E = mc^2$, I wondered what on earth does the relativity of space and time have to do with mass and energy? To understand this, we first take a look at what an object's mass is. We then explain the concepts of momentum and kinetic energy. Then we follow the path that Einstein took in coming up with his famous mass-energy relationship. Finally, we consider the profound implications of his remarkable equation.

Mass Hysteria

"Let's see. Your eight crates weigh a total of 289 mars-pounds. That's **732 earth-pounds**. I'll pay you 422 grand credits for the lot," Harley says.

"You cheating son-of-a-space flea," say the Zaslaw twins. "This cargo weighed **762 pounds on Earth** and you know it. You owe us 440 grand credits for this shipment."

"Take it or leave it," smiles Harley.

With a cold stare at the Mars docking agent, the twins reluctantly agree to the deal — they know they have no leverage here. What are they going to do, lug their shipment all the way to the Moon? Besides they are short on rocket fuel, and as usual short on cash, and Harley knows it.

The year is 2525. The Zaslaw twins make a living shipping cargo between the Earth, the Moon, and Mars. Everyone calls it the "tri-planet route," even though the Moon is not a planet. Typical of their breed, the twins are highly competitive and fiercely independent. They love the freedom and adventure of the job, but there is a problem. Disputes are constantly breaking out between freight carriers and docking station agents over the exact *weight* of their loads.

Shipments are paid for by weight, but cargo weight depends on where it is being weighed. For instance, a 100-pound cargo on Earth's surface weighs about 37.9 pounds on the surface of Mars and only about 16.6 pounds on the surface of the Moon — due to their respectively weaker gravity.

And the same cargo effectively weighs zero en-route due to the nearly zero gravity of interplanetary space.[4] Ground station personnel often make the conversion from one weight to the other incorrectly, and space teamsters always seem to be on the short end of the deal. (Especially on Mars for some reason.)

The Zaslaw twins decide to take matters into their own hands. They turn to their sister Pat — a physicist at Earth's International Weights and

Measures Agency (IWMA). The twins know they will have to put up with a lecture, but feel it is worth it. Pat patiently listens to their story, then tells them they need to estimate shipping costs by the freight's *mass*, not by its weight.

Pat explains that all objects have mass.[5] It is a measure of an object's resistance to being accelerated. This is called inertia (as we discussed in Chap. 2). The more mass, the more inertia — so the harder it is to get an object at rest to move, or to *change* its speed or direction once it is in motion. For example, a bowling ball at rest is much harder to move than a beach ball at rest. And a moving bowling ball is a lot harder to stop than a beach ball moving at the same speed. This is because a bowling ball has more mass, i.e., more inertia than a beach ball.

"The great thing about mass is that the same cargo has the same amount of mass everywhere — on Earth, on the Moon, on Mars, and even in space," Pat says.

"But because gravity on Mars is weaker than Earth's, the same mass doesn't get pulled down as hard on Martian weight scales as it does on Earth. Thus Martian scales give lower readings for weight. Gravity is even weaker on the Moon, so you get an even lower weight reading on the Moon for the same mass."

"As I said, the weight may be different, but a cargo's mass is the same on the surface of all three bodies. Let me put it in a table to help you understand."

Pat writes out a table of weights and masses for different locations and shows it to the twins. (See Table 7.1.)

"OK, enough with the explanations already. We get it," the twins say. "Just tell us how we can measure a cargo's mass, rather than its weight."

"Simple," Pat says. "Use an *Inertial Balance Scale* (Fig. 7.1). It's been around since ancient times.[6] Astronaut pioneers used it way back in the 20th century to measure their mass in space. I'm surprised you space nuts don't know about this." The twins shrug.

Table 7.1. Weight Changes with Location, but Mass is always the Same Value.

Location	Cargo Weight	Cargo Mass
Earth	100 pounds	45.5 kilograms
Mars	37.9 pounds	45.5 kilograms
Moon	16.6 pounds	45.5 kilograms
Outer Space	0	45.5 kilograms

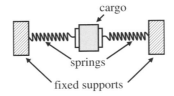

Figure 7.1.   The Inertial Balance Scale. *It measures an object's mass, not its weight.*

"It will measure the cargo's mass as the same value on Earth, on Mars, and the Moon, and even in outer space."

"How does this contraption work?" ask the twins.

"You put the cargo in between two springs, pull the cargo to one side, say to the left, and let go," says Pat. (The sequence is shown in Fig. 7.2.)

"The compressed left spring releases, and pushes the cargo to the right. The cargo then compresses the right spring. When the right spring releases, it pushes the cargo to the left, and so on. So the cargo swings back and forth between the two springs."

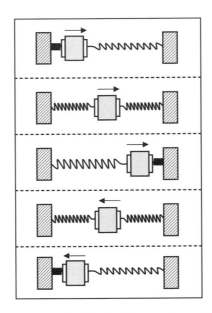

Figure 7.2.   Inertial Balance in Motion. *The time for a complete cycle back and forth is called the period of oscillation. The greater the mass, the slower the period of oscillation.*

"The idea is to time how long it takes to complete a full cycle.[7] The time interval is determined by two things; the cargo's mass and the strength of the springs."

"Typically, you measure a number of cycles to get an average reading. Say on average the cargo makes a complete cycle from the left side to the right side and back in a time interval of 1 second. This is called its period of oscillation.

"Cargo with a greater mass will travel more slowly between the springs. Thus its period of oscillation will be greater. Again say your cargo takes 1 second to complete a cycle. A cargo of twice the mass would make a complete cycle back and forth in 2 seconds. A cargo of three times the mass would complete a cycle in 3 seconds, and so on."

"So we just put the cargo on the Inertial Balance, pull it to one side, and let go?" the twins ask.

"Yes, and then time how long it takes to cycle back and forth."

"And it gives the same time interval for the same cargo on all the planets?"

"Yes," says Pat.

The twins like the idea. Under the auspices of the IWMA, the twins work with Pat to install identical Spring Balances at each docking station. Personnel are then trained in their use. To keep things simple, springs are chosen so that a period of oscillation of 1 second corresponds to a cargo *mass* of 100 kilograms. (This corresponds to an earth-weight of 220 pounds.)

It takes some time, but eventually the problem is resolved. For a given cargo, its measured period of oscillation, and thus its mass is indeed found to be the same value on the surface of Earth, Mars, the Moon, and even inside freight rockets in space. The measurements are independent of gravity. Space teamsters are thrilled.

"Why it's mass hysteria out there," say the twins.

"Very funny," Pat says.

An object's mass and how fast it moves is also involved in a concept called *momentum*. Let's consider two colliding vehicles to see how this works.

On Thick Ice

It's a typical February day in New England. Spot Pond is frozen solid. Oaks and maples at the pond's edge glisten with ice-coated limbs — bent branches of tall pines outline a pale grey sky. A brooding stillness fills the air.

Suddenly a car and truck appear on the ice. They head towards each other — the one-ton car at 50 miles an hour from the left and the ten-ton dump truck at 5 miles an hour from the right. (See Fig. 7.3.)

The car and truck collide! They lock bumpers.

Here's the question: After the collision, will the heavier truck move the lighter car to the left? Or will the faster car move the slower truck to the right?

Or will the two locked vehicles remain in place?

According to Newtonian physics, the vehicles will hit and remain in place. Why? Because they have equal and opposite amounts of momentum.

In Newton's world, momentum is equal to an object's mass times its velocity. (Recall that velocity is an object's speed and direction, so momentum has a magnitude and direction as well.)

The car's momentum is 1 ton times 50 miles an hour or 50 units of momentum. The truck's momentum is 10 tons times −5 miles an hour or −50 units of momentum. (Why the minus sign for the truck? Because it is going in the opposite direction from the car.)

So the two momentums (momenti?) cancel each other out — resulting in no movement of the locked vehicle pair after the collision. The car makes up for being only one-tenth the mass of the truck by going at ten times the truck's speed.

Conservation of Momentum

The law of conservation of momentum says the total momentum before the collision has to be equal to the total momentum after. Here the total momentum *before* is **50** for the car and **−50** for the truck — totaling zero.

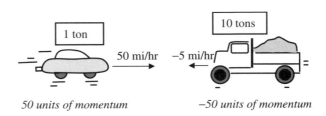

Figure 7.3. Car and Truck Collide on Ice. *The locked vehicles remain in place after the collision, because they have equal and opposite amounts of momentum.*

What is the total momentum after the collision? Also zero. Why? Because the car/truck pair is stopped. Zero velocity means zero momentum.

So the total momentum before the collision is the same as after the collision — in this case zero. This is conservation of momentum at work. Newton's momentum rules whenever two or more objects collide.

Or does it?

Einstein's Momentum

Momentum, the product of an object's mass times its velocity, and conservation of momentum were considered fundamental laws of physics — until Einstein. The young upstart maintained conservation of momentum but challenged the definition of momentum itself.

Per special relativity, an object's momentum isn't so simple. It is affected by its mass and velocity, *and* how fast it is moving with respect to the speed of light. Relativistic momentum is defined as mass times velocity *divided by the Lorentz Factor, F = sqrt (1- v²)*.[8]

What does dividing by the Lorentz Factor do? For slow speeds, it has very little effect. But remember, the Lorentz Factor becomes significant for speeds which are an appreciable fraction of the speed of light. So at relativistic speeds, the amount of momentum predicted by Einstein is *much, much larger* than predicted by Newtonian mechanics. The momentum of an object increases exponentially as it approaches the speed of light.

Was Einstein right?

Physicists conducted a series of experiments on electrons from 1909 to 1915 to test Einstein's version of momentum against Newton's. To most everyone's surprise, the results were in excellent agreement with Einstein's prediction, not Newton's.

Measurements showed that at speeds approaching the speed of light, momentum increased way beyond what the Newtonian formula predicted. Newton's simple mass times velocity formula was a very good approximation at slower speeds; but at relativistic speeds, only Einstein's formula gave the correct answers.

Does this increase in momentum have any real effect? Absolutely. Particle accelerators all over the world see tremendous collision effects due to the relativistic momentum increase of particles traveling near the speed of light. Cosmic rays from outer space, which also travel at nearly the speed of light, show this same effect when they collide with particles in our upper atmosphere.

Consider CERN's Large Hadron Collider (LHC).[9] At full power, it is designed to accelerate protons in opposite directions to an astounding 0.999 999 991c — only about 6 miles an hour slower than the speed of light. This gives a reciprocal Lorentz Factor of 7, 454. Thus protons moving at this speed have nearly *seven thousand five hundred times* the momentum predicted by Newton's formula. When two LHC protons collide, physicists see much, much greater impact — producing particles not seen since the extremely hot and ultra-dense environment of the big bang.

Mathematically, for a particle of mass, m traveling at 0.999 999 991c, its momentum (in units where the speed of light is 1) is:

Per Newton's formula:

Momentum = mass times velocity

$P = mv$

$P = 0.999\ 999\ 991\ m \approx m$

Per Einstein's formula:

Momentum = mass times velocity divided by the Lorentz Factor, F

$P = mv\ /\ sqrt\ (\ 1\ -\ v^2\ )$

$= 0.999\ 999\ 991\ m\ /\ sqrt\ (\ 1 - (0.999\ 999\ 991\ )^2)$

$= 0.999\ 999\ 991\ m\ /\ 0.000134$

$= 7454\ m$

See Appendix C for more on relativistic momentum.

Einstein's relativistic momentum is not just a mathematical abstraction; it governs all collisions in the universe. Now let's consider the concept of *energy* — the ability to do work.

Newton and Energy

The great Isaac Newton was not always right, even within the context of classical (pre-relativistic) physics — for example, in defining *kinetic energy*.

An object in *motion* has what physicists call "kinetic" energy; the faster the object moves the more kinetic energy it has. Newton believed this energy of motion was simply the product of an object's mass times its velocity.

His great nemesis, German mathematician and natural philosopher Gottfried Leibniz disagreed. He proposed that the kinetic energy of an object is proportional to its mass times the *square* of its velocity. (This is the same Gottfried Leibniz who had independently invented calculus, precipitating furious arguments over who had precedence — a bitter controversy which lasted well beyond the lives of both men.)

In 1730, Dutch scientist Willem 's Gravesande resolved the energy formula controversy with a simple experiment. He dropped small brass spheres into a soft clay floor, and measured their speed and how deeply they sank into the clay.

Let's say kinetic energy is proportional to velocity alone as Newton proposed. Then we would expect how deeply a sphere sinks into the clay would be proportional to its velocity. If the sphere were going twice as fast, it would sink into the clay twice as deeply. And "one going three times as fast would sink in three times as deep."[10]

But this is not what 's Gravesande found. A sphere going twice as fast sank *four* times as far into the clay. A sphere going three times as fast sank *nine* times deeper into the clay. The Dutch experiments showed that Leibniz was right — the kinetic energy of an object goes as the square of its velocity.

The classical equation for kinetic energy was later shown to be one-half times an object's mass times its velocity squared. [11]

In pre-relativistic physics:
Kinetic energy = one-half times mass times velocity squared
$$KE = \tfrac{1}{2}\, m\, v^2$$

To get a feel for this, imagine you are driving a car at **30 miles an hour** and you slam on the brakes, locking the tires.[12] It comes to a screeching halt. You measure your skid marks. Say the distance it takes this particular car to come to a complete stop is **45 feet**.

What if you go twice as fast or **60 miles an hour**. How far in distance does it now take the same car to come to a complete stop? Twice as long? 90 feet?

No. When you measure your skid marks, you find your car's braking distance is now **180 feet**! This is 2 times 2 or 4 times longer. Why? Because the car's accumulated energy has gone up by the square of its increase in speed. This is shown in Fig. 7.4.

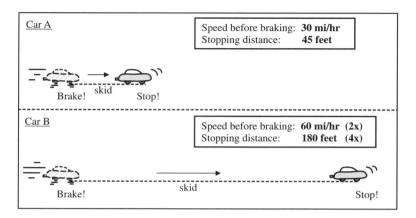

Figure 7.4. Energy of Motion (Kinetic Energy) Goes as the *Square* of the Velocity. *Car B goes twice as fast as car A, so it has four times the kinetic energy. Assuming identical cars, car B's braking distance is four times longer than car A's. It takes four times the distance to dissipate its kinetic energy.*

An object's energy of motion (kinetic energy) goes as the square of its speed. If you double an object's speed, its energy of motion becomes four times greater. If you triple the object's speed, its energy of motion is nine times greater. And so on.

What about when the car is standing still? What is its energy now? Newton would say if an object's speed is zero, its energy is zero too. So would Leibniz. In fact they would wonder why you would even ask such a question. (They would also wonder what a "car" is.)

The energy of any object at rest is zero. Zero speed, zero energy. Right? Ah, like so many "laws" of classical physics, this fundamental tenet was upended by Albert Einstein — changing the way we view mass and energy forever.

Eureka!

Einstein introduced $E = mc^2$ to the world in his September 1905 addendum to special relativity.[13] The title of his three-page paper was a question — "Does the Inertia of a Body Depend Upon its Energy Content?" He began his famous manuscript with the words:

> *The results of the previous investigation leads to a very interesting conclusion, which is here to be deduced.*

"Very interesting conclusion . . ." Talk about an understatement. He first tells us this work is based on Maxwell's equations and his relativity postulate. Then in classic Einstein fashion, he considers a deceptively simple thought experiment. An object emits two pulses of light in opposite directions. We can imagine it as a flashlight which shines light from both ends.

Why two pulses of light in opposite directions? So the object loses energy, but it does *not* move. The momentum of the two light pulses emitted in opposite directions cancel each other out. Thus the object remains at rest.

Einstein then presents equations for the energy of the "double-flashlight" and the energy of the light it emits. He looks at these energies from both a moving frame and one at rest (with respect to the flashlight). He combines his equations and does some algebra. Suddenly it appears. The change in kinetic energy of the flashlight, *KE*, is:

$$KE = \frac{1}{2}\,(E/c^2)\,v^2$$

Here E is the energy of the radiated light, c is the speed of light, and v is the relative velocity in the moving frame.

Now Einstein had his "eureka" moment. We can imagine his heart pounding, his body trembling with excitement. For of course he knew the classical equation for change in kinetic energy (for non-relativistic velocities),[14] which again is:

$$KE = \tfrac{1}{2} \, (\, m \,) \, v^2$$

Einstein saw that the m in Newton's equation is equal to the E/c^2 in *his* equation. So he concludes:

$$m = E \, / \, c^2$$

Einstein realized the revolutionary implications of this result. His flashlight had emitted light radiation. The energy of that emitted light (E) divided by the speed of light squared (c^2) is equal to the mass lost by the flashlight (m).

In other words, the flashlight's mass was reduced when it gave off energy in the form of light. Therefore *a flashlight weighs less after it emits light!* Einstein's wrote in his paper:

> *If a body gives off the energy E in the form of radiation, its mass is diminished by E/c².*

In yet another bold stroke, he interprets this result to have a simple yet profound, all-encompassing physical meaning:

> *The mass of a body is a measure of its energy content.*

As the title of his paper implies, Einstein was thinking about the *equivalence* of mass and energy, and, as noted, that energy, like, mass, has inertia. Thus energy, like mass, has weight (in a gravitational field).

At the end of his paper, Einstein suggested a possible test of this mass-energy relationship — invoking the recently discovered phenomenon called *radioactivity*. He identified the radioactive element radium as a possible source for such an experiment:

> *It is not impossible that with bodies whose energy content is variable to a high degree (e.g. radium salts) the theory may be successfully put to the test.*

Einstein's instincts were correct. Scientists working with radioactivity at the time had no idea these materials produce their radioactivity by converting a tiny amount of their matter into great amounts of radiating energy. We now understand radioactive decay to be a process in which an unstable atomic nucleus loses mass by emitting EM radiation. Measurements show its lost mass is equal to the energy emitted divided by the speed of light squared, precisely per Einstein's equation.

All-in-all, it was quite a curious paper.[15] His June paper on special relativity was the result of a decade of deep contemplation on the nature of light, time, space, and motion. (He had also touched on energy.)

However, his September paper on mass and energy was developed in a relatively brief period of time. Perhaps this is why he seems a bit tentative, unsure of the efficacy of his discovery. After all, he titles his paper with a question. And he concludes his manuscript with:

> *If the theory corresponds to the facts, radiation conveys inertia between the emitting and absorbing bodies.*

"*If* the theory corresponds to the facts . . .." We can see his doubt in this phrase. This was quite out of character for the usually confident young man.

The equation in the more familiar form, $E = mc^2$ did not appear until Einstein's 1907 review of relativity. This equation tells us energy equals mass times the speed of light squared.

Einstein had found a vast source of energy, as popular science writer David Bodanis put it, "hidden away in solid matter itself."[16] For example, the atomic bomb at Hiroshima contained only about two pounds of uranium.[17] Less than 1% of its mass was converted to the horrific radiation energy released via $E = mc^2$.

In 1906 and 1907, Einstein wrote several additional papers giving "more complete arguments" for the equivalence of mass and energy. In a talk in Salzburg, he emphasized that "mass (inertia) is associated with *all* forms of energy."[18] Therefore, he concluded, "electromagnetic radiation (light) itself must have mass (inertia)."

Let's take a closer look at what this all means.

When the Speed of Light is One

> *Things that seem incredibly different can really be manifestations of the same underlying phenomenon.*[19]
>
> Nima Arkani-Hamed

So what else is Einstein's equation telling us. Recall per Einstein's light postulate, the speed of light, c is a constant of nature. We can use this constant to convert conventional mass units to conventional energy units or vice versa.

Expressing mass and energy in equivalent units is not just a mathematical exercise. Historically, mass and energy were thought of as separate entities, so the *units* for each were developed independently. Now we know mass and energy are equivalent. It is a more accurate depiction of reality to represent them in the same units.[20] (See end note for example.)

We also want to change the units of distance and time so the speed of light, c equals one. Why? Because it makes Einstein's equation even simpler, and more revealing.

We can do this in a number of ways. One way is to express distance in light-years and time in years. Thus speed is given in terms of light-years per year. What is the speed of light in these units? It is one light year per year. Thus the speed of light equals one.

When we do all this, Einstein's famous equation becomes:

$$E = m$$

What are we to make of this? The equation makes it clear that matter and energy are *equivalent* — that every property which mass possesses is also a property of energy. For example, mass has inertia, mass has weight. Mass, like the mass of the Earth, is also a source of gravity. So, as noted, energy must also have inertia. Energy must also have weight (in a gravitational field). And energy is also a source of gravity. We can consider mass and energy as two forms of the *same entity*. That is why mass has been called "frozen energy".

Consider a matter particle such as an electron, which has a certain amount of *mass*. According to Einstein, this mass is a form of energy. How much energy? Measure the mass of the particle and multiply it times the speed of light squared. The calculated energy is called the particle's *rest energy*.

What about a particle with zero mass, like a photon of light?[21] Per physicist Art Hobson's terminology, it has a *non-material* form of energy.[22]

Faster than the Speed of Light?

According to special relativity, nothing can go faster than the speed of light. This is just one of the surprises to come out of Einstein's theory. Why should there be a universal speed limit?

Surely, if we apply enough force, enough energy, we could, at least in principle, make an object accelerate to any speed. That's what Newton would say. But Einstein tells us no object, no particle with mass can even reach the speed of light.

Here's why: According to special relativity, the total energy of a particle with mass is given by a simple formula: its rest energy *divided by the Lorentz Factor, F = sqrt (1- v^2)*. So the faster an object goes, the greater its energy (as seen from an observer at rest). And like relativistic momentum, relativistic energy increases exponentially as a particle's velocity approaches the speed of light.

Einstein's relativistic formula for energy is:
Total energy = rest energy divided by the Lorentz Factor, F
$$= E_0/sqrt\ (1 - v^2\ )$$
$$= m/sqrt\ (1 - v^2\ )$$
where: E_0 is rest energy,
         m is mass, and
         v is speed as a fraction of the speed of light.

See Appendix C for more on relativistic energy.

Imagine you are an operator of a particle accelerator. You pump more and more energy into your sub-atomic particles, trying to get them to go faster and faster. But at some point to double the particle's speed, you have to quadruple the energy. To double the object's speed again, you now have to increase the energy by eight times. Want to double it again? You need sixteen times the energy. And so on.

As the relative velocity, v of the particle approaches the speed of light, the energy you need approaches infinity. You find you can never get particles with mass to reach the speed of light because they require an infinite amount of energy. (See Table 7.2.)

Table 7.2. As a Particle's Speed Approaches c, Its
Energy Approaches Infinity.

Particle Speed	Energy (As Factor of Rest Energy)
0 .999c	22.4 ×
0 .999 999c	707 ×
0.999 999 999c	22,361 ×
c	∞

To get a quantitative idea of how this works, imagine a particle
with mass traveling at 0.999c. Per Einstein's relativistic energy formula,
it has an energy 22.4 times greater than its rest energy. This increases
dramatically as the particle approaches the speed of light, requiring
infinite energy at speed c, as shown in the above table.

This is yet another reason why, per to special relativity, nothing with
mass can ever reach the speed of light.

Every Move, Every Breath

A common misconception is that $E = mc^2$ applies only to nuclear processes, such as the production of sunlight and atomic energy. In fact,
Einstein discovered a relationship with universal applications. It applies
to all forms of energy.

Any process which results in a release of energy also produces a corresponding reduction in mass via $E = mc^2$. Say, for instance, we weigh an
unlit candle with great accuracy. Then we light it. Now as the candle
burns, we capture all the smoke, gases, etc. released in the process. Finally
we weigh the remaining candle and all the captured smoke etc. If we do
this with sufficient care and accuracy, we find that the weight of the candle and captured gases after burning is actually less than the original
weight of the unlit candle (by a very tiny amount).

Where is the missing matter? It has been converted to non-material
energy in the form of heat and light which was given off by the candle in
the burning process. When we look at the actual numbers, we find the
amount of energy given off by the candle is equal to the missing mass
times the speed of light squared, or $E = mc^2$.

Now let's consider some examples of the tremendous power of $E = mc^2$. If we burn 1/15 ounce of hydrogen gas, we get enough energy to keep a 100W light bulb lit for about 40 minutes. This burning process is very inefficient — only a very tiny amount of matter is converted to energy here.

What if we could somehow convert all the matter in the hydrogen gas, the entire 1/15 ounce into non-material energy via $E = mc^2$?[23] We would have enough energy to light the same 100 W light bulb for some 56,000 years.

A New Conservation Law

How does this matter/energy conversion affect the laws of *conservation of mass* and *conservation of energy*? Before special relativity, matter was thought to always be conserved. The conservation of matter was a cardinal law of physics. In other words, matter can neither be created nor destroyed.

For example, if you burn coal, it combines with oxygen in the air to form carbon dioxide. It was believed that if you weigh the coal before it is burned and then weigh all the escaping gases and residual ashes etc. after burning, you would find they are the same. The weight (and rest mass) before and after are equal. Matter is conserved.

There was also a corresponding law called the conservation of energy. Burning coal transforms chemical energy into EM radiation (heat and light). It was believed that the chemical energy in the coal before the burning equals the heat and light energy emitted by the burning. Thus the total energy before and after would be the same.

Right? Not quite. In the oxidization of carbon, for example, approximately a hundred millionth of a percent of the matter is converted into radiation energy via $E = mc^2$.[24] So the weight of the matter after is (very slightly) less than the weight of the matter before, the radiation energy after is more than the chemical energy before.

Once again Einstein's theory forced physicists to revise fundamental principles. Per special relativity, neither matter nor (non-material) energy is conserved.[25] It is *mass-energy* which is conserved. So we have a new conservation law: the conservation of mass-energy.

Note to reader: I'm tired of typing "non-material" before the word "energy". So from now on, when you see energy it means non-material energy.

Metamorphosis

In 1928, brilliant and socially challenged physicist Paul Dirac used his prodigious mathematical skills to unify quantum mechanics and special relativity. His grand marriage became known as "relativistic quantum mechanics".

Out of this work came the strangest of predictions. Dirac proposed that every fundamental particle has an almost twin — a doppelganger with identical mass but opposite electric charge. This new particle was dubbed an antiparticle.

For example, an electron has a charge of −1. Its corresponding anti-particle, called the positron, has the same mass but an electric charge of +1. Similarly, a proton, of electric charge +1, has a corresponding particle, the anti-proton of charge −1. However, the photon, with an electric charge of 0, is its own antiparticle.

Emotionally withdrawn to the extreme, Dirac studiously avoided the limelight, thus never received the public attention afforded many of his peers. As a result his name is little known outside scientific circles. He was, nonetheless, one of the greatest physicists of the modern era.

In 1928, while working with Neils Bohr, a principle founder of quantum mechanics, Dirac found a key connection between special relativity and quantum mechanics — his famous "spin-1/2 Dirac equation". With this in hand, Dirac merged quantum and special relativity into a single mathematical construct for the first time. He showed the marriage of the two great theories requires the existence of antiparticles.

Dirac also proposed a physical process which makes the metamorphosis of a caterpillar into a butterfly seem trivial. We saw that if you could somehow convert all of an object's matter into energy per $E = mc^2$, a stupendous amount of energy is produced. Dirac predicted just such a conversion is possible at the subatomic level. His mathematics showed if an electrically charged matter particle is made to collide with its *antiparticle* counterpart, they will annihilate each other — converting their matter into energy particles in the process.

The reverse is also true. Given enough energy, when two energy particles such as photons collide, they can produce matter particles.

Does this really happen? Do matter particles all of a sudden turn into energy particles? Do energy particles spontaneously transform into matter particles? Most definitely.

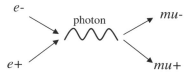

Figure 7.5. Matter/Antimatter Reaction Example. *Given enough initial energy, an electron and positron annihilate into a photon (non-material energy), which then materializes into a muon and antimuon.*

A typical example is shown in Fig. 7.5. It involves an electron and its antimatter particle, the positron. Here the electron and positron (two matter particles) collide, annihilate each other, and produce a photon. In other words, "the energy that was in the form of mass is converted to the (non-material) energy of the photon."[26]

The photon in turn spontaneously materializes into a muon and an anti-muon — two matter particles. The entire process is governed by $E = mc^2$.

Processes like this are standard fare in particle accelerators all over the world. Does this conversion occur naturally, that is outside of man-made facilities? Yes, but only where the energies are extremely high. It occurs in nuclear processes inside our Sun and stars, in supernova explosions, and in the neighborhood of black holes. It also happens on Earth in cosmic ray collisions with particles in our upper atmosphere and even in lightning.

Some 13.8 billion years ago, matter to energy and energy to matter transformations were commonplace — in the ultra-high energy conditions just after the Big Bang. So why don't we see energy spontaneously transforming into matter, and vice-versa, in our everyday lives? Why, for instance, doesn't a beam of light from our flashlight suddenly transform into matter before our eyes? Because the energies required for conversion are too high.

Say you calculate the amount of energy in the visible light you are using right now to read this page.[27] You would find it has way too little energy to spontaneously produce matter particles. Recall that EM radiation (light) energy increases proportionally with its frequency. So you would need photons of much higher frequency.

Photons of ultraviolet light can have a frequency on the order of 50 times greater than visible light, thus 50 times the energy. But this is still not nearly enough. You would need to go all the way to high-energy X-ray photons, which have frequencies and energy on the order of several hundred thousand times higher than visible light.

X-ray and gamma ray photons do have enough energy to spontaneously turn into electrons. Why do you need so much energy? Because of $E = mc^2$. The energy of the initial photons must be at least equal to the mass of the matter particles they are trying to produce times the speed of light squared. (This is called the *mass threshold*.)

Per physicist Neil deGrasse Tyson, "if you get high enough energy X-rays passing by your room, spontaneously, unannounced, unprompted, unscripted, they *will* make electrons." Photons of even higher energy produce even more massive particles, as long as that energy is "above the mass threshold for that particle." Matter into energy — energy into matter. A new understanding of reality discovered by Paul Dirac and governed by Einstein's $E = mc^2$.

Quark Weight

Too Many Quarks!

. . . 90 (to) 95% of the mass of matter as we know it comes from energy. We build it up out of massless gluons, and almost massless quarks, producing mass from energy. That's the deeper vision.[28]

Frank Wilczek

David splashes water on his face trying to wake himself up. "I hate mornings," he mutters. He steps on the bathroom scale — one of those new-fangled digital things that reads out numbers. "What was wrong with the old-fashioned dial scales?" he asks. "Why do they always have to change things?" He peeks reluctantly down at the numbers to see his current weight. "Oy!"

What David doesn't realize is that he is actually witnessing $E = mc^2$ at work. For it is the (non-material) *energy* inside his body, not his matter which is the primary source of his weight. What? Does this mean that the energy inside your body is what makes the numbers on your bathroom scale move? Yes, mostly. Remember, $E = mc^2$ tells us mass and energy are equivalent. Again, this means energy (like light) has weight, just like matter.

At the most fundamental level, everything inside your body is made of atoms and molecules, which in turn are made up of particles called quarks and electrons. (See Fig. 7.6.) If you add up the masses of all the particles contained in your body, they should give you your total body mass — hence your weight. But when you do, you find they add up to only a small amount of your body weight. So we ask the familiar question, where is the missing mass?

To get the answer, let's look at a typical atom. The vast bulk of an atom's mass is contained in its nucleus — its protons and neutrons. (The electrons are a very small part of its total mass.) Protons and neutrons are in turn made up of different kinds of *quarks*.

Experiments have determined the mass of protons and neutrons — and, independently, the masses of the quarks which make them up.[29] But the measured masses of the three quarks which make up a proton account for only a *small portion* of the proton's mass. The same is true for neutrons.

What is going on here? Quarks inside protons and neutrons are in constant motion. This quark motion is a form of kinetic energy. There are also electromagnetic (EM) and nuclear force fields inside atoms holding everything together. Art Hobson tells us that "quarks exert enormous forces on each other, and the *energy* in their force fields is enormous."[30]

All this energy from quark motion and EM and nuclear force fields has weight.[31] Calculations indicate at least 90% of the measured mass of

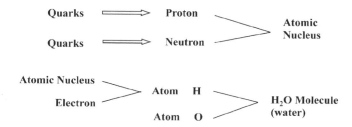

Figure 7.6. Summary of Ordinary Matter Build-Up. *Per the standard model of particle physics.*

protons and neutrons comes from the motion of quarks and field energies inside the nucleus.

So the primary source of our total body mass is not the rest mass of the matter particles inside our bodies. It is the energy from the motion of quarks and force fields inside us. This combined energy gives us almost all our weight — the same weight we see when we peek reluctantly at the numbers on our bathroom scale.

Evidence for $E = mc^2$

It wasn't until 1932, some 27 years after Einstein's famous paper, that *matter to energy* conversion was demonstrated experimentally.[32] These historic tests were performed at Cambridge University in the world's first "atom smasher" by British physicist John Douglas Cockcroft and Irish scientist Ernest T. S. Walton.

One year later French scientist Irène Joliot-Curie (daughter of Marie and Pierre Curie) and her husband Frédéric Joliot-Curie produced photographic evidence of the opposite effect — the conversion of *energy into matter*.

In this remarkable photograph (Fig. 7.7), a photon of light (invisible here) carries its energy up from beneath. The photon then spontaneously changes into matter (see the middle of the figure) — to form two new matter particles. These freshly created charged particles then curve away from each other under the influence of a magnet (see arrows).

Today there is a veritable catalogue of evidence confirming $E = mc^2$. In one notable 2005 experiment, researchers at the National Institute of

Paris,1933, by Irène and Frédéric Joliot-Curie : Photograph shows conversion of energy into matter.
• A photon of light (invisible here) carries energy up from beneath.
• In the middle it changes into matter.
• The two freshly created particles then curve away from each other under the influence of a magnet (dashed white lines marked by arrows).

Figure 7.7. Experimental Evidence for $E = mc^2$. *Creation of a pair of matter particles revealed by the fog spots they make in passing through the wet air of a cloud chamber.*

Standards and Technology (NIST) and Massachusetts Institute of Technology (MIT) compared measurements of energy emitted by silicon and sulfur atoms with measurements of their masses before and after emission.[33] Calculations confirmed $E = mc^2$ to an accuracy of better than *one part in a million.*

Good Morning Starlight

Occasionally Albert Einstein and pals Maurice Solovine and Conrad Habicht, the self-anointed "Olympia Academy", would hike up a mountain on the outskirts of Bern to watch the sunrise. "We would marvel at the Sun as it came slowly toward the horizon and finally appeared in all of its splendor to bathe the Alps in a mystic rose,"[34] Solovine later wrote. Little did they know on those fine mornings in Switzerland that amongst them was the one person who would explain to the world the mechanism behind how the Sun and all other stars shine in the sky.

In the early part of the 20th century, it was still a great mystery to scientists how the Sun managed to emit such copious amounts of energy day after day without burning out. Our Sun is a star in the center of our solar system. We now know it emits a staggering amount of energy — about 386 billion billion megawatts.

How has it been able to sustain this enormous energy output over its lifetime — an estimated 4.57 billion years? If, for example, "the Sun burned hydrogen fuel in an ordinary chemical reaction with oxygen," it would burn out in about a thousand years.[35]

The first plausible theory for solar radiation was offered in 1904 by the "father of nuclear physics," New Zealand physicist Ernest Rutherford. He suggested radioactive decay as the source of the Sun's energy. In the 1920s, scientists began to suspect Einstein's $E = mc^2$ had something to do with it. British physicist Arthur Eddington showed temperatures near the Sun's center were so high that hydrogen and helium atoms lose their electrons. Welsh astronomer and inventor Robert Atkinson was first to suggest the Sun's hydrogen to helium nuclear reaction in 1931.

We now know the Sun contains approximately two thousand billion billion billion (2×10^{30}) kilograms of mass — the equivalent of about 333,000 earths.[36] This stupendous mass of the Sun results in gravity so strong that matter in its center is compressed to a density 10 times greater than lead. This extreme compression produces super-hot, dense conditions inside the Sun's core — resulting in a process called *nuclear fusion*.

The nuclear furnace inside its core converts a very small portion of the Sun's mass to energy via $E = mc^2$. As a result, the Sun releases the energy equivalent of roughly 4 million tons of mass every second. About 160 tons of this sunlight is intercepted by our relatively tiny Earth each day.

The Sun's nuclear core heats to an estimated 27 million degrees F. In this severe environment, hydrogen atoms are stripped of their electrons, leaving bare protons. In the intense gravity pressing down on the Sun's core, protons overcome their electric repulsion and fuse together to produce helium nuclei.

This nuclear fusion occurs through a series of reactions called the proton-proton chain. In this multi-step process, four hydrogen nuclei (four protons) combine to eventually produce one helium nucleus (two protons and two neutrons).

Each helium nucleus produced has slightly less mass than the four original hydrogen nuclei. Where does this missing mass go? It is converted into energy — primarily in the form of high-energy gamma ray photons, via $E = mc^2$. Six high-energy photons (and two nearly weightless neutrinos) are generated for each helium nucleus produced.

David Bodanis suggests a simple way to quantify this. Let's assign a value of 1 to the mass of each hydrogen nucleus.[37] Four hydrogen nuclei add up to a total mass of 4. Using the same scale, the helium nucleus they produce has a mass of only 3.971. If we divide 3.971 by 4, we get about 0.993 or 99.3 percent. Where is the missing 0.7 percent? It is converted into gamma ray photons via $E = mc^2$.

Initially these high-energy photons are absorbed in only a few millimeters of solar plasma surrounding the Sun's core. They are then re-emitted in random directions and at slightly lower energies. This absorption and re-emission process continues throughout the Sun until photons of lower energy finally reach the Sun's surface — and are emitted into space as solar radiation.

A photon from the Sun's core scatters a tremendous number of times on the way out, on the order of 10^{20} times.[38] It takes a long time for this radiation to reach the Sun's surface — estimates range from seventeen thousand years to a million. The sunlight we see in the sky today began in its core sometime between the end of the last Ice Age (15,000 BC) and when our ancestor, *Homo Erectus*, first used fire a million years ago.[39]

How long will the Sun continue to shine? We don't have to find another solar system to live in — at least not yet. Scientists estimate the Sun has enough hydrogen left to fuel its nuclear reaction for about another five billion years or so.

The Joining of Space and Time

I'm exhausted. How 'bout you? But I must tell you one more thing about special relativity. It is just too important to leave out.

Albert Einstein disclosed the equivalence of mass and energy in September of 1905. Two years later, his former mathematics teacher at Zurich Poly revealed that space and time are also inextricably linked. From this work came the concept of *spacetime* — where all events in the cosmos occur not in space nor in time, but in spacetime.

This is the subject of our final chapter on special relativity (no cheering please).

Chapter 8

Spacetime

"The encounter could create a time paradox … that would unravel the very fabric of the space-time continuum!"

Doctor Emmett Brown (Christopher Lloyd) in the time-travel movie *Back to the Future*.

Time paradox? The unraveling of the spacetime continuum? Does "Doc" Brown's warning have any validity? Well, not really — it's only a movie. But there is a grain of truth to these far-fetched statements. According to relativity, the spacetime continuum does exist. And it is helpful to think of spacetime as a kind of fabric (especially in general relativity). Plus time travel into the future *is* real. As you will see, we do it all the time. This wild notion, as well as other curious predictions, begins with the concept of *spacetime*.

In the last chapter, we learned about a fundamental link between matter and energy. In this chapter we discuss how space and time are actually a single entity called spacetime. However, unlike mass and energy, the merger of space and time was not the invention of Albert

Einstein — it was in fact initially rejected by him. However, since its introduction in 1907, the concept of spacetime has become a core principle of modern physics. Spacetime is the universal background upon which all physical phenomena play out; the very "fabric of our cosmos."[1]

In this chapter, we meet the man primarily responsible for this new vision of reality — Einstein's math teacher Hermann Minkowski, and discuss its extraordinary implications.

The Long Wait

After publications in June 1905 of seminal papers on the particle nature of light, the size of atoms, and the relativity of time and space, Albert Einstein continued to go to the patent office day after day, dutifully performing his job as technical expert 3rd class, hoping for some reaction, some response to his revolutionary manuscripts.

Perhaps it was the lack of supporting evidence for his radical theories at the time, or the unconventional way in which his papers were presented, or that he was a complete unknown — for physicists reading through the German journal generally either skimmed or ignored his articles.[2] Einstein was "greatly disappointed when his paper was not even mentioned in the following issues of the *Annalen der Physik*."[3] We can imagine the 26-year-old checking the mail each day at his small second floor apartment in Berne — there is nothing.

Then in early 1906, Einstein received notification he has been awarded a Doctorate from the University of Zurich. In April of the same year, he was promoted to technical expert 2nd class at the patent office. Perhaps things were looking up.

In 1907, Einstein applied for a junior teaching position at the university in Berne — he included articles on relativity and others he had written with his application. He was rejected. He then applied for a job as a high school teacher. Three of 23 applicants were given interviews. Einstein was not one of them.

"During the years immediately following 1905, the concept of relativity percolated slowly through accepted ideas like the rain through limestone rather than breaking them down like the weight of water cracking a dam," writes biographer Roland C. Clark.[4] Gradually, a few scientists began to talk about his work. Some even wrote to Einstein and visited him at Berne to discuss his ideas.

Then in August of 1907, he heard the proverbial knock on the door. Physicist Max von Laue was in Berne to see Einstein — sent by none other than Max Planck, the most prominent physicist in Germany. (The same Max Planck who had first proposed the formula which Einstein used to explain the Photoelectric Effect.)

Einstein's paper on relativity had "immediately aroused my lively attention,"[5] Planck later recalled. He had given a lecture on the subject at the University of Berlin immediately after Einstein's paper was published, and had written a paper on special relativity in the spring of 1906. Ironically, however, Planck did not approve of Einstein's quantization of light.[6]

Albert felt he was at last being recognized. Perhaps his luck was turning for good. But as we shall see, two more years would pass before Einstein was finally offered a university professorship enabling him to work full-time on his beloved physics.

The Father of Spacetime

From henceforth, space by itself, and time by itself, have vanished into the merest shadows and only a kind of blend of the two exists in its own right.[7]

Hermann Minkowski

There was no love lost between Albert Einstein and Hermann Minkowski. During his college years at Zurich Poly, Einstein was required to take nine courses from Professor Minkowski. Einstein wanted to concentrate on physics, and did not yet understand the value of all these math courses. In addition, the young rebel did not appreciate his professor's rare mathematical talent or his accomplishments. Nor could he have known that his math teacher's work would later be a key to his greatest achievement — the theory of general relativity.

Born in 1864, Hermann Minkowski (Fig. 8.1) was a Lithuanian-born German of Jewish descent. He had a distinguished mathematics career in his too short life. At age 18, he shared the French Academy of Sciences Grand Prix award for mathematical science. He then went on to lay "the foundation for modern functional analysis" and, in his most original achievement, to develop the mathematical theory known as the geometry of numbers.[8] But it is for Minkowski's work in relativity

Figure 8.1. **The Father of Spacetime:** *Mathematician Hermann Minkowski (1864–1909).*

that he is most remembered, an extension of special relativity which made him immortal in the annuls of physics — the mathematics of *spacetime.*

When Minkowski first read Einstein's 1905 manuscripts, he was shocked. "It came as a tremendous surprise, for in his student days Einstein had been a lazy dog,"[9] the professor told physicist Max Born. "He never bothered about mathematics at all." Minkowski then began working on his own mathematical reformulation of special relativity.

On September 21, 1908, a sunny late-summer day in Cologne, Germany, Minkowski presented the results of his work to scientists from all over the country at the 80th General Meeting of the Society of Natural Scientists and Physicians. He titled his talk *Raum und Zeit* (Space and Time). In this now famous talk, Minkowski proposed the unification of space and time into a "four-dimensional entity dubbed 'space-time'."[10]

Minkowski declared that Einstein's theory of special relativity is best visualized in a four-dimensional "space-time" continuum. What are these four dimensions? They are the three space dimensions (up-down, left-right, and forward-back) and the time dimension. Minkowski proposed the revolutionary idea that time and space are not separate entities, but joined together mathematically.

Minkowski proposed his concept as an alternate to Einstein's theory rather than as a mathematical adjustment. Einstein was not amused. Minkowski's paper contained a single physical prediction. Einstein was quick to point out it "failed to account for a known phenomenon."[a,11]

---

[a]Einstein was referring to the polarization current produced by a current flowing in a wire in the presence of a magnetic field. (Polarization is the orientation of a wave.)

112

Minkowski in turn had said of Einstein; "The mathematical education of the young physicist [Albert Einstein] was not very solid, which
I am in a good position to evaluate since he obtained it from me in Zurich
some time ago."[12] The rivalry between Einstein and Minkowski "was
carried on at a level that few recognized."[13] The unpleasantness ended
with Minkowski's premature death of appendicitis in 1909 — he was
44 years old.

Wherewhen

What exactly does the term *spacetime* mean? To help visualize this, let's
first look at a plot of length versus width (Fig. 8.2(a)). Here the area
between the two axes represents *space*.

Now let's construct a *spacetime diagram* (Fig. 8.2(b)). What is a spacetime
diagram? It is simply a plot where one axis is time and the other axes are
space. (We only plot one of the three space dimension here for simplicity.) So
space is the horizontal axis and time is the vertical axis. What does the area
between the axes of space and time represent? It represents *spacetime*.[14]

Are we *in* spacetime right now? Yes, most definitely. But our common way of thinking is not conducive to the unification of space and time.
We have to think differently — not in terms of places in space or
happenings in time — but in terms of *events* which have a location in both
space and time, i.e., in spacetime.

Strictly speaking, an event is something that occurs at a single point
in space and at a single point in time. Thus an event is a single point in
spacetime. In addition, the very language we use to talk about events
needs modification. For example, if you are asked *where* you were born,

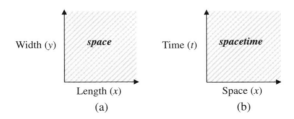

Figure 8.2. Picturing Spacetime. (a) *In a plot of length versus width, the area between the axes
represents space.* (b) *In a plot of space versus time, the area between the axes represents spacetime.*

you reply with a location in space, such as in San Diego, California. If you are asked *when* you were born, you reply with a date, a point in time — such as on June 15, 1985.

There is no word in the English language for your location in both space and time. So let's make one up. In the spirit of Minkowski's vision, we ask *wherewhen* were you born? Think about it. Your birth occurred in both a location in space and at a point in time. Your birth is an event in spacetime.

Say a light flashes two feet in front of you at 10 am. To get a visual picture, let's plot this event in a spacetime diagram. Figure 8.3 shows space in the horizontal axis (one spatial dimension for simplicity) and time in the vertical axis. Space represents where the event occurs and time represents when the event happens. The point (event) represents wherewhen the event is in spacetime — two feet away at 10 am.

Everything that takes place in our universe, from the mundane to the glorious, is an event in spacetime. Your departure from home at 8 am, your arrival back home at 6 pm, the birth of a child in Memorial Hospital room 515, the emission of a photon from the surface of the Sun, the collision of a meteor into the planet Jupiter, and a far-off supernova explosion are all events in spacetime. Each event occurs at a specific place and at a specific time — at a specific location in spacetime.

Thus, Minkowski advises us, we must think in terms of events, not in terms of places; in terms of four dimensions, not three; in terms of space and time together, united as part of a single structure — spacetime.

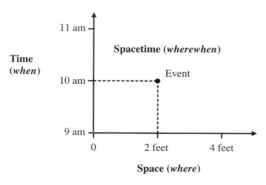

Figure 8.3.   An *Event* in Spacetime. *The spacetime co-ordinates of the light flash event are 2 feet and 10 am.*

The Metric of the Universe

Space is different for different observers. Time is different for different observers. Spacetime is the same for everyone.[15]

E. F. Taylor and J. A. Wheeler

Isaac Newton's universe is a straightforward, orderly one. Here the distance between two points in space is the same for everyone. The time interval between two events is the same for everyone.

In Newton's world, we can use measuring devices such as tape measures and rulers to determine distance without concern. (See Fig. 8.4.) They always give us the same value for the distance between the same two points, no matter how we are moving. Clocks and watches provide the same function for the measurement of elapsed time. Per Newton, all clocks run at the same rate, independent of their relative motion.

In Newton's cosmos, an inch is always an inch. A mile is always a mile. A second is always a second. No matter where you measure, no matter what your relative motion, the *units* of space and time are eternal. Here the distance in space and the interval in time are absolute. In other words they are reliable *metrics*.

What is a metric? Put simply, a "metric" is a quantity that does not change, so it can be used for measurement.

What is Einstein's answer to Newton's metrics? Space (distance) and time cannot be used as universal metrics because they are affected by relative motion. Distance contacts with relative motion (length contraction). Time slows down with relative motion (time dilation).

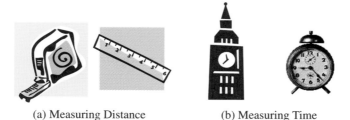

(a) Measuring Distance   (b) Measuring Time

Figure 8.4.   Newton's Metrics. *In Newtonian physics, (a) tape measures and rulers can be used to measure space because distance in space is the same for all observers, and (b) clocks can be used to measure time because time is the same for all observers.*

And per Einstein's relativity postulate, there is no "at rest" frame of reference. Everything in the universe is moving with respect to something else. According to special relativity, observers in all these different reference frames are in relative motion — thus they all measure different values for distance in space and elapsed time.

Plus there is a "blending" of space and time which Minkowski spoke of. Say you are at rest. There is no motion through space. But time still goes by. You are still aging. You experience a kind of *motion through time*.

As soon as you *move through space*, there is time dilation. The passage of time, your time, slows down (as seen by an observer at rest). And to this stationary observer, the faster you move through space, the more your motion through time slows down. Thus the two motions — through space and through time — are not independent. One affects the other.

So time and space are relative and interdependent. As far as being reliable metrics, they are out the window.

The Spacetime Interval

Are we left with no universal metric for space and time which is independent and the same for all observers? Not quite. Here's where Hermann Minkowski's discovery comes into play.

Imagine you are again in a classroom listening to one of my physics lectures. Assume we are all seated, thus stationary with respect to each other. In terms of relativity, since there is no relative motion between us, we are all in the same frame of reference. Let's call this the *classroom reference frame*.

I ask a student on the right side of the room to clap her hands together once. Then I ask a student on the left side of the room to clap his hands together once. These two hand-claps constitute two *events* in spacetime. In this case, they each occur at different locations in space and at different points in time.

Say we measure the separation in space (distance) between the two hand-claps in the classroom reference frame. We could do this, for example by using a ruler or tape measure. We call this distance in space between the two hand-claps the *space interval* between claps. During the hand-clapping, we also measure the elapsed time between the first hand-clap and the second. We call this separation in time between the two hand-claps the *time interval* between claps.

116

Assume we all have the same measuring devices and use the same diligence in making measurements. We find all of us sitting in the room measure the same space interval and same time interval between claps. Our values are the same because we are at rest with respect to each other. We are all in the same frame of reference.

Now imagine our fearless friend Crash flies a rocket ship across the classroom. Say he is moving (uniformly) at half the speed of light relative to the classroom. Per special relativity, Crash measures a different space interval and a different time interval between the same two hand-claps than we do. After all, he is in the *rocket ship reference frame*, which is in motion with respect to our classroom frame.

Let's say we take our classroom's measured values for the space interval and time interval between hand-claps and square them. That is we multiply the value for the space interval times itself, and we multiply the value for the time interval times itself. Then we subtract the two results. We call the square root of this difference the *spacetime interval*. Ok, let's write down the value we calculate for this so-called spacetime interval.

Crash inside the moving rocket ship does the same thing. He takes the values *he* measures for the space interval between hand-claps and squares it. He takes the value he measures for the time interval between hand claps and squares it. He then subtracts the two values, and calculates the square root. He writes down his value for the spacetime interval.

We meet with Crash to compare figures. When we look at both sets of numbers, we see, as expected, that Crash in the moving rocket ship has measured a different space interval than we did. And he has measured a different time interval than we did. Why? Again because he was in motion relative to us.

But, lo and behold, when we look at his value for the so-called spacetime interval — the square root of the difference between the squares of the space and time intervals — we find Crash's answer is the *same value* we calculated!

Our measured values for the space intervals between hand-claps are different, our measured values for the time-intervals between hand-claps are different. But the calculated spacetime interval is the same value for both Crash on the rocket and us in the classroom.

We have discovered Minkowski's great insight — if we square the space and time intervals and take the difference, we get an interval which does not change (is invariant) with relative uniform motion: the *spacetime interval*.

The formula for the spacetime interval (in units where the speed of light is 1) is:

The square of the spacetime interval is equal to the difference between the square of the time interval and the square of the space interval.[b]

(Spacetime Interval)² = (Time Interval)² − (Space Interval)²

$$\Delta S^2 = \Delta t^2 - \Delta x^2$$

where: Δt is the time interval between the two events, and
Δx is the space interval between two events

(There are actually three forms of spacetime interval. This equation here shows the *timelike* spacetime interval. All three forms are explained in Appendix B.)

Do you remember the Pythagorean Theorem from high school geometry? Yes? Good for you. No? It's not nice to sleep in geometry class. Recall that a right triangle is one where one of the angles is 90°. The hypotenuse is the side of the triangle opposite the right angle. Per Greek mathematician Pythagoras, the square of the hypotenuse of a right triangle is equal to the sum of the squares of the other two sides.

Minkowski's spacetime interval equation is sort of like the Pythagorean Theorem, except here you *subtract* the squares rather than add them. In fact, it is sometimes called the Modified Pythagorean Theorem.

Note to reader: We are able to subtract the square of the space interval from the square of the time interval by selecting compatible units — such as light-years for distance and years for time.[16] *As noted, this makes the speed of light, c equal to 1; so it drops out of the equation.*

How did Minkowski come up with this spacetime interval formula? He derived it from the Lorentz transform. And Einstein derived the Lorentz transform from the light postulate. So the absolute nature of the speed of light leads to the absolute spacetime interval — both are unaffected by uniform motion.

Now let's try to get a picture of what this spacetime interval looks like. Take a look at the spacetime diagram in Fig. 8.5. Here the horizontal

---

[b]In conventional units, the equation is: $\Delta S = sqrt\ (\ c^2\ \Delta t^2 - \Delta x^2\ )$.

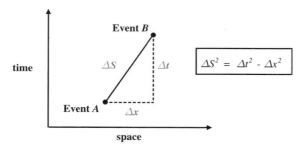

Figure 8.5. The Spacetime Interval, ΔS. *Two hand-clap events, A and B, each take place at different times and at different places. The space interval (distance) between the two events is Δx. The time interval between events is Δt. The spacetime interval between the two events, ΔS is calculated from Minkowski's equation:* $\Delta S^2 = \Delta t^2 - \Delta x^2$.

axis (x) represents space, the vertical axis (t) represents time, and the area between the two axes again represents spacetime.

Do you see anything strange in Fig. 8.5? Look at the solid diagonal line directly from A to B (the hypotenuse of the triangle). It represents the spacetime interval from event A to event B. It looks longer than each of the two dashed lines. Yet it represents the square root of the *difference* between the squares of the two dashed lines (the time interval and space interval respectively).

How can we subtract and get a *longer* line? We can't. The spacetime interval is actually shorter than both the space and time intervals. However, there is a kind of "distortion" when we plot spacetime diagrams on ordinary paper.[17] *Diagonal* distances appear longer than they really are. Please remember this point — it is key to visualizing spacetime diagrams.

The spacetime interval is analogous to distance in space. We can think of the spacetime interval as measuring a sort of "distance" between two events in spacetime.

As noted, the spacetime interval is not relative — it is absolute. It is the same for all observers in relative uniform motion. Thus it qualifies as a *metric*.[18] It can be used to measure the separation or interval between any two events in spacetime.

The interdependence of the space and time intervals and the absolute nature of the spacetime interval leads to the conclusion that we live in a universe where *space and time are inextricably linked*. And, as we shall see, this connection between space and time, this spacetime, has deep implications.

The Spacetime Interval at Work

"Oh, boy. This one is tougher. Gotta think. Gotta think."

Ethan, the astronaut "wanna be" is working his way through the second problem in his relativity 101 class. It's a little harder, because it is more abstract.

RELATIVITY 101:

Problem 2 — Assume the time interval and space interval between two events in the rest frame of reference are:

Time Interval: Δt_{rest} = 5 seconds

Space Interval: Δx_{rest} = 4 light-seconds (about 745 thousand miles)

(a) Using the Lorentz transform, calculate the values for the time interval and space interval for a _uniformly moving_ frame of reference, with relative velocity:

$$v = 0.25c \text{ or } 25\% \text{ the speed of light}$$

(b) Calculate the values for the spacetime intervals in _both_ the at rest and moving frames. Compare your result in a table.

Show all intermediate steps used to calculate your answers.

"C'mon, c'mon," Ethan thinks. "Calm down. You can do this," he tells himself. "OK, let's do the easy part first."

Rest Frame

Ethan writes down the time interval and space interval in the *rest frame* given in the problem: **5 seconds** and **4 light-seconds**, respectively. He then writes down the Minkowski equation for the spacetime interval. He plugs in these values for the time interval and the space interval, squares each, subtracts, and takes the square root. He calculates the spacetime interval in the rest frame as 3.

"But what are the units here?" Ethan mumbles. "OK, the time interval is in seconds, the space interval is in light-seconds. So I think here that all the units work out. The spacetime interval has to be in *seconds*. So it's **3 seconds.** (The details of Ethan's calculations are shown below.)

Moving Frame

"OK, now for the hard part. What are the time and space intervals for the *moving* frame? Do I use the time dilation equations? The length contraction equations? I'm in trouble here.

"Wait. Let me read the question again. Ah, it says to use the Lorentz transform. I think you have to use the full Lorentz transform equations here. I think. OK here goes."

Ethan writes down the Lorentz transform equations, which he has also memorized. (But he doesn't yet quite understand their physical meaning.) He puts the values for the space and time intervals for the *rest* frame into the equations.

"Hey, look at that. The value I get for the time interval in the *moving* frame depends on both the time and space intervals in the rest frame. Ya, I vaguely remember Prof telling us about this. This connection between time and space. OK, so given a relative velocity of 0.25c, what do I get?"

Ethan calculates the *time* interval in the *moving* frame to be: **4.13 seconds.**

"OK, now for the space interval. Hey, no surprise. It too depends on *both* the time and space intervals from the rest frame."

Ethan calculates the *space* interval in the *moving* frame to be: **2.84 light-seconds.**

"Oh, man. I better check my figures. I hope I didn't make some dumb math error here."

"OK, I think I'm over the hard part! Now I just have to calculate the *spacetime* interval for this moving frame. Let me see. I take the values, square them, take the difference, and then take the square root. I hope I'm right."

Ethan calculates the *spacetime* interval for the *moving* frame. He gets: **3 seconds**

"Wow! It works just like Minkowski said. The *spacetime* interval between the two events is the same value in both frames: *3 seconds.*"

Ethan's answers are summarized in Table 8.1.

Table 8.1. The *Spacetime* Interval: ΔS is the same value in both the stationary and moving frames.

Frame	Time Interval (Δt)	Space Interval (Δx)	Spacetime Interval (ΔS)
At Rest	5 seconds	4 light-seconds	*3 seconds*
Moving	4.13 seconds	2.84 light-seconds	*3 seconds*

As this example shows, Minkowski's formula works. The value for the time interval, Δt is different in the rest and moving frames: 5 seconds and 4.13 seconds respectively. The value for the space interval, Δx is also different in the two frames: 4 seconds and 2.84 light-seconds.

But the value for the *spacetime* interval, ΔS is the *same* in both the rest and moving frames: 3 seconds. So the time interval and space interval are affected by uniform motion, but the spacetime interval is not.

The details of Ethan's calculation are as follows:

In the Rest frame

The spacetime interval in the rest frame is

$$(\Delta S_{rest})^2 = (\Delta t_{rest})^2 - (\Delta x_{rest})^2 = 5^2 - 4^2 = 25 - 16 = 9$$
$$\Delta S_{rest} = sqrt\ (9) = 3\ seconds$$

In the Moving frame

At a uniform velocity of $0.25c$ the *time* interval in the moving frame is given by the Lorentz transform equations (as given in Appendix A) as:

$$\Delta t_{moving} = (\Delta t_{rest} - v\ \Delta x_{rest})/sqrt\ (1 - v^2)$$
$$= (\ 5 - 0.25 \cdot 4)/0.968 = (4)/0.968$$
$$= 4.13\ seconds$$

The *space* interval for the moving frame is:

$$\Delta x_{moving} = (\Delta x_{rest} - v\ \Delta t_{rest})/sqrt\ (1 - v^2)$$
$$= (4 - 0.25 \cdot 5)\ /\ 0.968 = 2.75/0.968$$
$$= 2.84\ light\text{-}seconds$$

The spacetime interval in the moving frame is:

$$(\Delta S_{moving})^2 = (\Delta t_{moving})^2 - (\Delta x_{moving})^2 = (4.13)^2 - (2.84)^2 = 17 - 8 = 9$$

$$\Delta S_{moving} = sqrt\ (9) = 3\ seconds$$

The set of numbers above is just one example of the absolute nature of the spacetime interval. It happens to be 3 in this example. It can be any number, but it is always the same number for any two given events, no matter what the uniform motion of the observer.

Minkowski (Fig. 8.6) proved mathematically that this is true for *any* two events in spacetime.[19] No matter what the space interval and time interval between any two events, no matter what the relative (uniform) motion of the reference frames, the spacetime interval between the same

Figure 8.6. What Hermann Minkowski May Have Thought About Einstein.

two events is always the same value. The space interval is relative, the time interval is relative, but the spacetime interval is absolute.

Minkowski's spacetime interval is a momentous conception. Why? Because it gives physicists a way to connect all events in the universe, independent of uniform motion. In the mathematics of spacetime physics, all the equations of special relativity are written in terms of four-dimensional spacetime.[20] And as we shall see in Part II, four-dimensional spacetime and the spacetime interval are at the very heart of general relativity.

Wristwatch Time

Perhaps the spacetime interval seems a bit abstract to you. You may be asking how it relates to real life, to every day experience? It turns out you can measure the spacetime interval directly, without doing any calculations.

How? Simply by looking at the elapsed time on your wristwatch.

Imagine it is sometime in the future and Marsmart, the largest store in the solar system, is having a terrific sale. So you decide to drive your fancy new rocket-car to Mars to pick up some special parts for your house robot.

Say you drive from Earth to the store on Mars at a uniform velocity of $0.8c$ or 80% the speed of light. At that speed, it takes you 15 minutes to get from Earth to Mars (as recorded on your wristwatch).

There are two events here: (1) leaving your house on Earth, and (2) arriving at the store on Mars. What are the time and space intervals between these two events in your reference frame?

As you drive your rocket car (in uniform motion), you feel as though you and your car are standing still. From your perspective, you see Mars ahead of you coming closer and closer and Earth receding in your rear view mirror. From your point of view, you are standing still, Earth is leaving you, and Mars is coming to you. With respect to your own "personal" frame of reference, you are always standing still and the world is going by you.

I try to imagine my personal reference frame as three perpendicular arrows representing space stuck to the top of my head and a clock attached at the origin representing time. (See Fig. 8.7.) Cool hat, huh! What can I say, I'm a nerd. Based on my point of view, my *personal* frame of reference, as I move about the day, the world is really moving about me. Hey, I like this. It's all about me. Oh, everyone else experiences the same affect. Never mind.

So, as measured in your personal reference frame, what are your time and space intervals in going from Earth to Mars?

Time Interval — In your frame, the time interval between the two events — leaving Earth and arriving on Mars — is simply 15 minutes, as recorded on your wristwatch.

Space Interval — What about the space interval in your frame? This takes a little more thought. You are at the first event, leaving your house on Earth. You are at the second event, arrival on Mars. Remember, in your reference frame you are at rest.

So Earth has left you and Mars has come to you. From your perspective, both events — leaving Earth and arriving on Mars — have occurred at the *same* location. What location is this? Where you are.

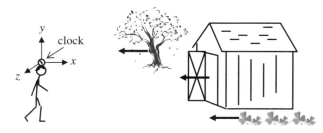

Figure 8.7. Your Personal Reference Frame. *You and your spacetime coordinates are always stationary. The rest of world is moving by you.*

Therefore you measure the separation in space between the two events as *zero*. The space interval in your personal frame of reference is zero. Strange as this may seem, this is what Einstein's relativity postulate tells us.

Spacetime Interval — So what is the spacetime interval in this case? Since the space interval is zero, the spacetime interval simply equals the time interval. Thus, in your personal reference frame, the spacetime interval between leaving the Earth and arriving on Mars is the elapsed time on your wristwatch — in this case 15 minutes! (This is called *proper time*.)

Mathematically, this is:

$$\Delta S^2 = \Delta t^2 - \Delta x^2$$
$$= (15)^2 - (0)^2$$
$$= (15)^2$$
$$\Delta S = 15 \ minutes$$

Figure 8.8 shows your trip from Earth to Mars in graphical form, in another "Minkowski" or spacetime diagram. The horizontal axis again represents space and the vertical axis time. Physicists call your travel through spacetime your "world-line". A so-called world-line is simply an observer or object's path from one event to another through spacetime.

Whenever you see a spacetime plot, it is important to ask; "What reference frame is it in?" In this case, the plot is shown in your *personal reference frame,* the one you always carry with you.

Since in your frame, you are standing still, you are not moving at all through space (from your point of view). But you *are* moving through

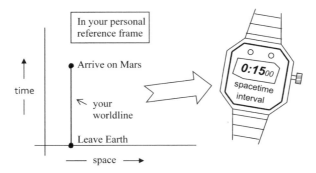

Figure 8.8. Wristwatch Time. *If you are present at both of two events, the spacetime interval between the two events equals the time interval between the two events (as recorded on your wristwatch).*

time. Thus your world-line in Fig. 8.8 is a straight vertical line through time only.

The key here is that you were present at *both* events — your departure from Earth and your arrival on Mars. Remember, from your perspective, you are at rest and Mars has traveled to you. So in your reference frame, the space interval between the two events is zero.

But what about the people on Mars? How do the people at Marsmart determine the spacetime interval for these same two events?

Marsmart Reference Frame — People at Marsmart measure both the time and space intervals in their frame, and then use Minkowski's formula to calculate the spacetime interval. Since they are in relative motion with respect to you, they measure different space and time intervals than you, but calculate the *same* spacetime interval you do: 15 minutes.

So again the space and time intervals are different, but the spacetime interval is the same for both reference frames, you in the rocket-car and the folks at Marsmart. This is summarized in Table 8.2.

The mathematics is as follows:

At your rocket-car speed of 0.8c, the Lorentz Factor, F is:

$$F = sqrt\ (1 - (0.8)^2) = 0.6$$

(A) <u>In Your Personal Reference Frame (inside rocket–car):</u>

The time interval is 15 minutes. The space interval is zero.
*So the spacetime interval, ΔS = **15 minutes**.*
And the distance from the Earth to Mars for you is computed as:
Distance = velocity times time = 0.8 × 15 minutes = 12 light-minutes

(B) <u>To the people in Marsmart (Earth-Mars Frame):</u>

(Assume that Earth and Mars are stationary with respect to each other for simplicity.)
The time interval is   15 minutes / 0.6 = 25 minutes (due to time dilation)
The space interval is 12 light minutes / 0.6 = 20 light-minutes (due to
length contraction)

The spacetime interval is:

$$\Delta S^2 = (25)^2 - (20)^2 = 625 - 400 = 225$$
So ΔS = sqrt (225) = **15 minutes**

Table 8.2. The Spacetime Interval is the Same in Both Earth-Mars (Marsmart) Frame and Your Rocket-Car Frame.

Frame of Reference	Time Interval	Space Interval	Spacetime Interval
Marsmart (Earth-Mars)	25 minutes	20 light-minutes	*15 minutes*
You (Rocket-car)	15 minutes	0 light-minutes	*15 minutes*

Imagine a distant future where space travel at relativistic speeds is commonplace. In this world, the Intragalactic Space Council adopts the spacetime interval as the single galactic measure of "distance". People on Earth, travelers on spaceships, and aliens on a far-away exoplanet argue about the correct time interval and the correct space interval from Earth to the planet. But they all agree on the same spacetime interval — the metric of spacetime.

The Twins Paradox

The Zaslaw twins are about to do the unthinkable. Our intrepid space teamsters are about to separate. The new Thousand-meter Space Telescope has detected mysterious signals from a distant Earth-like planet orbiting the dim star Gliese 581 — over 20 light-years from Earth.[21] The signals repeat every three days or so and seem to have some sort of pattern to them.

Is it a sign of intelligent life? Scientists are not sure. Based on the possibility, they have convinced the government of the United Planets to fund a mission to explore the source of the signals — the exoplanet everyone now calls Terra.

Both Zaslaw twins were selected to join the Terra mission's flight crew. They were chosen because of their youth, their extensive spaceflight experience, and the leadership they demonstrated in the Inertial Balance incident. But Steve is down with a nasty Martian respiratory tract infection, notorious for its intensity and duration.

"I feel awful. I can hardly hold my head up," says Steve. "There's no way I'll be able to go."

"Then maybe I shouldn't go," Arianna says.

Steve smiles weakly, "You don't sound like you really mean it. Hey, this is a once in a lifetime opportunity. Just go!"

Torn between guilt and desire, Arianna says "Oh, what the hell. I just have to do it!"

They both know what this means — the risk, the length of time they will be separated, and the permanent changes they will have to deal with when Arianna returns.

So Arianna signs up for the trip, while Steve remains at home. Fueled by the latest matter-antimatter engines, she and the rest of the flight crew travel on a new hyper-rocket at the incredible speed of 90% the speed of light (0.90c).

At a speed of 0.90c, it still takes over 22 years to reach Terra, and more than 22 years to return to Earth — a total trip of about **45.1 years** as seen in Earth's frame of reference.

Relative to Steve on the Earth, Arianna will go through significant time dilation. Here the Lorentz Factor, F is:

$$F = sqrt\ (1 - (0.9)^2) = 0.436$$

So to Arianna, the round trip for the voyage will take only:

45.1 *years times* 0.436 = **19.7 years.**

Thus, upon returning to the Earth, Arianna will have aged less than 20 years, while Steve will have aged over 45 years. They are both now 25 years old. On Arianna's return, Steve will be 25 plus 45.1 or over 70 years old, but Arianna will only be 25 plus 19.7 or 44 years old. This is why the trip is such a painful decision for both of them and their families.

Let's draw a spacetime diagram to get a picture of this so-called "Twins Paradox" (first proposed by French physicist Paul Langevin in 1911). Figure 8.9 gives us a pictorial history of Arianna's trip to Terra and back with respect to the *Earth reference frame*.[22]

We assume here for simplicity that (a) Earth and Terra are standing still with respect to each other, (b) Steve remains stationary on the Earth for the duration of Arianna's trip, and (c) Arianna's rocket returns to Earth as soon as it reaches Terra.

Steve's Path — Steve's path (world-line) through spacetime is a vertical line directly from *A* to *C* in the figure. Why? Because in the Earth reference frame, he is *standing still*. From his point of view, he is experiencing movement through time only, and no movement through space.

Arianna's Path — Arianna's trip, her world-line from Earth to Terra and back, is represented by path *ABC*. Arianna is moving along two diagonal paths, both going through time *and* space.

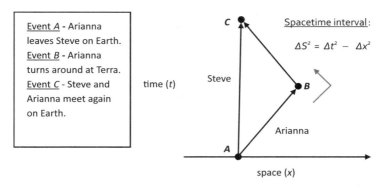

Event A - Arianna leaves Steve on Earth.
Event B - Arianna turns around at Terra.
Event C - Steve and Arianna meet again on Earth.

Figure 8.9. The Twins Paradox. *Steve's path is line AC. His world-line is in time only. Arianna's path is line AB and line BC. Her world-line has spatial components, which get subtracted from the temporal components. Therefore Arianna's path, her spacetime interval (wristwatch time) is less than Steve's. Thus she returns to Earth younger than her twin.*

Which path is longer, Steve's *AC* line or Arianna's *ABC* lines? Let's use the spacetime interval to find out.

The Spacetime Interval Redux

Steve's spacetime interval directly from event *A* to event *C* is simply his time interval or his wristwatch time (proper time): **45.1 years**. (Again since he has no motion through space, there is no space interval to square and subtract from the square of the time interval.)

But Arianna's path from *A* to *B* and from *B* to *C* goes through space and time. Thus Arianna's spacetime interval from events *A* to *B* and *B* to *C* requires that we *subtract* the square of the space interval from the square of the time interval.

This subtraction results in a *smaller* spacetime interval. This shorter spacetime interval means a smaller wristwatch time (proper time) for Arianna than for Steve.

This is shown mathematically as follows (in the Earth frame of reference):

Steve's World-line: The spacetime interval directly from event *A* (rocket leaves Earth) to event *C* (rocket returns to Earth) is calculated as follows:

The rocket velocity is 0.9c. Terra is a distance of 20.3 light-years from the Earth.

So the time it takes for the rocket to get from Earth to Terra is:

Time = distance / speed = 20.3 light-years / 0.9 l-yrs/yr = 22.6 years
*So the round-trip takes 2 times 22.6 = **45.1 years** (Steve's wristwatch time)*
Arianna's World-line: The spacetime interval from Event A (rocket leaves Earth) to event B (rocket arrives on Terra) is calculated as:

$$\Delta S^2 = \Delta t^2 - \Delta x^2$$
$$= (22.6)^2 - (20.3)^2$$
$$= 96.4$$
$$\Delta S^2 = sqrt\ (\ 96.4) = 9.82\ years$$

This is Arianna's wristwatch time from Earth to Terra
So, per Arianna, *the round-trip* from events A to B to C (Earth to Terra and back) takes:

*2 times 9.82 = **19.7 years***

The above calculation says that the spacetime interval or wristwatch time for *Steve* going directly from event A to event C is **45.1 years**. And the spacetime interval or wristwatch time for *Arianna* to go from events A to B to C is **19.7 years**. So Arianna ages less than Steve.

But all this was calculated in the *Earth* frame of reference. What would the calculations be in Arianna's *rocket* reference frame?[c]

The spacetime interval for Steve's world-line would be *same* value. The spacetime interval for Arianna's world-line would also be same value. Remember the spacetime interval is absolute. It is unaffected by uniform motion. So it does not matter which (uniformly moving) reference frame we use — the answers come out the same!

This is summarized in Table 8.3.

The Return

On a brilliant sunny mid-day in early August 2950, the great expedition to Terra returns to Earth. (It is always sunny at mid-day; the weather is programmed to rain only from 2 to 5 am.) Several hundred thousand people pack the roads and fields surrounding the landing area. The event is holo-cast across the Earth, and to humans on four planets, two moons, and seventeen space stations within our solar system.

---

[c] There are actually two reference frames for Arianna; Earth to Terra and Terra to Earth. Once she changes direction, it is a new frame of reference.

Table 8.3. The Twins Paradox. *After the trip, Steve is over 70 years old, but Arianna is still waiting to celebrate her 45th birthday.*

Twin	Wristwatch Time (round-trip)	Age (years) Beginning of Trip	End of Trip
Steve on Earth	45.1 years	25	Over 70
Arianna on rocket	19.7 years	25	Less than 45

Distance to Terra = 20.3 light-years (in Earth frame). Rocket speed = 0.9c.

Among the audience in the viewing stands at the Kennedy-Eagle Feather Space Center are Arianna's 70-year-old twin brother Steve, his wife, their two children, their spouses, and his four grandchildren.

The rocket ship lands and the crew slowly disembark. "They look so young," people say.

Arianna is one of the last to come down the gangway. Beside her are two 18-foot tall aliens encased in flexiglass suits to shield them from Earth's toxic atmosphere. Their multi-colored skin shimmers in the sunlight like living liquid. The crowd stares in wonder.

But Steve has eyes only for Arianna. She spots him in the crowd and waves. Tears flow down both their faces. They embrace. Steve introduces her to his family.

"This is your long lost Aunt Arianna, safe at home at last," he says, choking up. "You look great, Arianna."

"Thanks," she replies, but says nothing in return.

Arianna and the rest of the crew left the Earth in the year **2905**. To her and the crew on the rocket ship, time passes normally. When they return, to them it should be the year **2925** on Earth. After all, Arianna and crew have only aged about 20 years.

But calendars on Earth say it is the year **2950**. Even though they fully expected this, the crew still finds themselves shocked to be in the second half of the 30th century. They have arrived back on Earth some *25 years into the future*!

Theoretically, if her rocket moved fast enough Arianna could travel for say one year and arrive back on the Earth *thousands of years into the future*. If Arianna's rocket speed was 0.9999999c, the Lorentz Factor, F would be 0.0004472. If she traveled at that speed for one year, she would arrive back on Earth 1 divided by 0.0004472 or 2236 years later!

We must be careful here. According to special relativity, this time travel is a one-way trip. "You may be able to buy a round-trip ticket to (outer space)," write physicists Edwin F. Taylor and John Archibald Wheeler,[23] "but you get only a one-way ticket to the future." Arianna can travel into the future, but she *cannot* travel into the past.

Of course time travel effects are extremely small at every day speeds. But they are still real! Any time you are in motion, you experience this effect.

In fact, every time you leave a place, the slowing of time due to your relative motion means that you return to that same place a tiny fraction of a second into the future. We are all time travelers!

Who Aged and Why?

"I still don't get it," Steve says to Arianna. They tell us this time dilation works both ways. You know, if you and I are in relative motion, then I see your time slowing down and you see my time slowing down. Right?"

"Ya, I think that's it," says Arianna.

"Then how come it was you on that hyper-rocket who aged more slowly. I mean from your point of view, your rocket was standing still and I was in motion. So why wasn't it me who aged less?"

"Well," says Arianna, "We can't both be younger. I mean if there is a change in time, only one of us can be younger than the other."

"Ya, I know. But I still don't get it. You'd think after all the time I've spent on rockets, I'd understand the theory behind this stuff."

"I have an idea," Arianna says, "Let's ask Pat."

So once again the twins seek out their physicist sister. She begins with a question to Arianna.

"What did you feel on that rocket when you broke cruising speed and turned around at Terra?"

"When the forward thruster brakes were turned on to slow us down, I felt my body pushed forward against my seat harness."

"And once your rocket was turned around and pointed back towards Earth?"

"As we reaccelerated up to cruising speed, I felt my body pushed back against my seat."

"And Steve, did you feel anything like this during Arianna's trip?" Pat asks.

"No."

"You see, Arianna," Pat says, "you experienced the effects of *acceleration* during the turn-around — and Steve did not."

"The reason why Arianna's time slowed down is because of this acceleration. Remember in physics, both the rocket's braking to slow down and its accelerating to speed up are forms of acceleration."

"So . . . it was Arianna's turn-around that made all the difference?" says Steve.

"Yes, and the accelerations in that turn-around. That's why Arianna's time ran slower than yours."

"OK, thanks for that 'simple' explanation, Sis," the twins say, scratching their heads.

Verification

Still skeptical? Good for you. A true scientist doesn't accept a proposition just based on analysis of some imaginary space trip. In physics such issues are settled by experiment.[24] Let's look at one such experiment.

We don't have the technology (yet) to accelerate macroscopic objects such as rockets and people to relativistic speeds, but we can do it with microscopic objects. Let us turn again to our particle friend, the muon.

In 1975, an international team of physicists led by Italian particle physicist Emilio Picasso, sent muons on a series of "merry-go-round" rides around and around in circles. The muons were steered by magnets to follow a great circular path some 46 feet in diameter inside the then brand-new Muon Storage Ring at CERN. The test was conducted to check out a fundamental point in electron force theory, but it also tested the twins acceleration issue.

A circular path is one where the direction is constantly changing — and since change in direction is a form of acceleration, the orbiting muons were constantly undergoing acceleration.

The muons achieved speeds of some 99.94% the speed of light relative to the laboratory. Based on lifetimes of muons *at rest*, the traveling muons would typically live only long enough to make 14 to 15 trips around the Ring.

Now if Einstein is correct, we would expect the *accelerating* muons undergo a slowing of time, and thus have a longer lifetime (as observed in the laboratory frame of reference). Repeated testing showed the traveling muons lasted long enough to make on average about 400 orbits around the Ring. In other words, muon lifetimes were extended nearly

30-fold. Careful measurement showed this agreed with Einstein's prediction to 1 part in 500.

So it is the *accelerated* muons (or by analogy the accelerated twin) who experienced the slowing of time. Numerous laboratory tests since, as well as atomic clocks on airplanes, rockets, and satellites have all confirmed the same principle — the reference frame which experiences acceleration is the one which shows the slowing of time. Einstein is proven right again!

(The Twins Paradox can be explained using special or general relativity. See endnote for details.[25])

Spacetime and Gravity

When Einstein read Minkowski's paper on spacetime, he didn't think much of it at the time. He thought it was "just" a mathematics abstraction, without any particular application to the physical world. "With mathematics, you can prove anything," Einstein wrote derisively.[26] Perhaps his dislike for Minkowski colored his thinking.

Einstein came to regret these remarks. Working on his new theory of gravity, Einstein began to "appreciate the power of Minkowski's work and its deep philosophical implications."[27] He realized the mathematics of spacetime was essential to the development of his new theory of gravity. Einstein later admitted that "without the four-dimensional mathematics of Minkowski, relativity 'might have remained stuck in its diapers.'"[28]

The framework of spacetime became a centerpiece of Einstein's theory of general relativity. The absolute spacetime interval in particular provided Einstein with a *metric* in a world of relative motion — a universal "ruler" for all events in the cosmos.

Most striking of all, Einstein proposed that spacetime is not static, not rigid, but that it warps, curves, and bends in the presence of mass-energy. As we shall see, this "spacetime curvature" is what holds us to the surface of the Earth. It is the dynamic that controls the motion of all celestial bodies, orchestrating the cosmic dance of planets, stars, galaxies, and galaxy clusters. Spacetime curvature is gravity itself.

This is the subject of Part II of this book.

Imagine it is the year 3000, and space travel at relativistic speeds is commonplace. In such a world, our great-great grandchildren won't even think to question the slowing of time and who it applies to. They won't need to read this or any other book on relativity. To them, time dilation is just a common sense part of everyday experience.

A holo-ad (above) announces a party cruise to Jupiter and back to celebrate the new millennium. Traveled at a cruising speed of two-thirds the speed of light, or some 447 million miles an hour, it takes the rocket ship *two hours Earth time* to fly to Jupiter and back. But since — as everybody in the fourth millennium knows — time slows down with motion, the trip takes only *an hour and a half rocket time.*

PART II

Einstein Revealed: General Relativity, Gravity, and the Cosmos

Chapter 9

Einstein's Dream

I want to know how God created this world …
I want to know his thoughts. The rest are details.[1]

Albert Einstein

If you found the tenets of special relativity mind-boggling, wait till you read about *general* relativity. Special relativity told us how uniform motion squeezes space and slows time, how matter is "frozen" energy, and how the space interval (distance) and time interval are united under a single construct unaffected by uniform motion called the spacetime interval.

General relativity, on the other hand, tells us that space is stretched, time is slowed, and spacetime is "curved" in the presence of mass-energy; that gravity is not a force but the geometry of spacetime itself. These strange tenets reveal a brave new world of wonders which has revolutionized our perception of the universe and our place in it. Let's take a look.

Gravity and the Slowing of Time

General relativity predicts that gravity slows down the passage of time. To see how this works, raise your wristwatch above your head. Now hold the watch close to the ground. (Ignore those people giving you funny looks; what do they know?) Per Einstein, your watch runs *slower* nearer the source of the gravity — in this case, the Earth. The effect is so tiny you don't notice it, but it is real.

In a number of historic tests, physicists compared atomic clocks on Earth to identical clocks on airplanes, rockets, and satellites. They all demonstrated the closer you are to the Earth (lower altitude) the slower time runs. And the farther away from Earth (higher altitude) the faster time runs — all in concert with predictions of general relativity.

A recent test is closer in scale to our little watch-holding experiment:[2] In 2010, physicists at the National Institute of Standards and Technology in Boulder, Colorado placed two super-accurate aluminum ion atomic clocks one above the other and about a foot (33 cm) apart. The lower clock ran a tiny bit slower than the higher clock — adding up to a little over a billionth of a second per year — in excellent agreement with Einstein's formula.

Gravity and the Stretching of Space

Now take a pen, point it downwards, and hold it above your head. Then place it close to the ground (still pointing downward). As seen from far away, the distance from the tip of the pen to its tail is a tiny bit longer when it is close to the ground. This is because the closer you get to the Earth, the more space is stretched!

This stretching of space (and the slowing of time) was first measured during a 1919 solar eclipse. As we shall see, it made Einstein world famous.

And, as we shall see, this slowing of time and stretching of space — what physicists call spacetime curvature — is what causes objects to fall in a gravitational field. It is in fact gravity itself!

At the dawn of the third millennium, general relativity remains our most accurate theory of gravity. It continues to be the theoretical basis behind the marvels of modern cosmology — black holes where even light cannot escape, wormholes to perhaps another place in space and time, giant quasars which radiate more energy than an entire galaxy of stars, gravity waves, neutron stars, precession of planetary orbits, gravitational lensing, frame dragging, the expansion of space, and the origin and evolution of the universe in the big bang.

Albert Einstein's path to the theory of general relativity awaits us. In the vernacular of Al Jolson following a vaudeville act which brought down the house: "You ain't seen nothin' yet!"

The Quest for A New Theory

Albert Einstein's bold attempt to supplant Newton's 1687 "Law" of Gravity took great courage and no small measure of arrogance. "As an older friend, I must advise you against it for in the first place you will never succeed, and even if you succeed, no one will believe you," venerable physicist Max Planck told Einstein.[3] "(However) if you are successful, you will be called the next Copernicus."

Typical of Einstein, he began his pursuit with a universal question. His 1905 theory, what he began to call "special" relativity, is based on the principle that the laws (and equations) of physics are the same for all observers in *uniform* motion. He called this the Principle of Relativity.

Now in 1907, Einstein asked: Why should this grand principle apply only to observers whose speed and/or direction does not change? What about motion that is *not* uniform? What about an observer in a vehicle which is speeding up or slowing down? How about someone on a rotating platform? What do things look like from their point of view, from their *accelerating* frame of reference?

Shouldn't the laws of physics be the same for *all* observers, for *all* frames of reference; whether in uniform motion or not?

> Up to now we have only applied the principle of relativity, i.e. the presupposition that the laws of nature are independent of the state of motion of the reference system to (uniform motion) … Is it conceivable that the principle of relativity also holds for systems which are accelerating relative to each other?[4]

> Albert Einstein, 1907

Consider again two identical scientific laboratories which can perform any and all physics experiments to extraordinary accuracy. One lab is stationary on the ground and the other is in *uniform* motion. Per Einstein's principle of relativity, all experiments performed inside the uniformly *moving* laboratory get the same results as identical experiments performed inside the *stationary* laboratory.

But what if the moving laboratory's motion is *not* uniform? What if, for example, its speed is constantly increasing relative to the stationary lab? Will identical experiments give the same results inside *both* labs? What if we spin the second lab on a giant rotating platform? Will experiments inside both labs now give the same results?

We know from experience when we are inside a car traveling in *uniform* motion, we cannot tell (internally) whether it is moving or at rest. But when the driver steps on the brake, steps on the gas, or turns the wheel; our bodies lurch forward, back, or to one side. Acceleration is different. We *can* feel the effects of change in speed or direction. We feel accelerating motion — whereas we cannot feel uniform motion.

And what about gravity? What if the lab is falling in a gravitational field — why doesn't the principle of relativity apply to this point of view, this reference frame as well?

Einstein's search to include all frames of reference — acceleration, rotation, and gravity — in a general theory of relativity would prove the most difficult of his young life. It would challenge even his great imagination and keen scientific abilities, as well as his admittedly limited mathematical knowledge as never before.

In comparison with the present problem (general relativity), the theory of special relativity was child's-play.[5]

Albert Einstein

His journey began with conflicts between special relativity and Newton's Law of Universal Gravitation.

Troubles with Newton's Gravity

In the early part of the 20th century, no one questioned Newton's theory of gravity. It was considered the be-all, the end-all, the final word on the matter. Why? Because it worked so beautifully.

Newton's Law of Universal Gravitation explained the movements of planets around the Sun, the "precise motion of the Moon," the motions of the moons of Jupiter and Saturn, the eccentric orbits of comets due to the Sun's attraction, the equatorial bulge of Earth, the tides of Earth's seas due to the pull of gravity of the Moon and Sun, and the precession of the axis of rotation of the Earth.[6] It had even predicted the location of two new planets — Neptune and the dwarf-planet Pluto *before* they were spotted by telescopes.

There was one issue with Newton's theory — the tiniest of anomalies. Precise observations of Mercury, the planet closest to the Sun, showed its orbit ever so slightly off from Newtonian predictions. French mathematician Urbain Le Verrier tried to explain it as perhaps a disturbance from a tiny unknown planet inside the orbit of Mercury. But the planet "Vulcan" was never found. (Sorry, Spock.)

Mercury's measured orbit was such a small discrepancy in a veritable catalogue of successes that no one dared question the efficacy of Newton's theory. No one, that is, until Albert Einstein.

What made Einstein doubt the great Newton? He saw fundamental disagreements between Newton's theory of gravity and his new theory of special relativity. If Einstein's theory was correct, Isaac Newton had to be wrong!

Einstein saw three key issues in Newton's theory:

(A) Gravity is instantaneous — Imagine the mischievous and omnipotent immortal Q from Star Trek suddenly makes our Sun disappear. How long do we have before the skies go dark and the Earth begins to freeze?

The (very nearly) spherical Sun radiates light in all directions. As photons leave its surface, they radiate outward in an ever-growing sphere of light. Right now the space between the Sun and Earth is filled with photons all marching at the speed of light from Sun to Earth (and beyond).

If the Sun were to suddenly disappear, at that instance space between the Earth and Sun would still be filled with photons emitted by the Sun *before* it disappeared. And the last photons to be emitted before the Sun's disappearance would be just above the Sun's surface.

These last photons emitted from the Sun would take some 8.3 minutes to travel the approximately 93 million miles from the Sun to Earth. This means we would still see the Sun continuing to shine for 8.3 minutes after it had disappeared. Then and only then would the sky go dark.

What about gravity? Per Newton, the force of gravity holds Earth in orbit around the Sun. What if our Sun were to suddenly disappear? Would Earth *instantly* leave the Sun's orbit and fly off into space?

Newton would say yes. In Newton's theory, any changes in gravity are communicated *instantaneously*.[7] (See Fig. 9.1.)

But for Einstein, a gravitational disturbance traveling instantaneously is a serious problem. It violates special relativity's dictum that nothing can travel through space faster than the speed of light.

Plus, if gravity is instantaneous as Newton believed, you could use a gravitational disturbance to synchronize all clocks, including those in motion. You could establish a single absolute time for all observers. Time would not be relative. This would destroy Einstein's special relativity. Thus, Einstein theorized, gravitational disturbances are not transmitted instantaneously, but *at the same speed as light*.

Einstein's viewpoint is shown in Fig. 9.2. Here when the Sun disappears, a gravitational disturbance is emitted from where the Sun was. It travels outward in an ever expanding sphere, moving at the speed of

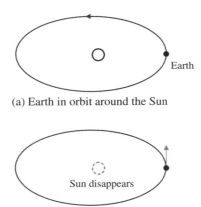

(a) Earth in orbit around the Sun

(b) Sun disappears; Earth *immediately* flies off into space

Figure 9.1. **Newton's View.** *If Sun were to suddenly disappear, Earth would leave its orbit instantaneously. (Not drawn to scale.)*

light. During this time, Earth continues in its orbit around where the Sun used to be.

A little over eight minutes after the Sun has disappeared, the disturbance finally reaches Earth. Then and only then does our planet leave its orbit around the Sun's former position and fly off into outer space.

Let's now look at the second issue Einstein had with Newton's theory of gravity.

(B) How to determine distance? — Newton's inverse square law says gravitational force between any two masses weakens as the square of the *distance* between them. If the distance between two stellar objects were to double, gravity between them would weaken by two times two or four times. Triple the distance and gravity would weaken by three times three or nine times. And so on.

But per special relativity, the distance between any two points in space *contracts* with relative uniform motion (in the direction of motion). And the planets are all moving at different speeds relative to the Sun and relative to each other.

Consider, for example, the distance between the Sun and Mercury.[8] It is a different value depending on where you choose your frame of

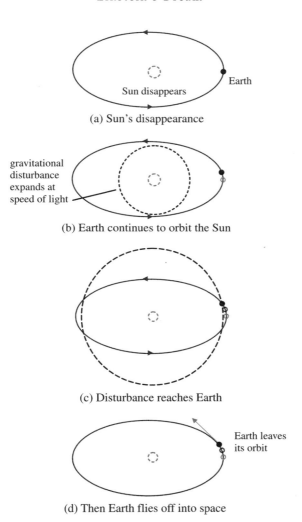

(a) Sun's disappearance

(b) Earth continues to orbit the Sun

(c) Disturbance reaches Earth

(d) Then Earth flies off into space

Figure 9.2. Einstein's View: *Sun disappears — Earth leaves Sun's orbit about 8 minutes later. (Diagrams not drawn to scale — Earth orbital speed greatly exaggerated.)*

reference. Say you are somehow riding on the Sun. From your point of view, the distance between the Sun and Mercury is different (by about one part in a billion) compared to the value you would measure if you were riding on Mercury. Yes this is a small difference in this case, but one that must be taken onto account in a comprehensive theory of gravity.

145

The third issue with Newton's gravity is *action at a distance.*

(C) Action at a distance — Unlike his three laws of motion, Newton's law of gravity describes an invisible force which "exerts control over matter without having any direct physical contact."[9] In other words, Newton's theory gives us a formula for the strength of gravity, but no explanation on how it is transmitted from place to place.

How does the Sun reach out some 93 million miles, grab Earth, and hold it in its orbit? What exactly *travels* from the Sun to Earth to make contact with our planet, telling it not to fly off into space?

Something has to be sent out from the Sun to make contact with Earth, doesn't it? Is it some form of matter or some type of non-material energy which goes from the Sun to Earth? Is it a particle? Is it a wave? Or is it something else entirely?

This issue is called "action at a distance" — the Sun some 93 million miles over there somehow controlling Earth's actions over here with an invisible force "transmitted through empty space, through nothingness."[10]

What was Newton's answer to this issue? Basically he said "I donno." Of course he phrased it in the more formal language of the time:

> *I have not been able to deduce . . . the cause of these properties*
> *of gravity, and I offer no hypothesis.*[11]

> Isaac Newton, *Principia*

"That gravity should be innate, inherent, and essential to matter, so that one body can act on another at a distance, through a vacuum," wrote Newton, "... is to me so great an absurdity that I believe no man, who has ... a competent facility of thinking can ever fall into it."[12]

Newton's theory was generally accepted despite this objection, because its predictions proved so accurate and universal. Over time, concerns with how gravity is transmitted receded into the background. But with Einstein's pursuit of a new theory of gravitation, they once again came to the forefront.

In summary, Einstein needed to resolve three issues: (1) the instantaneous transmission of gravitational disturbances, (2) the relative distance between masses, and (3) how gravity is transmitted from place to place. And hopefully, his new theory would explain the anomaly in

Mercury's orbit not accounted for by Newton. It was a tremendous challenge — one which began in earnest with Einstein's new career in academia.

Professor Einstein

It took some time for Einstein to comprehend the implications of his theory of special relativity. In December of 1907, he published his first detailed exposition on the subject. He also wrote about his first tentative steps toward a new relativistic theory of gravity. Einstein discussed methods for applying special relativity to acceleration, as well as some very early ideas on general relativity and his Equivalence Principle — which, as we shall see, connects acceleration to gravity.

In June of 1907, Einstein had applied for a post at Bern University in Switzerland. Despite the growing recognition of his work, he was turned down. Then some eight months later, he took the first step toward an academic career.

In February of 1908, the patent clerk was offered a position as a part-time lecturer at Bern. He became a "privatdozent", an unsalaried post-doc assignment paid directly from student fees. This standard European practice dating back to the middle ages gave universities a way to check out new applicants before offering them a full-time professorship.

For financial reasons, Einstein kept his job at the patent office and held classes in the evening.[13] Teaching was not one of his fortes — only three friends of Einstein attended the first term and one the second. The course was canceled.

University of Zurich

In May of 1909, 30-year-old Albert Einstein found himself on the short list for a full-time academic position — an associate professor in theoretical physics at the University of Zurich.[14] His primary competition was an old acquaintance, Friedrich Adler. Both were Jewish, a handicap — but Adler had the edge. Many faculty members were sympathetic to the Austrian Social Democratic Party and Adler's father was its founder.

The young Adler felt Einstein had far stronger physics abilities. So he wrote an eloquent letter to the faculty recommending Einstein for the post. Based on Adler's remarkable self-sacrifice, Einstein was given the job. He became a "professor extraordinarius," certainly a "step up from privatdozent but still not a tenured position."[15]

How did the now big shot professor present himself at his first lecture? "He appeared in class in somewhat shabby attire wearing pants that were too short," a student later recalled, "and carrying with him a slip of paper the size of visiting card on which he had sketched his lecture notes."[16]

So, now I too am an official member of the guild of whores.[17]

Einstein to Jakob Laub on becoming a professor

When Einstein told Friedrich Haller, his kindly director at the patent office he was resigning, Haller asked Einstein why he would leave such a promising career.[18]

In September of 1909, Einstein attended his first international conference, the annual congress of Germany National Scientists and Physicians.[19] He presented a paper on radiation theory (light quanta). His talk was the first to clearly discuss the issue of light having both wave-like and particle-like properties.

In October, Einstein received his first nomination for the Nobel Prize in physics.[20] (He would be nominated nine more times before finally receiving the award in 1921 for the Photoelectric Effect.)

While Einstein's star as a physicist was rising, his home life was deteriorating.[21] He and his wife Mileva Marić were becoming increasingly estranged during this period. Nonetheless, Albert fathered a second child with Mileva, their son Eduard, in July of 1910.

Prague

In April of 1910, the German University in Prague offered Einstein a position as full professor at twice the salary of Zurich.[22] To sweeten the deal, he was promised the directorship of the Institute of Theoretical Physics at the university. Einstein was recommended by none other than Max Planck, who wrote: "(Einstein's relativity) probably exceeds in audacity everything that has been achieved so far in speculative science."[23]

Einstein's position in Prague would be as "professor ordinarius",[24] a tenured position where he would no longer be required to teach. Even though the Prague University was not known for its physics, the ever restless Einstein accepted this promotion with glee. Now he could devote full time to his beloved physics.

His office overlooked a park attached to an insane asylum. Einstein "would point to the inmates and tell his visitors, 'There you see that fraction of the insane who are not working on quantum theory.'"[25]

In Prague, he worked on his pursuit of general relativity "with full vigor,"[26] writes Einstein historian and physicist John Stachel. Einstein wrote six papers on general relativity during this period plus "five on radiation (light quanta) and the quantum theory of solids."[27] Here he first proposed the bending of starlight due to the Sun's gravity.

> *Within the quiet halls of the Prague Institute of Theoretical Physics, (I) found the necessary equanimity to slowly give my earlier ideas a more definitive form.*[28]
>
> Albert Einstein

Einstein's work had become so well known by this time that whenever he gave a lecture to the public, it was standing room only.[29] He also found himself traveling in elite circles. In 1911, Belgian industrialist Ernst Solvay organized the first now legendary international scientific congress in Brussels. The gentle Henrik Lorentz was named its president.

Included in the invitation-only gathering were Einstein and a "who's who" of top European physicists — including Ernest Rutherford and James Jeans from Britain, Henri Poincaré, Marie Curie, Louis de Broglie, and Paul Langevin from Paris, and Walther Nernst, Max Planck, and Arnold Sommerfeld from Germany.

However, life in Prague was not so pleasant for Marić, with its "brown drinking water, fleas and bureaucracy."[30] And as a woman of

Serbian descent, she felt like an outsider in the German community of Prague. She was also jealous of the many hours her husband spent socializing with colleagues and friends.[31] This and the ever increasing amount of time he spent on his budding theory of gravity were taking a toll on their already rocky marriage.

When I think seriously day and night, I cannot engage in loving chatter.[32]

Albert Einstein

Near the end of 1911, his college friend Marcel Grossmann, now a Professor at Zurich Poly asked Einstein if he would be interested in a position at his alma mater.[33] Feeling isolated in Prague, Einstein said he would. Supported by letters of recommendation from a number of outstanding physicists (including Marie Curie), Grossman convinced the Institute to offer Einstein a full professorship. In the summer of 1912, after a mere seventeen months in Prague, the Einsteins moved to Zurich. Marić was thrilled.

How it must have felt for the now 33-year-old Albert Einstein to be appointed Professor of Theoretical Physics at Zurich Poly — the same college that had refused to hire him as an assistant upon his graduation 12 years earlier. Vindication indeed.

The Next Chapter

Could he do it? Could Einstein find a theory which would extend the relativity principle to all reference frames, including gravitational fields? In other words, could he come up with a *relativistic* theory of gravity? Einstein's path to this audacious goal began with a remarkable insight — the Equivalence Principle. This is the subject of the next chapter.

Chapter 10

"The Happiest Thought
of My Life"

*In all the years since Galileo and Newton, nobody before (Einstein)
had realized that there was something here worth noticing ...*[1]

Banish Hoffman

In his search for a relativistic theory of gravity, Einstein first attempted to treat gravity purely in terms of special relativity. He tried to replace Newton's instantaneous gravity with gravity traveling from place to place at the speed of light. His initial calculations showed something was wrong — under this construct, falling objects appeared to fall at different rates depending on their horizontal speed.

At least as far back as Galileo, it was known that a projectile shot out of cannon in a horizontal direction falls just as fast as one simply dropped from the same height. In other words, an object's horizontal speed has no effect on how fast it falls vertically. (See Fig. 10.1.)

This prompted Einstein to take a fresh look at Galileo's Principle: All objects fall at the *same* rate in a gravitational field, no matter what their weight or composition. "The law (of falling bodies) ... was now brought home to me in all its significance," Einstein later wrote.[2] "I was in the highest degree amazed at its existence and guessed that it must be the key to a deeper understanding of ... gravitation."

Once again, Einstein's intuitive feel for the physics was right on. Based on Galileo's Principle, he found a key relationship between gravity and acceleration — a connection which would become the physical

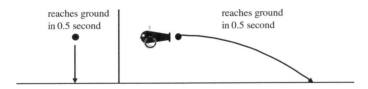

reaches ground
in 0.5 second

reaches ground
in 0.5 second

Figure 10.1. Per Galileo's Law of Falling Objects. *(a) Cannon ball dropped from a certain height (see left). (b) Cannon ball at same height and at same time shot out of cannon horizontally (see right). Both cannon balls drop at same rate and reach the ground at the same time, in this case a half-second.*

principle behind his theory of general relativity. He would call this relationship the *Equivalence Principle.*

The Hammer and the Feather

On August 2, 1971, Apollo 15 astronaut David Scott stood on the surface of the Moon at the end of his third and final EVA (extravehicular activity) and performed his final task — an experiment allegedly as old as Galileo.[3] In a TV broadcast live to Earth, Scott held a geological hammer in his right hand and a falcon feather in his left. With the lunar module (aptly named "Falcon") and the 13,000-foot-high Hadley Delta lunar mountains in the background, Scott released the hammer and feather at the same time. (See Fig. 10.2.)

Which hit the lunar dirt first? The hammer? The feather? Or did they both hit the ground at the same time?

The hammer and feather hit the lunar surface at the *same time.* Why? Because for one thing the Moon has gravity but virtually no air.[4] The smaller Moon's surface gravity is about one-sixth that of Earth's — so weak it has trouble holding on to its gases. As a result, it has an extremely thin atmosphere.

Thus the hammer and feather fell in a near-vacuum. The feather in particular encountered virtually no air resistance to make it float and bob as it would on Earth. It simply fell straight down along with the hammer.

But wait. Doesn't the feather *weigh less* than the hammer? Doesn't it have less mass? And wouldn't this mean that, even in a vacuum, the hammer would fall first because it is heavier? This is just what Aristotle believed, but it is incorrect. As Galileo pointed out, all objects fall at the

Figure 10.2. The Hammer and Feather Drop. *"In a live TV broadcast from the moon on August 2, 1971, astronaut David R Scott drops a hammer and feather simultaneously from the same height onto the lunar surface."*[5]

same rate (ignoring air effects) and hit the ground at the same time — no matter what they weigh.[6] This is Galileo's Principle for falling objects.

A number of modern experiments have confirmed Galileo's Principle to great accuracy. For instance, a group of scientists led by J. G. Williams at NASA Jet Propulsion Laboratory (JPL) used lasers to measure how fast the Earth and Moon are falling towards the Sun as they orbit our home star.[7] Even though Earth is about 80 times more massive than the Moon, they found the measured rate of fall or acceleration towards the Sun to be equal, within an accuracy of 0.00000000000015 or 1.5×10^{-13}.

What did Newton say about this counterintuitive notion in his great theory of gravity? Nothing. In Newton's theory, Galileo's Principle of falling bodies is an "isolated unexplained experimental fact".[8] In other words, it was accepted based on observation — Newton offered no theoretical basis for this behavior.

Einstein was deeply disturbed by this empirical fact unexplained by any theory. It seemed to him there must be some explanation for why all objects fall at the same acceleration in a gravitational field, some not yet recognized connection between acceleration and gravity.

As the American Institute of Physics puts it: "All bodies, however different, if released from the same height will fall with exactly the same constant acceleration (in the absence of air resistance)." Einstein puzzled over this *exact same* constant acceleration, this invariance (recall invariance means something that does not change). He had founded his special theory of relativity on an invariance — the speed of light. Perhaps, "here was an invariance that could be the starting point for a theory (of gravity)."[9]

> *This experience of the equal falling of all bodies in a gravitational field is the most universal which the observations of nature has provided us; (yet) this (empirical) law had not found any place in the foundations of our physical picture of the world.*[10]
>
> Albert Einstein

What is the connection? Why do all objects fall at the same acceleration in a gravitational field? What is this apparent link between gravity and acceleration? Pondering these questions led Einstein to what he called "the happiest thought of my life."

Einstein's Epiphany

One fateful day in November of 1907, Albert Einstein was sitting at his desk at the patent office, daydreaming about physics as usual. Perhaps he was leaning back too far in his chair. Maybe he almost fell over backwards. Whatever it was, a thought suddenly came to him, a great epiphany which went something like this; "If I were to fall, as I fall I would feel *weightless*."

In other words, in that brief moment of free-fall to the floor, it would seem to Einstein that he was stationary and the floor was rising up to meet him. It would feel as if he were *floating in zero gravity*. Einstein realized that falling in a gravitational field is physically equivalent to floating in the zero gravity of outer space.

He later explained this insight from the point of view of a painter falling from a roof.[11] Einstein allegedly said he had heard about a painter (or perhaps a roofer) who had fallen from a roof, so he went to the hospital to ask the painter what it felt like. The story has gained legendary status, but science historians generally believe it did not actually happen.

> *Then there occurred to me the happiest thought of my life ... The gravitational field has only a relative existence ... Because for an observer falling freely from the roof of a house there exists — at least in his immediate surroundings — no gravitational field ...*[12]
>
> Albert Einstein

154

Let us consider Einstein's unfortunate painter. Imagine he has just fallen off the roof of a house along with his hat, paint brush, and bucket. (See Fig. 10.3.) The painter and his paraphernalia are now in free-fall, accelerating at *1-g* towards the ground below.

What is *1-g*? Object's just above the surface of the Earth fall at an acceleration of about 32 feet per second every second. This is an acceleration of *1-g*. At this acceleration, the painter's speed increases 32 feet per second every second he falls. He starts out at zero. One second later he is traveling at a speed of 32 feet per second relative to the ground. Two seconds later, he is going 64 feet per second. Three seconds later, he is going 96 feet per second, etc.

Per Galileo's principle, the falling painter's paint can, paint brush, and hat all fall at this same rate, an acceleration of *1-g* toward the ground (again neglecting air effects). From the painter's perspective, he is stationary and the ground is rushing up towards him at *1-g* acceleration. He sees the paint can, brush, and hat *at rest* alongside him during free-fall. In fact, he feels as though he is weightless, as though there is no gravity at all.

> *If the (falling) observer drops some bodies, these remain relative to him in a state of rest or uniform motion, independent of their particular chemical or physical nature, (with) air resistance, of course, ignored. The observer has the right to interpret his state as "at rest".*[13]

> Albert Einstein

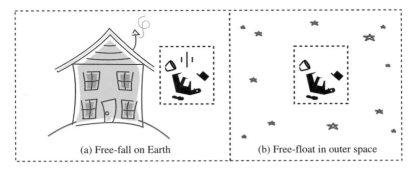

(a) Free-fall on Earth	(b) Free-float in outer space

Figure 10.3. Einstein's Epiphany. *Painter falling from roof. He feels his body is floating and the objects around him floating as well. Why? Because all objects fall at the same rate. Inside a box (dashed), he cannot tell whether he is (a) falling in a gravitational field, or (b) floating in the zero gravity of outer space.*

Now let's enclose the painter and his paint can, hat, and brush in a box (dashed lines in Fig. 10.3 above) so that he is unaware of his surroundings. He can no longer see the house passing by, the sky rushing away above him, or the ground rising up towards him.

His fear leaves him for a brief moment, replaced by a hopeful thought: "Maybe I am not falling. Maybe I am in outer space floating alongside my paint can, brush, and hat." Alas, he is in denial and will soon crash into the ground.

But the painter's hopeful notion does have a physical basis. If he *were* floating in outer space in zero gravity, he would feel weightless. And his paraphernalia would be floating alongside him as well, just like when he is falling. Einstein saw in a flash that there is no way for the painter inside the box to tell whether he is actually falling to the Earth or floating in outer space.

Now here is the key: why does the painter feel weightless when he is falling to the ground? Because his acceleration in free-fall cancels the effects of gravity.[14] Since they produce the same physical effects, they can cancel each other out. In other words:

Acceleration and gravity are equivalent.

What is the result of all this? For the painter falling inside the box, gravity is *zero*. There is no gravity in free-fall. This is why falling from the roof on Earth is equivalent to floating in outer space. Both situations are in effect in zero gravity.

Why? Again because in free-fall gravity is canceled out by acceleration.

Einstein realized there is no way to tell in a *closed* system (like inside the box) whether you are in free-fall in a uniform gravitational field or in free-float in the zero gravity of outer space.

Does this mean when you are falling, there is no gravity? Is he telling us that if you were to jump out of an airplane, there is no gravity on the way down? How can that be? If so, what makes you fall?

While you are falling, you feel an effect which is quite foreign to your experience, unless you are a sky diver. You feel weightless. (You also feel terrified.) Where else would you feel this weightlessness? In the zero gravity of outer space. The physical effects are the same. This is Einstein's point.

So are you really still falling from that airplane? Of course. But in your *personal* reference frame, you are stationary and the Earth is accelerating up towards you. And in this free-fall state, to you the effects of gravity are indeed zero. And from your perspective, the ground is rising up towards you. RELEASE THE PARACHUTE!

Now let's look at the Equivalence Principle the other way around.

The Alien Abduction Test

"These aliens look really weird," Aristox tells his commander.

"Yes, such small heads!" Commander Ignetzriblebop responds. "But even so, they have developed a primitive form of nuclear technology. We must study them."

"They think we fly around in disc-shaped space-ships they call flying saucers. Where in the name of Plipilmig did they get that idea?" says Aristox. "If they saw our rocket ships, they would think them quite conventional. And did you see what they think *we* look like? Emaciated bodies with bulbous heads and big sad eyes. How they ever ... "

"Enough!" says Ignetzriblebop. "Prepare for teleportation."

The two explorers from a great moon circling a planet orbiting a giant star 37 light years away in the Gemini constellation have been scouting Earth for some time. To learn more about our species, they implement their carefully thought-out abduction plan.

Imagine you are again in a classroom on Earth with a group of other students listening to one of my lectures. All windows in this classroom are covered and the single door to the classroom is closed. We cannot see outside the room.

On command, Aristox initiates teleportation. In an instant, we find ourselves in the alien spaceship. We are now in the zero gravity of outer space accelerating towards their home moon. (See Fig. 10.4.)

However, we are not aware that anything has changed. The aliens have configured the classroom on their ship to be identical in every detail to our classroom on Earth. The chairs, floor, walls, ceiling, even the writing on the whiteboard is the same. Air has been pumped into the room with the identical temperature and chemistry as on the surface of the Earth. No detail has been left unattended.

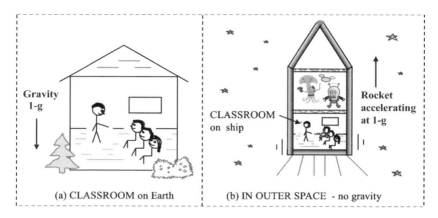

Figure 10.4. Alien Abduction. *Are we (a) in a classroom on Earth, or (b) in an identical classroom inside a spaceship accelerating at 1-g in outer space?*

What about *gravity*? The rocket ship is now in outer space far from any stellar objects. There is effectively no gravity. Shouldn't we all be floating weightless above the floor?

But you find yourself sitting in your chair and I find myself standing on the floor, just as though we were in the gravity at the surface of the Earth. How can this be? Because, to mimic the effects of Earth's gravity, Commander Ignetzriblebop has set the ship to accelerate at 32 feet per second every second or at *1-g*.

Is there any way to tell whether we are still in our classroom on the surface of the Earth or in the alien spaceship traveling at *1-g* acceleration in outer space?

Assume we have any device or scientific instrument at our disposal to make any measurements we wish. Except no measurements or observations are allowed exterior to the classroom. We can't, for example, look out the window or open the door. And no signals are allowed to be received from outside the room, such as a telephone call or TV/radio transmissions.

Again, is there any way to tell whether we are on Earth or in the alien rocket ship?[a]

At this point, I ask my students for ideas on how to tell the difference between gravity and acceleration. The most common suggestion is to let something fall to the floor.

---

[a]We ignore the effects of the earth's rotation, as it is only the Earth's gravitational field we are interested in here.

If we are on Earth, when we hold out an object and let it go, it will fall to the floor. But what will the same object do on the accelerating spaceship in outer space? Let's make it more interesting. Let's drop two objects of different mass — a light ball and a heavy cube. Now what happens? (Again ignoring air effects.)

Classroom on Earth's Surface (at rest in a gravitational field).

We are in the classroom on Earth. I hold the two objects out in front of me and let go. You record the experiment with your video camera. Per Galileo's Principle, the camera records both the light ball and heavy cube falling to the floor at the same *1-g* acceleration, as shown in Fig. 10.5. They hit the floor at the same time.

Classroom on Accelerating Rocket (in outer space — zero gravity).

Again I hold the two objects out in front of me and let go. What happens?

This is a little trickier. Both the ball and cube *float* in the zero gravity of outer space. But the floor of the spaceship is accelerating upwards at *1-g*.

Let's look at this from two points of view, outside the spaceship and inside the spaceship.

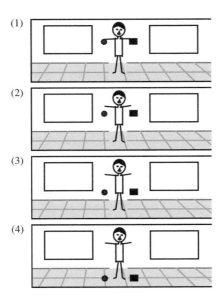

Figure 10.5. Classroom on Earth. *Light and heavy objects drop to floor at same rate (ignoring air effects). (See animation on the Equivalence Principle in marksmodernphysics.com.)*

View from Outside Spaceship. Assume astronaut Laura is outside the spaceship, floating at rest in space — as the accelerating ship passes by in front of her.

Astronaut Laura records the experiment on her video camera.[15] What does her video camera see? It records the ball and cube floating in space as the floor of the rocket rises up to meet them. This is shown in Fig. 10.6.

To Laura outside the spaceship, the released ball and cube are at rest — and the spaceship is accelerating upwards. She sees the floor of

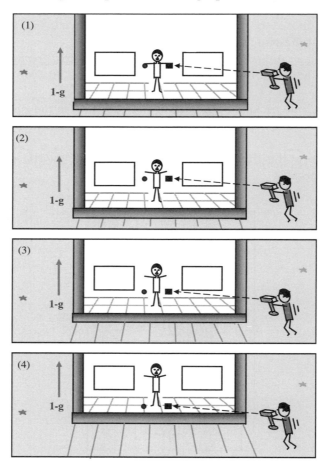

Figure 10.6. Outside View — Rocket Accelerating at 1-g in Outer Space. *Laura's "stationary" camera outside spaceship records released objects as stationary in space as floor rises up to meet them. But to students in rocket, it looks like the objects are falling to the floor. (See animation on the Equivalence Principle in marksmodernphysics.com.)*

the spaceship move up to meet the stationary ball and cube. How fast does the floor move up to meet the two objects? At *1-g* acceleration or 32 feet per second per second.

View from Inside Spaceship. All of us inside the spaceship are standing on the floor or sitting in chairs. From our perspective, we and the floor are standing still and the released ball and cube are moving *downwards.* To us, the ball and cube appear to fall to the floor at an acceleration of *1-g.*

On the Earth, the released ball and cube accelerate downward to the floor at the same rate. On the spaceship, the floor accelerates upward to the floating objects. But to us inside the classroom, *both situations look the same.* On Earth, we see the objects falling. Inside the spaceship, it appears to us that the objects are also falling.

Is this really so? Let's compare both "inside" cameras — the one inside the room on Earth and the one inside the rocket. We find they both show the same thing: the ball and cube falling together to the ground at an acceleration of *1-g.*

In fact there is no way to tell which camera recorded the event on Earth and which recorded the event on the accelerating spaceship. This in essence is Einstein's Equivalence Principle — gravity and acceleration produce equivalent physical effects.

Here Einstein realized something of great significance: the Equivalence Principle works *because* of Galileo's Principle — because all bodies fall at the same rate. Recall in our example the cube is heavier than the ball. On Earth they fall together to the floor, just as Galileo predicted. On the accelerating spaceship, once released, they float together in outer space. So to people inside the accelerating spaceship, it appears both the light and heavy objects fall together just like they do on Earth.

What if Galileo were wrong? What if a heavier object does fall faster than a lighter object? On Earth, the heavier cube would fall faster and hit the floor before the lighter ball. But in outer space, the ball and cube would still float together. If this were true, we could then *distinguish acceleration from gravity.*

If the cube were to fall to the floor before the ball, we'd know we are on Earth. If the cube and ball were to fall together, we'd know we are in the accelerating rocket ship in outer space.

But the ball and cube (and all objects, regardless of their mass) do fall together at same rate (neglecting air effects). And, of course, all objects float together in outer space. So we cannot tell whether we are in Earth's gravitational field or accelerating in outer space. The Equivalence Principle (EP) holds.

Thus Galileo's Principle, the fact that all objects fall at the same rate regardless of their mass or composition, is essential to the EP — and as we shall see, to the theory of general relativity upon which it is based.

In a bold generalization typical of Einstein, he proposed in 1907 that the Equivalence Principle (EP) applies to *all of physics*. And he now he had a basis for saying acceleration — like uniform motion — is *relative*. Why? Because the distinction between gravity and acceleration "depend on the frame of reference" chosen.[16] What looks like gravity from one point of view looks like acceleration from another.

From this, Einstein extended his Relativity Postulate to say that the laws of physics (and the mathematics which represent them) are indistinguishable, whether in an accelerating frame of reference or a gravitational frame of reference.[17]

He didn't have the mathematics yet — that would come much later. But Einstein had a basic principle of physics which no one before had fully appreciated. It would lead him to a new understanding of the behavior of light.

Light and Gravity

You understand, what I need to know is exactly what happens to the passengers in an elevator when it falls into emptiness.[18]

Albert Einstein to Madame Curie

"This is crazy," Bill says. "You are finally going to kill yourself! What if the elevator breaks apart when it falls? What if the cliff gives way? What if the glass breaks? What if you get crushed when it hits the ground?"

Bill's wife Sandy plans to ride one of the great Bailong Elevators in Zhangjiajie (pronounced Chung-cha-chia) in Hunan Province, China — situated over a thousand feet high on the side of a gigantic cliff.[19] Thousands of tourists have ridden these terrifying beasts, reportedly the highest and heaviest glass elevators in the world.

So what's the big deal? Sandy plans to ride one in *free-fall*.

The authorities are preparing to dismantle these controversial elevators. People argue they mar the pristine beauty of the mountain landscape of the Zhangjiajie National Forest Park and threaten the integrity of the great cliffs of this World Heritage Site.

Sandy, ever the daredevil, sees this as an opportunity for the thrill of a lifetime. She has convinced the authorities to let an elevator fall to the ground without any cables or attachments before they destroy it. How did she get the powers to be to go along with this crazy idea? By offering to perform experiments demonstrating Einstein's Equivalence Principle.

Sandy has tried skydiving, paragliding, and bungee jumping. She once even jumped out of an airplane without a parachute — diving to meet her jumping partner, holding on to him as they descended together. Bill always said that she had a screw loose, that somehow she was missing the fear of heights gene.

He, on the other hand, was happy to remain securely on the ground. He didn't even like flying in a commercial airplane. He somehow tolerated her thrill-seeking ways. Their relationship was about to receive its greatest test.

Sandy had read about Einstein's Equivalence Principle and she wanted to put it to the test. So she got her flight buddies to help with a real-life experiment before the great Bailong Elevators are torn down.

Together they beefed up an elevator at key points, with side and cross-braces, and placed a group of partially inflated air balloons at the base of the elevator to soften touchdown. They built a padded enclosure for Sandy to scramble into just before it hits ground zero. Sandy also secured instruments from a nearby university physics laboratory for the experiment — a laser, detector, two precision cameras and two spectrometers (a spectrometer measures light frequency.)

"Calm down, honey," Sandy says to Bill. "We've gone over every detail. And we're installing a back-up parachute just in case. We'll also test the elevator with no one in it. We plan to make three test drops to make sure it all works OK. We even put accelerometers inside the elevator to measure g-force."

Bill knows Sandy is dead set on this stunt, regardless of the risk. Or maybe because of it. Reluctantly, he agrees to perform the required ground measurements. He can't bear to watch, but can't bear to not watch either.

So Sandy and her team beef up the elevator with side bars and ell brackets, install the heavier glass doors, and build the enclosure. They then install the parachute and back-up, and are ready to go.

On the first few practice drops, they have trouble keeping the elevator glass from cracking when it lands, despite the air balloons at the bottom. So they rig up a spring system in addition to the air bags at the bottom of the elevator. This does the trick. The elevator comes to a halt with no further incidences. They repeat this procedure on a second back-up elevator.

What does Sandy plan to demonstrate? The effect of gravity on *light*. Her team rigs up a laser on one wall of the elevator and a detector on the opposite wall. The plan is to fire the laser upon release of the elevator and see what path the light takes. A special video camera inside the elevator will record the light path, and a special smoky concoction will be released to make sure the beam is visible. (We again ignore air effects, such as the elevator reaching terminal velocity in its fall.)

As the elevator falls to the ground, Bill on the ground will also record the path of the light beam with his video camera. The question is: will both Bill and Sandy observe the *same* light path?

From Sandy's Point of View — The EP says that free-fall is the same as free-float. So from her perspective in free-fall, Sandy and everything not tied down in the elevator will be weightless, as though floating in outer space.

All is ready. Sandy and the elevator are at the top of the cliff. She gives the thumbs up. The elevator is released and begins its terrifying fall. Sandy feels the floor give way beneath her.

"Yahoo!" she says as she floats in midair. A canister releases smoke to light up the path of the laser beam. The laser fires its beam. Sandy sees the light beam move in a *straight line* horizontally, across the elevator from the laser to the detector. This is shown in Fig. 10.7. (The path of a single photon of light is again depicted for clarity.)

From Bill's Point of View. What does Bill on the ground see? He sees the elevator fall, accelerating towards the ground at an ever increasing speed. His heart pounds as he records the event on his video camera. What light beam path does he see? He sees the photon follow a *curved path* as it travels across the elevator from laser to detector. (As shown in Fig. 10.8.)

The photon travels from the laser to the detector in both cases. From Sandy's point of view, the laser and detector are both *stationary*, so the photon travels in a straight line from one to the other.

But from Bill's point of view, the laser and detector are accelerating downward. Here's the key point: it takes a very short but finite amount of time for the photon from the laser to travel across the elevator and hit

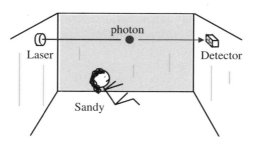

Figure 10.7. Sandy's View from Inside — Elevator Falling to Earth. *Per EP, free-fall is the same as free-float in zero gravity. So to Sandy, everything inside the elevator is standing still, in free-float like she is. Thus the photon from laser travels in straight line to the detector.*

the detector. During that time, the detector continues to fall (as Bill sees it). So the detector is in a *lower position* by the time the photon reaches it. Thus the photon has to curve, has to follow a bent path in order to hit detector. And this is just what Bill sees.

This also means once the photon is emitted from the laser, it is falling as well. From Bill's perspective, the photon in the accelerating elevator follows a curved path.

What does this imply? As seen by Bill, the elevator's downward acceleration causes the laser beam to follow a curved path. And per the

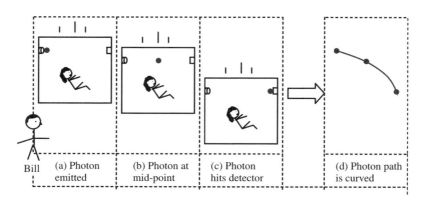

Figure 10.8. Bill's View from Outside — Elevator Falling to Earth. *As elevator falls, photon travels curved line from laser to detector. Light is bent by acceleration — thus, per EP, by gravity. (Bending greatly exaggerated in figure.)*

Equivalence Principle, what is true for acceleration is true for gravity. So, just as Einstein did in 1907, Bill concludes:

Light bends in a gravitational field![20]

Note to Reader: The elevator light experiment is rather impractical due to the enormous speed of light, but like the light-clock thought experiment, it demonstrates sound physics principles. The bending of the light due to gravity is real but miniscule over the width of an elevator.

Sandy's elevator comes screaming downwards. It hits the springs and air balloons at the bottom with a loud, heavy thud, bounces up slightly, and settles to the ground. The crowd is stilled. Sandy's hand peaks out from the padded enclosure and waves. The crowd roars.

She crawls out of the enclosure. A little wobbly, she pushes the elevator doors open. All smiles, she runs to Bill and gives her embarrassed husband a big hug.

Then to Bill's shock, Sandy climbs into the back-up elevator.

"What are you doing?!!" Bill asks.

"I am going to demonstrate *gravitational time dilation* with the laser pointed downward. Please set up the spectrometer, honey, and watch the beam from here."

Laser Pointing Downward. The crew mount the laser to the second elevator ceiling, pointed down towards a detector on the floor. They raise the elevator to the top of the cliff. It is released. At that same instant, the laser fires downward.

The elevator is in free-fall. Sandy again feels weightless as though in outer space. She sees the light beam proceed straight down to the floor, as shown in Fig. 10.9(a).

Sandy also sees the laser beam as bright red in color. Using her onboard spectrometer, she records its frequency. Her measurements indicate a wavelength of 0.6238 microns — the expected wavelength for a Helium Neon laser.

What does stationary Bill see? He measures the frequency of the laser light the instant it reaches the elevator floor. But to Bill, the laser is accelerating downward along with the elevator. Thus the laser, the source of the light beam, is moving towards him, as shown in Fig. 10.9(b). This motion of a light source towards Bill causes the Doppler Effect.

As noted, the Doppler Effect is where the frequency of light is affected by relative motion. The color or frequency of light appears higher

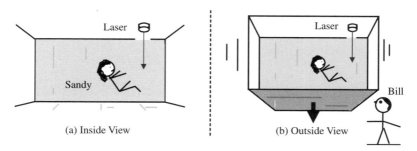

Figure 10.9. Vertical Laser Beam — Elevator Falling to Earth. *(a) Per the EP, the inside view is equivalent to free-float in zero gravity, so the light source (laser) is stationary to Sandy. She sees no change in the beam's frequency.(b) In the outside view, the light source is accelerating towards Bill, so he sees it at a higher frequency (blue-shifted).*

when the source of that light is moving towards you, and lower when its source is moving away from you. (The speed of the light is unaffected by this relative motion.)

Since the laser is moving towards Bill, he sees the laser beam's color move towards the blue end of the spectrum (blue-shifted). His spectrometer measures a *higher frequency* (shorter wavelength) than Sandy's for the same beam of light.

The elevator is accelerating from Bill's perspective, which again is equivalent to gravity. Thus he concludes (as did Einstein):

A gravitational field affects the frequency of light.

And per Planck/Einstein, light frequency is proportional to its energy. So gravity also affects the *energy* of a light beam.

To see how this works, let's look at two examples:

Blue-shift: Imagine a stationary spaceship in the zero gravity of outer space transmits a beam of light to us here on Earth. We see the beam shifted to a *higher* frequency or blue-shifted. Why? Because the beam gains energy traveling down through Earth's gravitational field.

The reverse is also true.

Red-shift: What if we on Earth were to send a beam of light into outer space? The beam loses energy as it climbs out of Earth's gravitational field. So an observer in outer space would see the beam from Earth shifted to a *lower* frequency or red-shifted. This is called gravitational red-shift.

Imagine how excited Einstein must have been when he first realized gravity affects the frequency of light. Why? Because it has profound implications regarding *time* itself.

Gravity Warps Time

Recall that light is an electromagnetic wave which goes up and down in regular intervals. The frequency of the laser beam in Sandy's elevator marks out equal increments of time just like the ticking of a clock. (Atomic clocks use this principle to tell time to extraordinary accuracy.)

To Sandy in the falling elevator, the frequency of the light beam is as expected. In her reference frame, time is running normally.

But to Bill, the beam in the elevator has a higher frequency. So from Bill's point of view, from his frame of reference, time on the elevator is running faster than time on the ground.

And, per the EP, acceleration produces the same physical effects as gravity. Thus the momentous conclusion of Einstein's elevator thought experiment:

Gravity affects the passage of time!

In Newton's universe, one second on Earth is one second in outer space — time is absolute everywhere in the cosmos, it always beats at the same rate.[21] Einstein first challenged this notion with special relativity, with his prediction that relative motion through space slows down time. Now, based on the EP, Einstein predicted that a *gravitational field* slows down time as well. So according to Einstein, time is relative — due to both motion and gravity.

For instance, Einstein predicts a clock on the surface of the Earth runs slower than the same clock at rest in the zero gravity of outer space by some two-hundredths of a second (0.02 seconds) per year. In fact, how fast we age and all other aspects of time run a tiny bit slower here on Earth than they would in outer space (all other things being equal).

In summary, Einstein's EP and his falling elevator thought experiment predict: (1) the path of a beam of light *bends* in a gravitational field, (2) the *frequency* of light is slowed by a gravitational field, and equivalently (3) the passage of *time* is slowed by gravity.

In November of 1907, Einstein published an update of his theory of special relativity in the *Yearbook of Radioactivity and Electronics*. He added a final section which discussed his latest thoughts on gravity. Using the Equivalence Principle, he predicted the gravitational bending of light and gravitational time dilation for the first time.[22]

Going in Circles

Through this, the whole structure of Euclidean geometry is made to totter.[23]

Max Born

Einstein arrived at a second epiphany in 1912 — gravity affects *space* as well as time. His brainstorm was based on a clever thought experiment proposed three years earlier by his friend physicist Paul Ehrenfest.[24]

The so-called "Ehrenfest Paradox" appears to defy a basic tenet of Euclidean geometry: the circumference of a circle divided by its radius always equals 2 times Pi or about 6.28. (The circumference is the distance along the edge of a circle once around, the radius the distance from its center to its edge.)

Physicists still argue about the subtleties of Ehrenfest's construct. Here is a simplified explanation:

Consider a spinning circular disc. Say scientist Noah is at rest above the disc, as shown in Fig. 10.10. From his perspective, the *circumference* of the disc rotates in the same direction of motion as the disc. According to special relativity, the length of a moving object contracts *in the direction of motion* (length contraction). So from Noah's perspective, the disc's circumference appears contracted — it is smaller than when it is at rest.

The radius of the spinning disc is *perpendicular* to the direction of the disc's motion. So, according to special relativity, it's length is unaffected by the disc's motion. It does not undergo length contraction.

Thus as Noah sees it, the circumference of the spinning disc is contracted and the radius is not. Standing above watching the disc spin, he concludes the circumference divided by the radius is *not equal to 2 times Pi!* In fact, the ratio is less than 2 times Pi, less than 6.28. (See end note for a more rigorous description.)[25]

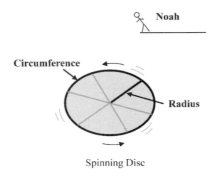

Spinning Disc

Figure 10.10. Rotating Disc. *As seen by Noah at rest, circumference is contracted due to length contraction, but radius is unaffected,. To him, ratio not equal to 2 times Pi.*

Thus per special relativity the spinning disc violates Euclidean geometry. In other words, the relative motion of the spinning disc causes a kind of *warping of space.*

In 1912 — armed with the Equivalence Principal — Einstein saw powerful implications in Ehrenfest's rotating disc thought experiment:

Any given point on the disc's circumference moves at a constant velocity of rotation, but it is always *changing* direction. Recall that acceleration in physics is a change in speed or change in direction. Therefore the disc's circumference is undergoing *acceleration*. And according to the Equivalence Principle, acceleration produces the same physical effects as gravity. So, Einstein deduced:

Space is warped in a gravitational field.

To see this, think about the spinning disc's circumference which appears contracted to Noah. Einstein tells us it is *space itself* which is contracted, warped, changed. More precisely, the *distance* between two points in space is changed by the spinning, by the acceleration.

And per the EP, the same is true in a gravitational field.

How does this work? Imagine you measure the distance between two points in space in a region of zero gravity. You then place the same two points in a gravitational field, oriented along the direction of gravity. You will find the distance between these points is no longer the same value, as seen from far away.

Recall the pen we held perpendicular to the ground in Chap. 9. The closer to Earth, the longer it measured (again as seen from far away). This so-called stretching of space was another example of space warp in a gravitational field.

From the Equivalence Principle, the elevator thought experiment, and the Ehrenfest Paradox, Einstein postulated that both *time and space* are warped in a gravitational field.

Is this true? We look at evidence for Einstein's radical vision in the next chapter.

Chapter 11

The Warping of Space and Time

*It doesn't matter how beautiful your theory is, it doesn't matter
how smart you are. If it doesn't agree with experiment, it's wrong.*[1]

Richard Feynman

It is the year 2525 and man is still alive.[2] Somehow our clever and con-
tradictory species has survived the threat of nuclear war, climate
change, ocean acidification, stratospheric ozone depletion, nitrogen and
phosphorus cycle imbalance, biodiversity loss, aerosol loading, global
viruses, global pollution, global starvation, depleted water supplies,
asteroid collisions, super-tsunamis, volcanic mega-eruptions, physical
atrophy, overpopulation, telephone texting, and mindless tweets.[3]

In this future world, super-accurate wristwatches are the latest rage.
These amazing timepieces use the latest quark separation technology to
offer the discriminating consumer accuracy beyond the best atomic
clocks. Older folks think the whole thing is silly, but teenagers just have
to have one.

One group of teens is practicing for an upcoming ice show. Of course
they all have a quark-watch or "quatch" on their wrists. One of them, a
16 year old named Levi, is a science nut. He has been learning about relativity in his "Physics-First" classes since kindergarten, and now decides
to conduct his own little experiment.[4]

Levi gets nine friends together. They shuffle onto the local ice rink,
put on their skates, and synchronize their watches. They hold hands and
begin skating in a great circle. Levi remains at rest on the sidelines to
observe. (See Fig. 11.1.)

Fastest speed; slowest time

Slowest speed; fastest time

Fastest speed; slowest time

Figure 11.1. Thought Experiment — Centrifugal Acceleration Warps Time. *After spinning around, times now disagree. The greater the velocity of rotation, the greater the slowing of time. Thus outer skaters' watches run slowest; center skater's watch is least affected.*

After spinning around for several minutes, they stop and compare watches. They find the times on their super-watches are no longer synchronized. Their watches have all slowed down relative to Levi's stationary watch. In fact, the disagreement correlates with their position in the circle. Abdus in the center finds his watch is the least affected. But Murray and Marie at the two far ends of the circle find their watches have slowed down the most.

Levi is thrilled. "This is just what I expected," he says. "Abdus, you were in the center of the circle, so you moved the least. That is why your watch shows the smallest slowing, as compared to my watch. Murray and Marie, you guys on the end had to move the fastest to keep the circle up." They both nod in agreement as they catch their breaths.

"Time slows down with relative motion through space," says Levi, "the more motion, the more slowing. That's why your clocks showed the greatest slowing. Einstein's time dilation works!"

Some of the group think the whole thing is a big waste of time and tell Levi. Then Marie says "Hey, I've got an idea. In class, they said that when you rotate, you are accelerating."

"What?" says Yoichiro, "I thought acceleration was when you speed up, like stepping on the accelerator in a hover-car."

"Ya, but acceleration is also slowing down, and changing direction," says Marie.

"This is so unrad," says Zhores. (Unrad is teen slang for boring.)

Marie ignores him and goes on. "Anyway, Einstein's ancient Equivalence Principle says acceleration is equivalent to gravity, right." Only Levi nods in agreement. "So if time is slowed down due to our acceleration, then it should also slow down due to gravity."

"And," Levi says, "time should slow down more and more the lower you are in a gravitational field." Marie smiles at Levi. "How come I never noticed her before?" Levi thinks.

Levi and Marie convince the group to do another experiment. Even Zhores agrees to come along (under protest). After skating practice, the gang traipses out to the hover-bus and heads downtown. They pile out of the bus and run over to the famous Minkowski Spacetime Building, a 90-story high rise (Fig. 11.2).

They gather at the street-level lobby and again synchronize their watches. Levi stays in the lobby, and the others get on the hover-lift. Per plan, Abdus goes to the 10th floor, Murray to the 20th, Marie to the 30th, and so on. Zhores, the last to get off the lift, goes to the 90th floor. They remain at their posts for a few hours, allegedly doing their homework while listening to space-rap-rock-fuzz on the sound chips implanted behind their ears. Several hours later the group meets again at the street-level and compare watches.

So will their watches agree or disagree? (We ignore here the effect of motion up and down the high rise.)

Per Einstein, time lower in a gravitational field runs slower than time higher up.[5] Thus their watches now all disagree. Levi on the street-level experienced the greatest slowing of time, because he was closest to the Earth. Abdus on the 10th floor experienced less slowing of time, Murray on the twentieth even less, Marie on the 30th even less, and so on. Zhores on the ninetieth floor experienced the least slowing of time. His watch ran the fastest because he was the highest up in the gravitational field of Earth.

"Again this is just what Einstein predicted," says Marie. "The higher you go, the less time slows down. On the 30th floor, even my heart was beating faster than you guys on the floors below. Zhores aged the fastest because he was on the highest floor."

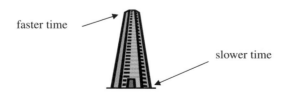

Figure 11.2. Time in a High Rise Building on Earth. *Per the Equivalence Principle, time lower in a gravitational field runs slower than time higher up.*

"Ya," Levi says, "and my heart beat the slowest. I aged the slowest because I was on the street floor, lowest in the gravitational field of Earth."

Even Zhores was impressed. "Do you mean that we all age less here at sea-level than we would on a mountain-top?"

"Ya, you got it," Marie says, "I mean ignoring other stuff like the cold or the rare atmosphere, you would age faster up there. All this is called "gravitational time dilation."

Is Gravitational Time Dilation True?

Einstein first predicted the frequency of light — and equivalently the passage of time — is affected by a gravitational field with his Equivalence Principle in 1907. The validation of Einstein's epiphany had to wait for science and technology to catch up. Gravitational time dilation was first put to the test some 52 years later.

Harvard Tower Test

Imagine a beam of light of a certain frequency. Einstein predicts an observer on Earth sees that light beam coming towards her from above has a *higher* frequency. An observer located at a higher altitude sees the light beam traveling up from Earth has a *lower* frequency.

In 1959, physicists Robert Pound and G. A. Rebka Jr. at Harvard University set out to test Einstein's prediction.[6] They placed a light source made of radioactive iron (^{57}Fe) at the bottom of a 22.5-meter tower in the Jefferson laboratory. They placed a detector, also made of radioactive iron, at the top of the tower.

The two physicists measured how much the light's frequency decreased from the bottom to the top of the tower as it climbed up through Earth's gravitational field. (See Fig. 11.3.)

They repeated the experiment in reverse — with the radioactive source at the top of the tower and the radioactive detector at the bottom. Now the light's frequency increased as it climbed down through Earth's gravity. Then they averaged the results (with the sign of the second experiment reversed).

For the 22.5-meter distance, Einstein predicts a difference in light's frequency due to Earth's gravity of a miniscule 2.45 parts in a thousand trillion (2.45 parts in 10^{15}). Pound-Rebka's measurements matched

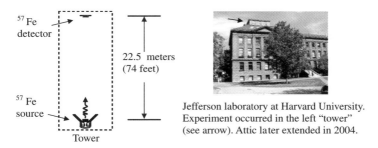

Jefferson laboratory at Harvard University. Experiment occurred in the left "tower" (see arrow). Attic later extended in 2004.

Figure 11.3. Harvard Test Confirms Gravitational Redshift — Time Runs Slower with Lower Altitude. *Results agreed with General Relativity predictions to 99.9%.*

Einstein's prediction to within 10%. Pound and J. L. Snider repeated the experiment in 1964, improving the agreement to within 1%.

As noted, light frequency can be thought of as a clock. In other words, gravitational red-shift is equivalent to gravitational time dilation. Evidence that gravity slows the frequency of light also says gravity slows down *time*.

A number of tests and observations since have confirmed Einstein's predictions. Several are listed below.

Flying Clocks

In the fall of 1971, two scientists demonstrated gravitational time dilation with real clocks.[7] Joseph C. Hafele of Washington University in St. Louis and astronomer Richard Keating at the US Naval Observatory placed highly accurate Cesium-beam atomic clocks on commercial airplanes and booked flights which circumnavigated the globe.

They had to take two effects into account: (1) special relativity predictions that the clocks in the *moving* airplanes run *more slowly* than an identical one at rest on the ground, and (2) general relativity predictions that the flying clocks run *faster* due to their altitude. With the effect of altitude on time dominating, Hafele and Keating's results agreed with Einstein's predictions to about 10%.[8]

Rocket Clocks

On June 8, 1976, Robert Vessot and Martin Levine of Smithsonian Astrophysical Observatory at Harvard University placed a newly invented hydrogen maser atomic clock on a Scout D rocket — and compared it to an identical clock on the ground.[9] (See Fig. 11.4.) The experiment

Hydrogen Maser
Clock

Typical Scout Rocket Launch

Figure 11.4. Rocket Clock Verifies Time Dilation Due to Both Motion and Gravity.
In 1976, R. Vessot and M. Levine of Smithsonian Astrophysical Observatory compared Hydrogen Maser clock in nose-cone of Scout D rocket to clock on the ground.

confirmed Einstein's predictions of the warping of time per special and general relativity to 70 parts per million!

Standard Time

Today, atomic clocks take the effects of gravitational time dilation into account to meet accuracy requirements for world standard time. For example, an atomic clock at the US National Bureau of Standards in the foothills of the Rocky Mountains of Boulder, Colorado, is situated at an altitude of 5400 feet. A second atomic clock can be found a short boat ride from London down the Thames at Great Britain's Royal Greenwich Observatory. The Greenwich atomic clock is nearly at sea level, at an altitude of only 80 feet.[10]

The higher altitude Colorado clock gains 5 microseconds (5 millionths of a second) per year relative to the Greenwich clock, just as Einstein's theory of gravity predicts.[11]

Global Positioning Satellite (GPS)

Today's Global Positioning Satellites provide a *continuous verification* of gravitational time dilation. On-board clocks are corrected for the effects of altitude on time relative to ground clocks per general relativity, and motion on time per special relativity. If the system ignored these effects, a navigational fix from GPS would be false after only 2 minutes.[12]

In the Lab

In 1997, three physicists — Holger Müller of the University of California Berkeley, Achim Peters of Humboldt University in Berlin and Steven Chu, previously at Berkeley but then US Secretary of Energy — used quantum techniques to carry out the most accurate tests to date.[13] Their measurements confirmed gravitational time dilation to an incredible seven parts in a billion!

So Einstein's gravitational time dilation is real. Thus, as we shall see, time travel is not only possible — it happens all the time.

Time Travel with Altitude

"I just can't bear it," Maynar says. "They are so little, so helpless."

"Now dear one, you know The Law. The twins must be separated," Kaleb says. "Here, here, our beautiful Tina will go to Mount Neutron. There are families up there who are in great need of a child. They will care for our little one just as we would. And we shall still have our sweet Sammy. We must bear it. And we will. Let us prepare dear Tina for transport."

Wealthy surface citizens somehow find a way to keep all their children, but Maynar and Kaleb have very little money. And so the twins, Sammy and Tina are separated at birth, as The Law decrees. Sammy will continue to live on the surface, but Tina is to be transported to a pioneer family on the top of the great mountain.

The stellar object on which these beings live is called Neutronium (as translated into English). This remnant of a supernova explosion is *extremely* massive and dense. Thus gravity on its surface is much greater than gravity here on Earth. And the great mountain on its surface is of tremendous height — its top called Mount Neutron.

Overcrowding on the surface has forced pioneers to emigrate to the top of the great mountain. They are able to survive, but the greatly reduced gravity so far from the surface has for some reason made them infertile — they cannot bear children.

Twins are a common occurrence on the surface. Thus "The Law" — twins are separated at birth, one left with its family on the surface and one sent to live with an adopting family on the top of the mountain.

The great difference in gravity on the surface versus gravity on Mount Neutron causes another effect — severe gravitational time warp.[14] Clocks on the mountain top runs *twice as fast* as clocks on the surface. This means that all aspects of time run faster on the mountain top than on the surface. (See Fig. 11.5.)

179

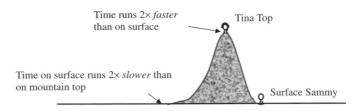

Time runs 2× *faster* than on surface

Tina Top

Time on surface runs 2× *slower* than on mountain top

Surface Sammy

Figure 11.5. Time Travel with Altitude. *The surface of Neutronium and Mount Neutron.*

Beings on the surface see their time running normally and time on Mount Neutron running fast. Beings on the mountain top see the reverse — their time runs perfectly normally, but time on the surface runs twice as slow.

As Sammy on the surface grows up, he learns of his twin sister living on Mount Neutron. He takes to calling her Tina Top. And Tina Top is told she has a twin brother — she refers to him as Surface Sammy.

As is customary on Neutronium, Tina Top is initiated into adulthood at age 30. Her wealthy adoptive parents love their only child with great intensity and can't help spoiling her. Tina's lavish 30-year ceremony is like a combination coming-out party, Bas-Mitzvah, and inauguration.

Now considered an adult, Tina Top can make her own decisions. Her first desire is to look down the mountain at the surface of Neutronium. She uses some of her 30-year gift credits to buy time on the giant telescope at the Mount Neutron Observatory. Instead of pointing it out at the heavens, she requests that it be pointed down at the surface.

She was told what to expect, but still finds the sight a great shock. Everything on the surface appears to be moving in slow motion. Vehicles and beings on the surface move at half speed. "So this is gravitational time dilation," Tina Top says to herself.

And the surface has a funny color to it — a dramatic shift to the red. The frequency of the light from the surface appears at a lower frequency as viewed in the Mount Neutron telescope. "Ah, so gravitational red-shift is also true," Tina Top says to herself.

Looking at the strange images below, Tina Top is filled with a sudden desire to see her birth family, to meet her biological parents and her twin brother. She takes the rest of her loot from the 30-year bash and buys a ticket on the next transporter to the surface.

Tina Top's Trip to the Surface [a]

When she arrives on the surface, even though she has read about the differences, Tina Top is shocked to see how crowded everything is. Plus the vehicles and people are moving at normal speeds, not the slow speeds she saw through the mountain-top telescope. And there is no red-shift — the colors all now appear perfectly normal.

She immediately proceeds to the Hall of Records and searches for her birth certificate, her original family name, and where her parents live now. The assistant recording clerk asks Tina Top when she was born. "June 19, 3700," Tina says. The clerk gives her a funny look. He hasn't seen many mountain-top dwellers. Here on the surface it is the year 3715 — which means according to her birth certificate she should be 15 years old. But Tina is 30 years old and looks it.

Tina knows she was born in the surface year 3700. But since time runs twice as fast on Mount Neutron, to her 30 years have gone by. So it should be the year 3730 — but it is only the year 3715 here on the surface. Tina Top has effectively traveled *15 years into the past*.

Despite knowing about these effects in advance, Tina feels disoriented. She pulls herself together and goes through the archives at the Hall of Records. There it is — her birth parents' names and their current address. "I hadn't expected it would be so easy," she says to herself.

With great excitement and some trepidation, Tina takes a squeaker-tram to the address listed. Maynar, her birth mother and Kaleb, her birth father welcome her with tears and hugs. They all start laughing because they can't seem to stop crying.

"Where is my brother?" Tina Top asks.

"Oh, Sammy is at particle-ball practice, but he should be home soon."

In the midst of all this, Sammy Surface saunters in. He sees this strange woman in his house. "I am your twin sister," Tina says, her voice choking.

"But you are so . . . old," Sammy says.

"How old are you, Sammy?" Tina asks.

"I just turned 15."

"I just turned 30," Tina says.

---

[a] We ignore here effects on time due to motion up and down the mountain (special relativity).

"Is this because of that relativity stuff they talk about in science class?" Sammy asks.

"Yes," Tina says, "But we're still twins, no matter what."

Sammy is a good boy. He gives his twin sister a big hug.

Tina knows she can't stay on the surface for very long. For one thing, her body isn't accustomed to the stronger gravity. The added weight is making her very tired. She also wants to get back to her life on Mount Neutron.

After all, her friends and family on the mountain-top are aging at twice the rate she is for every moment she stays on the surface. She wants to get back before these gravity time warp effects are significant.

She says a teary goodbye to her surface family. As she is leaving, Sammy promises to visit her on Mount Neutron to celebrate coming of age on his 30th birthday.

Surface Sammy's Trip to the Mountain-top

What happens when Surface Sammy visits Tina Top on his 30th birthday? Before he goes, he looks through a surface telescope pointed up at Mount Neutron. He sees the vehicles and people on the mountain-top moving in *fast* motion, like a movie that has been speeded up. And there is a strange shift towards the blue in the image in the telescope.

But when Surface Sammy arrives on the mountain-top, he sees everything moving normally. Colors looks quite normal too — no blue-shift at all. He meets his twin sister Tina Top. She is now 60 years old. Everything on the mountain-top has aged 60 years since Sammy was born.

The time interval between his and Tina's birth to now is 30 years on the surface, but 60 years on the mountain-top. To Sammy Surface, it is as though he has traveled *30 years into the future*!

Time Travel Paradox?

Wait a minute. Hold your horses. What about the classic time travel conundrum — you know, the one where you travel into the past to before you were born and accidently cause the death of your birth mother. But if your mother died before you were born, how can you exist? And if you don't exist, how could you have travelled into the past to cause your mother's death?

Have we finally tripped up Dr. Einstein? Have we found a logical inconsistency in one of his predictions? No, he is much too clever for that.

The time travel matricide conundrum is avoided in the physics of gravitational time dilation.

Per Einstein, Tina Top can travel into the past, but she cannot travel to a point in time before she left the surface. Thus she cannot affect circumstances before that point in time, that is before she was born. No matter what the mass-energy density of Neutronium and the resultant gravitational time dilation relative to Mount Neutron, she can never return to a point in space at a time earlier than when she left it. Causality is maintained.

Earthly Considerations

Of course this is just a fanciful story. But the phenomenon it demonstrates is real. The effects of gravitational time dilation are miniscule on Earth because Earth's gravity is relatively weak. Nevertheless, every time we change altitude we experience the same time travel effects as Tina Top and Sammy Surface. It's just the effects are so small we don't notice them.

What about space? How is it affected by gravity? Let's take a look.

Euclid Doesn't Live Here Anymore

Amongst the books family friend Max Talmud gave young Albert Einstein was a text on Euclidean geometry. To 12-year-old Albert, the clear logic and visual nature of the geometric arts was a revelation. He called it his "holy geometry book."[15] Later in life he wrote: "If Euclid failed to kindle your youthful enthusiasm, then you were not born to be a scientific thinker."[16] The adolescent Einstein had no idea his greatest achievement — general relativity — would come to overthrow the towering edifice of Euclidean geometry.

In Newton's world, Euclidean geometry (Fig. 11.6) holds throughout all space. In 1912, Einstein concluded from the rotating disc thought experiment that gravity warps space. This meant Euclid's postulates are violated where gravity is present. Einstein realized he needed a new geometry.

Euclidean plane geometry applies to a plane, a flat surface. What if the surface is curved? Consider the spheres shown in Fig. 11.7. When we examine lines and circles and triangles drawn on a spherical surface, we see: (1) the sum of the three interior angles of a triangle is *not* equal to 180°, (2) parallel lines *meet*, (3) the shortest path between two points is *not*

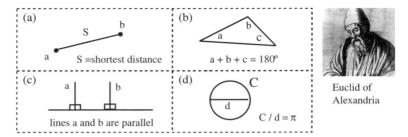

Euclid of
Alexandria

Figure 11.6.   Examples of Euclidean Geometry. *(a) The shortest distance between two points is a straight line. (b) The sum of the interior angles of any triangle equals 180°. (c) Two straight lines perpendicular to a third straight line are parallel. (d) The circumference of any circle divided by its diameter equals Pi (π).*

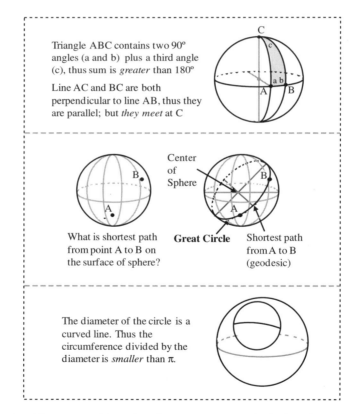

Figure 11.7.   Examples of Geometry On a Spherical Surface.

a straight line, and (4) the ratio of the circumference to the diameter of a circle is *not* equal to *Pi* — all violations of Euclidean plane geometry.

Einstein concluded that these same violations applied where ever gravity is present. Since all matter and non-material energy — including subatomic particles, atoms, molecules, rocks, people, buildings, meteors, comets, asteroids, moons, planets, stars, and galaxies — are sources of gravity, we live in a world which is *non-Euclidean.*

For example, the ratio of the Sun's circumference to its diameter is less than Pi by several parts per million. This is because the Sun's presence warps space in its vicinity. The effect is more pronounced in more massive stars.[17]

The Eddington solar eclipse expedition of 1919 was the first evidence for the warping of space. As we shall see in Chap. 15, it confirmed general relativity over Newton's theory of gravity by a factor of two and made Einstein world famous.

The Next Chapter

Time is warped. Space is warped. But how to represent this warpage due to the presence of mass-energy *mathematically*? This was Einstein's dilemma. In the search for a solution, he looked at the four-dimensional mathematics of his former math professor, Hermann Minkowski. After careful consideration, Einstein swallowed his pride and accepted that spacetime and the spacetime interval were the best way to represent the warping of time and space. This is the subject of the next chapter.

Chapter 12

Stitching Spacetime

The spacetime continuum obeys the laws of Euclidean geometry in small limited regions, but not on a large scale.[1]

Max Born

By the summer of 1912, Albert Einstein had established the warping of space and time per the Equivalence Principle. Now he needed a formula which modeled this so-called warping. Years earlier he had denigrated the spacetime construct of Poincaré and Minkowski, calling it a mathematical curiosity with no physical relevance — perhaps in part because he did not think of it himself.

Now some four years later, Einstein saw the error of his ways. He realized the merit of representing the warping of time and space in a gravitational field with the mathematics of four-dimensional *spacetime*.

He also saw limitations in his Equivalence Principle. Einstein found it only holds over a limited region of spacetime — it applies only over a space which is small enough and over a time which is short enough. He called this a *local* region of spacetime.

The brilliant Dr. Einstein saw this restriction not as a hindrance, but as a critical tool in the development of general relativity. He proposed mathematically "stitching" local spacetime regions together in order to represent gravity on a global scale.

How did he come up with this idea? And what does it mean? We examine Einstein's thinking and his new picture of gravity in this chapter.

What is Local Spacetime?

Imagine we are again in our classroom trying to determine whether we are (a) stationary on the surface of the Earth or (b) accelerating at 1-*g* inside that alien rocket ship in outer space.

It turns out there are ways to tell whether we are on Earth or in the rocket ship, if our classroom is large enough. Say I stand way over on the left side of the room and one of my students stands way over on the right. We each hold a ball in our hand and release the two balls at the same time from the same height.

What does this look like from inside the rocket?

Accelerating in Outer Space (no gravity) — After we release the two balls, they float in the same place as we and the floor accelerate upwards at 1-*g*. Now this is key: Because they are in free-float in outer space, the two balls remain *the same distance apart* over time. After all they are floating in outer space where there is no gravity. So they remain floating in the same locations as the floor rises up to meet them.

From our point of view inside the accelerating rocket ship, we are stationary on the floor and the two balls appear to accelerate downward at 1-*g*. To us, it looks like the balls are falling together to the floor. As the balls appear to fall, the horizontal separation between the two objects remains constant.

How would things look on Earth?

Stationary on the Surface of the Earth — When we let the two balls go here on Earth, they of course fall to the ground at 1-*g* acceleration. But the objects do not fall straight down. They fall at *a slight angle* towards the center of the Earth, as shown in Fig. 12.1. (Hey, I look pretty good, except for the skinny legs.)

Figure 12.1. Two Objects Separated Horizontally Above Earth's Surface. *They do not fall straight down. They fall towards the center of the Earth and converge over time. (Angles of fall in left figure greatly exaggerated.)*

The further apart I and my student are when we release the two balls, the greater the angles. In a wide enough room, this motion towards the center of the Earth is not negligible — it can be measured.

As the two balls fall toward the center of the Earth they converge. The horizontal separation between the two falling objects decreases over time.

Aha, this gives us a way to tell whether we are on Earth or in the accelerating rocket! If we carefully measure the distance between the two balls before they fall and then again at a later time, say just as they hit the floor, we see one of two outcomes: (a) the balls are still the same distance apart, or (b) they are closer together.

If the balls stay the same distance apart, we know we are accelerating in the zero gravity of outer space. If the two balls come closer together as they fall, we know we are on Earth. So here the Equivalence Principle — gravity and acceleration produce the same physical effects — breaks down.

But if the separation between the balls is small enough, the difference between the angles at which they fall is negligible. Their convergence as they fall is also negligible. So for a small enough room, the Equivalence Principle still holds: there is no way to tell whether we are accelerating or in a gravitational field.[a]

Vertical Separation

Now let's consider the same thought experiment with the balls positioned *vertically* or one above the other:

Accelerating in Outer space (no gravity) — I stand on a chair and hold one ball above my head and the other down below (see Fig. 12.2). When I let go of the two balls, in the zero gravity of outer space they simply float where they are — one above the other.

Here again is the key point: After being released in the zero gravity of outer space, the two floating balls *remain the same distance apart over time.*

As I see it, the floor accelerates upwards at 1-g. So the two balls appear to accelerate downwards towards the floor. But they fall at the same rate and remain the same distance apart.

Stationary on the Surface of the Earth — What if I am at rest on Earth's surface? If the room is high enough, the vertical separation of the two

---

[a]We again ignore the effects of Earth's rotation here.

Figure 12.2. Two Objects Separated Vertically. On Earth's surface (shown here), the lower object falls a little faster than the higher object because gravity is stronger closer to Earth. Thus the objects diverge over time. But in the accelerating rocket ship in zero gravity, they remain the same distance apart as they appeared to fall. (Arrow differences greatly exaggerated.)

balls has a noticeable effect. The higher ball is a little bit further from the Earth, thus gravity is slightly weaker there. So the higher ball falls at an acceleration which is less than the lower ball.

Conversely, since the lower ball is closer to Earth, it sees stronger gravity than the upper ball. It falls with a greater acceleration. So as the two balls fall, the lower ball pulls away from the upper ball. The separation between the two vertical balls *increases* over time.

Say we measure the vertical separation of the two balls when we release them and again just as the lower ball hits the floor. If the vertical separation of the two balls is the same during the fall, we know we are in the accelerating rocket ship in outer space. On the other hand, if the vertical separation between the two balls increases as they fall, we know we are in a gravitational field — in our classroom on the surface of the Earth.

We do need a large enough initial vertical distance between the two balls so the difference in the strength of gravity is great enough to make the balls' divergence over time measureable.

But over a small enough space, the difference in gravity and divergence of the vertical balls is too small to measure. The same holds if we conduct the experiments over a small enough time. The change in distance between the two balls is negligible.

In summary, *locally* — over a small enough space and time, a small enough spacetime — we can't tell whether the balls have converged horizontally or diverged vertically. We can't tell whether we are on Earth or in the accelerating rocket in zero gravity. Thus gravity and acceleration are equivalent only locally.[2]

Globally — over a large enough space and time, a large enough spacetime — we can tell the difference between gravity and acceleration.

What is Einstein telling us here? That gravity does not show its effects *locally* — over a small enough space and time. The effects of gravity are only seen on a *global* scale.

Gravity and the *Spacetime* Interval

To understand where Einstein is going next, we must again put on our *spacetime* thinking caps. It may seem awkward to think in this way, but if we want to understand Einstein's construct, it is well worth the effort.

We learned that according to special relativity, the space interval (distance) and time interval between any two events are both relative — they are affected by uniform relative motion. But a particular mathematical combination of space and time intervals called the *spacetime interval* is absolute — it is not affected by uniform motion.

Again this spacetime interval is equal to the square root of the difference between the square of the time interval and the square of the space interval.

> The spacetime interval equation is repeated here for convenience (in units where the speed of light is one):
>
> *(Spacetime Interval)² = (Time Interval)² – (Space Interval)²*
>
> $$\Delta S^2 = \Delta t^2 - \Delta x^2$$
>
> *where: Δt is the time interval between the two events, and*
> *Δx is the space interval between two events*

In 1912, Einstein proposed that space and time are also changed or warped in a gravitational field. In other words, the separation in space (space interval) and the separation in time (time interval) between the same two events are different values in a gravitational field than when no gravity, no mass-energy is present. More specifically, an observer far away from any mass-energy will measure a *different* space and time interval between the same two events than an observer in the gravitational field.

What about the spacetime interval? We know it is absolute — it is unaffected by uniform motion. Ah, but we said *uniform* motion. What about when motion is not uniform? What about acceleration?

Acceleration and the Spacetime Interval

Say our intrepid race car driver Crash is in a rocket which is going faster and faster or accelerating with respect to Steady Eddie on the Earth.

What does Steady Eddie on Earth observe? At any instant in time, Eddie measures Crash's rocket having a certain velocity — its so-called instantaneous velocity. At that moment in time, Crash's rocket is going at a single speed relative to Eddie. Thus in that single instant, all the rules of *special* relativity apply.

This is in fact a *local* point in spacetime. And within that small enough moment, Crash has a constant speed and direction; i.e. he is in uniform motion. So here the spacetime interval is the same for both Crash and Steady Eddie.

What about the next instant in time? Because he is accelerating, Crash's speed is now different. As a result, the spacetime interval is no longer the same value.[3]

So over any instant in time (locally), the spacetime interval is unaffected by uniform motion. But over a number of different times (globally), the spacetime interval changes under acceleration. Thus the spacetime interval *is affected* by acceleration or *non*-uniform motion.

And per the Equivalence Principle, what is true for acceleration is true for gravity. So gravity affects the spacetime interval. Like the space interval and time interval:

> *The spacetime interval is warped or changed in a gravitational field.*

Please take a little time to fully appreciate the above statement. It is a key to understanding general relativity.　　　　　　　　·

Local versus Global Spacetime

Einstein saw a deep connection between warping of the spacetime interval in a gravitational field and the local and global behavior of gravity. In a small enough region of spacetime or *locally*, there are no gravity effects — the spacetime interval between the same two events does not change. But over a large enough region of spacetime or *globally*, the spacetime interval does change. This is summarized below:

Locally — Over a small enough space and time interval, there are no measurable gravity effects. Here free-fall in a gravitational field is equivalent to free-float in the zero gravity of outer space. Here the laws of special relativity hold — the spacetime interval is absolute.

This local region of spacetime, this free-float frame, is called *"flat"*.

Globally — Over a large enough region of spacetime, gravity effects are discernible. Here the effects of gravity are evident over *multiple* free-float frames. Globally, the laws of special relativity break down — the spacetime interval is warped or changed in the presence of mass-energy, in a gravitational field.

Since the spacetime interval changes globally, spacetime here is called *"curved"*.

Locally flat and globally curved. This is Einstein's grand vision of the spacetime interval in a gravitational field.

Surface of Earth Analogy

Consider the surface of Earth (again assume it is perfectly spherical). As shown in Fig. 12.3(a), the surface of Earth appears flat over a small enough distance, i.e., locally. But when we look at the Earth over a large enough distance or globally, we see, of course, that the Earth is curved. The surface of the Earth is locally flat and globally curved.

If we take a set of straight lines and stitch them together, we get an approximation of a curved surface, as in Fig. 12.3(b).[4] If we use lines of smaller length, the approximation is an even better one. Given small enough lines, the difference between the actual curved surface and the one stitched together from straight lines becomes negligible.

So you can stitch a bunch of local straight lines together to represent a global curved surface. Similarly, you can stitch a bunch of local free-float frames together to represent the global curved spacetime of a gravitational field.

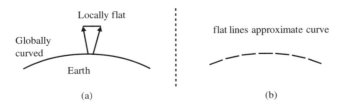

Figure 12.3. Example of Global versus Local Curvature. *(a) Earth's surface appears flat locally, but curved globally, (b) a set of flat lines stitched together approximate a curve.*

Show Me

By the summer of 1912, Albert Einstein had formulated the core concepts of his new theory of gravity within a spacetime framework.

But it isn't enough to just come up with concepts in physics — you have to produce equations which tell exactly how these concepts work quantitatively. In the business world, it is "Show me the money!" In physics, it is "Show me the equations!" Maybe that's why most physicists are not rich.

Thirty-three-year-old Einstein was now ready to take the first step towards modeling his grand vision mathematically. He needed to find the correct formula for "stitching" the spacetime intervals for each local frame into a global construct. And he needed to find equations which described exactly how this global tapestry, what he called *spacetime curvature*, is affected in the presence of mass-energy.

This is the subject of the next two chapters.

Chapter 13

What is Spacetime Curvature?

What holds the Earth in its path around the Sun?

*What reaches out through the vacuum of space to grab
and hold the Earth in its orbit?*

Spacetime curvature — the "fabric" of the universe.

As the summer of 1912 turned to fall, Albert Einstein was working exclusively on the "gravitation problem".[1] The now Professor of Theoretical Physics at Zurich Poly soon hit upon his first major stumbling block.

The Problem Facing Einstein

In Newtonian physics, space and time can be represented by an *equally-spaced* coordinate system. This simple approach works because, in Newton's world, space and time are absolute. That is the distance between two points in space is the same value for everyone everywhere, and time passes at the same rate for everyone everywhere.

Thus one can divide both unchanging space and unchanging time into equal increments — to represent space and time throughout the universe. The same equally-spaced co-ordinate system extends forever.

Spacetime Co-ordinates

Einstein's special relativity adds a twist to this scenario: space and time intervals are affected by uniform motion through length contraction and time dilation.

Consider a single observer in uniform motion; i.e. in a single uniformly moving reference frame. For this individual, a series of identical rulers can be laid out dividing space into equal increments. Similarly, clocks record the passage of time in equal increments. That is as long as the clocks and rulers are at rest with respect to the observer. In special relativity, the observer can still divide the universe into equal space and time intervals.

These spacings are different values for someone *moving* (uniformly) with respect to the first observer. So each observer in relative uniform motion constructs a different coordinate system to represent space and time. Each observer's coordinate system has its own unique equal spacings in space and time. And, as in Newton's construct, each coordinate system may be extended across the entire universe (for that particular reference frame).

To get a visual picture of this, let's construct a typical spacetime diagram. (See Fig. 13.1.) Once you choose the (uniformly moving) frame of reference, you can divide space and time into equal increments forever.

What about clocks, rulers, and *gravity*? Ah, now we have a problem. Einstein's Equivalence Principle says space and time are warped in a gravitational field. Within this gravitational field, the very "units" of space and time themselves change with location.[2] Where there is gravity, an equally-spaced grid is no longer a valid representation of space and time intervals, no longer an accurate depiction of reality.

We learned earlier that space and time intervals vary with altitude. For Levi and his friends inside the high-rise building, identical clocks run slower at lower floors, i.e. as they get closer to the Earth. Identical rulers

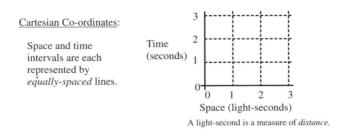

Figure 13.1. An Equally-spaced Spacetime Co-ordinate System of Special Relativity.

placed vertically at each floor would be stretched to longer lengths as they get closer to the Earth (as seen by an observer far away).

Imagine a billion rulers laid out end-to-end in a great three dimensional grid, like the beams of a gigantic mega-structure. This skeleton, this tinker-toy arrangement is set up with identical-length rulers which mark out equal spacings in all three spatial dimensions.

Let's put clocks at each intersection of rulers. Then let's place this edifice in empty space far away from any stellar objects — a location where gravity is effectively zero. Here the rulers measure out equal increments of space and the clocks all tick out equal increments of time.

What if we place this grid of rulers and clocks near a massive stellar object, like the Sun — in other words in a gravitational field? The same rulers no longer mark out equal increments of space everywhere, as seen from far away. And identical clocks no longer run at the same rate everywhere. They are changed, warped, curved — depending on their location in the gravitational field.

How then are we to construct a co-ordinate system which represents time and space in a gravitational field? The very background upon which all physical phenomena play out is no longer static, it is not always the same. It is in fact *dynamic* — it changes with location in space, and if the source of that gravity is moving, over time. In other words, the background changes with its location in space and time or *spacetime*.

Consider the solar system, where the Sun and planets are always moving. The combined gravitational field they generate continually changes from place to place and over time. Time and space intervals within our solar system are not only unequally spaced; these unequal spacings are constantly changing over time.

This was the dilemma facing Einstein in 1912 — how to construct a *continuously-changing* spacetime coordinate system to represent the warping of space and time in a gravitational field?

Locally

There was one place where Einstein could begin to build his new theory of gravity — a place where the co-ordinates are equally–spaced, where the simpler rules of special relativity hold. Where? *Locally,* that is in the conditions of free-fall/free-float — a local free-float frame of reference.

For here in this small enough region of spacetime, gravity is effectively uniform. It has the same strength and direction. So all particles within this local region move in unison. Thus gravitational effects within this local frame are negligible (like for Einstein's falling painter).

And since special relativity holds within this local free-float frame, space and time can be marked out in equal increments. And here simple Euclidean geometry also holds.

So Einstein latched onto Minkowski's mathematics of 4-D spacetime and the spacetime interval. Why? Well, for one thing, the spacetime interval in a gravitational field is *absolute* locally. It is the same value for all uniformly moving observers in a small enough space and over a small enough time. This simplified things dramatically.

There was another major advantage. The spacetime interval encompassed both the time and space interval within it. So Einstein could represent the warping of space and time inside a gravitational field with a single expression.

As we saw, he could then stitch together a series of local spacetime intervals to construct a global gravitational field.

Globally

A number of different free-float frames over a large enough region of spacetime show the *global* effects of gravity. Here the particles are so far apart they see different strengths and/or directions of gravity, as in the widely separated dropping balls in the previous chapter. You can tell they are in a gravitational field.

What about the spacetime interval? As we saw, it is a different value from one local free-float frame to another, i.e. it changes globally. And globally, Euclidean geometry no longer holds.

Einstein knew he needed a new geometry to represent this global gravity, this global change in the spacetime interval — one which allowed for continuously-changing spacetime coordinates. In this new vision of the universe, in a gravitational field the interior angles of triangles would not add up to 180°. In addition, the circumferences of a circle divided by its diameter would not equal Pi, and two parallel lines would not remain parallel.

Where to find such a *non-Euclidean* geometry? For once Einstein's prodigious genius, remarkable physical intuition, and stubborn persistence were not enough. He simply lacked the mathematical knowledge to solve the problem himself. His cavalier attitude towards esoteric forms of mathematics had come back to haunt him.

Grossman to the Rescue

Never in my life have I tormented myself anything like this ... I have become imbued with a great respect for mathematics, the more subtle parts of which I had previously regarded as sheer luxury. Compared to this problem, the original (special) relativity theory is child's play.[3]

Einstein in letter to Marcel Grossman

Fortunately for Einstein, he had attended some college lectures on non-Euclidean geometry some 14 years earlier given by mathematics professor Carl Friedrich Geiser.[4] In early August 1912, Einstein recalled Geiser's lectures on Gauss's theory for modeling two-dimensional curved surfaces. Perhaps, he thought, this was the way to represent the continuously varying space and time co-ordinates in a gravitational field. He worked out some of the basics of this approach, but was now stuck. He was in over his head and he knew it.

Grossman, you've got to help me or I shall go crazy.[5]

Albert Einstein

By a most fortuitous co-incidence,[6] Einstein's long-time friend and former classmate Marcel Grossmann had become a professor of mathematics at Zurich Poly, specializing in geometry. This was the same Grossman who had arranged for Einstein's job at the patent office and had told Einstein's mother "something very great" would someday happen to her son.[7]

When Einstein skipped math classes at Zurich Poly, he borrowed Grossmann's notes to catch up. Einstein got a grade of 4.25 (out of 6) on the two geometry courses he took, while Grossmann scored a perfect 6. "He (Grossman), on good terms with the teachers and understanding everything," Einstein later wrote, "I, a pariah, discounted and little loved."[8] And to top it off, Grossman's dissertation was on non-Euclidean geometry. He had "published seven papers on the topic, and was now chairman of the math department."[9] (See Fig. 13.2.)

Figure 13.2.   Albert Einstein with his Friend Marcel Grossman, circa 1899.

Grossmann is getting his doctorate on a topic that is connected with fiddling around and non-Euclidean geometry. I don't know exactly what it is.[10]

Einstein to Mileva Marić, 1902

Einstein asked his friend for help. "Instantly (Grossman) was all afire," Einstein later recalled.[11] The mathematician introduced Einstein to the intricacies of non-Euclidean geometry, with the agreement that he, Grossman, would "bear no responsibility for the physics."

A branch of mathematics developed by 19th century German mathematicians Carl Friedrich Gauss, Bernhard Riemann and others for continuously varying co-ordinate systems, non-Euclidean geometry is typically applied to curved surfaces. (See Fig. 13.3.) These days it is called "differential geometry."[12]

Gauss

Born in 1777 in the Duchy of Brunswick (now part of Germany),[13] Johann Carl Friedrich Gauss is generally consider by mathematicians to be amongst the three greatest of their kind, along with Archimedes and Newton.

Termed the "wonder child" for his prodigious mathematical talents, at age three Gauss allegedly identified an error in one of his father's financial calculations.[14] In primary school, the class was told to add up all the numbers from 1 to 100 as busy work. The story goes that Carl gave the correct answer in a few seconds.

Carl Friedrich Gauss   Bernhard Riemann
(1777 – 1855)   (1826 – 1866)

Figure 13.3.   The Fathers of Curved Surface Geometry.

It is believed Gauss simply added the numbers 1 through 100 from opposite ends, as:

1 + 100 equals 101,
2 + 99 equals 101,
3 + 98 equals 101,
and so on.

There are 100/2 or 50 such sets. Thus the answer is 50 times 101 or 5050.

The reserved Gauss had very few close relationships, one being former classmate and lifelong friend Hungarian mathematician Farkas Bolyai. Farkas's son János, also a mathematician, became obsessed with coming up with a geometry that was not Euclidean. It was a most difficult mathematical task, but János eventually succeeded — a breakthrough which had eluded other mathematicians for two millennium.[15]

> *I have discovered things so wonderful that I was astounded … out of nothing I have created a strange new world.*[16]
>
> János Bolyai to his father Farkas

Gauss had developed non-Euclidean geometry years earlier, but ever the perfectionist, held back on publishing his work because he felt it was not yet in perfect form. When Farkas sent a copy of his son János's discovery to his friend, Gauss responded: "To praise it would amount to praising myself, for the entire content of the work…coincides almost exactly with my own …"[17]

János Bolyai was crushed.[18] He never published again and eventually gave up mathematics all together. His father suspected Gauss of plagiarism (unjustly) and their relationship suffered an irreparable blow.

Today the development of non-Euclidean geometry is credited to both Gauss and János Bolyai,[19] as well as to Russian mathematician Nikolai Lobachevsky, who had published a similar work independently in 1829. Gauss, Bolyai, and Lobachevsky showed that Euclid's axioms are not the only way to produce a self-consistent geometry.

In their new geometry, the three angles of a triangle did not always add up to 180°, a circle's circumference divided by its diameter did not always equal Pi, and two parallel lines could converge or diverge. This was a paradigm shift — a major achievement in the field of mathematics, and as Einstein later revealed, a major change in our view of reality.

Riemann's Multi-dimensional Geometry

Born in 1826, Georg Friedrich Bernhard Riemann studied under Gauss at the University of Göttingen.[20] In 1854, with Gauss in attendance, Riemann gave a now famous talk on extending Gauss's *2-D* geometry to any number of dimensions; e.g. *3-D, 4-D, 5-D,* etc. His mathematics described a continuous (and differentiable) surface, even if it varied from one point to the next in form e.g. from spherical to flat to hyperbolic.[21] Riemannian geometry has since been called "one of the greatest masterpieces of mathematical creation and exposition."[22]

(He demonstrates) a gloriously fertile originality.[23]

Gauss on Riemann's PhD thesis

One item in Riemann's lecture must have shocked and impressed Gauss. In a private letter to a colleague some three decades earlier, Gauss had dared to suggest that space itself might be *curved*: "I have from time to time in jest expressed the thought that Euclidean geometry would not be correct."[24] Now in his lecture, Riemann asked whether non-Euclidean geometry is restricted to abstract mathematics, or whether it is applicable to the real world.[25]

In 1903, along with his companions of the "Olympia Academy," Einstein read Riemann's masterpiece *On the Hypotheses which Determine the Foundations of Geometry.*[26] Nine years later, in his search for a relativistic theory of gravity Einstein recalled the differential geometry of Gauss and

Riemann. It was to become the mathematical foundation for general relativity, fulfilling the prophetic vision of Gauss and Riemann — we live in a non-Euclidean universe.

Potato Mapping

When he served as advisor for a geodetic survey of the Kingdom of Hannover, Gauss applied non-Euclidean geometry to mapping the hilly countryside.[27] Here he developed the concept of a "curvilinear" (rather than straight line) coordinate system. He applied a network of what are now called *Gaussian coordinates* directly to the curved land surface itself.

To see this, imagine throwing a fishnet over a potato (as suggested by physicist James Hartle).[28] This fishnet represents a "coordinate system" applied directly to the potato's surface, as shown in Fig. 13.4.

Notice the spacings between grid lines on the potato. They vary over the surface — some are smaller, others larger. This is a continuously-changing co-ordinate system applied to a curved surface.

What if we took a fishnet with *finer spacings* and threw it over the potato? Each local segment of the grid is now smaller, as shown in Fig. 13.5. And the surface area enclosed by each segment is now closer to a *flat* surface.

An even finer grid would give us even smaller segments. Each segment would be even closer to flat. Do you see it? The finer we make the grid, the better each segment approximates a flat surface.

Roughly speaking, the four sides of each segment make up a kind of *parallelogram* (also shown in the figure). What is a parallelogram? It is a four-sided figure where opposite sides are parallel.

As you can see, the parallelograms don't fit each segment exactly. If you want more accuracy, just use more grid lines with a finer spacing. To

Fishnet thrown
over a potato

Figure 13.4. Continuously Changing Co-ordinate System for a Curved Surface. (*Artist drawing; not mathematically precise.*)

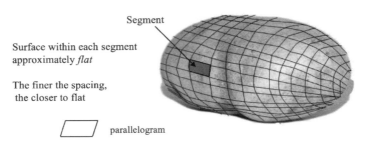

Figure 13.5.   Finer Mesh Fishnet Over Potato. (*Artist drawing; not mathematically precise.*)

get an exact solution, you have to go to line spacings which are infinitesimally small. But you need calculus for that.

We can describe each parallelogram segment with three parameters: length, width, and interior angle. Mathematically they are represented by three "*g's*" — the so-called Gaussian metrical coefficients. The three *g's*, length width, and angle (cross-term) tell us the size or scale of a parallelogram.

Again, if we make the grid lines fine enough, each local segment is essentially flat. So we can use the plane geometry of Euclid *within* each segment.

Say we construct a list of the three *g's* — length, width, and angle (cross-term) — for *all* parallelogram segments. We can then give this list to someone else. From it that person can mathematically stitch together all the *locally flat* segments and construct a *global* map of the entire curved surface of the potato. In other words, the list of *g's*, the so-called Gaussian coefficients, gives us a map of the potato's surface!

Locally flat. Globally curved. Sound familiar?

Any Reference Frame Will Do

What if we choose to throw the fishnet over the potato from a different angle or with the net rotated or shifted in position? We would of course get a different set of curved lines covering the potato in each case.

Which set of fishnet lines is valid? Any set is as good as any other. The orientation of the fishnet and its location on the potato is *completely arbitrary.*

This feature of Gauss's unequally-spaced co-ordinate systems had special appeal to Einstein. Recall his 1905 Relativity Postulate: the laws of physics are the same for all reference frames in uniform motion. Now in

1912 he sought to extend this principle to reference frames in any kind of motion and within any gravitational field.

In other words, Einstein wanted his coordinate system, his reference frame to be located anywhere at all and be moving in any way possible — such as in uniform motion, acceleration, rotation, or in a gravitational field. He wanted to represent the continuously changing co-ordinates of space and time in a gravitational field in a way which was completely arbitrary. In mathematics, this is called "generally covariant."

This means the underlying physics is unaffected or does not vary with the location or transformation of the coordinate system in spacetime. He called this deceptively simple tenet his *Principle of General Covariance.*

Einstein felt no matter where he chose to place his coordinate system, the laws of physics should stay the same. This may seem obvious, even trivial, but Einstein did not know how to generate the mathematics to obey this principle. It was the primary reason he sought the help of Marcel Grossman.

His friend introduced Einstein to the mathematics of Bernhard Riemann. And as we shall see, adhering to the Principle of General Covariance — throwing the proverbial fishnet over the potato in whatever way one chooses — proved to be Einstein's most difficult challenge in coming up with the mathematics of general relativity.

Note to reader: The next section contains more detailed mathematics. If you wish, you may skip it and go to the following section; What is Gravity?, and still maintain the essence of the exposition.

Mapping Spacetime[29]

In a brilliant stroke, Einstein took curved surface geometry, the non-Euclidean geometry of Gauss and Riemann, and applied it to *spacetime* itself.

Mapping Spacetime - in 2-D

In the potato mapping, the three *g's* give us the *x*-length, *y*-length, and cross term (angle) for each local subsection. In general relativity, the three *g's* give us the time interval, space interval, and space multiplied by time cross-term for each *local* subsection of two-dimensional spacetime. They define the spacetime interval for each local subsection.

Recall that two points in space are separated by a certain distance, the *space interval*. Two points in time are separated by the *time interval*. Two events in spacetime, are separated by the *spacetime interval*.

As we saw, within a local region of spacetime (small enough in space and short enough in time), gravity effects are effectively zero. So the spacetime interval between any two events is the same value within this local region.

But in a gravitational field, the spacetime interval changes globally over a number of local regions.

In Einstein's construct, the three g's of Gaussian geometry represent each local spacetime interval — one g for the space interval, one g for time interval, and one for the cross-term. This is the *generalized* spacetime interval. In a gravitational field, the three g's vary with location in the spacetime continuum — that is they vary *globally*.

Generalized Spacetime Interval — *two dimensions*

(Spacetime interval)^2 =

(space interval term)^2 + *space times time interval term* + *(time interval term)*^{2}

$$dS^2 = g_{xx}\, dx^2 + 2g_{xt}\, dx\, dt + g_{tt}\, dt^2$$

where: g_{xx}, g_{xt}, and g_{tt} are metrical coefficients, and
dx and dt represent the percentage or ratio for any given
point in spacetime within the region.

Mapping Spacetime - in 4-D

To represent spacetime in four dimensions, we extend the mathematics to three dimensions of space (x, y, and z) and one dimension of time (t) — the four dimensions of spacetime.

Here there are *ten g's*. Why ten? Because the four-dimensions of the generalized spacetime interval has four times four equals sixteen terms: *xx*, *yy*, *zz*, *tt*, plus cross-terms. But there are six redundant terms. For example the *x times t* term is the same as the *t times x* term. This leaves only ten independent terms.

Thus we have a ten-component equation representing 4-D spacetime with ten Gaussian coefficients. Again the values of the g's are the same within each local region, but change globally in a gravitational field. This is the global change in the spacetime interval.

Generalized Spacetime Interval — four spacetime dimensions

$(Spacetime\ interval)^2 = (x\ space\ interval\ term)^2 + (y\ space\ interval\ term)^2$

$+ (z\ space\ interval\ term)^2 + (time\ interval\ term)^2$

$+ all\ the\ cross\text{-}terms$

$$dS^2 = g_{xx}\ dx^2 + 2g_{xy}\ dxdy + 2g_{xz}\ dxdz + 2g_{xt}\ dxdt +$$

$$g_{yy}\ dy^2 + 2g_{yz}\ dydz + 2g_{yt}\ dydt + g_{zz}\ dz^2 + 2g_{zt}\ dzdt + g_{tt}dt^2$$

where: again the g's are metrical coefficients,
and dx, dy, dz, and dt represent the percentage or ratio
for any given point in spacetime within the region.

What is Gravity?

In the previous section, we presented Einstein's mathematics for the global change in the *spacetime interval* in a gravitational field. Now let's see how this relates to spacetime curvature and gravity itself:

Have you come to terms with the fact that we live on the surface of a gigantic ball? Why don't we fall off? Or for that matter, why is it when we jump up from the ground, we fall back down? We label this phenomenon "gravity". Most of us have been taught that, per Isaac Newton, gravity is a force; a mysterious attraction between all objects in the universe.

Einstein says this is wrong. Gravity is not a force. He proposes that an object such as the Earth's mass-energy stretches space and slows down time in its vicinity. He represents this warping of space and time with the global change in the spacetime interval. And, Einstein declares, this changing spacetime interval, this so-called *spacetime curvature*, governs how all objects move through spacetime.

So it is spacetime curvature which holds our bodies to the surface of the Earth, holds the moon in orbit around the Earth, holds the planets in orbit around the Sun, keeps the Sun and several hundred billion other stars within the great spiral galaxy we call the Milky Way. It holds galaxies within great global clusters millions of light years across. It is the cosmic glue which holds our universe together on the grandest of scales.

But isn't it *gravity* which makes objects fall to the Earth. Isn't it gravity which holds planets in solar orbits and binds galaxies together?

Yes, it is. You see; *the warping of space and time is the global change in the spacetime interval, is spacetime curvature, is gravity!*

They are all names for the same thing.

The stretching of space and slowing of time by the mass-energy of the Earth is what holds you down in your seat right now as you read this book. This global change in the spacetime interval, this spacetime curvature, this gravity is what keeps you tied to the surface of the Earth. It is the cosmic bond which holds the universe together. This is Einstein's radical vision of reality.

Now let's see how this spacetime curvature works.

Of Golf and Curvature

I am on the green in 7. It's a 3-par hole and I still have a long putt, about 15 feet. The shot looks easy. I take out my putter and try to look like I know what I am doing. I bend down and eye the green. It's not flat! It's curved. Now when I hit the ball, where it goes will be determined by how hard I hit it, the direction I hit it in, and the *curvature* of the green (as well as friction and the ball's spin).

If the green is curved downward to my right, the ball will roll to the right. If it is curved downward to the left, the ball will roll to the left.

I practice my stroke. Then I address the ball (golf jargon). I tap the little pimply orb firmly. Too firmly. Way too firmly. It follows the curvature of the green, rolls to the left, then slightly to the right, then merrily past the hole, continues on a downhill slope past the green and plops into the water.

"Nice shot," my partner says.

There are two salient points here. First, next time someone suggests a game of golf, stay home and play checkers. Second, once the ball is in motion, friction and the *curvature* of the green determine the path of the ball.

This is an analogy for the global change in the spacetime interval or *spacetime curvature*. Because the Sun's mass-energy produces a gravitational field, because it warps space and time, because it curves spacetime, the Earth orbits the Sun. The Earth wants to travel in a straight line through space, and if the Sun were not there, it would. (We ignore the effects of the other planets here.) But like the golf ball which follows the curved surface of the green, the Earth follows warped space and time, the spacetime curvature (gravity) produced by the Sun.

Picturing Spacetime Curvature

In his book, *A Journey into Gravity and Spacetime*, John Archibald Wheeler gives us a way to picture spacetime curvature and how it is transmitted across empty space.[30] Imagine a trampoline with nothing on it (Fig. 13.6(a)). The surface of the trampoline is flat because there is nobody on it — just like spacetime is flat when no mass-energy is present, when there is no gravitational field.

Notice how the trampoline lines in the left figure mark out a uniform, equally-spaced grid. This represents a Cartesian coordinate system. The mathematics of Euclidean geometry work just fine here. If we think of each rectangular section as a "local" representation of the surface, we see that all the local areas are the same — no different spacings, no curvature. Looking at all the rectangles, we see that the surface is globally flat as well.

Imagine a bowling ball on the trampoline representing the Sun (Fig. 13.6(b)). The bowling bowl causes the surface of the trampoline to curve where it is. As a result, the grid lines are no longer the same spacing. They are continuously changing. Now we need a Gaussian coordinate system.

Notice how the grids are stretched near the bowling ball. As we proceed outward from its location, we see this stretching grow less and less.

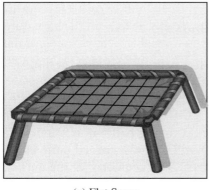
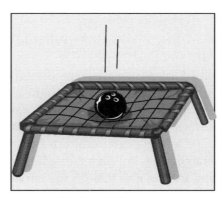

(a) Flat Space　　　　　　　　　　　(b) Curved Space

Figure 13.6.　Trampoline Fabric Represents Space. (*a*) *With no mass-energy present, trampoline fabric is flat,* (*b*) *Bowling ball (mass-energy) curves trampoline fabric in its vicinity.*

Far away from the bowling ball, near the edges of the trampoline, the surface is pretty much flat. The grid lines are of equal spacing.

Similarly, the Sun's mass-energy causes local spacetime to stretch, warp or curve where it is. Close to the Sun, spacetime curvature is strong. But as it spreads out through space, it becomes weaker. The stretching gets less and less.

How is this spacetime curvature *transmitted* from the Sun to Earth? Spacetime curvature has energy. So spacetime curvature produces space-time curvature!

When the bowling ball hits the trampoline surface, it stretches the fabric where it is. This in turn stretches adjacent fabric, and so on, all the way out to the edge of the trampoline. Similarly, Wheeler tell us, "the mass-energy in the Sun curves spacetime where the Sun is.[31] This curves spacetime just outside the Sun. That curvature curves spacetime still further out, and so on (until it reaches Earth)."

Like each local grid of the trampoline fabric, spacetime curvature from the Sun is transmitted from local frame to local frame across space to the Earth and beyond. How fast is this spacetime curvature transmitted from the Sun to Earth? At the speed of light. Or to be more precise, at the same speed as light travels, c.

How do objects *travel* through this spacetime curvature? They take a path called a geodesic.

What is a Geodesic?

Non-Euclidean geometry says the shortest path between two points on a curved surface is not a straight line. It's a curved line called a *geodesic*. This geodesic is the "natural" path which all objects take on a curved surface — the "curve of least effort."[32]

On a perfectly uniform flat surface, a rolling ball will continue in a straight line. But on a curved surface it will follow a curved path, as we saw for the golf ball on the curved green. The geometry of the surface decides what direction the ball takes. This curved path is a geodesic through space.

(A simple example on how to construct a geodesic is given in Appendix D.)

When Einstein applied curved surface geometry to spacetime, he saw that moving objects continue on a straight line *through space* as long as there is no gravity. But when mass-energy is present, when there is a gravitational field, moving objects follow a curved path through space.

What about the object's path *through spacetime*? When gravity is present, an object moves through four-dimensional spacetime in a *straight line*! And this geodesic path is not the shortest, but the longest path through spacetime. It is the path of greatest wristwatch (proper) time. British philosopher and mathematician Bertrand Russell called this "the law of cosmic laziness."[33]

So when you jump off that diving board, the geometry of spacetime curvature "decides your direction for you," just as the geometry of spacetime curvature decides what path planets take around the Sun. And not just any path, but the longest possible path — the laziest path — through curved spacetime.

Basketball Geodesics

To get a visual picture of a geodesic in spacetime, imagine we are at a WNBA basketball game. Superstar Candace Parker has the ball in the far corner. She pivots to the left. She stops. She shoots. She scores!

Let's consider the basketball's path from two points of view:

An "Unnatural" Reference Frame — Seated in the stands, we see the basketball rise up and then fall into the basket. To us, the ball follows a curved path to the basket. (See Fig. 13.7(a).) What causes this curvature? Is it some mysterious force of gravity? No, Wheeler tells us, "it is the fault of us — the viewers."[34] In other words, the curvature we see is due to our point of view, our frame of reference.

In a Free-Fall Reference Frame — Daredevil Sandy is hanging precariously from the rafters high above the court. At the instant Parker shoots the ball, Sandy lets go and falls towards the floor. From her perspective, she is at rest in free float, and the basketball court and all on it are rising up towards her.

Sandy sees the flight of the basketball quite differently than we in the stands do. To her in free fall, the basketball transverses a *straight line* path to the basket. (See Fig. 13.7(b).)

Because we are on the ground, "we are not in a 'natural' state of motion." Thus we see a curved path. On the other hand, Sandy in her free-float-frame is in the "natural" state of motion. To her, the geodesic, the path of the basketball (or any falling object) is a straight line.

211

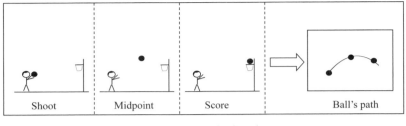

(a) View from the Stands:

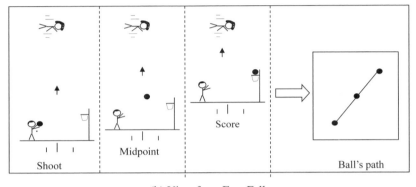

(b) View from Free Fall:

Figure 13.7.   Path is Relative. *(a) People in stands see basketball follow curved path. (b) Sandy in free-fall sees ball follow straight line.*

Thus, as Wheeler points out, "the ball's 'arc' is an illusion."[35] So in this sense "'gravity' is an illusion. When we are in free float, neither exists (locally)." Only globally do we see the effects of gravity, of spacetime curvature.

The Search for a Solution

In 1912, Albert Einstein came up with a new paradigm for gravity — not as some mysterious Newtonian force but as the curvature of spacetime itself. Einstein found he could best model this newfound vision with the curved surface geometry of Gauss and Riemann.[36]

He represented the distortion or warping of space and time with the global change in the spacetime interval. And he realized this *spacetime curvature* determines how objects fall to the Earth, how planets move around the Sun.

Yet, despite all he had accomplished, the hardest part of his quest was yet to come. Years of arduous effort awaited him. Einstein's final journey to "the equations of the universe" is the subject of the next chapter.

Chapter 14
Einstein's Masterpiece

In the light of knowledge attained, the happy achievement seems almost a matter of course. ... But the years of anxious searching in the dark with their intense longing, their alternations of confidence and exhaustion and the final emergence into the light — only those who have experienced it can understand that.[1]

Albert Einstein

Einstein's famous collaboration with Marcel Grossman began in earnest in the summer of 1912. Together they tried to come up with mathematics which connected spacetime curvature (the gravitational field) with the source of gravity (an object's mass-energy). At its core was a trio of ambitious goals for his new theory.[2]

Major Objectives

Einstein had three key aims in mind for his new relativistic theory of gravity. First it had to be in the *same form* for all frames of reference, i.e. obey his Principle of General Covariance. In addition, his theory had to obey conservation of mass-energy and momentum. And lastly, it had to give predictions which agreed with Newton's theory for "weak" gravity and "slow" speeds.

Attempts to meet these objectives would at times provide key insights and simplifications, but more often prove extremely difficult. They became an ongoing source of frustration in his quest.

Let's look at each issue:

General Covariance — Einstein envisioned a theory of gravity which was totally relative — one which met his Principle of General Covariance. His would be a theory where the laws of physics are the same in *all* reference frames — the location and orientation of the reference frame (coordinate system) would be completely arbitrary.

Einstein felt that "coordinates do not exist *a priori* in nature," that they are only "a tool used (by humans) to describe nature."[3] Thus the choice of coordinate system must play "no role in the formulation of fundamental physical laws."

Of all his goals, this would prove the most difficult to understand and satisfy mathematically.

Conservation — Einstein strived to develop a theory which obeyed certain conservation "laws" of physics — namely the conservation of mass-energy and the conservation of momentum. This criterion had a great simplifying effect on the search for the equations of general relativity, significantly narrowing possible mathematical solutions.

Newtonian Limit — Einstein knew his new theory of gravity would have to agree with the predictions of Newton's theory in two situations: weak gravity and slow speeds (as compared to the speed of light). This generally meant for observations within our solar system.

Why? Because over two centuries of observations and measurements of the motion of our Sun, planets, moons, and comets very closely matched Newton's predictions. Einstein's new theory had better agree with these known empirical results as well.

General relativity would be expected to break new ground particularly outside our solar system, in places where gravity was especially strong, and/or where the speeds of stellar materials were an appreciable fraction of the speed of light.

What defines "weak" gravity? One way is to compare a stellar object's *escape velocity* to the speed of light. Here on Earth, if you shoot an object straight up in the air at a speed of about 25,000 miles per hour (11 km per sec) or greater, it will overcome Earth's gravity and escape into outer space. Anything slower and the object will fall back to the ground.

Because it is so massive, the Sun has an escape velocity of about 1.4 million miles an hour (618 km per sec). Recall the speed of light is about 670 million miles an hour — so even the Sun's escape velocity is only a mere 0.2% the speed of light.

Thus gravity produced by the Sun — the most massive object in our solar system — is still so "weak" that Newton's law of gravity is an excellent approximation for nearly all observations. Only when a stellar object's escape velocity or its relative motion is a significant fraction of the speed of light can we expect Einstein's general relativity to give predictions which are significantly different from Newton's.

The Mercury Test

As noted in Chap. 9, there was one known phenomenon in the weak gravity of our solar system where Newton's theory of gravity failed to agree precisely with existing observations: the so-called perihelion shift of Mercury.

The tiny planet Mercury is the closet planet to the Sun, thus it experiences the greatest solar gravity effects. Since its orbit is elliptical (like all planets), Mercury is sometimes closer and sometimes farther away from the Sun. The closest point in its orbit to the Sun is called the *perihelion*, as shown in Fig. 14.1.

Mercury's elliptical orbit rotates or precesses around the Sun ever so slightly over time. Per Newton's theory, this is due to gravitational disturbances from the other planets on Mercury. As shown in Fig. 14.2, this precession forms a sort of "rosette pattern".

Newton's theory predicted that Mercury's closest point to the Sun shifts in angle by **531** arc seconds per century.[4] But telescopic observations showed a shift of some **574** arc seconds per century. Newton's prediction

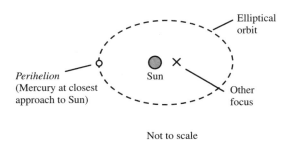

Not to scale

Figure 14.1. Mercury's Orbit Around the Sun. *Mercury orbits the Sun in an elliptical orbit (as do all the planets). The Sun is at one of the two foci of the ellipse. The perihelion is the point at which Mercury is closest to the Sun. (Ellipse greatly exaggerated.)*

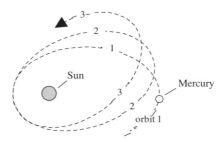

Figure 14.2. Rotation (Precession) of Mercury's Orbit Around Sun. *(Elliptical orbit and precession greatly exaggerated.)*

was too small by a **43** arc seconds. (An arc second is 1/60 of an arc minute. An arc minute is 1/60 of a degree. So an arc second is 1/3600 of a degree.)

This missing 43 arc seconds was a deep puzzle. Every other observation of our solar system agreed remarkably well with Newton's great theory. This admittedly miniscule shift could not be explained. Could Einstein's new theory of gravity explain this tiny excess in the precession of Mercury's orbit — and meet his three major objectives?

The Lost Years

> *I am now working exclusively on the gravitation problem and I believe that, with the help of a mathematician friend here, I will overcome all difficulties.[5]*

Albert Einstein, October 1912

First Attempt — Ricci Curvature

In August of 1912, Einstein began a dedicated search for the gravitational field equations of general relativity with great confidence. Under Grossmann's tutelage in Zurich, he worked to understand the mathematics of non-Euclidean geometry and its application to spacetime curvature.

In addition to Gauss and Riemann, Grossmann introduced Einstein to later advances in differential geometry by 19th century German mathematician Elwin Christoffel, and Italian mathematicians Gregorio Ricci-Curbastro and Tullio Levi-Civita.

218

Ricci in particular had developed surface curvature mathematics based on the Riemann tensor which was covariant. Grossman recommended Einstein use this so-called *Ricci Curvature Tensor* to represent spacetime curvature — the global change in the spacetime interval due to the presence of mass-energy. With this suggestion, Einstein began to make progress.

By the end 1912, Einstein had developed his first version of the field equations for general relativity.[6] Did he have the solution? Einstein thought so, but when he evaluated his new equations, he found the same mass-energy gave multiple solutions for the gravitational field.

In other words, a specific mass-energy gave a number of different but apparently equally valid solutions for the spacetime curvature.[7] This was a real problem. If there is no unique solution, a one-and-only-one spacetime curvature for a given mass-energy, then the equations were useless.

Einstein abandoned this approach and reduced his reliance on a mathematical strategy.[8] Reluctantly, with Marcel Grossman he pursued a more limited solution which did not fully obey his Principle of General Covariance.

Second Attempt: The Entwurf

In May of 1913, Einstein published a paper on the Einstein–Grossman approach titled "Outline of a Generalized Theory of Relativity and of a Theory of Gravitation."[9] The theory became known as the *Entwurf* (German for outline). Einstein admitted in the paper that this limited theory had serious issues.

As the spring of 1914 approached, Einstein had convinced himself he had a viable solution. But despite another year of effort, his Mercury shift calculations were still way off. He began to question his own arguments.

While still in a state of general confusion, Einstein received a fateful invitation to lecture at the University of Göttingen. The rather innocent Dr. Einstein did not see the distress this request would cause him.

The Göttingen Lectures

> In Göttingen, I had the great pleasure of seeing that everything was understood down to the details. I am quite enchanted with Hilbert.[10]
>
> Albert Einstein

In June of 1915, Einstein gave a series of two-hour invited lectures on the status of his theory at the University of Göttingen. Why did he choose to publicly present a theory still beset with so many problems? And why to the great mathematical minds at Göttingen? Einstein was, by nature, totally forthcoming, almost childlike concerning both his successes and failures. And perhaps he could not resist the chance to enter the same halls that Gauss and Riemann had walked.

Naively, Einstein laid out his approach in great detail, including the problems with his gravitational equations.[11] After listening to Einstein's lecture, the great German mathematician David Hilbert decided to see if he could find the correct field equations. To his great consternation, Einstein found himself in a race with Hilbert to the final theory of general relativity.

In early September, Einstein discovered additional problems with his *Entwurf* theory. He came to the conclusion that the mathematics were fundamentally flawed. After some three years of struggle, he was effectively back where he started.

> *I don't believe I am able to find the mistake myself, for in this matter my mind is too set in a deep rut.*[12]

Albert Einstein, September 30, 1915

Ironically, at around that time, Einstein was offered the most prestigious job of his life.

Berlin

In July 1913, Max Planck and Walther Nernst approached Einstein with a tantalizing offer — a professorship in Berlin, the "world-capital" of physics, and membership in the prestigious Prussian Academy of Sciences.[13,14] At age 34, he would be appointed to Director of the Kaiser Wilhelm Physical Institute and Professor in the University of Berlin, and become the youngest member of the Prussian Academy of Sciences — the "premier scientific society of all Europe."[15] In addition, he would have no teaching responsibilities nor any real administrative duties.

After five months of consideration, Einstein accepted the offer. He left Zurich Poly the following spring, and moved back with his family to the country of his birth. On arrival in Berlin, he remarked:

> *The Germans are gambling on me as they would on a prize-winning hen, but I don't know if I can still lay eggs.*[16]

On June 28, 1914, four days before Einstein gave his inaugural address to the Prussian Academy, a Serbian nationalist assassinated

Archduke Franz Ferdinand, heir to Austria-Hungary's throne, and his wife, Sophie, while they were visiting Sarajevo.[17] With the pretext he had been looking for, Austro-Hungarian Emperor Franz Joseph declared war on Serbia a month later. World War I, the "War to End All Wars," had begun.

On July 31, Serbian ally Russia mobilized its armed forces. The next day, Austria-Hungary's ally Germany declared war on Russia. Two days later, she declared war on France, and then on neutral Belgium to flank France. In response, Britain declared war on Germany. On August 6, Austria-Hungary declared war on Russia. The continent was soon ablaze with the bloodiest and most inexplicable war in its history.

In September of 1914, 93 prominent German scientists, scholars, and artists, including Max Planck, signed a manifesto which declared support for the Kaiser and the war effort.[18] Albert Einstein refused to sign. Two months later, he put his signature on a counter-manifesto calling for peace. Only four others dared sign.

> *Europe in her insanity has started something unbelievable. At such times as this one realizes what a sorry species of animal one belongs to.*[19]
>
> Albert Einstein

To make matters worse, Einstein's marriage to Mileva Marić was on the rocks. As his fame grew, her resentment over the time he spent outside the home and on his physics grew accordingly.

In the spring of 1912, while a professor in Prague, Einstein had reconnected with his cousin Elsa Löwenthal, a divorcée with two grown daughters who lived in Berlin.[20] Unhappy at home, he began a romantic correspondence.

After several failed attempts at reconciliation, Mileva left Berlin in July of 1914 and returned to Zurich with the two boys. (See Fig. 14.3.) Seeing his sons off at the station, Albert "bawled like a little boy."[21] He wrote to Elsa; "They used to shout with joy when I came ... Now they will be gone forever."

Einstein's mother Pauline was delighted with the news. She had always disliked Marić intensely. "Oh, if your poor Papa had only lived to see it!" she told her son.[22]

In the bitter summer of 1915, Albert Einstein found himself at the lowest point of his adult life. Not since his parents had left him in the hated Munich gymnasium and moved to Italy had he felt such despair. With the continent and much of the world raging with war, his health

Figure 14.3.   Eduard Einstein, Mileva Einstein, and Hans Albert Einstein, 1914.

deteriorating due to lack of food, his children virtually unreachable in Zurich, and his new theory of gravity at a dead end, his only solace was the growing attentions of Elsa.

But for Einstein it was literally the dark before the dawn.

The Solution

In late September of 1915, Einstein made what was perhaps the most difficult and important decision of his career.[23] Completely frustrated with the Einstein-Grossmann approach, the so-called *Entwurf theory*, now convinced that it was not the path to a relativistic theory of gravity, he abandoned it.

Einstein took a second hard look at the approach he had rejected in 1912 — gravitational field equations using Riemann and Ricci tensors to represent spacetime curvature.

Those years of searching in the dark were not completely in vain. Einstein had developed the skills to truly understand the problem, to use and manipulate the complex mathematics of differential geometry and tensor analysis. Now, after re-examination, he found, per his Principle of General Covariance, the solutions he thought were different were in fact *mathematically and physically equivalent*. In other words, they actually represented the same solution.

Like a nasty four-dimensional jigsaw puzzle of many tiny pieces, everything was finally falling into place. His senses heightened, his power of mind concentrated as never before, the 36-year-old could sense victory at last. He worked himself at a fever pitch to the exclusion of all else and took the final step of his epic journey in a mere three months. But it was still not easy by any stretch of the imagination.

Beginning on November 4, 1915 — in a series of four now famous weekly lectures — Einstein presented the step-by-step progress of his reconstituted approach to the Prussian Academy of Sciences. He began by divulging all the issues with the *Entwurf theory*. He then presented his new approach using Ricci curvature. In his second lecture, he showed that, unlike the *Entwurf*, this new approach was generally covariant. It conformed to his dream of a truly general theory where any reference frame will do.

Then, in a painstaking trial and error process, he tried to find the final field equations which produced the observed perihelion of Mercury.[24] Each examination required calculation of first order approximations to each of ten complicated field equations. Somehow he completed this "exhaustive, almost Herculean task" in time for his third lecture.[25]

On November 18 he announced the results — a value for the added perihelion shift of Mercury of *42.9 arc seconds*! It was a great triumph for the former patent clerk.

I was beside myself with joy and excitement.[26]

Albert Einstein on Mercury calculation

In his calculations, Einstein found Mercury's elliptical orbit naturally rotates around the Sun — independent of gravitational perturbations from other planets.[27] In other words, Mercury's orbit precesses *on its own* — at a rate of *42.9* arc seconds per century. So Mercury's inherent orbit is not stationary as Newton thought, but a rotating ellipse.

This effect is true for all planets. But the farther away from the Sun, the less the inherent rotation. For example, the perihelion of Venus shifts only 8.6 arc seconds per century, Earth's a mere 3.8 arc seconds per century, and Mars less than 1.4 arc seconds.

In his third lecture, Einstein also presented his new prediction for the bending of starlight near to the Sun. Taking both the warping of time and space into account, he calculated a value of 1.7 arc seconds. This was the first true prediction to come out of his new field equations — a calculation for the value of a phenomenon which had yet to be observed.

The Final Lecture

On November 25, 1915, Einstein presented his solution to the Academy. He announced "finally the general theory of relativity is closed as a logical structure."[28] His equations were completely independent of reference frame, in other words of choice of coordinate system. They maintained the same form under any and all forms of motion. "The general laws of nature ... hold true for all systems of coordinates," Einstein later wrote.[29] Einstein's precious Principle of General Covariance had been satisfied.

> *The theory is of incomparable beauty.*[30]
>
> Albert Einstein

His equations also obeyed conservation of mass-energy and momentum. Plus they reduced to Newton's equations under both weak gravity conditions and non-relativistic speeds. The long journey from his 1907 Equivalence Principle was over. A new paradigm, a new model of universal gravitation was born.

Einstein then wrote a letter to his 11-year-old son Hans Albert in Switzerland:

> *I will try to be with you for a month every year so that you will have a father who is close to you and can love you.. . . In the last few days I completed one of the finest papers of my life. When you are older I will tell you about it.*[31]

In the midst of his elation, Einstein learned that David Hilbert had published his own solution to the gravitational field equations in a Göttingen science journal on November 21, some four days before Einstein's final presentation.

Had Hilbert beaten Einstein to the finish line?[32] A team of scholars in 1997 determined that Hilbert's original equations in fact were not generally covariant.[33] Apparently he sent a revised version to his publisher after seeing Einstein's correct solution, appropriately adding the words "first introduced by Einstein."

Even so, Einstein felt betrayed and let Hilbert know it. To his credit, David Hilbert's response was most gracious. In the end, he acknowledged Einstein as the sole author of the theory of general relativity.[34] Nevertheless, Einstein was now wary about divulging unpublished results.[35]

Albert Einstein's presentation of his field equations of general relativity to the Prussian Academy of Sciences was a seminal moment in the annals of science — the culmination of nearly a decade of struggle. This was his greatest triumph, the supreme accomplishment of a lifetime, his masterpiece, and he knew it.

Let's take a look at his great achievement.

The Equations of the Universe

When I introduce Einstein's masterpiece in class, I feel like a roaring symphony should be playing over the loud-speakers — as in the opening to the movie *2001:A Space Odyssey*:

Trumpets: Daah, Daaah, Daaaah, Dah Daaaaaah!
Drums: Dum dum . . dum dum . . dum dum . . dum dum . . dum dum.[a]

I know I am prone to hyperbole, but I feel the enthusiasm is justified. These equations gave the world its first model for the origin, structure, and evolution of our cosmos. They are in fact the equations of the universe.

Let's examine Einstein's field equations in their simplest form:

Spacetime Curvature = Mass-energy Density

In the succinct (and slightly modified) words of relativist John Archibald Wheeler:

Mass-energy grips spacetime, telling it how to curve. Spacetime grips mass-energy, telling it how to move.[36]

In other words, mass-energy produces spacetime curvature (gravity). More precisely, the distribution of mass-energy density and its movement through spacetime produces the curvature of spacetime, i.e. the gravitational field.

And spacetime curvature in turn governs the movement of mass-energy. More precisely, spacetime curvature governs the movement of matter and non-material energy in that gravitational field.

---

[a]It is recommended that you play this music while reading this section. Link: http://www.youtube.com/watch?v=SLuW-GBaJ8k. Last accessed July, 2013.

In Newton's universe, one body exerts a force on another. But in Einstein's world, one body causes spacetime to curve, and another body moves "in response to that curvature,"[37] as physicist Bernard Schutz put it. For example, the mass-energy of the Earth curves spacetime in its vicinity. An object thrown into the air, like Candace Parker's basketball, follows the path of greatest wristwatch time (proper time) through that curved spacetime — the geodesic.

The Einstein Equation

Einstein's gravitational field equations are written in the shorthand of tensor notation as a single equation called the Einstein equation:

Curvature Tensor = *a constant times the* **Momenergy Tensor**

(Put simply, a tensor is a mathematical array which obeys certain transformation rules.)

Note to reader: The next subsection also contains more detailed mathematics. You may skip it and go to the subsection, The Left Side, if you wish.

The Einstein Equation is actually a set of ten (second-order differential) equations. When written out in full detail, the ten equations "fill three large book pages in small, tight print."[38] To this day, physicists are still learning things from these highly complex and difficult equations.

Mathematically, the Einstein Equation is:

$$G_{ab} = K T_{ab}$$

where

G_{ab} *is the ten-component* **Curvature Tensor** *representing spacetime curvature,*

K is a constant $8\pi\ G/c^4$ *where G is the gravitational constant, and*

T_{ab} *is the ten-component* **Momenergy Tensor** *representing mass/ energy/momentum density*

The **Curvature Tensor** *is further broken down as:*

$$G_{ab} = R_{ab} - \tfrac{1}{2}\,R g_{ab}$$

where

R_{ab} is the **Ricci Tensor**, *which represents the rate of change of space-time curvature (2nd derivative),*

R *is the Ricci scalar, which represents the radius of curvature of this spacetime curvature*[b], *and*

g_{ab} *is the* **Metric Tensor** *(the 10-g's which represent all the "stitched together" local spacetime intervals).*

The subscripts *a* and *b* refer to the four spacetime coordinates, *x, y, z,* and *t* respectively; e.g. xx, xy, xz, xt, etc.

(For more on the Einstein Equation, its history, and how it represents space and time curvature, see Appendix E.)

Now let's see what each side of the Einstein Equation is telling us.

The Left Side

The **Curvature Tensor** on the left-side of the Einstein's Equation represents spacetime curvature (gravity) and how it changes from place to place (in space) and over time (in time) — in other words how it changes in space-time. It contains the global change in the spacetime interval within it.

The Right Side

The **Momenergy Tensor** on the right-side of the Einstein Equation is the *source* of gravity, of spacetime curvature. More precisely, the **Momenergy Tensor** represents the distribution of matter and non-material energy and their movement through spacetime.

What is *momenergy*? It is mass, relativistic momentum, and relativistic energy combined into one mathematical expression. And, like the space-time interval, momenergy's magnitude is unaffected by uniform motion. Conservation of mass-energy and momentum become conservation of momenergy.

(See Appendix C for more details on momenergy.)

---

[b]A scalar is a quantity which has single value only; its magnitude. *Temperature* is an example of a scalar, e.g. 72°F, whereas *wind* is not a scalar but a vector because it has a magnitude and direction, e.g. 15 mph from the West).

The *Momenergy Tensor* contains three sources of gravity or space-time curvature: mass density, energy density, and momentum density.

Mass Density — This source of spacetime curvature is a particle's mass (or equivalently its rest energy). By mass *density*, we mean the amount of mass contained within a certain volume of space.

Energy Density — Energy in all its forms is also a source of spacetime curvature.

Momentum Density — Momentum, the *movement* of matter and non-material energy through space, also produces spacetime curvature.

Per the Einstein Equation, a stellar object with greater momenergy density produces greater spacetime curvature (stronger gravity) at its surface. Consider an extreme example — a neutron star.

A neutron star is the highly compressed remnant of a giant star.[39] It is condensed to such an extreme degree that a large portion of its electrons and protons are squeezed together to form neutrons. A neutron star can be a staggering one hundred trillion times as dense as the Sun. To escape this neutron star's gravity, an object emitted from its surface would have to reach an escape velocity of some 335 million miles an hour or half the speed of light.

This dramatic increase in spacetime curvature also affects time on the surface of a neutron star. Compared to a clock in the zero gravity of outer space, time on the neutron star's surface runs slower by about a month per year.[40] In comparison, time on the Sun's surface runs slower by about six seconds per year.

Also contained within Einstein's field equations is a striking feature which simply does not exist in Newton's universe.[41] In physics, the flow of a particle's momentum is its *pressure*. And since momentum is a source of spacetime curvature, pressure is also a source. Thus pressure produces a gravitational field!

Are we talking about the same pressure that keeps automobile tires inflated? Yes. According to the Einstein Equation, the higher the air pressure, the more the tire weighs! (By a minuscule amount.)

Momentum and thus pressure is due to the motion of particles through space, like the movement of the molecules of air in that tire. But the particles inside a tire move around very slowly compared to the speed of light, so here the effect of pressure on spacetime curvature is extremely tiny.

Where does this pressure effect become significant?[42] In conditions where particles move at *relativistic* speeds — such as inside the collapse of very massive stars. The role of pressure in producing gravitational effects has proved critical in understanding the dynamics of very massive star collapse — and the resulting neutron stars and black holes they produce.

Another Source of Gravity — Gravity Itself!

Einstein's field equations are extremely difficult to solve. Why? Because, as noted, spacetime curvature has energy — and energy is a source of spacetime curvature. Thus spacetime curvature itself produces spacetime curvature. In other words, *gravity itself creates gravity*! Today, computers and often supercomputers are needed to solve the non-linear equations of general relativity.[43]

Goals Met, Issues Resolved

As discussed in the beginning of this chapter, Einstein had three major goals for his new theory of gravity. His field equations met them all:

Conservation — The equations obey the law of Conservation of Mass/Energy and Momentum (Conservation of Momenergy).

Covariance — The transformation laws are the *same* for both the Curvature Tensor and Momenergy Tensor. In other words both tensors are transformed from one coordinate system (reference frame) to another using the same mathematical rules. Thus if we set the Curvature Tensor equal to the Momenergy Tensor in a certain coordinate system, this equality automatically holds, per physicist Peter Bergmann, in *"all conceivable coordinate systems."*[44] The Principle of General Covariance is satisfied — Einstein's equation works for all frames of reference!

Weak Gravity — The predictions of Einstein's field equations are nearly identical to Newton's theory for "weak" gravity and non-relativistic speeds — such as within our solar system.

Newton's Gravity Issues

Einstein's general theory of relativity also resolves the three issues with Newton's Theory of Universal Gravitation identified in Chap. 9:

Action at a distance — Recall Newton tells us nothing about how gravity is transmitted from place to place. What, for example travels from the Sun to the Earth through some 93 million miles of space, grabs our planet, and holds it in orbit? Einstein's answer? *Spacetime curvature.*

As we learned, the mass-energy of the Sun causes spacetime to curve where it is. This in turn produces spacetime curvature just outside its surface. And this spacetime curvature distorts spacetime just a little further away, and so on. So, like the bending of a trampoline fabric by a bowling ball, spacetime curvature is transmitted from one local region to another, expanding outward from the Sun in all directions until it reaches Earth and beyond.

Length contraction — How does general relativity deal with the notion that distance is relative? In Einstein's construct, there is no need for a global distance between the Sun and Earth. Spacetime curvature is local.

The change in the spacetime interval from local free-float frame to adjacent local free-float frame is transmitted from the Sun bit by bit, piece by piece, until it reaches the Earth. Again, this "stitching of spacetime" from local frame to local frame produces the *global* gravitational field.

Instantaneous gravity — Once completed, Einstein evaluated his field equations of general relativity to determine the speed of transmission of spacetime curvature from place to place. To his delight, the answer showed gravity does not travel instantaneously as Newton proposed, but at *the speed of light!*[45]

Einstein's Cosmos

At first generally ignored by most physicists, over time Einstein's relativistic theory of gravity proved monumentally successful. Not since Isaac Newton had a single scientist conjured up such an accurate and far-reaching model of reality. General relativity soon became the theoretical foundation for the great cosmological revolution of the 20th century.

Now some 100 years after Einstein's breakthrough, nearly every prediction of his general theory has been verified to impressive accuracy, directly or indirectly, by empirical evidence. We discuss Einstein's wondrous new universe and its mind-boggling implications in the final two chapters.

Chapter 15

The Universe Revealed

There are more things in heaven and earth, Horatio,
Than are dreamt of in your philosophy.

William Shakespeare, *Hamlet, Act 1 scene 5*

On March 20, 1916, Albert Einstein published his now famous exposition on general relativity. The manuscript was presented in *Annalen der Physik*, the same prestigious German physics journal in which he had published his theory of special relativity a decade earlier.

What was the physics community's general reaction to Einstein's new theory? Skepticism. Yes, his theory apparently corrected a tiny anomaly in Newton's theory regarding the perihelion shift of Mercury. But Newton's Law of Universal Gravitation has successfully explained the behavior of objects here on Earth and in the heavens for over 200 years.

"Should we abandon the seminal creation of Isaac Newton," they asked, "because of a single anomaly?" After all, Einstein's first theory, his radical theory of special relativity had yet to be fully embraced. And there was no evidence supporting a single prediction of his wild new theory of relativistic gravity.

The key word here is "prediction". It is one thing to come up with a new set of mathematics which matches existing measurements, as in general relativity calculating the additional perihelion shift of Mercury. Scientists are particularly adept at getting their mathematics to fit known data. It is quite another thing to predict the future outcome of a yet to be performed experiment.

It's hard to make predictions, especially about the future.[1]

Yogi Berra

But when a scientist does make a prediction based on his/her new theory, and another scientist independently confirms this prediction through careful observation and measurement — then others stand up and take notice.

Einstein's proposition that light is quantized energy, based on Max Planck's formula, helped spark the quantum revolution. Thinking about the speed of light led Einstein to his theory of special relativity. And now, the first true prediction of general relativity to be tested involved the bending of light in a gravitational field.

Forgive Us, Sir Isaac

On May 29, 1919, British astrophysicist Arthur Eddington — fellow pacifist and ardent fan of Einstein's new theory of gravity — led an expedition to Principe in the Gulf of Guinea off the west coast of Africa. His goal: To measure how much starlight is bent by the Sun's gravity during a total solar eclipse.

As a back-up, Eddington sent a group led by astronomer Andrew Crommelin to the village of Sobral in the Amazon jungle of northern Brazil where the eclipse would also be visible.

Why an eclipse?[2] During the day, the Sun is so bright you can't see the stars in the sky, especially those very near the Sun. So Einstein suggested to astronomers they test his theory on the bending of light during a full solar eclipse when stars are visible even in the middle of the day.

For light from a star grazing the limb of the Sun along its way to the Earth, Newton's theory of gravity predicted a bending or displacement angle of **0.875** arc seconds.[3] Einstein's new theory of general relativity predicted a displacement angle of **1.75** arc seconds — half due to time warp and half due to space warp. (See Fig. 15.1.)

Fortuitously, the solar eclipse of 1919 would occur with the Hyades cluster directly behind it. This especially dense grouping of stars is roughly at the center of the constellation Taurus.[4]

Eddington's plan was simple: compare photographs taken during the eclipse (with the Sun present) to photographs of the same Hyades cluster taken at night six months before in England (with no Sun present).

232

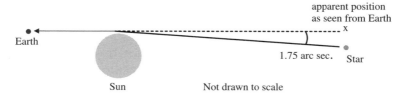

Figure 15.1. **Bending of Starlight by the Sun's Gravity.** *Newton's gravity predicts a displacement angle of 0.875 arc seconds. Einstein's general relativity predicts 1.75 arc seconds.*

The idea was to measure any apparent changes in position of stars near the Sun's limb. Results are shown in Table 15.1.

The Principe data showed an average displacement of 1.6 arc seconds. The data from Sobral gave a higher value of 1.98 arc seconds. Einstein's prediction of 1.75 arc seconds fell within the two data sets, in agreement within 20% or so. The Eddington eclipse data were the first measurements to support a prediction of Einstein's new theory of gravity.

Table 15–1. **Results of 1919 Solar Eclipse.**[5] *Reported results support Einstein's prediction over Newton's.*

Measurement	Usable Photos	Stars per Photo	Displacement (arc seconds)
At Principe	2	5	1.60 ± 0.31
At Sobral	8	At least 7	1.98 ± 0.12
		Newtonian Prediction:	0.875
		Einstein's Prediction:	1.75

What was one of the first things Einstein did when he heard the news? He cabled his mother:

Dear Mother — Today some happy news. Lorentz telegraphed me that the British expeditions have verified the deflection of light by the Sun.[6]

Pauline Koch Einstein

A formal announcement of the Eddington results followed at Burlington House in the grand hall of Piccadilly in London on November

6, 1919. The elderly J. J. Thomson, Royal Society president and discoverer of the electron spoke last:

> This is the most important result obtained in connection with the theory of gravitation since Newton's day . . . If it is sustained that Einstein's reasoning holds good . . . then it is the result of one of the highest achievements of human thought.[7]

He then added "I have to confess that no one has yet succeeded in stating in clear language what the theory of Einstein really is." Thompson then allegedly turned to the portrait of Isaac Newton hanging in the hall and said; "Forgive us, Sir Isaac, your universe has been overturned."[8]

The Times of London covered the Eddington announcement in its November 7, 1919 edition.[9] Sandwiched between two articles on page 12 — the price of New Zealand Mutton and the US embargo of bunker coal — was the small headline: "Revolution in Science. Einstein *vs* Newton". *The New York Times* picked up the story the following day. It soon spread to newspapers around the world.

Einstein found himself inundated with requests from the (mostly) adoring public. He was both irritated and intrigued by this sudden world-wide fame. The consummate loner found not even he could resist all the attention.

> Since the flood of newspaper articles, I have been so swamped with questions, invitations, challenges, that I dream I am burning in Hell . . . This world is a curious madhouse . . . I feel now something like a whore. Everybody wants to know what I am doing.[10]
>
> Albert Einstein

Over the following years, Einstein attended public events celebrating his new theory in Europe, the United States, and the Far East. In venue after venue, there was the irreverent, informal, "genius of our age" entertaining a huge crowd with his quick wit and self-effacing charm. This celebrity status fed his ego, but spoiled the privacy he so needed to concentrate on his work.

> With fame I become more and more stupid, which of course is a very common phenomenon.[11]
>
> Albert Einstein

The public had embraced Einstein as "the new Copernicus", as Max Planck had foretold. But the scientific community was not so sure. Some questioned the accuracy of Eddington's experiment, including the poor quality of star images and measurement issues. American astronomer and Lick Observatory director William Wallace Campbell, in particular, was "not impressed with the British results."[12]

Determined to do a more accurate measurement, Campbell led a team to desolate Wallal in the Kimberley region of Western Australia for the solar eclipse of September 21, 1922.[13] With improved telescopes, Campbell recorded star positions on four photographic plates, with between 62 and 85 stars each. Measurements indicated an average displacement of *1.72 ± 0.11 arc seconds* — in very close agreement with the Einstein's prediction. A second set of plates from a University of Toronto team got similar results, but with less accuracy.

Just as the 1919 eclipse had rallied the public, the 1922 results united most scientists behind the validity of Einstein's new theory of general relativity.[14]

Modern radio interferometry has since provided even more accurate verification. In a 1975 experiment, physicists obtained a value of *1.75 ± 0.019 arc seconds*.[15] In 2005 astrophysicist Edward Fomalont and his colleagues — using the Very Long Baseline Array (VLBA) and four distant quasars — confirmed Einstein's prediction to within an accuracy of three-hundredths of one percent.[16]

Thus, we are faced with compelling evidence that the world is not at all as we had believed. Space *is* "curved". Time *is* "curved". The verification of this so-called spacetime curvature is seen in the bending of light by stellar objects, precisely as predicted by Albert Einstein.

Now let's consider another prediction of Einstein's — one of the strangest and most difficult to accept.

That Spinning Feeling

Einstein's Law of General Covariance extended his Principle of Relativity from uniform motion to any and all kinds of motion. It says the laws of physics are the same in *any* frame of reference.

Perhaps you are thinking, "Physics should be the same no matter what your point of view. So what's the big deal?" It turns out it is a very big deal. The compliance of general relativity to this principle requires a fundamental shift in how we view space and time — and results in a most profound prediction.

Let us consider a famous thought experiment called "Newton's bucket" (based on a discussion in Brian Greene's book, *The Fabric of the Cosmos*).[17]

Fill a bucket with water, place it on a turntable, and start the turntable spinning. The water doesn't do much at first. But soon the friction between the water and the walls of the rotating bucket cause the water to spin along with the bucket. The water begins to climb up the sides of the bucket and a depression forms in the center. The surface of the spinning water is now concave.

Isaac Newton used this experiment to defend his notion that space is "absolute". "What is the bucket rotating with respect to?" he asked. His answer: "With respect to absolute space."

Einstein says there is no such thing as absolute space. He tells us we would see the same concave water surface whether we choose a frame of reference on the ground or on the bucket. His Law of General Covariance requires that either perspective predicts the same results.

Let's look at things from each point of view to see what Einstein is saying here.

The Ground Reference Frame — Imagine Little Miss Muffet sitting on her tuffet at rest on the ground. From her perspective the bucket and water are rotating. As a result, the water surface inside the bucket is concave. (See Fig. 15.2(a).)

The Bucket Reference Frame — Imagine Tom Thumb sitting on the side of the bucket. From his perspective, the bucket and water inside it are

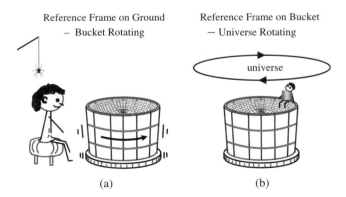

Figure 15.2. Any Reference Frame Will Do. (*a*) *Miss Muffet on ground sees bucket rotating. This rotation causes the water to become concave.* (*b*) *To Tom Thumb sitting on the bucket; it and the water is at rest, and the rest of universe is rotating. But the water surface is concave in either case.*

stationary — and *the rest of the world is rotating*. But from his point of view, Tom still sees the water inside the bucket form a concave surface. (see Fig. 15.2(b).)

How? From Tom's perspective, from his reference frame, the bucket and the water are *stationary* and the rest of the universe is rotating. So what makes the water surface concave?

We have another question. Tom also feels his body being pushed away from the center of the bucket. But if the bucket is stationary, what is producing this outward force on Tom's body?

Newton would say, "That's my point." Obviously, the bucket is rotating. And so is the water. That is why its surface is concave. That's also why Tom feels an outward push. You can't just use any reference frame like Tom's on the bucket. You have to use Miss Muffet's reference frame. Why? Because it is the one where the physics makes sense, where the equations represent what is actually happening. It is a special reference frame — one which is stationary with respect to absolute space.[a]

But per Einstein's Law of General Covariance, any and all reference frames are equally valid. This means there is no special point of view, that Tom Thumb's reference frame on the bucket is just as valid as Miss Muffet's.

So the question we have for Einstein is: Would the water surface still be concave if the bucket is really "stationary" and the rest of the universe is truly rotating around it?

I mean if the bucket is not moving in any way, is just sitting there — but all the rest of the universe is somehow made to rotate in the other direction around the bucket — will the water in the bucket still be concave? After all, that's what it looks like from Tom Thumb's point of view.

Sounds ridiculous, doesn't it. Have we finally trapped Einstein? Have we at last ensnared him in his own logic? Well, no, the master once again manages to escape what appears to be an inescapable conundrum. The explanation is nothing short of bizarre.

Einstein's gravitational field equations indeed say that in Tom's case, *the rotation of the rest of the universe* causes the water surface to become concave! So, per general relativity, the water surface is concave in both Miss Muffet's and in Tom Thumb's reference frame.

How? Through a prediction of general relativity called *frame dragging*.[18]

---

[a] Again the effects of the rotational and orbital motion of Earth are negligible, so are ignored here.

Frame Dragging

In 1918, Austrian physicists Joseph Lense and Hans Thirring used general relativity to make a most unusual prediction: since objects warp space and time, a rotating object *drags* space and time around with it — like a spinning stone in a bucket of syrup.[19]

Imagine a massive rotating object, a huge hollow sphere (a shell).[20] Newton would say rotation of the sphere in empty space has no effect on things near the sphere. But the particles which make up this rotating hollow sphere are moving through space, and particles moving through space have momentum — which per Einstein is a source of spacetime curvature or gravity. The equations of general relativity show space and time or spacetime inside and outside the hollow sphere are *dragged* by the rotational motion of the sphere. In other words, just as neighboring spacetime is warped by an object's momentum, *it is made to rotate by an object's rotating momentum.*

As a result, space inside and outside the hollow sphere starts to spin in the same direction as the sphere. So if, for example, we place a bucket filled with water inside the rotating sphere, the spinning sphere will exert a force on the stationary water. This in turn will cause the water surface to form a concave shape.

And here's the most amazing part. Calculations show for a hollow sphere with mass-energy on par with that contained in the universe, frame dragging produces the same concave water surface as when the universe is stationary and the bucket is rotating. So it does not matter whether you think the bucket is spinning inside a stationary universe or the universe is spinning around a stationary bucket — the results are the same![21]

The next time you decide to spin around, remember in your personal frame of reference, you are stationary. From your point of view, that dizzy feeling you feel is caused by the spinning of the mass-energy of the rest of the universe.

That is the power of Einstein's Law of General Covariance — any reference frame *will* do!

Is Frame Dragging Real?

Frame-dragging effects are extremely small within our solar system, thus extremely difficult to measure. Physicists, nonetheless, now have tantalizing evidence in support of frame-dragging.

In 2004, the Gravity Probe B satellite was launched in orbit some 400 miles above the Earth. The goal: to measure both spacetime curvature due to the Earth's mass-energy and frame-dragging due to Earth's rotation. In December 2008, the GP-B team reported spacetime curvature measurements — the so-called geodetic effect — agreed with general relativity to within five-tenths of one percent.

After several more years of painstaking data analysis, the team announced the results of the much more difficult frame-dragging experiment in May of 2011.[22] General relativity predicts a drift of on-board gyroscopes of a mere **0.0392** arc seconds per year due to frame-dragging from Earth's spin. The average measured value from GP-B was **0.0372** arc seconds per year **± 0.0072** arc seconds. This agreed with Einstein's prediction to within a statistical uncertainty of about 18%.

Not great accuracy, but still a most remarkable result considering the extraordinary accuracy required to measure such a miniscule effect. It verifies once again that Einstein's wild universe is our universe — *empty space itself* does indeed rotate in sympathy with a distant spinning object.

More Cosmic Marvels

General relativity predicts the existence of other strange wonders, such as gravitational lensing and gravity waves. Let's take a look:

Gravitational Lensing

Consider a far-away quasar. Say a massive galaxy is between the quasar and us here on the Earth. The galaxy in the foreground hides the distant quasar in the background, sort of like a cosmic "eclipse".

But according to general relativity, light from the distant quasar is *bent* by the intervening galaxy's spacetime curvature (gravity), just like starlight is bent as it passes near to the Sun.[23] As a result, this quasar light curves around the intervening galaxy, producing strange optical effects as seen from Earth. Examples of this cosmic optical illusion — so-called *gravitational lensing* — are shown in Fig. 15.3.

On the left side of the figure is gravitational lens B1938+666. Here the background galaxy and foreground "lensing galaxy" are precisely aligned with Earth's line-of-sight. As a result, light from the background galaxy is distorted into a nearly perfect giant ring around the foreground massive galaxy. The effect is called an Einstein Ring.

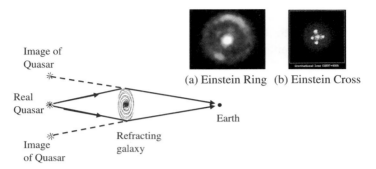

Figure 15.3. Gravitational Lensing. *As viewed from Earth:* (a) *Distant galaxies form a ring of light around intervening galaxy.* (b) *Intervening spiral galaxy produces multiple images of same quasar.*

When the alignment is not perfect, multiple images of the background object can be formed. In gravitational lens G2237+0305 (see right side of Fig. 15.3), a quasar is some eight billion light-years from Earth. Due to the intervening lensing galaxy some 400 million light years away, four images of this *same* quasar are seen on Earth. This effect is called an Einstein Cross.

Gravitational Waves

In 1916, Einstein discovered something in his equations of general relativity which Newton hadn't thought of in his wildest dreams — gravity *radiates*. Ripples in spacetime propagate at the speed of light through otherwise empty space. Einstein called these ripples *gravitational waves*.

Einstein's mathematics showed any accelerating mass — with the exception of an object in spherically or cylindrically symmetric motion — produces gravity waves. Gravity waves are not waves which travel through spacetime, they are *"waves of the spacetime fabric itself!"*[24]

Gravity waves alternately squeeze and stretch objects as they pass through them. (See Fig. 15.4.)[25] Why don't we notice this effect? Because spacetime is such a stiff medium. Even though gravity waves carry significant energy, the amount of squeezing and stretching they produce is way too small for us to perceive.

We live in the pioneering age of gravity wave exploration. A number of extreme sensitivity sensors have been built in an attempt to do what has never been done before: detect gravity waves directly. Among these are LIGO in the US, VIRGO in Italy, and Germany's GEO. A number of

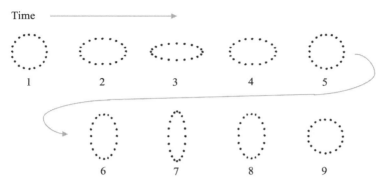

Figure 15.4. Gravity Wave Time Sequence. *A circle of ball-bearings (test masses) is in a plane transverse to the direction of propagation. As gravity waves pass through, the ball-bearing configuration is squeezed and stretched, becoming elliptical in one direction then elliptical in another.*

other state-of-the-art instruments are now or soon to be operational all across the globe.

Why bother?[26] Besides confirming yet another prediction of general relativity, these sensors promise to give us a deeper understanding of binary star systems, supernova explosions, and black holes — as well as greater insight into the creation of the universe itself. What new wonders await us if and when we detect the *cosmic gravity wave background* created just an instant after the big bang?[27]

Now let's take a look at what Stephen Hawking called "the most mysterious objects in the universe" — black holes.[28]

Where Time Stands Still

The detailed mathematics of Einstein's field equations are quite complex and well beyond the scope of this book — not to mention the abilities of the author. A remarkably simpler representation of Einstein's general theory was developed by a German army lieutenant who also just happened to be a renowned astrophysicist.

At the advent of World War I, Karl Schwarzschild — a 41-year-old German-Jewish father of three — volunteered for service in the Imperial German Army.[29] Assigned to an artillery unit in Russia, in late 1915 Schwarzschild managed to obtain copies of Einstein's Prussian Academy lectures on his new theory of general relativity. Just two short months later, Schwarzschild sent Einstein a letter in which he proposed the first *exact solution* to Einstein's field equations.

> *I had not expected that one could formulate the exact solution of the problem in such a simple way.*[30]
>
> Albert Einstein

Schwarzschild used an approach echoing Newton. To simplify things, he assumed that all of the mass-energy of a stellar object like the Sun was concentrated in a point at its center, like Newton's center of mass method. But there was a problem. Schwarzschild's solution showed that, as astrophysicist John Gribbin put it, "any mass concentrated into a single point distorts spacetime so much that space closes up around the mass and pinches it off from the rest of the universe."[31]

Schwarzschild found this so-called "pinching off" extends to a spherical region — with the point mass at its center. Within this region, *nothing can escape to the outside world*. And the more mass-energy concentrated at the center point, the greater the size of its surrounding pinch-off sphere.

Karl Schwarzschild had inadvertently discovered the mathematical basis for what John Archibald Wheeler later dubbed a "black hole".[32]

What is a black hole? Let's look at the simplest example: a non-spinning, uncharged black hole. At its center is an infinitesimally small point called a *singularity*. General relativity says this strange singularity possesses *infinite* mass-energy density and *infinite* spacetime curvature.[b]

What does this mean? When you get infinity for answers, it means the equations have broken down. They don't work. General relativity — our current best theory of gravity — simply cannot tell us what happens at the very center of a black hole. (For this we need new physics.)

Whatever it is, the so-called singularity is surrounded by the pinch-off sphere — a one-way spherical barrier to the outside world called the *event horizon*.[33] Any spacetime event that is inside this sphere cannot be observed by the outside world. Nothing, not even light can escape from within this event horizon. It is called a horizon, because like the horizon on Earth, we cannot see beyond it. (See Fig. 15.5.)

Why is a black hole *black*? Because this ultimate source of gravity produces the ultimate gravitational red-shift. The frequency of all light inside the black hole's event horizon is stretched to zero! (See Fig. 15.6.)

---

[b] A *finite* amount of mass-energy is concentrated within a singularity's infinitesimally small volume, producing an infinite amount of mass-energy density and spacetime curvature..

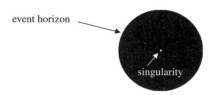

event horizon

singularity

Figure 15.5. Non-spinning Black Hole. *All the mass of a non-spinning black hole is concentrated in a single point called a "singularity" (not visible to the outside world). The spherical boundary around the singularity is called the "event horizon". Nothing, not even light, can escape from inside the event horizon.*

What does this imply for time? As we discussed, the regular up and down movement of a light beam's electromagnetic wave is a kind of clock. So a light frequency of zero implies zero time. Thus, as seen from far away, *time is frozen* at the event horizon of a black hole!

All this may sound like science-fiction to you. If so, you are in good company. Both Einstein and Schwarzschild felt black holes were a mathematical construct with no physical meaning. Were they right? In other words:

Are Black Holes Real?

According to modern cosmology, a stellar black hole forms when a star roughly some 20 times the mass of the Sun or greater runs out of nuclear fuel. The heat and outward pressure from its dying nuclear furnace is no longer able to stave off the inward crush of its own gravity. As a result, the

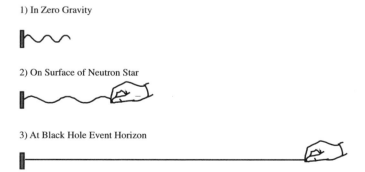

1) In Zero Gravity

2) On Surface of Neutron Star

3) At Black Hole Event Horizon

Figure 15.6. The "Hand" of Spacetime Curvature. *Light inside the event horizon of a black hole is stretched to zero frequency.*

243

giant star implodes, its core collapses, and its outer layers rebound in the shock wave to produce a spectacular supernova explosion.

If the remaining core's mass is between 1.4 and 2 times the mass of the Sun, a neutron star is formed. But if the core's mass is greater than 2 solar masses (the exact value is uncertain), a black hole is created.[34]

In black hole formation, the imploding star's crushing gravity is so great it's core overcomes all atomic and nuclear forces and undergoes a "never-ending collapse" to form an infinitesimally small point — a singularity.[35] At least that's what general relativity and quantum mechanics tell us.

So where are these black holes? It is impossible with current technology to see a stellar black hole directly. It's like trying to locate a far-away tiny black disc against a black sky. So how do astronomers find evidence for something they cannot see?

Consider a bathtub with an *invisible* drain hole filled with soapy water. How can you tell whether this invisible drain is open or closed? By observing the motion of the soap bubbles, the swirling of the water, and the movement of your Rubber Ducky — especially near the drain. They all circle around the unseen drain and fall into this spacetime curvature "gravity well". So *indirectly*, you know the drain is open.

Similarly, a number of modern astronomical observations show compelling evidence — albeit indirect — for the existence of black holes. They include (1) the motion of neighboring stellar gases and dust particles as they rush towards the invisible hole, (2) the telltale high-energy EM radiation these extremely fast moving stellar materials give off, and (3) the ultrahigh speeds of nearby stars as they orbit these massive unseen objects.

The most dramatic evidence for black holes is within so-called quasi-stellar radio sources or *quasars*. A single quasar typically radiates more light than billions of stars. They are powered by supermassive black holes billions of times the mass of the Sun. Where are such formidable beasts found? At the center of massive galaxies formed when the universe was very young.

And, unlike Schwarzschild's idealized black hole, these black holes *spin*. Why? Because they retain the angular momentum of the matter that formed them. Like a spinning ice skater pulling her arms in, matter spins faster and faster as it collapses to form a black hole.

A spinning black hole also causes neighboring space to spin around the hole per *frame-dragging*.[36] This in turn makes in-falling material rotate around the hole to form a "thick, hot doughnut of gas" called an *accretion disc*. The material within the accretion disc spins so fast — typically millions of miles an hour — that its internal friction produces tremendous heat. Great twisting magnetic fields accelerate this hot material outward, generating enormous *jets* of matter perpendicular to the disc which blast into space at nearly the speed of light.

Figure 15.7 shows just such a black hole jet produced by an ultraluminous quasar found in the constellation Virgo. From the measured distance to the quasar (redshift) and the amount of light we receive here on Earth, astrophysicists calculate this quasar has a seemingly impossible energy output of *trillions* of times the luminosity of our Sun.[37] That means it is *100 times brighter* than all the stars in the Milky Way combined.

If we had X-ray vision like Superman, recent sky surveys by NASA's Chandra X-ray telescope and others tell us above the Earth's atmosphere we would see millions upon millions of points of light in the heavens — a dazzling ultra-high-energy glow from material falling into supermassive black holes at the centers of distant galaxies.[38]

How many black holes are out there?[39] NASA astrophysicists estimate each galaxy typically has one super-massive black hole at its center and some 100 million stellar black holes. Since there are well over 100 billion galaxies in our visible universe, this says there are more than 10,000,000,000,000,000,000 or ten billion billion black holes in our observable universe.

Strange stuff? Well, it's about to get even stranger. Let's look at another wild phenomenon predicted by general relativity: a "wormhole".

Wormholes and Embedding Diagrams

To help us picture a wormhole, let's first look at what physicists call an *embedding diagram*.

Quasar 3C 273 and its jet

Figure 15.7. Observation of a Black Hole Jet. *From the black hole within quasar 3C 273 recorded by the ESO New Technology Telescope at La Silla, Chile.*

245

Consider two points connected by a straight line in one-dimensional space. (See Fig. 15.8(a).) Say we place a stellar object like the Sun between the two points. Einstein tells us the space between the two points is now warped or curved — that is the *distance* between these same two points is *stretched* due to the presence of the Sun (as seen from far away).

How are we to show this increase in distance, this so-called space curvature? One way is to draw a *curved* line between the two points, as in Fig. 15.8(b). The line from point A to point B is now longer. This is because the distance between point A and point B is longer due to the curvature of space, due to the presence of the Sun.

The line does not really curve down. It curves into a fictitious mathematical space called *hyperspace*. So we have one dimension of real space and one dimension of hyperspace. This is an example of an embedding diagram. (We could have shown the line curving up — the direction makes no difference.)

The Sun Embedding Diagram in 3D — Now let's extend this diagram to *two* dimensions of real space, with a third dimension of hyperspace. Without the Sun present, uncurved space would be a flat sheet. But the Sun's presence distorts neighboring space, as shown in Fig. 15.9. This illustration depicts the Schwarzschild solution of general relativity's field equations for an idealized Sun — one which is perfectly round, uniformly distributed, non-rotating, and uncharged.

Imagine a huge circle surrounding this idealized Sun in the figure. How does the Sun's presence affect this circle? Distances in space *parallel* to the Sun's surface (tangential) are unaffected by the Sun's presence. Thus the *circumference* of the circle remains the same.

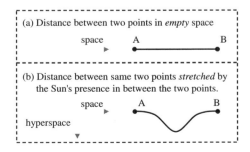

Figure 15.8. Embedding Diagram in 2D. *How to show increase in distance (curvature of space) due to presence of mass-energy.*

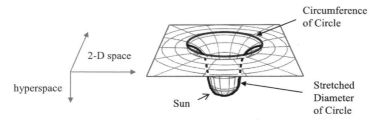

Figure 15.9. Embedding Diagram in 3D - Circle in Space with Sun at Center. *Diameter of circle is longer due to stretching of space by Sun's mass-energy. Circumference is unaffected. Ratio is not equal to Pi. (Effect exaggerated.)*

But distances in space *perpendicular* to the Sun's surface (radial) are affected. They are in fact stretched by the Sun's mass-energy. Thus the *diameter* of the circle is larger due to this stretching of space (as seen from far away). So when we divide the circumference of the circle by this stretched diameter, we get a value *smaller* than Pi. The space surrounding the Sun is non-Euclidean.

General relativity predicts the Sun's *diameter* is some 2.5 miles (4 km) *longer* due to the stretching of space.[40] For the much less massive Earth, its diameter is stretched by little less than a tenth of an inch (2.2 mm).

Now let's look at what a non-rotating black hole does to space.

Black Hole Embedding Diagram in 3D - General relativity has "an extra version of spacetime" built into its equations.[41] This suggests spacetime inside a black hole opens up into a throat or "wormhole". And this so-called wormhole may be a gateway into some other spacetime point in our universe.

The black hole Schwarzschild embedding diagram in Fig. 15.10 implies that if an astronaut were somehow able to survive the crushing gravity of a black hole and travel through its wormhole, she would end up in a different place and time in our universe — or, as some physicists suggest, a *different universe!*[42]

But before we go out and buy a ticket for a ride through a wormhole, we must consider that the collapse of a star is more complicated than Schwarzschild's idealized model — its spin for example. University of Colorado physics professor Andrew Hamilton tells us "when a *realistic* star collapses to a black hole, it does not produce a wormhole."[43]

And analysis by eminent relativist Roger Penrose says even if a Schwarzschild wormhole were somehow formed, it would still be impossible to travel through it to another universe. Why? Because EM radiation

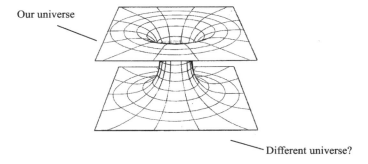

Our universe

Different universe?

Figure 15.10. **Black Hole Embedding Diagram** *The extra version of spacetime built into the equations of general relativity indicates a throat or "wormhole".*

and quantum effects are accelerated so enormously by the black hole they "destroy the little closed universe."[44] (Not to mention the astronaut.)

What kill-joys. I so wanted to visit another universe.

Creation

Of all the revelations of general relativity, perhaps the most profound is our current understanding that the universe had a *finite* beginning in time and space. What exactly is this cosmological event which created our universe, this so-called "big bang"? And what caused it? Is our universe really expanding as a result? If so, what is it expanding into? And what are dark matter and dark energy? Do they determine the future of our universe?

These cosmic issues are addressed in the next and final chapter.

Chapter 16

In the Beginning

In the beginning God created the heavens and the earth.[1]

Genesis 1.1

In the beginning were only Tepeu and Gucumatz. These two sat together and thought, and whatever they thought came into being.

Mayan Creation Story

In the beginning the earth was a bare plain. All was dark. There was no life, no death. The sun, the moon, and the stars slept beneath the earth.

Australian Aboriginal: *The Dreamtime*

In the beginning there was only darkness, water, and the great god Bumba

Boshongo, *Bantu tribe of Central Africa*

Peering into the night sky on a clear night, the stars shimmering like jewels against the blackness of space, we find ourselves asking: How did we get here? Was the universe always as it appears today? What is its future? In this chapter we discuss these profound questions based on the first *scientifically* substantiated theory on the origin, structure, and evolution of the universe — the big bang theory.

The development of this theory involves a cast of characters even a Hollywood writer could not dream up — an unpaid lab assistant, a former law student and Spanish teacher, a former janitor, a brilliant Russian mathematician, a Catholic priest, a jokester physicist, and of course, a former patent clerk named Albert Einstein. This is their story.

Cosmic Discoveries

In 1917, Einstein tried to model the entire universe with his new theory of general relativity.[2] From astronomical data at the time, he estimated the overall mass-energy density of the universe. With this as input, he used general relativity to calculate the overall spacetime curvature of the universe. (In those days, the known universe consisted of only our Milky Way galaxy.)

The results troubled him deeply. His equations said a universe which contains mass-energy cannot stay the same size — it has to either expand or contract. This is similar to throwing a ball into the air.[3] It can move upward or come back down, but cannot remain in a fixed position.

This idea of a "non-static" universe ran contrary to prevailing beliefs. Scientists at the time, including Einstein, thought our universe had existed for all time — that it had always been the same size in the infinite past and will always be the same size in the infinite future.

Without observational evidence to the contrary, Einstein refused to believe what his own equations were telling him. So he added what has been called the most famous "fudge factor" in the history of physics: the *cosmological constant*. With this added term, his equations now modeled a static universe.

The revised Einstein Equation became[4]:

Curvature Tensor + cosmological constant = a constant times the Momenergy Tensor

Mathematically, in the shorthand of tensor notation, this is:

$$G_{ab} + \Lambda g_{ab} = K\, T_{ab}$$

where

G_{ab} *is again the Curvature Tensor,*
Λ *is the cosmological constant,*
g_{ab} *is the Metric Tensor,*
K *is again the constant* $8\pi\, G/c^4$ *where G is the gravitational constant, and*
T_{ab} *is again the Momenergy Tensor.*

What did this so-called cosmological constant do? It added an *outward pressure* term to Einstein's field equations to balance the inward squeeze of spacetime curvature (gravity). Einstein cleverly chose a value for the cosmological constant so the net result was a balanced universe, neither contracting nor expanding, but static. And its small value didn't affect our solar system — it only became significant over vast astronomical distances.[5]

Einstein's brilliant fudge factor had "fixed" his equations — a step he would come to regret.

A Cosmic Yardstick

Let's wind the clock back to 1895. The same year 16-year-old Albert Einstein imagined riding a light beam in Italy, a young woman named Henrietta Swan Leavitt was hired as a "computer" at the Harvard College Observatory in Cambridge, Massachusetts. Her tedious job was to count the number of star images on photographic plates. Amongst the stars she recorded were *Cepheid variables*. These are supergiant stars whose brightness varies over time — they pulsate at regular intervals, typically from a few days to a few months.

Leavitt noticed a pattern, a correlation between a star's brightness and its frequency of pulsation: the brighter a Cepheid variable was the slower it pulsated. She published her findings in 1908, but received almost no credit for this accomplishment during her lifetime.

Before Leavitt's discovery, astronomers used *parallax* to determine star distance.[6] Telescopic images of the same star were taken at different times, typically six months apart. From the distance between the two Earth positions and the measured angles to the star, astronomers could calculate the distance to the star. This geometric triangulation method was accurate for star distances to around a hundred light-years.

In 1913, Danish astronomer Ejnar Hertzsprung calibrated "Leavitt's Law."[7] Too far away to use the parallax method, he determined rough distances to thirteen Cepheid variables with an ingenious method. Hertzsprung estimated each star's overall velocity from its blueshift or redshift. Then he examined star atlases to determine how fast each star had moved across the sky over the years, at right angles to Earth's line of sight.

A star *appears* to be moving faster across the sky the closer it is, and slower the farther away it is. (Just like an airplane up close appears to be roaring across the sky, while one far away seems to be progressing slowly.) Using this approach, Hertzsprung estimated the approximate distance to each Cepheid variable star — calibrating Leavitt's frequency-brightness relationship.

Now, by measuring *any* Cepheid's period of oscillation and apparent brightness, astronomers could determine its true brightness and thus its approximate distance from Earth. How does this work? A star's *apparent* brightness — how bright it appears to be in our telescopes — drops off as the square of its distance from us. Its *true* brightness or luminosity is how much light it actually gives off at its source. By comparing a Cepheid's apparent brightness (from observation) to its actual or true brightness (from its observed blinking rate and Leavitt's Law), astronomers could determine how far away it is.

This new "standard candle" for Cepheid variable stars extended astronomical distance measurements to some 10 million light-years!

Hubble's Breakthrough

Again, most astronomers at the time believed our Milky Way galaxy was the entire universe. They did see a number of faint spiral-shaped objects in their telescopes. What exactly were these so-called *nebulae*? Were they interstellar dust or perhaps the beginnings of new solar systems? Surely they were objects inside our galaxy.

Not all agreed. American astronomers Heber Curtis, Vesto Slipher, and others proposed the controversial notion that these nebulae were "island universes" — independent galaxies beyond our Milky Way.[8]

In 1924, American astronomer Edwin Hubble — former athlete, law student, Spanish teacher, and Rhodes Scholar — pointed California's new 100-inch Hooker Telescope on Mount Wilson at a faint spiral-shaped "nebula" called Andromeda. (See Fig. 16.1.) The largest telescope in the world at the time revealed individual stars on the outer edges of what most thought was just a collection of interstellar dust.

Some stars were Cepheid variables![9] Using Leavitt's frequency-brightness relationship, Hubble determined the distance to these stars in Andromeda. He found they were over a million light-years away. But the Milky Way galaxy is only about a hundred-thousand light-years across. Hubble concluded Andromeda cannot be inside our Milky Way galaxy. (Modern observations put the distance to the Andromeda galaxy at some 2.5 million light-years from Earth.)

Hubble then searched for Cepheid variable stars in other nebulae. Distance calculations showed these nebulae were also too far away to be

Figure 16.1. Edwin Hubble (1889–1953). *Discovered that the universe is filled with other galaxies beyond our own Milky Way galaxy.*

part of the Milky Way. He concluded Curtis and Slipher were right — these nebulae were *other galaxies.*

Just as Copernicus had shown we are not at the center of the universe, Hubble showed we live inside just one of what we now know to be over several hundred billion galaxies in our observable universe.

Friedmann's Dynamic Universe

In 1922 — the same year the Soviet Union was established — Russian mathematician Alexander Friedmann published his own set of cosmic solutions to Einstein's field equations of general relativity. They revealed a universe which, as mathematician Ari Belenkiy put it, "can expand, contract, collapse, and might even be born in a singularity."[10] In other words, Friedmann raised the possibility of a *dynamic* universe, one which changes in size over time.

What was Einstein's reaction? He called Friedmann's non-stationary world "suspicious."[11] He later retracted his comments, but still felt Friedmann's solutions held no physical meaning.

Alexander Friedmann died from typhoid fever in 1925 at age 37. He never lived to see evidence for the expansion of the universe. Nor did he live to learn of Arthur Eddington's proof that Einstein's static universe solution is unstable.

Lemaître

Enter Abbé Georges Lemaître, a Roman Catholic priest from Belgium — who also happened to be a professor of physics at the Catholic University of Leuven and a former pupil of Eddington.[12] Unaware of Friedmann's work, Lemaître independently came up with his own more limited dynamic solution to Einstein's field equations. In 1927, he published his findings in an obscure Belgian journal in French.

From his model, Lemaître proposed — as Willem de Sitter had suggested — that a linear relationship exists between a galaxy's distance and its redshift. What does this mean? It says that in general, the further away a galaxy is, the greater its light is shifted towards the red end of the spectrum (lower frequency).

What causes this shift? Lemaître argued that on its long journey to the Earth, a galaxy's light is stretched in frequency *by the expansion of space itself*. The longer the light's journey, the more the universe has expanded — thus the greater the light is stretched or redshifted.

Lemaître backed up his theory with empirical evidence.[13] He showed a correlation existed between *galaxy redshift* observations recorded by astronomers Vesto Slipher and Gustaf Strömberg and Hubble's *galaxy distance* measurements. The data showed the further away a galaxy is, the greater its observed redshift, just as Lemaître's theory predicted. The Abbé had made a most profound discovery: the universe is expanding.

That same year, Einstein was in Brussels to attend the prestigious Solvay Conference. The excited Lemaître collared the great physicist to explain his model. Einstein responded: "Your calculations are correct, but your grasp of physics is abominable."[14] (See Fig. 16.2.)

Two years later, Edwin Hubble — who, like most scientists, had not read Lemaître's paper — began his own investigation of galaxy redshift

Figure 16.2.   Fr. Georges Lemaitre & Albert Einstein.

and distance.[15] He determined distances to 24 galaxies while astronomer Milton Humason examined redshifts. A former mule driver with an eighth grade education, Humason had started out as a janitor at the Observatory and had worked his way up to become Hubble's assistant.

Hubble published their findings in a landmark 1929 paper. The data showed a general trend: distance to a far-away galaxy is proportional to its redshift. Ignorant of Lemaître's precedence, astronomers labeled the relationship "Hubble's Law".

Based on Lemaître and Hubble's compelling evidence, Einstein later said he had made the biggest blunder of his life.[16] His fudge factor, the cosmological constant, was unnecessary. Had he stuck to his original equations, *he* could have predicted the expansion of the universe. In 1931, a humbled Einstein traveled to the top of Mount Wilson and personally thanked Edwin Hubble for "delivering him from folly."[17]

Mathematically, Hubble's Law (non-relativistic) is given by[18]:

Recession Velocity = Hubble's constant times distance to galaxy
$V = H_0 \times d$

where

$H_0 = 67.15 \pm 2 \ km/sec/Mpc$, *and*
$V = z \ c$ *(where z is the red-shift and c is the speed of light)*

Thus a galaxy far away is moving away from us at a velocity which is equal to Hubble's constant times the distance to that galaxy.

Where the recession velocity is a significant percentage of the speed of light (relativistic), Hubble's Law becomes:

$$V = [\ (z+1)^2 - 1 \ ] \ c \ / \ [\ (z - 1)^2 - 1 \ ]$$

Our Expanding Universe

Does everything in the universe expand?[19] Not quite. The expansion of space only affects distances between *galaxy clusters*. These concentrations of some tens to hundreds of galaxies are held together by mutual gravity, with vast amounts of almost empty space between each cluster.

The expansion force is weak. It is easily offset by gravity within a galaxy cluster. So space is not expanding where we are inside the Milky Way galaxy, inside our Local Group cluster. The expansion force only becomes significant over the huge astronomical distances between clusters — where the expansion of the universe takes place.

But what is the universe expanding into? The answer is as strange as any in relativity. According to Einstein, the universe contains *all* space-time, that is all space and all time. Therefore the universe "is not expanding into anything."[20]

Per general relativity, the expansion of the universe is a "metrical" expansion.[21] This means the local distance between two points in space far away from galaxies or clusters of galaxies increases over time. Imagine two ball bearings at rest with respect to each other in this "empty" space. As time goes by, the two objects drift apart. But they themselves are not in motion. It is the local distance or space between the two points which is constantly stretching — an effect inherent to space itself.

Faster than Light?

Wait a second. Isn't there something amiss here? Per Hubble's law, as the distance to a galaxy increases, its recession speed (speed away from us) increases proportionally. So eventually won't the recession speed become greater than the speed of light? Yes. But didn't Einstein say that nothing can go faster than the speed of light? Have we finally trapped him in a logical conundrum?

No, Einstein manages to wiggle out of this one too. According to his theory of special relativity, nothing can go faster than the speed of light *through* space. But per general relativity, *space itself* has no limit as to how fast it can expand. Space can and does expand faster than the speed of light.

Galaxy clusters far enough away are indeed receding from us at speeds faster than the speed of light. But it is actually the space between these galaxy clusters which is expanding. Per Brian Greene, "galaxy (clusters), on average, hardly move through space at all. Their motion is due almost completely to the stretching of space itself." And this stretching of space has no speed limit.[22]

Now let's look at the implications of the expansion of the universe on its creation.

The Cosmic Egg

In 1927, Einstein introduced Lemaître to Friedmann's dynamic universe papers. Four years later, the Belgian priest proposed the universe began as a "single quantum".[23] If the universe has been continually expanding, it must have been smaller and smaller in the past. Thus it must have had a finite beginning. "We could conceive the beginning of the universe in the form of a unique atom," wrote Lemaître, "the atomic weight of which is the total mass of the universe."[24]

How was Lemaître's idea received? Many physicists were suspicious of a beginning of the universe proposed by a Catholic priest. The idea was too close to the Genesis story in the Bible. To make matters worse, Pope Pius XII latched onto Lemaître's theory as confirmation of the biblical description of creation. Lemaître argued it was just a scientific theory and nothing more — neither confirming nor denying religious beliefs. He later said:

> As far as I can see, such a theory remains entirely outside any metaphysical or religious question . . . It is consonant with Isaiah speaking of the hidden God, hidden even in the beginning of the universe.[25]

> *George Lemaître*

In 1933, Lemaître and Einstein gave a series of lectures in California. Recanting his earlier objections, Einstein now called Lemaître's theory "the most beautiful and satisfactory explanation of creation to which I have ever listened."[26]

Lemaître's ideas were vindicated in 1964 with the discovery of the cosmic microwave background (CMB) — the first evidence in support of the big bang theory. His successor at Louvain, Odon Godart, told him of the discovery in 1966 while Lemaître was in Hospital Saint Pierre suffering from a heart attack.[27] The man called "the father of the big bang" died two weeks later at the age of 71.

The Big Bang

Infamous jokester Russian-American physicist George Gamow extended Lemaître's theory in 1948.[a] Gamow proposed the universe was created in a gigantic explosion, later dubbed the big bang.[28] According to Gamow, the big bang was not a bomb which exploded in the center of the universe; it was an *explosion of space itself.*

Where in the universe did this so-called big bang happen?[29] It happened here. It happened there. It happened everywhere. It happened on

---

[a] Gamow arranged for an additional physicist along with colleague Ralph Alpher to be listed as author in one of their papers — Hans Beta. The author list thus read: Alpher, Beta, Gamow, after the first three letters of the Greek alphabet, Alpha, Beta, Gamma.

the tip of your nose, it happened in China, it happened on the star Betelgeuse, it happened in the Andromeda galaxy, and on the other side of the universe. Just as there is no "center" on the surface of a balloon, there is no center of the universe. The mysterious event called the big bang was "an explosion of space which happened everywhere."[30] (This is true whether the universe is finite or infinite.)

And importantly, Gamow's brilliant collaborator, Ralph Alpher, made a *prediction* which could be measured. The theory proposed the very early universe was extremely hot and dense, and as it expanded, it cooled. Some 380,000 years after the big bang, the universe was cool enough so that atomic nuclei (protons and neutrons) could now capture electrons and form the simplest atoms — mostly hydrogen, some helium, and traces of lithium and beryllium.[31]

Photons of light could now move freely for the first time. Why? The earlier universe contained isolated protons and electrons — electrically charged particles which tend to absorb photons. Now the universe contained *neutrally-charged* atoms, which are far less likely to absorb photons. So most photons "stopped bouncing from particle to particle" and traveled freely through the cosmos.[32] These free-moving primordial photons filled the universe with high-energy light.

Alpher predicted this light should still exist today. But over the billions of years of expansion, the universe stretched the frequency of this light to a much longer wavelength — low energy microwaves.[33] Alpher and American physicist Robert Herman calculated the current temperature of this ancient light should now be some five degrees above absolute zero or **5 Kelvin**.

First Light

In 1965, American physicists Arno Penzias and Robert Wilson of Bell Labs were studying radio emissions from the Milky Way using an ultrasensitive cryogenic microwave receiver in Holmdel, New Jersey. Their instruments recorded an annoying background radio noise which they couldn't seem to get rid of. It showed up no matter where they pointed their receiver.[34]

They checked for urban noise, seasonal variations, and even residuals from a 1962 above-ground nuclear test. They removed pigeon dung from the dish, thinking maybe that was the source of the hiss. But no matter what they did, this noise seen everywhere in the sky would not go away.

Penzias and Wilson called the lab at nearby Princeton University. They were put in contact with physicist Robert Dicke, who happened to be leading a team trying to find Alpher's ancient cosmic photons. "Well boys, we've been scooped," Dicke told his colleagues.[35] Penzias and Wilson had inadvertently discovered what Dicke's team had been looking for; the residual radiation from some 380,000 years after the big bang.[36] The so-called Cosmic Microwave Background (CMB) had been found. (If you disconnect the cable from your TV, switch to antenna mode and to a channel with no signal, about 5 to 10% of the noise or snow on the screen is from the CMB.)[37]

Penzias and Wilson measured a temperature value for the CMB of a little under **3 Kelvin** — in close agreement with Alpher's original prediction of 5 Kelvin.[38] This represented the first empirical evidence for a scientific theory on the origin and evolution of our universe.[39]

Today the big bang theory is widely accepted by physicists as our best current explanation for the geometry, composition, and history of the cosmos.[40] Why? Because a number of independent measurements from vastly different observations agree with big bang theory predictions to a precision of 10% or better. This is most remarkable considering the measurement challenges for something which began some 13.8 billion years ago.[41]

Modern evidence for the big bang includes: the homogeneity of the universe, the expansion of the universe, the amount and abundance of hydrogen, helium and other light elements in our universe, the CMB and the fluctuations in the CMB, the large scale structure of the universe, the age of stars, the evolution of galaxies, and a number of other more esoteric measurements.

OK, so evidence for the big bang is quite compelling. But what caused the big bang? This is a question we all ask. Unfortunately, no one knows. The big bang theory tells us what happened immediately after the big bang, but nothing about *time zero* itself. The equations of general relativity again break down at this singularity — giving infinity for answers. So in physics, what caused the creation of the universe or what, if anything, happened before the big bang remain open questions.[42]

Science can't tell us what happened at the very beginning of the universe (yet), but what about its future?

The Geometry and Future of the Universe[43]

As each second passes, per John Archibald Wheeler, our expanding universe adds "billions upon billions of cubic light years of space" to its volume.[44] Recall a billion light years is nearly 6 billion trillion miles or 10 billion trillion kilometers.

The great question is: Will our cosmos continue to expand forever? Or will it eventually stop expanding and remain the same size from then on? Or like a leaky balloon, will it begin to contract at some point, becoming smaller and smaller, eventually compressing all its matter and energy into a single point, a new singularity — the so-called Big Crunch. Or is there some other fate awaiting our cosmos?

According to general relativity, the future of the universe is determined by its overall mass-energy density. Why? Because this determines its overall spacetime curvature. Remarkably, in the Friedmann-Lemaître picture, there are only three possible curvatures for this overall cosmic "geometry": positive, flat, or negative.[45]

Let's look at a two dimensional analogy (Fig. 16.3). *Positive* curvature is represented by the surface of a spherical Earth.[46] Here we imagine two sail boats on the equator moving parallel to each other heading north. If they continue in the same exact direction, due to the curvature of Earth they will converge over time and eventually meet.

A plane surface represents *zero* curvature. Here if two initially parallel sail boats travel in the same exact direction, they stay the same distance apart indefinitely. A saddle-shaped surface represents *negative* curvature. Here the two initially parallel sail boats diverge — their separation increases over time.

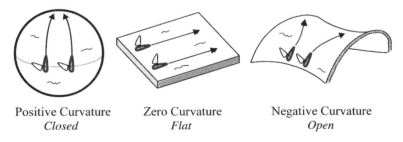

Positive Curvature
Closed

Zero Curvature
Flat

Negative Curvature
Open

Figure 16.3. The Geometry of the Universe Analogy. *Two sail boats start out parallel and never change direction. On a spherical Earth they converge over time. On a flat Earth they remain parallel. On a saddle-shaped Earth they diverge over time.*

What if we send two parallel beams of light out into the universe? If the spacetime curvature of the universe is *positive*, they will eventually meet. This is called a *closed* universe. (In this geometry, a single beam of light would eventually curve around the entire universe and return, hitting you on the back of the head!)

If universal spacetime curvature is *zero*, the two beams will remain parallel forever. This is called a *flat* universe. If spacetime curvature is *negative*, the two beams will diverge — the distance between them increasing over time. This is called an *open* configuration.

Per general relativity, this overall spacetime curvature not only determines the geometry and fate of the universe, it also tells us the extent of the universe, that is whether it is finite or infinite. This is summarized in Table 16.1.[47]

According to modern cosmological models,[48] a universal mass-energy density of about **10^{-23} grams per cubic meter** produces an overall *zero* spacetime curvature — a flat configuration. This is about five hydrogen atoms per cubic meter. Physicists label this the *critical density*. If the overall density of the universe is any greater than this critical value, its curvature is positive. If the overall density of the universe is any less than critical, its curvature is negative.

A Flat Universe?

What is the overall curvature of our universe? One place astrophysicists find the answer is in the Cosmic Microwave Background. The geometry of space affects the observed sizes of hot and cold spots within the CMB. Measurements of these variations indicate our *observable* universe is flat to

Table 16.1. **The Configuration and Future of Universe is Determined by its Overall Mass-energy Density.**

Mass-energy Density	Overall Curvature	Configuration	Size	Future of the Universe
Less than critical	Negative	Open	Infinite	Expands at same rate forever
Exactly critical (10^{-23} g/m³)	*Zero*	*Flat*	*Infinite*	*Expansion slows over time*
More than critical	Positive	Closed	Finite (but has no end)	Expansion stops and universe contracts

an accuracy of about 1%. (See Fig. 16.4.) A number of other observations also point to a flat observable universe.

How big is our observable universe?[49] Because the speed of light is finite, it takes time for light from distant stellar objects to travel across the vastness of space to Earth. We can't see anything so far away that its light has not had time to reach us here on Earth. What we can see is called the observable universe.

Recall the universe is estimated to be some 13.8 billion years old. So you'd think we could see objects close to 13.8 light-years from Earth. But because of the expansion of space, we see objects which are *now* much further away. Physicists calculate the edge of the observable universe today to be about 47 billion light-years away.

But why is our observable universe flat?[50] Why is its overall mass-energy density just the right value to give zero spacetime curvature? A smidgen higher and it's positive. An iota lower and it's negative. This seems to be a most extraordinary coincidence. The answer to this cosmic question comes from a wild theory called *inflation*.

Inflation to the Rescue

Inflation theory is a modification to the big bang theory. It proposes that a miniscule moment after the big bang, about 10^{-32} seconds after time zero, the universe expanded exponentially — more than a billion billion billion billion billion billion billion billion times over much less time than the blink of an eye.[51]

Imagine an (unbreakable) balloon suddenly expanding more than 10^{78} times in size.[52] That's 1,000,000,000,000,000,000,000,000,000,000,00

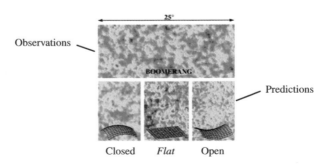

Figure 16.4. Cosmic Microwave Data (top) Versus Closed, Flat, and Open Universe Predictions (bottom). *Flat universe predictions (bottom middle) are the best match to hot and cold spot observations in the CMB. Image courtesy of NASA/JPL.*

0,000,000,000,000,000,000,000,000,000,000,000,000,000 times. Imagine you are placed on the surface of this super-colossal balloon. Like an ant in the middle of the Bonneville salt flats on curved Earth, the very small part of the overall surface you can see appears flat.

This is the idea with inflation.[53] Over an extremely brief period, space was stretched by such an enormous factor that our visible universe today is but a tiny pinpoint within a gigantic cosmos. Even though the entire universe may be curved, the *visible* universe — the part we can see — appears flat.

Since our observable universe is "flat", it should have the so-called critical value for its density. But data from the Wilkinson Microwave Anisotropy Probe (WMAP) and more recent Planck Space Telescope indicate the total mass of ordinary matter from stars and other stellar material we can see is only about **5%** of the critical density.[54] Where is the rest of the mass-energy?

Invisible Matter

In the 1930's, American physicist Fritz Zwicky made the revolutionary proposal that galaxies harbor a huge quantity of unseen matter. Based on his study of the motions of "outlying galaxies in the Coma cluster,"[55] Zwicky concluded there was not enough visible matter to hold these fast-moving galaxies together. He insisted something unseen was producing additional gravity out there in the heavens. He called it *dark matter*. But because of his penchant for radical ideas coupled with a pugnacious personality, Zwicky was generally ignored.

Over the next 30 years, evidence for dark matter began to build. In the 1970s, American astronomer Vera Rubin along with W. K. Ford and others "clinched the case" when they measured the rotations of individual galaxies.[56] They found outer stars were orbiting so fast they should be flying off into space — if nothing held them but the gravitational pull of visible stars.[57] There had to be more matter, thus more gravity, more spacetime curvature out there than could be accounted for by stars we can see.

Numerous astronomical surveys since have confirmed that stars moving within galaxies and galaxies moving within clusters of galaxies are going faster than they should. Gravitational lensing also indicates enormous amounts of invisible matter throughout the universe. Physicists

Fritz Zwicky   **Vera Rubin**

have proposed a number of exotic possibilities, but no one knows what the source of this additional gravity, this dark matter is.

The leading candidate is clusters of yet to be discovered particles dubbed Weakly Interacting Massive Particles, or WIMPs. These are "massive, slowly moving electrically neutral particles" which may interact via the weak force.[58] A number of experiments are searching for these mysterious particles. Recent data at DAMA in Italy and the SuperCDMS and CoGent in Minnesota, as well as from the Alpha Magnetic Spectrometer on the International Space Station, show hints of WIMP effects. Hopefully, more sensitive detectors coming on line soon will give us a clearer picture.

What ever dark matter is, estimates from the Planck Telescope say it accounts for about **27%** of our visible universe. So about 5% of the critical density is attributed to ordinary matter, and some 27% is made of dark matter. We are still missing some 68%.

Mysterious Energy

> *Our universe isn't just getting bigger, it's getting bigger faster,*[59]
>
> Roger Penrose

Physicists in the late 20th century believed that if the visible universe is flat; i.e., has zero overall spacetime curvature, then per cosmological models gravity should be *slowing* the expansion of the universe. What was needed was some observational data to confirm this theoretical prediction.

In 1998, two independent teams — one led by Saul Perlmutter at Lawrence Berkeley National Laboratory, the other by Brian Schmidt at the Australian National University and Adam G. Riess of the Space Telescope

Science Institute and Johns Hopkins University — searched the heavens to measure how much the expansion of the universe is being slowed by gravity. They were shocked by the results.

Upon examination of data from some 100 or so supernovae, the astrophysicists found distant supernovae were fainter than expected.[60] This meant they were further away than they should be — implying greater expansion. After careful evaluation, the two teams concluded the expansion of the universe did slow down for the first seven billion years or so after the big bang, but has been *speeding up* ever since!

Recent data from over 200 supernovae and other observations confirm the Perlmutter-Schmidt-Riess measurements: the expansion of the universe is indeed accelerating.[61] What makes expansion speed up? Physicists don't know. Many postulate our universe is filled with a kind of "repulsive energy," which University of Chicago astrophysicist Michael Turner dubbed *dark energy*. He called it "the most profound mystery in all of science."[62]

Einstein had said his cosmological constant was the greatest blunder of his life. Now a cosmological constant of much larger magnitude appears necessary to model this so-called dark energy, this accelerating expansion of the universe. It seems Einstein is such a genius that even when he makes a mistake, he turns out to be right after all — sort of.

How does dark energy work? As ordinary matter spreads out, its gravitational inward pull diminishes — but the repulsive outward *push* of the cosmological constant does not diminish with expansion. Hence the expansion slows at first, then dark energy overcomes gravity and the expansion accelerates.

And per Planck Telescope data, dark energy makes up some **68%** of the critical mass-energy density of the current visible universe. Voila! Some 5% "ordinary" matter plus some 27% dark matter plus about 68% dark energy gives us a total of around 100%.

In other words, the amount of ordinary matter, dark matter, and dark energy we measure in our observable universe adds up to an overall mass-energy density of about 10^{-23} **grams per cubic meter**, the critical density value necessary for a flat observable universe. Amazing!

Before we congratulate ourselves and break out the champagne, we have to remember, as of this writing, we still do not know what dark matter and dark energy are.

So where does this all lead us? Let's take a look.

The Future of the Universe

This is the way the world ends

This is the way the world ends

This is the way the world ends

Not with a bang but a whimper.

T. S. Eliot, *The Hollow Men*, 1925

The Sloan Digital Sky Survey has examined over 35% of the heavens and some 500 million objects to date. Over a decade's worth of data tells us that dark energy is best represented by an *unchanging* cosmological constant. If dark energy continues to behave this way in the future — a big assumption since we don't know what it is — cosmological models predict our cosmos will expand forever.[63]

Under this scenario, the most likely fate of the universe is as follows:

The expansion of the universe will continue to accelerate; until some 100 billion years from now, all but the closest galaxies will recede from us faster than the speed of light — making them impossible to see.[64] In something like a trillion years, generations of stars will have used up all the hydrogen and helium gases in the universe. With no more fuel to power them, no more stars will form, galaxies will go dim, and matter will consist of dead stars, cold planets and spent meteorites, etc.

Random collisions of stellar objects will eventually drive many stars to lower galactic orbits. As they circle black holes at the center of galaxies, they will give off even stronger gravitational waves. This loss in energy will drive stars closer and closer to black holes, ultimately to be absorbed. When our universe is about a billion billion years old, galaxies will consist of enormous black holes surrounded by dead stars.

Be not totally dismayed, my friends — there is still some hope for our universe.

The end (or the beginning?) — In an estimated 10^{97} to 10^{106} years (that's some billion billion billion billion billion billion billion billion billion billion billion years), black holes will finally evaporate due to Hawking radiation. And per Hawking's theory, during the final moments of evaporation, these black holes will perhaps become *white* holes, "pumping new matter into the universe in an unpredictable fashion."[65] So at least theoretically, our universe will continue to exist in some strange new way.

We must keep in mind, however, that predictions for the future of our universe are very much a work in progress. There are still major questions to be resolved; such as what dark matter and dark energy actually are, and whether inflation will occur again.

Future research and observations in physics have the potential to shed new light on both how the big bang came to be as well as the ultimate fate of the universe. But until our understanding of dark energy improves and/or a new theory replaces general relativity and quantum mechanics, the future of our universe remains speculative at best.

Stay tuned.

Epilogue

To punish me for my contempt for authority, fate made me an authority myself.[1]

Albert Einstein

Our story began with a young boy enthralled by a compass, a teenager pondering the nature of light. It ended with a revolution in thought which forever changed our conception of reality. Albert Einstein's struggles and triumphs along the way demonstrate that even the most brilliant among us errs, and despairs of reaching his goal — that it is persistence and strength of will even more than prodigious talent which ultimately leads to success.

The Later Years

In 1917, suffering from digestive problems and "the poor food of wartime Berlin," 38-year-old Albert Einstein experienced a near breakdown.[2] He lost 56 pounds in just two months and became so weak he could not leave his apartment. He feared he was dying of cancer; he was diagnosed with a stomach ulcer. Cousin Elsa devoted full-time to nursing Albert back to health. It took him four years to recover fully.

In February of 1919, three months after the end of World War I, Einstein was granted a divorce from Mileva Marić. Confident he would win a Nobel Prize at some point, he offered her the prize money as part of the divorce settlement. (He had been nominated for the prize nearly every year since 1910.) Mileva took the bet. Albert married Elsa four months later.[3]

Einstein finally won the Nobel Prize in physics in 1921 for the Photoelectric Effect.[4] Christopher Aurivillius, secretary of the Swedish Academy, wrote in a letter to Einstein:

> *(The Nobel Prize) is awarded . . . without taking into account the value which will be accorded your relativity and gravitation theories after these are confirmed in the future.*[5]

In awarding the prize for the Photoelectric Effect, the Nobel committee pointedly ignored Einstein's seminal achievements in special and general relativity. Why? Admittedly, the theories were strange, but no stranger than the quantization of light in the Photoelectric Effect. And evidence supporting relativity had begun to mount. According to Science historian Robert Marc Friedman, it was "an intentional snub fueled by the biases of the day; a prejudice against pacifists, Jews, and, most of all, theoretical physics."[6]

A year after winning the Nobel Prize, Einstein published his first paper on his *unified field theory*. His goal was the unification of electromagnetism and general relativity into a single theory which encompassed electricity, magnetism, light, and gravity. In this pursuit, Einstein deliberately avoided quantum mechanics — whose principles he helped found yet argued against his entire life. His stubbornness cost him. It put him for the most part outside the mainstream of modern physics and its remarkable progress.

A New Form of Matter

> *I have (read) your paper . . . It is a beautiful step forward.*[7]
>
> Albert Einstein to S. N. Bose

In 1925, literally out of the blue, Einstein made yet another major contribution to quantum theory. Indian physicist Satyendra Nath Bose had developed a statistic method for counting photons, but had trouble getting his theory published. Because Einstein had worked on the subject, Bose wrote to the famous scientist asking for help. Einstein read Bose's paper and in a brilliant stroke, surmised Bose's theory might also apply to atoms.[8] Together they had discovered a new form of matter: Bose-Einstein condensates (BEC).

In solids, liquids, and gases, each atom has a different location, each atom is separated in space from other atoms. But according to BEC theory, at extraordinary low temperatures atoms adopt the lowest energy level allowed by quantum mechanics. As a result, the atoms are not spread out in space but all occupy the same location.

In 1995, Eric Cornell and Carl Wieman at the University of Colorado NIST-JILA lab produced the first Bose-Einstein condensate gases.[9] They cooled some 2000 rubidium atoms down to an incredible 20 nanokelvin or 0.00000002 degrees above absolute zero. Microscopic observations verified that all the atoms *occupied the same place!*

Personal Difficulties

With his marriage to Elsa Löwenthal, Einstein's family troubles were far from over.[10] His relationship with his elder son was particularly rocky. Hans Albert was disturbed by his father's treatment of his mother during the divorce and his isolation afterwards. Einstein in turn was distraught by separation from his boys. He considered moving back to Zurich to be closer to them, but could not bear the thought of being in such close proximity to his first wife. Elsa, appalled by the idea, put a final kibosh to the notion.

As time passed, Mileva worked to improve her boys' relationship with their father. Albert managed to find time to vacation with his children, as well as keep up a steady correspondence. "Our two sons," he told Mileva, are "the best part of my inner life."[11] Despite periodic tensions between two stubborn personalities, Einstein's relationship with Hans Albert grew to be more positive.

The boy gives me indescribable joy.[12]

Albert Einstein on Hans Albert

His second son Eduard developed schizophrenia in the late 1920's. Mileva Marić dedicated the rest of her life to caring for him.[13] She died in Zurich in 1948 at the age of 73, suffering a stroke after Eduard, in a schizophrenic state, ravaged their apartment. Eduard passed away in 1965.

The rise of Hitler in the 1930's made living in Germany untenable for Einstein. Many German Jews decided to wait out the Nazi's, either in denial over the ever increasing anti-Semitism in what was once relatively liberal Germany or not having the means to emigrate. The highly visible Einstein found himself a particular target of Nazi hate-mongers. He knew he must leave the land of his birth once again.

In 1932, Einstein secured a position at the Institute for Advanced Study in Princeton, New Jersey. He left Germany the following year — the same year Hitler became chancellor — and never returned. Einstein lived and worked in Princeton for the rest of his life.

> *Arrows of hate have been shot at me too; but they never hit me, because somehow they belonged to another world, with which I have no connection whatsoever.*[14]

Albert Einstein

Once in the United States, Einstein was far from universally revered. He was vilified by right-wing elements as "a pacifist, a democrat and civil libertarian, a radical, and a socialist," as physicist John Stachel put it.[15] His call to "young men to refuse military service" angered people in America as well as in other countries. And "America Firsters" attacked him for aiding numerous Jewish and non-Jewish refugees from fascist regimes.

Quantum Entanglement[16]

In 1935, 56-year-old Einstein along with young Princeton colleagues Boris Podolsky and Nathan Rosen (EPR), raised a challenge to quantum mechanics which reverberates to this day. Say we measure a *random* attribute of a photon, such as its polarization. Standard quantum mechanics says this *act of measurement* immediately determines both its polarization — *and* the polarization of its entangled partner in another location in space, no matter how far away. Instantly. Faster than the speed of light. Even if the two particles are separated by miles or even light-years. In other words, the universe is what physicists call "non-local."

Einstein derided this notion as "spooky action at a distance." He felt quantum theory must be wrong, or at the very least incomplete. The EPR paper postulated there must be something beyond our quantum understanding which governs this behavior.

To everyone's surprise, in 1964 Irish physicist John Bell proposed an experiment to determine whether EPR or quantum theory was right. Tests performed in the 1980's by French physicist Alain Aspect and collaborators (and later by others) confirmed that the universe is not local! The outcome of what you do at one place, as Brian Greene wrote, "*can* be linked to what happens at another place, even if nothing travels between

272

the two locations!"[17] In other words, two random events separated in space are somehow instantly correlated. This is the essence and mystery of quantum entanglement.[18]

The Letter

In 1936, after only a few years in the United States, Albert's second wife Elsa passed away at the age of 60. That same year Einstein learned his lifelong friend and collaborator, Marcel Grossman had also died. The following year, Einstein's oldest son Hans Albert immigrated to America, where he was welcomed by his father. And in 1939, Einstein's sister Maja left Mussolini's Italy and moved in with Albert.

The year Maja joined him, Einstein faced the most difficult moral decision of his life. Over the years, he had spoken out against war in all of its forms. He felt nationalism which pits one country against another was at best a foolish waste of energy and at worst the cause of incalculable human suffering.

In the summer of 1939, Hungarian-Jewish nuclear physicist Leó Szilárd asked Einstein to sign a letter urging President Roosevelt to develop an atom bomb. After fleeing Nazi Germany, Szilárd ended up in England for a time. There he came up with the idea of a nuclear chain reaction. While at Columbia University in Manhattan, he learned of physicist Lise Meitner's discovery of nuclear fission — based on German chemist Otto Hahn's uranium experiments.

This news alarmed Szilárd and his close friend, fellow Hungarian physicist Eugene Wigner.[19] They worried that a nuclear chain reaction could produce bombs of unheard of destructive power. Fearing Nazi Germany might be developing such a bomb, Szilárd and Wigner wanted to warn the world.

But how? They needed someone who could draw the attention of higher powers (and understand the physics). Who better than the originator of $E = mc^2$, Szilárd's old friend from Berlin, Albert Einstein.

On July 16, 1939, Szilárd and Wigner drove to the north fork of eastern Long Island where Einstein was renting a vacation cottage. There they explained to Einstein that neutrons released from uranium layered with graphite could produce an explosive chain reaction through nuclear fission. "I never thought of that!" Einstein replied.[20]

Such was Einstein's fear of Hitler that it overcame his lifelong objection to war. At a second meeting attended by Szilárd and Hungarian-Jewish physicist Edward Teller, Einstein signed the now famous letter to Franklin

Delano Roosevelt. It warned the president of the possible creation of "extremely powerful bombs" and that German scientists might be pursuing such devices.[21]

In late August of 1939, Germany announced a pact with Stalin and invaded Poland. World War II had begun. Six weeks later, prominent economist Alexander Sachs, a friend of Roosevelt, delivered the Einstein-Szilárd letter to the president and read it out loud. "This requires action," Roosevelt told his personal assistant.[22] The Einstein-Szilárd letter and three follow-up letters helped prompt US Government-sponsored research into nuclear fission.

The government had already been secretly informed of Enrico Fermi's work at the University of Chicago on the "first controlled nuclear chain reaction," as well as the potential danger of atomic bombs.[23] Nonetheless, research proceeded at a slow pace, as the practicality of developing an atomic weapon was questioned.

Then in October 1941, British intelligence forwarded a classified report to the US government, based on the work of German-Jewish refugee physicists Rudolf Peierls and Otto Frisch, now living in England.[24] Their research showed only several pounds of the rare element uranium-235 — rather than many tons as had been thought — was sufficient to produce a nuclear bomb of immense destructive power. The British "MAUD Report" warned that "an atomic bomb could be built (by Germany) and that it might be ready for use by late 1943."[25]

On December 6, 1941, the day before the Japanese attack on Pearl Harbor, the US government initiated a secret program of highest national priority — code-named the Manhattan Project.[26] Over the next three-and-a-half years, an international team of renowned scientists would build mankind's first atom bombs.

Einstein came to lament his letters to Roosevelt. "Had I known that the Germans would not succeed in producing an atomic bomb," he said, "I never would have lifted a finger."[27]

An American Citizen

> *At the time (I left Germany), I did not understand how right I was in my choice of America as such a place. On every side I hear men and women expressing their opinions on candidates for office and the issues of the day without fear of consequences.*[28]
>
> Albert Einstein

In the United States, Einstein grew to appreciate the country's "tolerance of free thought, free speech and non-conformist beliefs."[29] In his adopted country, he was free to argue for the ideals of world peace and an "international federation of nations." He became a US citizen in 1940.

After World War II, he lobbied for world government and nuclear disarmament.[30] In 1952, he wrote a controversial open letter which condemned the McCarthy committee's communist witch hunt and supported civil rights. Einstein remained a proponent of world peace, internationalism, and human rights for the rest of his life.

Einstein dedicated his remaining years to the pursuit of his elusive unified field theory. Whether it was because he no longer had the innovative spark of youth or because the task was simply too difficult even for Einstein, his efforts proved futile. After some three-and-a-half decades of work, more and more alone and virtually ignored by the rest of the physics community, the great scientist never found a viable solution.

> I live in that solitude which is painful in youth but delicious in the years of maturity.[31]
>
> Albert Einstein

In his final years, Einstein led a quiet life in Princeton — working on his unified field theory, answering letters, and occasionally speaking out on issues of the day. He continued to dress shabbily, live modestly, and, as Spanish physicist Antonio Gonzalez put it, fiddle with "his beloved pipe . . . even after he had been ordered to stop smoking."[32] He was "an *Einspänner*, a loner in all his behavior, among his students, his colleagues, his friends and his family."

> I am a completely isolated man and though everybody knows me, there are very few people who really know me.[33]
>
> Albert Einstein

On March 14, 1954, his 75th birthday, Einstein received a note addressed to the "President of the Olympia Academy". It was a birthday card from old friends Conrad Habicht and Maurice Solovine. On April 18, 1955, Einstein passed away at age 76. His notebook indicates he worked on his unified field theory till the very end.[34]

"To the whole of mankind Albert Einstein's death is a great loss,"[35] the great quantum physicist Neils Bohr eulogized, "and to those of us

who had the good fortune to enjoy his warm friendship, it is a grief that we shall never more be able to see his gentle smile and listen to him."

A New Reality?

Today, the "Holy Grail" of theoretical physics research is the unification of quantum mechanics and general relativity under a single construct termed "quantum gravity."[36] There are a number of approaches. String theory is by far the most active and most heavily funded.

It is the fervent hope of string theorists that their grand quest will unite all quantum forces (electroweak and strong nuclear) and *gravity* into a single force, explain why the numerous properties of matter are as they are, tell us what dark matter and dark energy are, shed new light on quantum entanglement, and place all the laws of the universe under a single theory.

String theory offers other tantalizing prospects — explanations for what caused the big bang, how spacetime itself came into being, and what (if anything) happened before the big bang.[37] String theory may also reveal the physics of black hole interiors and whether they truly allow wormhole time machines. And it may give us a definitive answer to the most profound physics question of all: are there really multiple universes?

There are hints. Yet, despite some 40 years of effort, there is not a single piece of clear empirical evidence in support of string theory.[38] Until a prediction of string theory is confirmed by measurement, it remains merely a possibility.

Epilogue

The great physics question for the 21st century is: will string theory or any other quantum gravity approach eventually succeed? Despite the formidable difficulties and decades of unresolved effort, our intuition says "yes". We have come to expect strange cosmic revelations in modern physics. Surely there must be an even more bizarre reality waiting just beyond our grasp.

Who will dissipate the fog we seem to find ourselves in? Who will make the next world-shattering breakthrough? If history is any judge, it will be someone who does not follow the crowd, an individual with the temerity to reject conventional thinking, the courage to challenge deeply held beliefs, the brilliance of mind to see beyond all others, and a passion for physics bordering on obsession. Who will shed new light on our universe? Who, indeed? We need another Einstein.

Appendix A

The Lorentz Transform

Assume two reference frames are in uniform motion with respect to each other at a velocity v *along the x-axis*. Consider two events in spacetime. The three space intervals and one time interval between these two events in the first frame of reference, S are labeled as:

$$\Delta x, \Delta y, \Delta z, \text{ and } \Delta t,$$

The three space intervals and one time interval between the *same* two events as observed in the second frame of reference, S' are labeled as:

$$\Delta x', \Delta y', \Delta z', \text{ and } \Delta t'$$

Using the notation above, the four-dimensional *Galilean* transform equations are:

Galilean transform:

$$\Delta x' = \Delta x - v\Delta t$$
$$\Delta y' = \Delta y$$
$$\Delta z' = \Delta z$$
$$\Delta t' = \Delta t$$

Using the same notation, the Lorentz transform equations in all four dimensions of spacetime are:

Lorentz transform:[1]

$$\Delta x' = (\Delta x - v\Delta t)/F$$

$$\Delta y' = \Delta y$$
$$\Delta z' = \Delta z$$
$$\Delta t' = (\Delta t - v\Delta x/c^2)/F$$

where

The Lorentz Factor, F is

$$F = sqrt\ (\ 1 - v^2/c^2),\ and$$
$$c = the\ speed\ of\ light.$$

Here the velocity, v is in standard units such as miles per hour or kilometers per second, not as a percentage of the speed of light as in the text. In standard units, the speed of light, c is not equal to 1, so it must be included in the equation.

The Galilean Transform Approximates the Lorentz Transform
for Small Velocities:

For a velocity v which is small compared to the speed of light, the Galilean transform is an excellent approximation of the Lorentz transform. For example, assume a velocity of 5% the speed of light. Then:

$$F = sqrt\ (1 - v^2/c^2) = sqrt\ (1 - (0.05)^2) = sqrt\ (1 - 0.0025)$$
$$= sqrt\ (0.9975) = 0.9987$$

So the Lorentz transform equation for $\Delta x'$ becomes:

$$\Delta x' = (\Delta x - v\Delta t)/F = (\Delta x - v\Delta t)/0.9987$$
$$= 1.001\ (\Delta x - v\Delta t) \approx \Delta x - v\Delta t$$

which is the first *Galilean* transform equation.
In this case, the Lorentz transform equation for time is:

$$\Delta t' = (\Delta t - v\Delta x/c^2)/F = 1.001\ (\Delta t - x\ \Delta v/c^2)$$
$$= 1.001\ (\Delta t - (0.05/c)\ x)$$
$$= 1.001\ (\Delta t - 7.5 \times 10^{-11}\ x) \approx \Delta t\ (where\ c\ is\ in$$
$$units\ of\ miles\ per\ hour)$$
$$So\quad \Delta t' \approx \Delta t$$

which is the last *Galilean* transform equation.

Time Dilation

The time dilation equation is derived from the Lorentz transform above as follows:

Time Dilation (in one spatial dimension)[2]

If the two events occur in the same *location* in frame S, then:

$$\Delta x = 0$$

Thus the *fourth* Lorentz transform equation becomes:

$$\Delta t' = (\Delta t - v\Delta x/c^2)/F = (\Delta t - v\,(0)/c^2)/F = \Delta t/F$$
$$\text{or } \Delta t' = \Delta t/\text{sqrt}\,(1 - v^2/c^2)$$

In units where the speed of light equals 1, the equation becomes:

$$\Delta t' = \Delta t/\text{sqrt}\,(1 - v^2)$$
$$\text{or } \Delta t = \text{sqrt}\,(1 - v^2)\,\Delta t'$$

This is the form of the equation used in the text.

Length Contraction

The length contraction equation is derived from the Lorentz transform equations as follows:

Length Contraction (in one spatial dimension)

If the two events occur at the same *time* in frame S, then:

$$\Delta t = 0$$

The *first* Lorentz transform equation becomes:

$$\Delta x' = (\Delta x - v\Delta t)/F = (\Delta x - 0)/F = \Delta x/F$$
$$\text{or } \Delta x' = \Delta x/\text{sqrt}\,(1 - v^2/c^2)$$

Reversing, we get:

$$\Delta x = \text{sqrt}\,(1 - v^2/c^2)\,\Delta x'$$

This is the form of the length contraction equation *along the direction of motion* used in the text.

Combining Velocities

Let's compare Einstein's equation to Newton's:

Adding Speeds per Galileo/Newton:

$$V = v_1 + v_2$$

where v_1 and v_2 are the speeds in question, and
V is the result of combining the two speeds

Combining Velocities per Einstein:

$$V = \frac{v_1 + v_2}{1 + v_1 v_2 / c^2}$$

where v_1 and v_2 are the speeds in question,
c is the speed of light, and
V is the result of combining the two speeds

Deriving Einstein's Combining Speeds Formula from the Lorentz Transform

If we divide the first Lorenz transform equation by the fourth, the F cancels and we get:

$$\Delta x' / \Delta t' = (\Delta x - v\Delta t)/(\Delta t - v\Delta x/c^2)$$

Dividing all terms on the right side by Δt gives:

$$\Delta x'/\Delta t' = (\Delta x/\Delta t - v\Delta t/\Delta t)/(\Delta t/\Delta t - v\Delta x/\Delta t/c^2)$$
$$= (\Delta x/\Delta t - v)/(1 - v\Delta x/\Delta t/c^2) \qquad (1)$$

Now $\Delta x/\Delta t$ is the average velocity of the object in the S frame over the time interval Δt. In the limit as Δt approaches zero, the average velocity in this frame is the *instantaneous* velocity, $u = dx/dt$.

Using similar reasoning, $\Delta x'/\Delta t'$ is the average velocity in the S' frame and the instantaneous velocity in this frame is $u' = dx'/dt'$.

So equation (1) above becomes:

$$dx'/dt' = (dx/dt - v)/(1 - v\, dx/dt/c^2)$$
$$\text{or } u' = (u - v)/(1 - u\, v/c^2)$$

Moving the denominator on the right to a numerator on the left, we get:

$$u' (1 - u\, v/c^2) = (u - v)$$
$$\text{so } u' - u\, u'\, v/c^2 = u - v$$

Rearranging we get:

$$u' + v = u + u\, u'\, v/c^2$$
$$= u (1 + u'\, v/c^2)$$

Solving for u, we get:

$$u = (u' + v)/(1 + u'\, v/c^2) \tag{2}$$

This is the relativistic equation for combining velocities.

If we change notations, so that $u = V$, $u' = v_1$, and $v = v_2$, then equation (2) above becomes:

$$V = (v_1 + v_2)/(1 + v_1\, v_2/c^2)$$

In units where the speed of light is 1, we get:

$$= (v_1 + v_2)/(1 + v_1\, v_2)$$

This is the form of the equation given in the text.

Appendix B

Spacetime Interval Categories

There are three categories of spacetime interval:[1] timelike, spacelike, and lightlike. They measure the separation between two events in spacetime. For a *timelike* spacetime interval, you can determine the space-time interval directly from the elapsed time on your wristwatch, as long as you are present at both events (as discussed in Chap. 8).

For a *spacelike* spacetime interval, the spacetime interval can be measured directly by laying a *ruler* between the locations in space of two events, as long as they occur at the same time. For a *lightlike* spacetime interval, the spacetime interval is always zero. Details follow.

Given two events in spacetime, we label the *time interval* between the two events as the customary Δt, and the *space interval* between the two events Δx. We again use the symbol ΔS to represent the *spacetime interval*.

(To simplify the equations, units are chosen where the speed of light is 1, as in light-years per year.)

Timelike

Here the time interval is always greater than the space interval, or:

$$\Delta t > \Delta x$$

For instance, say it takes five years to get from Earth to a distant star which is 2 light-years away (in the Earth frame). Then Δt is five years and Δx is two light-years. The spacetime interval is calculated as[a]:

Spacetime interval = sqrt (time interval squared − space interval squared)

$$\Delta S = sqrt (\Delta t^2 - \Delta x^2)$$

---

[a] We again use compatible units, such as light-years for distance and years for time, so the speed of light, c is 1. Recall, in conventional units, the equation is: $\Delta S = sqrt (c^2 \Delta t^2 - \Delta x^2)$.

Since in this category the time interval is always greater than the space interval, it is called *timelike*.

Figure B.1 shows a spacetime diagram of a timelike spacetime interval. Because we represent space and time in equivalent units (like light-years and years), the angle of the world-line is always *greater* than 45° from horizontal for timelike separations.

On the left of Fig. B.1, two events (the two points on the graph) are shown in an arbitrary reference frame. Here Δt is greater than Δx, so when we square, subtract, and take the square root, we get a *positive* spacetime interval.

Timelike spacetime intervals permit causality. This means that one event may influence another, because the speed through space required to get from one event to the other is less than the speed of light. There is enough time for something or someone to travel from one event to another.

What about the *special* reference frame where two events occur in the same place? As discussed in Chap. 8, this is the "personal" reference frame you carry with you as you travel through spacetime. This is shown on the right of Fig. B.1.

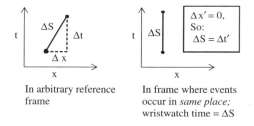

In arbitrary reference frame

In frame where events occur in *same place;* wristwatch time = ΔS

Figure B.1. **Timelike**. Time interval greater than space interval: $\Delta t > \Delta x$.

In your personal frame, you are standing still and everything else moves relative to you. Here the space interval or spatial separation between any two events in which you are present is *zero*. Thus your *wristwatch time* equals the spacetime interval. This is called *proper time*.

Spacelike

Here the space interval is always greater than the time interval, or:

$$\Delta x > \Delta t$$

This is called a *spacelike* separation. The spacetime interval is calculated as:

Spacetime interval = sqrt (space interval squared − time interval squared)

$$\Delta S = sqrt (\Delta x^2 - \Delta t^2)$$

The time interval and space interval reverse places so we still get a *positive* difference.

Figure B.2 shows a spacetime diagram of a spacelike separation. Because we represent space and time in units where the speed of light is 1, e.g. light-years per year, the angle of the world-line from horizontal is always *less* than forty-five degrees for spacelike separations. Two events are plotted in an arbitrary reference frame on the left of the figure. A special reference frame is shown on the right, where the two events occur *at the same time*. In this case, a ruler laid out between the two events is a direct measure of the spacetime interval. This is called *proper distance*.

In the spacelike category, speeds greater than the speed of light are required to get from one event to another. Since nothing can exceed the speed of light, no object or signal can get from one event to the other in the spacelike category. Thus there is *no causality* between events in spacelike separations.

Imagine an explosive device has been set up on the Moon which can be triggered remotely by radio signal from Earth. (Assume the Earth and Moon are at rest with respect to each other for simplicity.) Consider two events:

(1) A radio signal is sent from the Earth to the explosive device on the Moon, and
(2) the device on the Moon explodes 0.5 second later.

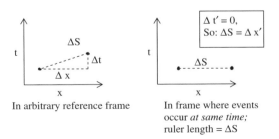

In arbitrary reference frame   In frame where events
                                            occur *at same time;*
                                            ruler length = ΔS

Figure B.2. **Spacelike.** Space interval greater than time interval: $\Delta x > \Delta t$.

There is no way the first event could have caused the second. Why? Because it takes about 1.28 seconds for a radio signal (which travels at the speed of light) to cover the distance from Earth to the Moon. Something else must have triggered the explosion. Since nothing can travel faster than the speed of light, the two events are *not* causally related. So we know the explosion was triggered by some other mechanism, such as a fault in the device.

In the Earth-Moon frame of reference, the space interval between the two events is 1.28 seconds, which is greater than the time interval between the two events of 0.5 second. So the *spacetime* interval between these two events is *spacelike*.

Lightlike

What if the space interval *equals* the time interval? For example, say the separation between two events is 5 light-seconds in space and 5 seconds in time. The square of the difference between the two is therefore zero. (See Fig. B.3.)

Because we choose units where the speed of light is 1, the angle of the world-line between two events is always equal to 45° in a lightlike spacetime plot. Here:

$$\Delta x = \Delta t \text{ for lightlike spacetime intervals}$$

Thus $\Delta S = \text{sqrt} (\Delta x^2 - \Delta t^2) = 0$

For a particle to travel five light-seconds in distance in five seconds of time, it has to travel at the speed of light, *c*. Thus only massless particles such as photons (electromagnetic force messenger particles) and gluons (strong force messenger particles) experience lightlike separations between events in spacetime. For these particles, the spacetime interval is always zero.

Figure B.3. **Lightlike.** *Time interval equals space interval:* $\Delta t = \Delta x$, *so* $\Delta S = 0$.

Summary

The three spacetime interval categories are summarized in Table B.1.

Table B.1. The Three Spacetime Interval Categories. *Direct measurement of the spacetime interval is only possible in the special frames noted.*

			Direct Measurement	
Category	Relationship	Spacetime Interval	Metric	Special Frame
(a) *Timelike*	$\Delta t > \Delta x$	sqrt $(\Delta t^2 - \Delta x^2)$	wristwatch carried between events	events occur at same place
(b) *Spacelike*	$\Delta x > \Delta t$	sqrt $(\Delta x^2 - \Delta t^2)$	ruler laid out between events	events occur at same time
(c) *Lightlike*	$\Delta x = \Delta t$	zero	—	—

Appendix C

Momenergy

In spacetime physics, the mass, energy, and momentum are given in a single expression called *momenergy*. It is a vector (possesses both magnitude and direction). Since there are four dimensions in spacetime (three space and one time), the momenergy vector has four dimensions. It is called the momenergy 4-vector.

Momenergy is shown graphically in Fig. C.1 (in one spatial dimension for simplicity). It contains:

The Momenergy Vector

- Energy — the time-component
- Momentum — the space-component
- Mass — the *magnitude* of the momenergy vector

Magnitude of Momenergy Vector

The magnitude of the momenergy vector is the particle's *rest mass*. And since the rest mass does not change with motion, it is always the same for

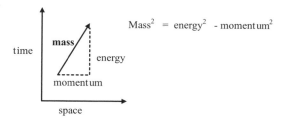

$$Mass^2 = energy^2 - momentum^2$$

Figure C.1. The Momenergy Vector (in 2-D). *Energy and momentum vary with relative motion, but mass does not change.*

a given particle. Thus the rest mass or magnitude of a particle's momenergy is invariant.

(In the modern spacetime interpretation, mass *always* refers to the rest mass. From now on, when we use the term *mass*, we mean a particle's rest mass.)

Direction of Momenergy Vector

The direction of a particle's momenergy vector is simply the particle's direction in spacetime, i.e. the direction of its world-line.

Calculating the Components of Momenergy Vector

The *energy* and *momentum* components of the momenergy vector can be separated out from the momenergy vector. For a free-float frame and two nearby events, the spacetime separation of momenergy resolves into four different components:

- Laboratory time (time in the observer's reference frame)
- Three perpendicular space directions

Energy: The energy component of momenergy is the particle's mass multiplied by its motion through *time*. More formally:

$$\text{Energy} = \text{mass} \times (\text{co-ordinate time/proper time})$$

where:
  the co-ordinate time is the time interval in the chosen (inertial) reference frame, and
  the proper time is the spacetime interval in time units.
  Thus energy is the *time component* of the momenergy vector.

Momentum: The momentum component of momenergy is the particle's mass multiplied by its motion through *space*. More formally:

Component of momentum in x = mass times displacement in x /proper time interval
(Similar for momentum (y) and momentum (z).)
Thus momentum is the *space component* of the momenergy vector.

The Momenergy Equation

The relationship between mass, energy, and momentum of the momenergy vector is similar to the spacetime interval.[1] It is:

Mass squared equals energy squared minus momentum squared

$$m^2 = E^2 - p^2$$

The momenergy of a particle has existence *independent* of any inertial frame of reference since it is invariant (similar to the invariant spacetime interval). However, both the energy *component* and the momentum *component* are relative, rather than absolute quantities — they vary with relative motion. In other words, momenergy has different energy and momentum components depending on frame of reference, but always has the *same* magnitude (mass).

The equations for the *momentum* and *energy* components of the momenergy vector are given below.

The Momentum Equation:

The magnitude of the momentum of a particle is the Newtonian momentum divided by the Lorentz transform factor:

$$P = mv/\text{sqrt}\,(1 - v^2)$$

The Energy Equation:

For a particle at rest, its rest energy, E_0 equals its mass, m:

$$E_0 = m$$

For a particle moving in a given (inertial) reference frame, its total energy is its mass times the particle's motion through time, or more formally:

$$E = E_0\, dt/d\tau$$
$$= E_0/\text{sqrt}\,(1 - v^2)$$
$$= m/\text{sqrt}\,(1 - v^2) \tag{1}$$

where:

t is co-ordinate time (time interval in the inertial frame chosen)
τ is proper time (spacetime interval in time units), and
v is relative velocity

From this, we derive the relativistic equation for *kinetic* energy, the energy of motion of a particle, as follows:

Kinetic Energy (Newtonian):

In Newtonian physics, kinetic energy, K is one-half times a particle's mass times its velocity squared, or:

$$K = \tfrac{1}{2}\, m\, v^2$$

Kinetic Energy (Relativistic):

Per Einstein, a particle at rest has a non-zero energy, $E_0 = m$. So a particle's total energy is its rest energy *plus* its kinetic energy, K, due to motion. A particle's *total energy* E, is:

$$E = E_0 + K$$
$$= m + K$$

Solving for K, we get:

$$K = E - m$$

Substituting equation (1), we get the *relativistic kinetic energy* equation:

$$K = m/\mathrm{sqrt}\,(1 - v^2) - m$$
$$= m\,[(1/\mathrm{sqrt}\,(1 - v^2) - 1)]$$

In "conventional" units where the speed of light $c \neq 1$, relativistic kinetic energy is:

$$K = mc^2/(\mathrm{sqrt}\,(1 - v^2/c^2)) - mc^2$$

Appendix D

Constructing a Geodesic

To get a feel for what a geodesic looks like, take a standard piece of 8 ½ by 11 inch paper, and:

(1) cut out a long rectangular strip,
(2) lie the paper down on a flat surface and mark two points on it,
(3) draw a straight line between the two points,
(4) bring the long ends of the paper together to make a cylinder, and
(5) tape the two ends together.

This is shown in Fig. D.1.

On the *flat* piece of paper, the straight line is of course the shortest path between the two points. It is a geodesic on a plane surface.

This same straight line becomes a *curved* line once the paper is shaped into a cylinder. This curved line is still the shortest path between the two points. It is a geodesic on a curved surface.

(a) Draw a straight line connecting two points on a flat strip of paper

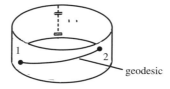

(b) Fold paper into cylinder and tape ends

Figure D.1. Constructing a Geodesic. (a) *The straight line is the shortest path from point 1 to 2 on a plane, and* (b) *the shortest path from point 1 to 2 on a curved surface. Both are geodesics.*

The Einstein Equation

A Little History

Einstein's original field equations of 1912 used the Ricci Tensor to represent spacetime curvature. In the shorthand of tensor notation:

Ricci tensor = a constant times Momenergy Tensor

$$R_{ab} = K\,T_{ab}$$

Why did Einstein chose to model spacetime curvature using the *Ricci Tensor*?[1] To meet the Principle of General Covariance, Einstein and Grossman had searched Riemannian geometry for mathematical entities which are "generally covariant", that is expressions which don't change with a co-ordinate (reference frame) transformation. Only two are: the *volume* of curved space and *curvature* (called Ricci curvature). The Ricci Tensor represents these two entities, thus is generally covariant.

As noted in Chap. 14, Einstein abandoned the Ricci tensor approach in 1912 because he mistakenly believed it gave multiple solutions for the same mass-energy.

When Einstein returned to these field equations in late September, 1915, he found there were still problems.[2] They violated conservation of energy and momentum (momenergy) and disagreed with Newton's gravitational theory for "weak" gravity and non-relativistic speeds. After searching around for a while, he arrived at a "slight modification". He added a term to the *left* side of the equation, which now read:[3]

Ricci Tensor − ½ curvature invariant = a constant times Momenergy Tensor

$$R_{ab} - \tfrac{1}{2} R\,g_{ab} = K\,T_{ab}$$

The left side now included the Ricci Tensor *minus one-half the Ricci scalar times the Metric Tensor*. This new equation showed the laws of conservation of energy- momentum *must* hold for the source of spacetime curvature — mass-energy. (More properly, the source is momenergy and it is the conservation of momenergy which must hold.)

And the new equation agreed with Newton's equations for weak gravity and non-relativistic speeds.[4]

In simpler form, we write the "Einstein equation" as:

Curvature tensor = a constant times Energy Tensor

$$\mathbf{G}_{ab} = K \, \mathbf{T}_{ab}$$

where:

$$\mathbf{G}_{ab} = \mathbf{R}_{ab} - \tfrac{1}{2} R \, \mathbf{g}_{ab}$$

Spacetime Curvature — Newton versus Einstein[5]

The elevator in free-fall thought experiment (Chap. 10) takes into account *time warp only*.[6] It ignores the effects of the warping of space. If we evaluate Einstein's gravitational field equations for time warp only, we get solutions for gravitational fields which are identical to Newton's.

Einstein initially thought including space warp violated Newton's theory for "weak" gravity conditions. But it is, in fact, the *only* way to distinguish Einstein's gravity from Newton's. Let's look at this in terms of the spacetime interval.

The spacetime interval in *flat* spacetime (zero gravity) is simply the Minkowski metric of special relativity:

Spacetime Interval — Zero time or space warp

(Spacetime interval)^2 = (space interval)^2 − (time interval)^2

$$ds^2 = (dx^2 + dy^2 + dz^2) - (dt)^2$$

(In units where the speed of light is 1, such as in light-years per year.)

Now assume a uniform density, non-rotating, uncharged spherical star (ala Schwarzschild). How does the spacetime interval change globally due to this idealized stellar object? If we include the curvature of *time only*, we get the following equation from *both* Newton's and Einstein's gravitational theories:

Spacetime Interval in Gravitational Field — Time warp only
(Newton and Einstein)[7]

$$ds^2 = (dx^2 + dy^2 + dz^2) - (1 - 2GM/r)\,(dt)^2$$

where

G is the gravitational constant,
M is the mass of a Newtonian star, and
r is the distance from the star to a particular point in space.

If we include the curvature of time *and* space, we get the full solution to Einstein's field equations, which no longer agrees with Newton's theory. The approximation to the Schwarzschild metric in Cartesian co-ordinates is:

Spacetime Interval in Gravitational Field — Time and space
warp (Einstein only)

$$ds^2 = (1 + 2GM/r)\,(dx^2 + dy^2 + dz^2) - (1 - 2GM/r)\,(dt^2)$$

So it is the space interval which distinguishes Einstein's equation from Newton's.

The Effects of Time and Space Curvature

Let's look at how time and space warp affect Einstein's first two major predictions, as compared to Newtonian predictions for the same phenomena. Figure E.1 shows two spacetime diagrams (space and time are plotted in equivalent units such as light-years and years, as usual).

Planet's Orbit: Time Warp Dominates — The world-line of a planet orbiting the Sun is shown in Fig. E.1(a) (solid curved line). The dashed vertical straight line in the figure represents the world-line of the Sun. (With respect to a reference frame where the Sun is stationary.)

Notice how close to the dashed vertical line the planet's orbit is. This tells us the planet moves mostly *through time* and very little through space. This is because our planets move at very slow speeds compared to the speed of light. So they have a small value of *dx* (space interval) for a given spacetime interval. The *dt* term (time interval) dominates.

The Mercury Prediction — Like all planets, Mercury's path around the Sun is determined primarily by the warping or curvature of time. Thus

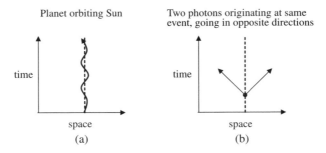

Figure E.1.   Spacetime Diagrams — Orbiting Planet and Photons. (a) *Planet moves mostly through time and very little through space.* (b) *Photons move equally through time and space.*

the orbit of Mercury around the Sun predicted by *Newton's* equations (equivalent to time warp only) is a very good approximation.

But Einstein's full time *and* space warp calculations showed a tiny additional advance in each of Mercury's orbits of about 0.1 arc second. Since Mercury orbits about 415 times in 100 Earth years, then:

0.1 arc second per orbit times 415 orbits = 41 arc seconds per century

This rough calculation here is very close to Einstein's additional 43 arc seconds per century prediction for the perihelion shift of Mercury.

Bending of Light by the Sun: Time and Space Warp Have Equal Effect — Figure E1(b) shows the world-lines of two photons in flat space-time (no gravity). They are emitted from the same spacetime location (event) and move in opposite directions.

Because space and time are plotted in equivalent units, e.g. light-years and years, both photons move through spacetime at a 45-degree angle. Per physicist Bernard Schutz, the fact that the photons travel at the speed of light, c means "the contributions to the spacetime interval of the terms involving dx (space interval) are comparable to those of dt (time interval)."[8]

So space warp and time warp have equal effect on the bending of light in a gravitational field. Thus Newton's prediction (equivalent to time warp only) for the bending of starlight grazing the limb of the Sun is only *half* the value of Einstein's prediction — which includes both time and space warp.

Newton's and Einstein's predictions are 0.875 and 1.75 arc seconds respectively. The fact that Einstein's prediction matches observations to extraordinary accuracy verifies that the presence of mass/energy warps both time and space.

And the fact that Newton's gravity is equivalent to time warp only explains why it works so well within our solar system. The speeds of stellar objects in our solar system (and their escape velocities) are so slow compared to the speed of light that time warp only predictions yield an excellent approximation for their gravitational behavior.

Acknowledgements

First and foremost, I wish to thank my wife Pat for her unwavering encouragement, loving support, and invaluable assistance during the writing of this book. At a time when I was advised to cut the book down dramatically, she stepped in and edited the entire manuscript — identifying where I had been repetitious, wordy, or overly complicated. Her wisdom and common sense editing skills have made *Einstein Relatively Simple* a better and simpler book. Pat also created both my web-sites: iramarkegdall.com for the book and marksmodernphysics.com for my courses. She has been a great partner in this journey. And best of all, she still laughs at my jokes.

I'd also like to thank those who took time out of their busy lives to review drafts of this book. They are: Patricia Ahern, Joel Backer, Victor Bennett, Donnis Benson, Ralph Burns, John DeChancie, Randy Hernandez, Darold Rorabacher, and James R. Webb. Their criticisms (ouch) and wise council have helped shape the book — a number of their recommendations have been incorporated into the text. Special thanks to Victor Bennett and James Webb for their review of the physics. I have learned much from their discerning questions and patient guidance. Any remaining issues in the text are due to my deficiencies alone. Particular thanks to John DeChancie for his astute critique of the first few chapters. His advice on form and style has greatly enhanced the presentation.

I owe a great debt to authors and educators — often eminent physicists — who have written text books, popular expositions, and web articles on relativity. I am self-taught in Einstein's great theories, so what-ever knowledge and comprehension I have is due to their explanations and insights. Amongst them are Jonathan Allday, John Baez, P. G. Bergmann, David Bodanis, Max Born, Arnold R. and David E. Brody,

Nigel Calder, Paul Davies, Albert Einstein, Lewis C. Epstein, Michael Fowler, Roger A. Freedman, Martin Gardner, Stan Gibilisco, Brian Greene, Paul Halpern, James B. Hartle, Art Hobson, Banesh Hoffmann, Roger S. Jones, Michio Kaku, William J. Kaufmann III, Lillian Lieber, Ernie McFarland, Hans Ohanian, Barry Parker, Roger Penrose, Wolfgang Rindler, Bernard Schutz, John Stachel, Daniel F. Styer, Kip Thorne, John Archibald Wheeler, Clifford M. Will, and Richard Wolfson. I would like to thank Brian Greene in particular for his lucid explanations of Einstein's theories. His eloquence has been an inspiration to me.

I'd also like to extend my appreciation to Susan Jay and Clara Barman at Florida International University, Noreen Frye and Julia Rose Cayuso at the University of Miami, and Edward Aqua and Linda Maurice at Nova Southeastern University, and their staffs for giving me the opportunity to do what I love: teach modern physics to interested lay students. Thank you to George Alexandrakis and James Nearing of the University of Miami for invaluable guidance on course content and timing. Thanks also to my "writing buddy" Steve Benson for his encouragement and willing ear.

I am particularly indebted to my students at the Osher Lifelong Learning Institutes. Their enthusiasm and kind evaluations of my courses have surprised and encouraged me. Their responses to the material and sharp questions have forced me to think more deeply on the subject-matter and helped shape the book.

Thank you to my fellow members of scienceforums.net for many helpful discussions and insights. I also want to acknowledge the greatest library in the world: the world-wide-web. Used judiciously, it has been a great aid and constant source of material literally at my fingertips.

Thank you to Kok Khoo Phua, Chairman and Chief Editor at World Scientific Publishing, for selecting *Einstein Relatively Simple* for publication. He has made a lifelong dream come true. Special thanks to my editor at World Scientific, Rhaimie Wahap, for his patience, attention to detail, and steadfast collaborative efforts.

Finally I'd like to thank my family and friends for all their encouragement and support. Special thanks to my dear sister, Sandy Taffin; and to my brother-in-law, Bill Taffin who, when told about my courses, said "You should write a book."

Notes with Sources

Abbreviations

CPAE — *Collected Papers of Albert Einstein series,*
  Diana Kormos Buchwald, General Editor, Princeton University Press
AEA — *Albert Einstein Archives, Hebrew University of Jerusalem*

Notes to Chap 1

1. Einstein, Albert. *The World As I See It* (New York: Philosophical Library, 1949. Based on *Mein Weltbild*, edited by Carl Seelig). As quoted in Patrick, George Thomas White and Chapman, Frank Miller. *Introduction to Philosophy* (London: George Allen & Unwin, Ltd., 1935).
2. Michele Besso (private communication), May, 1905. Recalled during Einstein's lecture in Kyoto, Japan. Source: Einstein, Albert. "How I Created the Theory of Relativity." Talk in Kyoto, Japan, Dec. 14, 1922. As cited in Calaprice, Alice, Ed. *The Ultimate Quotable Einstein* (Princeton: Princeton University Press, 2011), p. 354; Howard, Don and Stachel, John Ed. *Einstein, the Formative Years, 1879–1909* (Boston: Birkhäuser, 1994), p. 162. http://photontheory.com/Einstein/Einstein02.html. Last accessed June 2013.
3. Calder, Nigel. *Einstein's Universe: A Guide to the Theory of Relativity* (London: Penguin Books, 1982), p. 13.
4. French physicist Henri Poincaré is credited with first proposing the possibility of relative space and time. His paper at the first International Congress of Mathematicians in Zurich 1897 stated, "Absolute space, absolute time, even Euclidean geometry, are not conditions to be imposed on mechanics." Einstein was a first-year student at Zurich Poly at the time. There is no evidence that he attended the conference or heard this particular paper. Source: Clark, Roland C. *Einstein: The Life and Times* (New York and Cleveland: The World Publishing Company, 1971), p. 37.
5. Schutz, Bernard. *Gravity from the Ground Up* (Cambridge, England: Cambridge University Press, 2003), p. 188.

6. Ibid.
7. With the exception of magnetism. It is a relativistic effect which is noticeable at every day speeds. Consider an electric field at rest with respect to you. If you move, you will see both an electric *and* magnetic field. The faster you move, the weaker the electric field and the stronger the magnetic field. At the speed of light, you will see only a magnetic field. So "whether or not a field is electric or magnetic depends on your motion relative to it." Source: Parker, Barry. *Einstein's Brainchild: Relativity Made Relatively Easy* (Amherst, New York: Prometheus Books, 2000), p. 64.

In more technical language, "relativistic length contraction along with Coulomb's law accounts for the force on a charged particle as it moves relative to a current-carrying wire. We call that force magnetism (as seen from the reference frame of the wire)." It is measurable down to "on the order of $10^{-12}c$" or about 3.5 feet per hour. Source: Piccioni, R. G. "Special Relativity and Magnetism in an Introductory Physics Course," *Phys. Teach.* **45** (March 2007) 152.
8. Reiser, Anton and Kayser, Rudolf. *Albert Einstein: A Biographical Portrait* (A. & C. Boni, 1930), p. 28–29. As cited in Stachel, John. *Einstein from 'B' to 'Z'* (Boston: Birkhäuser, 2001), p. 13.
9. Einstein's message for Ben Scheman, dinner, March 1952, AEA 28–931. As cited in Isaacson, Walter. *Einstein: His Life and Universe* (New York: Simon & Schuster, 2008-pbk), p. 13.
10. Isaacson, Walter. *Einstein: His Life and Universe* (New York: Simon & Schuster, 2008-pbk), p. 10; Ohanian, Hans C. *Einstein's Mistakes: The Human Failings of Genius* (New York: Norton, 2008), p. 6.
11. Einstein to Sybille Blinoff, May 21, 1954, AEA 59–261. As cited in Isaacson, Walter. *Einstein: His Life and Universe* (New York: Simon & Schuster, 2008-pbk), p. 8–9. Isaacson states Einstein had a mild form of echolalia, causing him to repeat phrases to himself.
12. Einstein, Albert. "Autobiographical Notes." In Schilpp, Paul Arthur, ed. *Albert Einstein: Philosopher-Scientist* (La Salle, III: Open Court Press, 1949), p. 3–94. As cited in Isaacson, Walter. *Einstein: His Life and Universe* (New York: Simon & Schuster, 2008-pbk), p. 13.
13. Mamola, Karl C. "Editorial: Einstein in the Classroom," *Phys. Teach.* **43** (November 2005) 486.
14. Berkson, William. "Einstein's Religious Awakening," REFORM JUDAISM, Winter 2010, p. 67.
15. Schilpp, Paul Arthur, ed. *Albert Einstein: Philosopher-Scientist* (La Salle, Ill: Open Court Press, 1949), p. 5. As cited in Kaku, Michio. *Einstein's Cosmos: How Albert Einstein's Vision Transformed our Understanding of Space and Time* (London: Phoenix, 2005-pbk), p. 15.
16. Einstein, Albert. "Autobiographical Notes." In Schilpp Paul Arthur, ed. *Albert Einstein: Philosopher-Scientist* (La Salle, III: Open Court Press, 1949), p. 3–94. As

cited in Isaacson, Walter. *Einstein: His Life and Universe* (New York: Simon & Schuster, 2008-pbk), p. 21.

17. Isaacson, Walter. *Einstein: His Life and Universe* (New York: Simon & Schuster, 2008-pbk), p. 23. Isaacson notes that it is not clear whether Einstein wanted to leave the Gymnasium or was forced to leave.

18. Now the *Eidgenössische Technische Hochschule* (ETH) or Swiss Federal Institute of Technology.

19. Isaacson, Walter. *Einstein: His Life and Universe* (New York: Simon & Schuster, 2008-pbk), p. 36.

20. Harris, Kevin. "Collected Quotes from Albert Einstein," 1995. http://rescomp. stanford.edu/~cheshire/EinsteinQuotes.html. Last accessed August 2013. Whether Einstein actually said these words is an open question. I could not find an original source for the quote, nor could Barbara Wolff, Einstein Information Officer, AEA.

21. Isaacson, Walter. *Einstein: His Life and Universe* (New York: Simon & Schuster, 2008-pbk), p. 2.

22. A year later, his college sweetheart, Mileva Marić became pregnant from a spring tryst with Albert at Lake Como. She returned to her family home in Hungary to have the baby in secret. Their daughter Lieserl was is born in 1902 and reportedly given up for adoption. Einstein did not tell his parents or his sister about Marić's pregnancy or the birth of Lieserl, never saw his daughter, nor publicly acknowledged her existence. Letters between Albert and Mileva published twenty years after Einstein's death revealed the secret of Lieserl's birth for the first time. What actually happened to Lieserl has been lost to history. Source: Ohanian, Hans C. *Einstein's Mistakes: The Human Failings of Genius* (New York: Norton, 2008), p. 13; Isaacson, Walter. *Einstein: His Life and Universe* (New York: Simon & Schuster, 2008-pbk), p. 84–88.

23. Ohanian, Hans C. *Einstein's Mistakes: The Human Failings of Genius* (New York: Norton, 2008), p. 13.

24. Einstein to Hans Wohlwend, autumn 1902; Fölsing, Albrecht, Eward Osers trans. *Albert Einstein: a Biography* (New York: Viking, 1997), p. 102. As cited in Isaacson, Walter. *Einstein: His Life and Universe* (New York: Simon & Schuster, 2008-pbk), p. 78.

25. Isaacson, Walter. *Einstein: His Life and Universe* (New York: Simon & Schuster, 2008-pbk), p. 85.

26. Mileva Marić to Helene Savic, June 14, 1904; Popović, Milan. *In Albert's Shadow: The Life and Letters of Mileva Marić*, (Baltimore: Johns Hopkins University Press, 2003), p. 86. As cited in Isaacson, Walter. *Einstein: His Life and Universe* (New York: Simon & Schuster, 2008-pbk), p. 88.

27. German mathematician Gottfried Leibniz invented calculus independently in the same era as Newton.

28. Per Isaacson, this quote is attributed in a variety of sources to an address by Lord Kelvin to the British Association for the Advancement of Science in 1900, but he found no direct evidence for it. Source: Isaacson, Walter. *Einstein: His Life and Universe* (New York: Simon & Schuster, 2008-pbk), p. 90.

29. Kaku, Michio. *Einstein's Cosmos: How Albert Einstein's Vision Transformed our Understanding of Space and Time* (London: Phoenix, 2005-pbk), p. 10.

30. This refers to blackbody radiation. A blackbody is an object which absorbs all electromagnetic radiation impingent upon it. It is also a perfect emitter. 19th century theory predicted a blackbody would emit an *infinite* amount of radiation — the so-called ultraviolet catastrophe. Max Planck solved the problem in 1900 with his equation, $E = h\nu$, where E is energy, h is Planck's constant, and ν is frequency. The equation proved an excellent fit to blackbody radiation measurements. Planck postulated that "all atoms vibrating with a given frequency could exchange energy only in discrete (*quantized*) amounts." Hence the birth of quantum mechanics. Source: Schutz, Bernard. *Gravity from the Ground Up* (Cambridge, England: Cambridge University Press, 2003), p. 122.

    In his 1905 photoelectric effect paper, Einstein proposed *light* contained quantized packets of energy (photons) proportional to its frequency, precisely per Planck's equation.

31. Einstein wrote a fourth paper in the spring of 1905. "*A New Determination of Molecular Dimensions,*" completed on April 30, provided a method to determine the dimensions of atoms. The least significant of his 1905 papers, it was submitted and accepted by the University of Zurich as Einstein's doctoral dissertation.

32. Einstein to Conrad Habicht, May 1905. As cited in Isaacson, Walter. *Einstein: His Life and Universe* (New York: Simon & Schuster, 2008-pbk), p. 1.

33. Clark, Roland C. *Einstein: The Life and Times* (New York and Cleveland: The World Publishing Company, 1971), p. 73. Historian Peter Galison shrewdly points out "the absence of footnotes and references make Einstein's early papers look more like patent applications than scientific writings." This suggests Einstein's style came from reviewing and writing patent applications, where footnotes and references were typically omitted. Source: Galison, Peter Louis. *Einstein's Clock, Poincaré's Maps: Empires of Time* (New York: Norton, 2003), p. 291. As cited in Ohanian, Hans C. *Einstein's Mistakes: The Human Failings of Genius* (New York: Norton, 2008), p. 91.

34. Einstein to Conrad Habicht, May 1905. As cited in Calaprice, Alice, Ed. *The Ultimate Quotable Einstein* (Princeton: Princeton University Press, 2011), p. 355; Isaacson, Walter. *Einstein: His Life and Universe* (New York: Simon & Schuster, 2008-pbk), p. 2.

Notes to Chap 2

1. *The Rubaiyat of Jalal al-Din Rumi.* Translation by A. J. Arberry. http://www.art-arena.com/rumi2.htm. Last accessed June 2013.

2. Galilei, Galileo. *Dialogue Concerning the Two Chief World Systems — Ptolemaic and Copernican*, first published 1632; translation by Stillman Drake (Berkeley: University of California Press, 1962), p. 186ff. As cited in Taylor, Edwin F. and Wheeler, John Archibald. *Spacetime Physics: Introduction to Special Relativity — Second Edition* (New York: W. H. Freeman and Company, 1992), p. 53–54.

3. Lentini, Liza, "20 Things You Didn't Know About... Galileo," discovermagazine.com, July 2, 2007. Source: http://discovermagazine.com/2007/jul/20-things-you-didn2019t-know-about-galileo#.UaWALtL3CfJ. Last accessed June 2013.

4. Ohanian, Hans C. *Einstein's Mistakes: The Human Failings of Genius* (New York: Norton, 2008), p. 16.

5. Galilei, Galileo. *Dialogue Concerning the Two Chief World Systems — Ptolemaic and Copernican*, first published 1632; translation by Stillman Drake (Berkeley: University of California Press, 1962), p. 220. As cited in Ohanian, Hans C. *Einstein's Mistakes: The Human Failings of Genius* (New York: Norton, 2008), p. 49.

6. Sobel, Dava. *Galileo's Daughter: A Historical Memoir of Science, Faith, and Love* (New York: Walker, 2011), p. 273–280.

7. More formally, a reference frame is a *coordinate system* which can be used to measure the location and/or motion of an object. All reference frames in this book are *inertial* reference frames (unless stated otherwise). Why inertial? Because they are in relative *uniform* motion and thus obey Newton's Law of Inertia.

8. Needham, Joseph; Wang, Ling. *Science and Civilization in China*, 2. *History of Scientific Thought* (Cambridge University Press, 1956).

9. Salam, Abdus (1984), "Islam and Science". In C. H. Lai. *Ideals and Realities: Selected Essays of Abdus Salam*, 2nd ed. (Singapore: World Scientific, 1987), p. 179–213.

    Medieval French "thinker" John Buridan also wrote on inertia (and momentum) in the 1300's. Some science historians propose Buridan's writings influenced 17th century "scientists such as Galileo". Source: Graney, Christopher M. "Mass, Speed, Direction: John Buridan's 14th Century Concept of Momentum," *Phys. Teach.* **41** (Oct. 2013) 411.

10. Wolfson, Richard. *Simply Einstein: Relativity Demystified* (New York: Norton, 2003), p. 29.

11. For a detailed explanation of Newton's Laws of Motion in everyday language, see Hobson, Art. *Physics: Concepts and Connections* (New York: Addison Wesley, 2009), Chaps. 3 and 4.

12. For example, if we apply the Galilean transform to $F = ma$, we get the same equation out. Let's call Newton's second law *in the stationary frame* $F = ma$. We label the variables in the *moving frame* at constant velocity v with respect to

the stationary frame as: $F_{moving} = F'$, $m_{moving} = m'$, and $a_{moving} = a'$. So in the *uniformly moving frame*: $F' = m' a'$.

Now since acceleration is change in velocity, which in turn is change in position over time, we get: $F' = m' d^2x'/dt'^2 = m' d/dt' (dx'/dt')$. Per Newton, neither the mass of an object nor space or time are affected by motion. So $m = m'$ and $t = t'$. Thus the equation becomes: $F' = m d/dt (dx'/dt)$. Now we invoke the *Galilean transform* by substituting $x + vt$ for x' in the above equation. We get: $F' = m d/dt (d (x + vt)/dt) = m d/dt (dx/dt + d(vt)/dt) = m d/dt (dx/dt + v)$. Since v, the relative velocity between the stationary and moving frame is a *constant* velocity, its derivative with respect to time is zero. So $F' = m d/dt (dx/dt) = m a$. Thus: $F' = m a = F$. Source: Connell, Simon, "The Galilean Transformation," February 2, 2006. http://psi.phys.wits.ac.za/teaching/Connell/phys284/2005/lecture-01/lecture_01/node5.html. Last accessed June 2013.

13. McFarland, Ernie. *Einstein's Special Relativity: Discover it for yourself* (Toronto: Trifolium Books, 1997), p. 4.

14. Ørsted would not have used this terminology. The concept of magnetic *fields* was developed later by Michael Faraday.

15. Gbur, Greg, "The Birth of Magnetism," http://skullsinthestars.com/2011/04/03/the-birth-of-electromagnetism-1820/. Last accessed June 2013.

16. Isaacson, Walter. *Einstein: His Life and Universe* (New York: Simon & Schuster, 2008-pbk), p. 91.

17. This is actually a comment by Einstein on his first paper on the relationship between "the coefficients of viscosity, heat conduction, and diffusion" in the kinetic theory of gases. I have taken the liberty of applying it to Maxwell's theory. Source: Einstein to Marcel Grossman, 14 April 1901. As cited in Stachel, John. *Einstein from 'B' to 'Z'* (Boston: Birkhäuser, 2001), p. 122.

18. Rigden, John S. "The mystique of physics: Relumine the enlightenment", *Am. J. Phys.* **73** (12) (December 2005) 12.

19. Maxwell's four equations show (1) An electric charge produces an electric field, (2) A magnetic field exists between the poles of a magnet, (3) *Changing* magnetic fields produce electric fields (as in Faraday's electromagnetic induction experiment), and (4) *Changing* electric fields and electric currents produce magnetic fields (as in Ørsted's experiment). Source: Brody, D. E. and Brody, A.R. *The Science Class You Wish You Had...: The Seven Greatest Scientific Discoveries in History and the People Who Made Them* (New York: Perigee Trade, 1997), p. 165.

Maxwell's original version contained 20 differential equations in 20 variables. The well-known simpler form of the four differential equations was grouped together later "as a distinct set in 1884 by Oliver Heaviside, in conjunction with Willard Gibbs." Source: Nahin, Paul J., *Oliver Heaviside: The Life, Work, and Times of an Electrical Genius of the Victorian Age* (Baltimore: Johns Hopkins University Press-pbk, 2002) p. 108–112.

20. Wolfson, Richard. *Simply Einstein: Relativity Demystified* (New York: Norton, 2003), p. 43. The "spin" of electrons in atoms produces magnetic fields. (Spin is a measure of the angular momentum of a particle.) In most materials spins are oriented randomly, so the individual magnetic fields do not line up. They tend to cancel each other out so the net magnetic field is negligible. In bar magnets, however, the spins of most electrons are oriented in the same general direction. Thus their magnetic fields add up to a net magnetic field of significant strength. (An electron's motion with respect to the atom's nucleus can also affect a material's magnetic field.)

21. Kaku, Michio. *Einstein's Cosmos: How Albert Einstein's Vision Transformed our Understanding of Space and Time* (London: Phoenix, 2005-pbk), p. 9.

22. Wolfson, Richard. *Simply Einstein: Relativity Demystified* (New York: Norton, 2003), p. 49.

23. The EM wave is a sinusoidal function.

24. Maxwell calculated the speed of EM radiation from two numbers previously determined experimentally: (1) the *electrical number*, ε_0 which is the permittivity of vacuum derived from experiments on "the electric force between charge objects", and (2) the *magnetic number*, μ_0 which is the permeability of vacuum derived from experiments "with electric circuits and the magnetism they produced". The equation is: $c = 1/sqrt\ (\varepsilon_0\ \mu_0)$. Source: Wolfson, Richard. *Simply Einstein: Relativity Demystified* (New York: Norton, 2003), p. 50; McFarland, Ernie. *Einstein's Special Relativity: Discover it for Yourself* (Toronto: Trifolium Books, 1997), p. 15–16. For a detailed mathematical derivation of the speed of light from Maxwell's Equations, see Fowler, Michael, "Maxwell's Equations and Electromagnetic Waves," Physics Department, University of Virginia, May 9, 2009. http://galileo.phys.virginia.edu/classes/109N/more_stuff/Maxwell_Eq.html. Last accessed June 2013.

25. Einstein, Albert. "Autobiographical Notes." In Schilpp, Paul Arthur, ed. *Albert Einstein: Philosopher-Scientist* (La Salle, Ill: Open Court Press, 1949), p. 33. As cited in Howard, Don and Stachel, John Ed. *Einstein, the Formative Years, 1879–1909* (Boston: Birkhäuser, 1994), p. 66.

26. Einstein, Albert. "On the Generalized Theory of Gravitation", *Sci. Am.* **182** (4) April, 1950, 27.

27. Calder, Nigel. *Einstein's Universe: A Guide to the Theory of Relativity* (London: Penguin Books, 1982), p. 54.

28. Wolfson, Richard. *Simply Einstein: Relativity Demystified* (New York: Norton, 2003), p. 61.

29. In fairness to physicists of the time, H. A. Lorentz's interpretation of Maxwell's theory seemed "compatible with (almost) all the known experimental results." Einstein himself cited its success in explaining the aberration of starlight and the results of Fizeau's experiment on light velocity in flowing water. Source: Stachel, John. *Einstein from 'B' to 'Z'* (Boston: Birkhäuser, 2001,

p. 160; Einstein, Albert, "Ether and the Theory of Relativity", an address delivered on May 5, 1920, at the University of Leyden. http://www.tu-har-burg.de/rzt/rzt/it/Ether.html. Last accessed June 2013.

30. The Michelson-Morley experiment, a very clever one for its time, set out to find evidence for the ether. An *interferometer* was used to compare the speed of light in two perpendicular directions to great accuracy. The device split a monochromatic light beam into two perpendicular parts, used mirrors to recombine the two beams, and sent the resultant beam to a detector. It was expected that a slight difference would be observed between the light's speed in the direction of Earth's motion around the Sun (moving through the ether) and the speed of the light in a perpendicular direction. This would affect the interference of the two recombined light waves at the detector. The two beams traveled a distances "on the order of a few meters." The expected "difference in time for the two round trips (was) only on the order of a millionth of a millionth of a second," still within the interferometer's ability to detect. No such difference was found. Source: knowledgerush.com, "Michelson-Morley experiment". http://www.knowledgerush.com/kr/encyclopedia/Michelson-Morley_experiment/. Last accessed January, 2013.

31. Browne, Malcolm W., "In Centennial of One of its Biggest Failures, Science Rejoices," nytimes.com, April 28, 1987. http://www.nytimes.com/1987/04/28/science/in-centennial-of-one-of-its-biggest-failures-science-rejoices.html?pagewanted=all&src=pm. Last accessed June 2013.

Michelson's daughter recounted her father's explanation in her biography of him: Swimming upstream obviously slows the swimmer and swimming downstream speeds the swimmer up. One might think the two effects cancel each other. But, in fact, the round-trip against and with the current takes *longer* than swimming the same distance in still water. There is a *reciprocal* relationship between speed and time. Assuming a one-way distance d, the times for the trip *with the current* and the trip *against* are: $t_{with} = d/(s - c)$, and $t_{against} = d/(s + c)$ respectively, where s is the swimmer's speed and c is the speed of the current. So swimming with the current does *not* cancel out swimming against it — it takes *longer* to swim up and back than if there were no current. Source: Livingston, Dorothy Michelson. *Master of Light: A Biography of Albert A. Michelson* (Chicago: University of Chicago Press, 1979), p. 77. For a detailed explanation, see Michael Fowler, "The Michelson-Morley Experiment," University of Virginia Physics. http://galileo.phys.virginia.edu/classes/109N/lectures/michelson.html. Last accessed Aug, 2013.

32. Charap, John M. *Explaining the Universe: The New Age of Physics* (Princeton: Princeton University Press, 2004) revised 9/23/08, p. 13.

33. Wolfson tells us this so-called ether was required to have very unusual properties. It had to be a fluid rather than a solid since all the planets and stars move through it. It had to be a very tenuous fluid since it apparently offers

no resistance to the motion of these bodies. But the great speed that light travels at says the ether also had to be very stiff! (By analogy, "send a wave pulse down a (stretched) spring by disturbing it briefly and then letting go." The more the spring is stretched, the faster the pulse will travel.)

Einstein wrote because light can be polarized, the ether must be a solid body, since "transverse waves are not possible in a fluid, but only in a solid." In summary, the ether had to be a very stiff, tenuous fluid-solid — a strange material indeed. Source: Wolfson, Richard. *Simply Einstein: Relativity Demystified* (New York: Norton, 2003).

34. Einstein to Erika Oppenheimer, 13 September 1932. As cited in Stachel, John. *Einstein from 'B' to 'Z'* (Boston: Birkhäuser, 2001), p. 197.

Notes to Chap 3

1. Hoffman, Banesh. *Relativity and Its Roots* (Mineola, NY: Dover-pbk, 1983), p. 92.
2. Einstein's father Hermann's business difficulties were partly rooted in his generosity. He was "always helping those in financial trouble", writes Michio Kaku. "He wasn't tough-minded like most successful business men. (Albert would inherit this generosity of spirit.)" Source: Kaku, Michio. *Einstein's Cosmos: How Albert Einstein's Vision Transformed our Understanding of Space and Time* (London: Phoenix, 2005-pbk), p. 18.
3. Einstein also left Germany to avoid military service. Source: Galison, Holton, Gerald, and Schweber, Silvan S., Eds. *Einstein for the 21st Century: His Legacy in Science, Art, and Modern Culture* (Princeton: Princeton University Press, 2012), p. 220.
4. Brody, D. E. and Brody, A.R. *The Science Class You Wish You Had...: The Seven Greatest Scientific Discoveries in History and the People Who Made Them* (New York: Perigee Trade, 1997), p. 106.
5. Bodanis, David. $E = mc^2$: *A Biography of the World's Most Famous Equation* (New York: Walker and Company, 2000), p. 49.
6. Epstein, Lewis C. *Relativity Visualized* (San Francisco: Insight Press, 1997), p. 32.
7. Einstein, Albert. "Autobiographical Notes." p. 53. In Schilpp, Paul Arthur, ed. *Albert Einstein: Philosopher-Scientist* (La Salle, Ill: Open Court Press, 1949), p. 3–94, As cited in Brody, D. E. and Brody, A.R. *The Science Class You Wish You Had...: The Seven Greatest Scientific Discoveries in History and the People Who Made Them* (New York: Perigee Trade, 1997), p. 121.
8. Stachel, John. *Einstein from 'B' to 'Z'* (Boston: Birkhäuser, 2001), p. 166.
9. Contrary to what some popular science writings may imply, the Michelson-Morley (MM) experiments *do not* demonstrate the invariance of the speed of light. To do this, an observer must be in relative uniform motion with respect to the source of that light. There is no such "moving observer" in the MM experiments. The source, interferometer and observer (detectors) are all in the

same frame of reference, the Earth frame, i.e. they are all standing still with respect to each other. Ref: Conversation with Robert Murphy.

"*Without exception*, MM is cited (by Einstein) as evidence for the relativity principle, and is *never* cited as evidence for the principle of the constancy of the velocity of light." Source: Stachel, John. *Einstein from 'B' to 'Z'* (Boston: Birkhäuser, 2001), p. 179.

10. Einstein, Albert. "On the Electrodynamics of Moving Bodies." English translation of original published in *Annalen der Physik*, 17:891, which appears in W. Perrett and GB Jefferey, *The Principle of Relativity: A Collection of Original Memoirs on the Special and General Theory of Relativity* (London: Methuen, 1923).

11. Calder, Nigel. *Einstein's Universe: A Guide to the Theory of Relativity* (London: Penguin Books, 1982), p. 174.

12. If Newton were correct and star motion does affect light speed, other optical illusions are possible in observing binary star configurations. These include an apparent wobble in a star, or "ghost" images of the same star, or a star appearing to move backwards while it orbits. We could also see a star disappear, or delays in the eclipse as one star passes behind the other. Earth telescopes viewing the orbits of binary stars see no such anomalies. Sources: Hey, Anthony J. G. and Walters, Patrick. *Einstein's Mirror* (Cambridge, UK: Cambridge University Press, 1997), p. 71; Sartori, Leo. *Understanding Relativity: A Simplified Approach to Einstein's Theories*, (Berkeley: University of California Press, 1996), p. 42; Rindler, Wolfgang. *Essential Relativity: Special, General, and Cosmological* (London: Springer-Verlag, 1977), p. 24; Calder, Nigel. *Einstein's Universe: A Guide to the Theory of Relativity* (London: Penguin Books, 1982), p. 177.

13. Alväger *et al.*, "Test of the second postulate of special relativity in the GeV region," *Physics Letters*, **12** (1964) 260–262. As cited in Styer , Daniel F. *Relativity for the Questioning Mind* (Baltimore: The Johns Hopkins University Press, 2011), p. 17.

14. Brecher, Kenneth, "Is the Speed of Light Independent of the Velocity of the Source?", *Phys. Rev. Letters* **39** (17) (1977) 1051–1054.

15. Lorentz's interpretation was a precursor to Einstein's length contraction prediction. Thus it is commonly called the Lorentz-FitzGerald contraction or simply the Lorentz contraction.

16. Many physicists, including Fitzgerald, Larmor, Lorentz and Woldemar Voigt had been discussing the physics behind these equations since 1887. Source: Brown, Harvey R., "The origins of length contractions: I. The Fitzgerald-Lorentz deformation hypothesis," *Am. J. Phys.* **69** (10) (October 2001) 1044.

17. Einstein later recalled that *electromagnetic induction* led him to propose his Relativity postulate. Consider a bar magnet with a coil of wire circling around it, with the ends of the wire connected to an electric voltage meter. If we *move the bar magnet* through the coiled wire, a current flows in the wire and we

observe a momentary rise in voltage on the meter. What if we keep the bar magnet stationary and *move the coiled wire* in the opposite direction? As Einstein knew from his experience with generators in his family's business, a current again flows in the wire and we see the *same* amount of momentary voltage rise on the meter. The magnitudes of the voltages are the same in both cases, but they were predicted at the time by totally different sets of equations. "The idea that these two cases should essentially be different was unbearable to me," Einstein said.

"The observable phenomenon here depends only on the *relative motion* of the conductor and the magnet," Einstein wrote in his 1905 relativity paper. (My italics.) From the point of view of the magnet, it is stationary and the coil is moving. From the point of views of the coil, it is stationary and the magnet is moving. Which view is correct? They both are. Both produce identical results. Only *relative* motion matters. Source: Einstein, Albert. "On the Electrodynamics of Moving Bodies, 1920." English translation of original published in *Annalen der Physik*, 17:891, which appears in W. Perrett and G. B. Jeffery, *The Principle of Relativity: A Collection of Original Memoirs on the Special and General Theory of Relativity*, (London: Methuen, 1923), p. 1; Einstein, Albert. "Fundamental Ideas and Methods of the Theory of Relativity," 1920; unpublished draft of an article for *Nature*, Vol 7: Doc. 31. http://www.fourmilab.ch/etexts/einstein/specrel/www/. Last accessed June 2013; Stachel, John. *Einstein from 'B' to 'Z'* (Boston: Birkhäuser, 2001), p. 163; Wheeler, John Archibald. *A Journey into Gravity and Spacetime* (New York: Freeman, 1990), p. 8; Isaacson, Walter. *Einstein: His Life and Universe* (New York: Simon & Schuster, 2008-pbk), p. 115.

18. Einstein, Albert. "On the Electrodynamics of Moving Bodies." English translation of original published in *Annalen der Physik*, 17:891 (1905), which appears in W. Perrett and GB Jeffery, *The Principle of Relativity: A Collection of Original Memoirs on the Special and General Theory of Relativity*, (London: Methuen, 1923), p. 1.

19. In his June 1905 paper, Einstein mentioned the Relativity Postulate *before* the Light Postulate. Thus the Relativity Postulate is commonly referred to as Einstein's first postulate and the Light Postulate his second.

20. Clark, Roland C. *Einstein: The Life and Times* (New York and Cleveland: The World Publishing Company, 1971), 133.

21. Henri Poincaré was particularly prophetic. Although unable to dismiss the existence of the ether, "in 1904 he spoke of 'a principle of relativity' and suggested there be a new mechanics in which nothing could exceed the speed of light." Source: Hoffman, Banesh. *Relativity and Its Roots* (Mineola, NY: Doverpbk, 1983), p. 86.

22. Isaacson, Walter. *Einstein: His Life and Universe* (New York: Simon & Schuster, 2008-pbk), p. 133.

Notes to Chap 4

1. Clark, Roland C. *Einstein: The Life and Times* (New York and Cleveland: The World Publishing Company, 1971), p. 89.
2. Based on a story in Greene, Brian. *The Elegant Universe, Superstrings, Hidden Dimensions, and the Quest for the Ultimate Theory* (New York: Vintage Books-pbk, 2000), p. 26–27.
3. In physics text books and technical papers, the reciprocal of the Lorentz Factor, F is commonly represented by the Greek letter γ (gamma).
4. The full quote is: "Common sense is nothing more than a deposit of prejudices laid down in the mind before you reach 18," as quoted in Hartman, Lee Foster and Allen, Frederick Lewis; "Harper's Magazine, Volume 196" (1948) 473; and later in Bell, Eric Temple, *Mathematics, Queen and Servant of the Sciences* (1952), p. 42. Per quoteyard.com, "it appeared in (Bell) without any citation so its accuracy is questionable." http://www.quoteyard.com/common-sense-is-nothing-more-than-a-deposit-of-prejudices-laid-down-in-the-mind-before-you-reach-eighteen/. Last accessed July 2013.
5. "The Progression of Javelin Throw World Record," 2011. http://www.javelinthrowmagazine.com/poster/javelinthrowmagazine.do. Last accessed June 2013.
6. Einstein, Albert. "How I Created the Theory of Relativity." Talk in Kyoto, Japan, Dec. 14, 1922. As cited in Isaacson, Walter. *Einstein: His Life and Universe* (New York: Simon & Schuster, 2008-pbk), p. 121.
7. Styer, Daniel F. *Relativity for the Questioning Mind* (Baltimore: The Johns Hopkins University Press, 2011), p. 100.
8. The *Fizeau experiment* confirmed Einstein's velocity combining formula over Galileo/Newton's simple addition. Consider light traveling in a *motionless liquid* with a measured velocity, w with respect to the tube containing the liquid. How quickly does light travel if the *liquid is now moving* at velocity v with respect to the tube? The velocity of the light, W, relative to tube agreed with Einstein's formula, $W = (v + w)/(1 + vw/c^2)$ to within 1 percent. Source: Einstein, Albert. *Relativity, The Special and General Theory: A Popular Exposition* (New York: Crown, 1956), p. 40.

Notes to Chap 5

1. Davies, Paul. *About Time: Einstein's Unfinished Revolution* (New York: Simon & Schuster-pbk, 1996), p. 51.
2. Greene, Brian. *The Elegant Universe, Superstrings, Hidden Dimensions, and the Quest for the Ultimate Theory* (New York: Vintage Books-pbk, 2000), p. 38.
3. The Lorentz factor is derived from the geometry of a moving light clock in uniform motion as follows: Imagine two light-clocks; one at rest and one in uniform motion, as shown in Figure N5.1.

Figure N5.1. Geometry of Stationary and Moving Clock.

Clock at Rest: The distance between M1 and M2 is labeled L. How long does it take the photon to go from M1 to M2? Let's label this as time interval, T. Distance = speed x time, so time = distance/speed. The time interval, T is then: Eq. (1) $T = L/c$ where c is the speed of light.

Moving Clock: We label the distance between M1 and M2 as L'. Assume the light-clock is moving to the right at speed v. The distance that mirror M2 moves in a time interval of t is: distance = speed times time = v *times* $t = vt$. The Pythagorean Theorem is: (Hypotenuse)² = (side one)² + (side two)². So the equation for L' is: Equ (2) $(L')^2 = L^2 + v^2 t^2$. Now the photon goes from M1 to M2 in a time interval of t. So time = distance/speed, or $t = L'/c$. Squaring both sides gives: $t^2 = (L')^2/c^2$. Substituting Eq. (1) gives: $t^2 = (L^2 + v^2 t^2)/c^2$. Solving for t^2, we get: $t^2 = L^2/c^2 + v^2 t^2/c^2$ which is: $t^2 - v^2 t^2/c^2 = L^2/c^2$. Now factoring, we get: $t^2 (1 - v^2/c^2) = L^2/c^2$. Thus $t^2 = (L^2/c^2)/(1 - v^2/c^2)$. Recall Eq. (1) $T = L/C$. So $t^2 = T^2 (1 - v^2/c^2)$. Finally $t = T/sqrt (1 - v^2/c^2)$. If we use units where $c = 1$, such as light-years per year, v is given as a fraction of the speed of light. Here $t = T/sqrt (1 - v^2)$.

4. This section is based on Fowler, Michael, "Experimental Evidence for Time Dilation, Special Relativity: What Time is it?" University of Virginia, 2008. http://galileoandeinstein.physics.virginia.edu/lectures/srelwhat.html. Last accessed June 2013.

5. Frisch, D. H. and Smith, J. H. in *Am. J. Phys.* **31** (1963) 242–355.

6. "'Particle decay' refers to the transformation of a fundamental particle into other fundamental particles . . . The end products are not pieces of the starting particle, but totally new particles." (Source: particleadventure.org, "The Standard Model — Particle decays and annihilations — What is decay?" The Particle Adventure. http://particleadventure.org/frameless/decay_intro.html. Last accessed June 2013.

7. "Almost 90% of all incoming cosmic ray particles are protons, about 9% are helium nuclei, and about 1% are electrons." Cosmic rays primarily come from several sources: (1) galactic cosmic rays from outside the solar system, such as from rotating neutron stars, supernovae, and black holes; (2) anomalous cosmic rays which come from interstellar space at the edge of our solar system's heliopause; and (3) solar energetic particles associated with our

sun's solar flares and other energetic solar events. Source: NASA, "Cosmic Rays," Cosmicopia, May 11, 2012. http://helios.gsfc.nasa.gov/cosmic.html. Last accessed June 2013.

8. Davies, Paul. *About Time: Einstein's Unfinished Revolution* (New York: Simon & Schuster-pbk, 1996), p. 118–119; Frisch, D.H. and Smith, J. H. in *Am. J. Phys.* **31** (1963) 242–355. Frisch and Smith made a film of the experiment, *Time Dilation — An Experiment with mu-Mesons* (Educational Development Center, 1963).

9. The muon detector was shielded such that it only recorded muons around a speed of $0.994c$ or about 978 feet per microsecond.

10. Will, Clifford M. *Was Einstein Right? Putting General Relativity to the Test* (New York: Basic Books, 1993), p. 255.

11. McFarland, Ernie. *Einstein's Special Relativity: Discover it for yourself* (Toronto: Trifolium Books, 1997), p. 62. Original paper: Kaivola, M., *et al.*, *Phys. Rev. Lett.* **54** (1985) 255.

12. When excited by a laser, neon atoms emit light of a precise frequency. This extremely regular variation of light amplitude with time provides a very accurate clock. Researchers compared the change in the emitted light's frequency (clock rate) with the speed of the atoms (relative to the laboratory). Source: McGowan, Roger W. *et al.*, "New measurement of the relativistic Doppler shift in neon," *Phys. Rev. Lett.* **70** (1993) 251–254.

13. Styer, Daniel F. *Relativity for the Questioning Mind* (Baltimore: The Johns Hopkins University Press, 2011), p. 36.

14. Based on table in Jones, Roger S. *Physics for the Rest of Us* (New York: McGraw-Hill, 1993), p. 23.

15. Review comment by Joel Bacher. Strictly speaking a photon does not have an inertial reference frame. If a photon had its own reference frame, it would be at rest with respect to that frame. But per Einstein's light postulate, light travels at c with respect to *all* frames of reference. Hence the contradiction: A photon cannot be both at rest and moving at the speed of light. Source: D H, "Rest frame of a photon," Physics Forum, January 26, 2011. http://74.86.200.109/showthread.php?s=ec37843963efdd472da13b3ceaa83b97&t=511170. Last accessed June 2013.

16. Isaacson, Walter. *Einstein: His Life and Universe* (New York: Simon & Schuster, 2008-pbk), p. 128.

Notes to Chap 6

1. As quoted in Davies, Paul. *About Time: Einstein's Unfinished Revolution* (New York: Simon & Schuster-pbk, 1996), p. 70.

2. As opposed to Einstein's 1905 paper, I have introduced time dilation *before* relativity of simultaneity because I believe it is easier to understand this way.

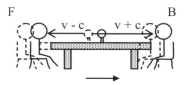

Figure N6.1. Moving — If light speeds added per newton

3. Greene, Brian. *The Elegant Universe, Superstrings, Hidden Dimensions, and the Quest for the Ultimate Theory* (New York: Vintage Books-pbk, 2000), p. 36.
4. Schutz, Bernard. *Gravity from the Ground Up* (Cambridge, England: Cambridge University Press, 2003), p. 189.
5. Greene, Brian. *The Elegant Universe, Superstrings, Hidden Dimensions, and the Quest for the Ultimate Theory* (New York: Vintage Books-pbk, 2000), p. 36.
6. Newtonian physics predicts the speed of the light adds or subtracts to the speed of the vehicle (see Fig. N6.1). For the right beam, speeds would add per $c + v$, where c is the speed of light and v is the speed of the vehicle. Thus the right beam *goes faster*. Similarly, speeds subtract for the left beam, so the left beam *goes slower*. Its speed is $c - v$. So the added speed of the light beam to the right makes up for the added distance to the right. And the reduced speed of the light beam to the left compensates for the shorter distance to the left. The net result per Newton is that the light beam reaches both presidents at the *same time*.

    Newtonian physics predicts people on the vehicle and people on the roadside both see the presidents sign simultaneously. Thus, if light speed *were* affected by motion, there would be no relativity of simultaneity.
7. Schutz, Bernard. *Gravity from the Ground Up* (Cambridge, England: Cambridge University Press, 2003), p. 202. Similar to length contraction, relativity of simultaneity varies as the cosine of the angle between the direction of motion of the observer and the line in space connecting the two events. Thus for two events whose connecting line is *parallel* to the direction of motion, relativity of simultaneity is a maximum. When the line connecting the two events is *perpendicular* to the direction of motion, there is no relativity of simultaneity.
8. Einstein to Rudolph Carnap, as noted in Carnap, Rudolf , "Autobiography," in *The Philosophy of Rudolf Carnap*, A. Schlipp, ed. (Chicago: Library of Living Philosophers, 1963), p. 37. As cited in Greene, Brian. *The Fabric of the Cosmos: Space, Time, and the Texture of Reality* (New York: Vintage Books-pbk, 2005), p. 141.
9. Ibid., p. 134.
10. Ibid., p. 141.
11. Lieber, Lillian. *The Einstein Theory of Relativity* (Lieber Press, 2007), p. 43–44. A number of observations have been made which give *indirect* evidence for length contraction. The muon experiment in Chapter 5 is one example. Here

is another: In particle accelerator experiments, "a spherical bunch of particles coming at you looks like a flattened ellipsoid due to relativistic shortening, and the detection probabilities and expected directions of ejecta are affected." Source: Self-adjoint, physicsforum.com, March 9, 2004. http://www.physics-forums.com/archive/index.php/t-15958.html. Last accessed June 2013.

In 1959, James Terrell of Los Alamos Scientific Laboratory explained, though length contraction is the actual effect, it is not what we would see. For astronomical observations (where the incoming light is essentially parallel), objects appear *rotated* due to relativity effects. Why? Because we do not see all the light rays from the object *at the* same instant in time. (Source: Terrell, James, Invisibility of the Lorentz Contraction, *Phys. Rev.* **116** (1959) 1041–1045. (The phenomenon was also derived independently by Roger Penrose.) An excellent animation of this effect is presented in Harrison, David M. "ContractInvisible," March 2003. http://faraday.physics.utoronto.ca/PVB/Harrison/SpecRel/Flash/ContractInvisible.html. Last accessed June 2013.

12. Based on table in Jones, Roger S. *Physics for the Rest of Us* (New York: McGraw-Hill, 1993), p. 23.

13. The demonstration and explanation works equally well for a pole of any size larger than the barn, assuming its relative speed is enough to contract it to the length of the stationary barn or less per the Lorentz Factor. For a more detailed explanation of the barn-pole paradox, see Einsteinlight, "The pole and barn paradox (ladder and garage paradox)." http://www.phys.unsw.edu.au/einsteinlight/jw/module4_pole_paradox.htm. Last accessed June 2013.

14. Thorne, Kip. *Black Holes & Time Warps: Einstein's Outrageous Legacy* (New York: W. W. Norton, 1994), p. 79. As quoted in Isaacson, Walter. *Einstein: His Life and Universe* (New York: Simon & Schuster, 2008-pbk), p. 133.

15. Einstein, Albert. "On the Electrodynamics of Moving Bodies." English translation of original published in Annalen der Physik, 17:891 (1905), which appears W. Perrett and GB Jeffery, *The Principle of Relativity: A Collection of Original Memoirs on the Special and General Theory of Relativity*, (London: Methuen, 1923), p. 1.

16. Zionism-israel.com, "Albert Einstein — Zionism and Israel — Biographies," Project Einstein. http://www.zionism-israel.com/bio/Albert_Einstein.htm. Last accessed June 2013.

17. Hume, David. Treatise on Human Nature, book 1, part 2; Norton, John D. "How Hume and Mach Helped Einstein Find Special Relativity," July 1, 2005. As cited in Isaacson, Walter. *Einstein: His Life and Universe* (New York: Simon & Schuster, 2008-pbk), p. 82. http://www.pitt.edu/~jdnorton/pap,rs/HumeMach.pdf. Last accessed June 2013.

18. Stenger, Victor J. *Quantum Gods: Creation, Chaos, and the Search for Cosmic Consciousness* (New York: Prometheus Books, 2009), p. 66.

19. Leibniz, G. W., *Philosophical Papers and Letters*, ed. L. E. Loemker (Reidel, Dordrecht, 1969). As quoted in Wheeler, John Archibald. *A Journey into Gravity and Spacetime* (New York: Freeman, 1990), p. 5.

Notes to Chap 7

1. Kaku, Michio. NOVA, "Einstein's Big Idea, E=mc² Explained", pbs.org. http://www.pbs.org/wgbh/nova/einstein/experts.html. Last accessed August, 2013.
2. Greene, Brian, *That Famous Equation and You*, edge.org, Oct. 6, 2005. http://www.edge.org/3rd_culture/greene05/greene05_index.html. Last accessed June 2013.
3. Einstein to Conrad Habicht, end of June-end of September 1905. As cited in Stachel, John. *Einstein from 'B' to 'Z'* (Boston: Birkhäuser, 2001), p. 202.
4. A gravitational field still exists in interplanetary space. The primary source is the Sun, which holds the planets in their orbits.
5. Again we are referring to *inertial* mass rather than *gravitational* mass.
6. Story based on Gibilisco, Stan *Understanding Einstein's Theories of Relativity: Man's New Perspective on the Cosmos* (Mineola, NY: Dover, 1983), p. 64–66. A version of the Inertial Balance was used by astronauts to monitor changes in their mass aboard space station "Skylab" launched in 1973. http://www-istp.gsfc.nasa.gov/stargaze/Sgloss.htm#v25. Last accessed June 2013.
7. The period of oscillation, P is equal to the mass times the spring constant, K: Here period = spring constant times mass or $P = Km$, where K is the spring constant for those particular springs, and m is the mass of the cargo.
8. A related concept in special relativity is *relativistic mass*; an increase in a particle's mass with relative motion. This so-called apparent mass is equal to a particle's rest mass divided by the Lorentz factor, sqrt $(1-v^2)$. You can see the similarity between this and relativistic momentum. We can assume the mass of a particle increases by the reciprocal Lorentz Factor due to relative motion (apparent mass), or we can assume the *mass stays the same* but the momentum of the particle increases due to relative motion. Each gives us a valid way to calculate the physics. Most modern physicists prefer the latter approach (as did Einstein), where mass is invariant — it gives a clearer picture of the underlying physics and is particularly useful when applied to spacetime physics and general relativity. http://math.ucr.edu/home/baez/physics/Relativity/SR/mass.html.

In 1901, four years before Einstein published his paper on special relativity, German physicist Walter Kaufman, "experimenting with fast moving electrons, found that the mass of a moving electron is greater than that of one at rest — a result which seemed very strange at the time." Source: Lieber, Lillian. *The Einstein Theory of Relativity* (Lieber Press, 2007), p. 78.

The concepts of relative mass (and relative momentum) were initially developed between 1905 and 1909 by Max Planck and American physical chemists Gilbert N. Lewis and Richard C. Tolman. Source: Gibbs, Philip *et al.*, "What is relativistic Mass?" Physics FAQ, Updated 2012. http://math.ucr. edu/home/baez/physics/Relativity/SR/mass.html. Last accessed June 2013.

9. "Facts and figures," CERN: European Organization for Nuclear Research, 2008. http://home.web.cern.ch/about/accelerators/large-hadron-collider. Last accessed June 2013.

10. Willem 's Gravesande story based on Bodanis, David. *E = mc²: A Biography of the World's Most Famous Equation* (New York: Walker and Company, 2000), p. 65.

11. Per the work-energy theorem, to determine the change in kinetic energy we integrate the net force of an object over the distance traveled: Per Newton's second law, the force is: $F = m\, dv/dt$. Integrating the force over distance we get: $\int F\, dx = \int m\, (dv/dt)\, dx = m\int (dx/dt)\, dv = m\int v\, dv = \frac{1}{2}\, m\, v^2$. Source: Doc Al, physicsforums.com, February 18, 2006. http://www.physicsforums.com/ showthread.php?t=111162. Last accessed June 2013.

12. Bodanis, David. *E = mc²: A Biography of the World's Most Famous Equation* (New York: Walker and Company, 2000), p. 68.

13. Einstein, Albert. "Does the Inertia of a Body Depend upon its Energy-Content?" Based on the English translation of his original 1905 German-language paper. (Published as *Ist die Trägheit eines Körpers von seinem Energiegehalt abhängig?* in *Annalen der Physik*. **18**:639 (1905). http://www. fourmilab.ch/etexts/einstein/E_mc2/www/. Last accessed June 2013.

14. Physicist John Stachel points out that the Newtonian kinetic energy equation is justified here because the moving frame was introduced only for comparison and can be arbitrarily slow. For a detailed mathematical explanation of Einstein's 1905 $E = mc^2$ paper, see Stachel, John. *Einstein from 'B' to 'Z'* (Boston: Birkhäuser, 2001), p. 215–222.

15. The association of (inertial) mass with electromagnetic energy "was often discussed before 1905." For example, attempts were made to "derive the entire inertial mass of the electron from the energy associated with its electromagnetic field." Physicists in fact showed that a container filled with EM radiation "manifests an apparent inertial mass (increase) . . . proportional to the energy of the enclosed radiation." Source: Stachel, John. *Einstein from 'B' to 'Z'* (Boston: Birkhäuser, 2001), p. 203.

The issue over whether any other physicist discovered $E = mc^2$ before Einstein is muddy. See, for example: Ball, Philip, "Did Einstein Discover $E = mc^2$?" physicsworld.com, April 23, 2011. http://physicsworld.com/cws/ article/news/46941. Last accessed June 2013.

16. Bodanis, David. *E = mc²: A Biography of the World's Most Famous Equation* (New York: Walker and Company, 2000), p. 26.

17. Strictly speaking, mass to energy conversion plays only a small part in the atomic bomb nuclear fission process. Nuclear force fields and various electromagnetic (EM) forces in the bonds between protons and neutrons — so-called

binding energies — are the dominant source of the energy released. Binding energies are also the chief source of the initial uranium's weight. Source: Pössel, Markus. "From E = mc² to the atomic bomb." Einstein Online Vol. 4 (2010), 1004.

18. Stachel, John. *Einstein from 'B' to 'Z'* (Boston: Birkhäuser, 2001), p. 203.

19. Nima Arkani-Hamed. *NOVA*, "Einstein's Big Idea, E = mc² Explained", pbs. org. http: //www.pbs.org/wgbh/nova/einstein/experts.html. Last accessed August, 2013.

20. For example, if we divided energy in kilogram-meters² per second² by c^2 (the speed of light squared) in meters² per second², we get energy in kilograms. Source: Taylor, Edwin F. and Wheeler, John Archibald. *Spacetime Physics: Introduction to Special Relativity — Second Edition* (New York: W. H. Freeman and Company, 1992), p. 190 and 203.

21. How much energy does a photon have? Multiply the photon's frequency times Planck's constant, per his formula, $E = h\nu$, where h is 6.62606957 × 10⁻³⁴ joule-second.

22. Hobson, Art. *Physics: Concepts and Connections* (New York: Addison Wesley, 2009), p. 299.

23. Brody, D. E. and Brody, A.R. *The Science Class You Wish You Had...: The Seven Greatest Scientific Discoveries in History and the People Who Made Them* (New York: Perigee Trade, 1997), p. 87.

24. McFarland, Ernie. *Einstein's Special Relativity: Discover it for Yourself* (Toronto: Trifolium Books, 1997), p. 57.

25. Physicist Art Hobson defines matter as rest-mass, and mass as inertia. So matter (rest-mass) can be converted to "non-material forms of energy via $E = mc^2$." Thus matter is not always conserved, but mass (inertia) is. Source: Hobson, Art. *Physics: Concepts and Connections* (New York: Addison Wesley, 2009), p. 299.

26. Swansont, thread #40, ScienceForums.net, 4/14/2012.

27. Neil deGrasse Tyson. *NOVA*, "Einstein's Big Idea, E=mc² Explained", pbs. org. http: //www.pbs.org/wgbh/nova/einstein/experts.html. Last accessed August, 2013.

28. Frank Wilczek. *NOVA*, "Einstein's Big Idea, E=mc² Explained", pbs.org. http: //www.pbs.org/wgbh/nova/einstein/experts.html. Last accessed August, 2013.

29. A proton is made of two up quarks and a down quark. A neutron contains an up quark and two down quarks. "The up and down quark's masses are, respectively, 0.3% and 0.6% of a proton's mass." Source: Hobson, Art, "Millikan Award Lecture, 2006: Physics for All" *Am. J. Phys.* **74** (12) 1048, Dec. 2006.

30. Hobson, Art. *Physics: Concepts and Connection*, 5th edition (New York Addison Wesley, 2010), p. 246.

31. Ibid. Hobson notes that particle interactions with the Higgs field (which gives particles their rest mass) explain the remaining 10% or so energy.

32. Cockcroft and Walton bombarded the nuclei of the element lithium with protons. The force of the collisions split the nuclei. Lithium then fused into two helium nuclei, with a resultant release of radiation. Source: Encyclopedia Britannica, "Sir John Douglas Cockcroft". http://www.britannica.com/eb/topic-123640/Sir-John-Douglas-Cockcroft. Last accessed June 2013.

33. NIST, "Einstein Was Right (Again): Experiments Confirm that $E = mc^2$," Dec. 21, 2005. http://www.nist.gov/public_affairs/releases/einstein.cfm. Last accessed June 2013.

34. Solovine, Maurice. *Albert Einstein: Letters to Solovine* (New York: Philosophical Library, 1987). p. 11–14. As cited in Isaacson, Walter. *Einstein: His Life and Universe* (New York: Simon & Schuster, 2008-pbk), p. 80–81.

35. Calder, Nigel. *Einstein's Universe: A Guide to the Theory of Relativity* (London: Penguin Books, 1982), p. 35.

36. Sun statistics from various NASA websites: Solarscience.msfc.nasa.gov, "The Solar Interior," Solar Physics, Dec. 2011; Graps, Amara," How old is the Sun?" solar-center.stanford.edu, accessed February 2013; Helios.ssfc.nasa.gov, "Ask Us: Sun," Cosmicopia, June, 2012.

In nuclear *fission*, an unstable atomic nucleus transforms into lighter nuclei, releasing high energy photons and often free neutrons in the process. Binding energies — force fields and various electromagnetic (EM) forces in the bonds between protons and neutrons in the original nucleus — are the dominant sources of the energy released, rather than mass to energy conversion. Source: Pössel, Markus. "From $E = mc^2$ to the atomic bomb." Einstein Online Vol. 4 (2010), 1004. http://www.einstein-online.info/spotlights/atombombe. Last accessed June 2013.

37. Bodanis, David. *E = mc²: A Biography of the World's Most Famous Equation* (New York: Walker and Company, 2000), p. 182.

Specifically, the energy released in the Sun's fusion process is as follows: Four ¹H nuclei (protons) possess a mass of *6.693 x 10⁻²⁷ kg*. One ⁴He nucleus (two protons and two neutrons) possesses a mass of *6.645 x 10⁻²⁷kg*. This gives a mass loss of *0.048 x 10⁻²⁷ kg*. This lost mass is converted to non-material energy as $E = mc^2 = (0.048 \times 10^{-27} \, kg) \times (3 \times 10^8 \, m/s)^2 = 4.3 \times 10^{-12} \, joule$. Source: Freedman, R. A. and Kaufmann III, W. J. *Universe*, 6th Edition (New York: W. H. Freeman, 2002), p. 392.

38. von Fáy-Siebenbürgen, Róbert (Erdélyi), Sheffield University, sunearthplan. net, 2007; Holladay, April, "Photon on a drunk walk, Why severed lizard tails keep twitching," Wonderquest, Cyberspeak, usatoday.com, November 2006. http://usatoday30.usatoday.com/tech/columnist/aprilholladay/2006-11-06-sun-lizards_x.htm. Last accessed July 2013.

39. Berna, Francesco *et al.*, "Microstratigraphic evidence of in situ fire in the Acheulean strata of Wonderwerk Cave, Northern Cape province, South Africa," *Proceedings of the National Academy of Sciences*, April 2, 2012. As cited

in sciencedaily.com, "Evidence That Human Ancestors Used Fire One Million Years Ago," April 2, 2012. http://www.sciencedaily.com/releases/2012/04/120402162548.htm. Last accessed July 2013.

Notes to Chap 8

1. Based on title of Greene, Brian. *The Fabric of the Cosmos: Space, Time, and the Texture of Reality* (New York: Vintage Books-pbk, 2005).
2. Bodanis, David. $E = mc^2$: *A Biography of the World's Most Famous Equation* (New York: Walker and Company, 2000), p. 78.
3. Stachel, John. *Einstein from 'B' to 'Z'* (Boston: Birkhäuser, 2001), p. 201.
4. Clark, Roland C. *Einstein: The Life and Times* (New York and Cleveland: The World Publishing Company, 1971), p. 108.
5. Fölsing, Albrecht, Ewald Osers trans. *Albert Einstein: A Biography* (New York: Viking, 1997), p. 202; Max Planck, *Scientific Autobiography and Other Papers* (New York: Philosophical Library, 1949), p. 42. As cited in Isaacson, Walter. *Einstein: His Life and Universe* (New York: Simon & Schuster, 2008-pbk), p. 140.
6. Max Planck did not accept Einstein's 1905 light quantization proposition. In 1908 he "warned the young patent clerk that he had gone too far". Five years later, Planck proposed Einstein for a "coveted seat in the Prussian Academy of Sciences". Planck's letter of recommendation said of Einstein: "That he might have overshot the target in his speculations, as for example in his light quantum hypothesis, should not be counted against him too much." Source: Isaacson, Walter. *Einstein: His Life and Universe* (New York: Simon & Schuster, 2008-pbk), p. 100.
7. Minkowski, H. A., "Space and Time," in H. A. Lorentz *et al.*, *The Principle of Relativity* (New York: Dover, 1952), p. 75. As cited in Taylor, Edwin F. and Wheeler, John Archibald. *Spacetime Physics: Introduction to Special Relativity — Second Edition* (New York: W. H. Freeman and Company, 1992), p. 15.
8. Bookrags.com, "World of Mathematics on Hermann Minkowski," 2006.
9. Seelig, Carl. *Albert Einstein: A Documentary Biography*. Translated by Mervyn Savill. (London: Staples Press, 1956). (Translation of *Albert Einstein: Eine Dokumentarische Biographie*, a revision of *Albert Einstein und die Schweiz*. Zürich: Europa-Verlag, 1952), p. 28. As cited in Isaacson, Walter. *Einstein: His Life and Universe* (New York: Simon & Schuster, 2008-pbk), p. 132.
10. "100 Years of Space-Time," Sept. 21, 2008, http://backreaction.blogspot.sg/2008/09/100-years-of-space-time.html. Last accessed June 2013.
11. In 1908, Einstein in "a short paper written with collaborator Jakob Laub". Source: Pyenson, Lewis, "Hermann Minkowski and Einstein's Special Theory of Relativity," Communicated by J. D. North, Springer, Archive for History of Exact Sciences: 31. V. 1977, Volume 17, Issue 1, pp 71–95 rp. 73.

12. Newman, J. R. *The World of Mathematics* (Mineola, NY: Dover, 1956).

13. Bookrags.com, "World of Mathematics on Hermann Minkowski," 2006.

14. This was suggested by a student of mine as a way to visualize spacetime.

15. Taylor , Edwin F. and Wheeler, John Archibald. *Spacetime Physics: Introduction to Special Relativity — Second Edition* (New York: W. H. Freeman and Company, 1992), p. 18.

16. We can express distance and time in the same units by using the speed of light, c as the conversion factor. For example, a time of 30 nanoseconds times the speed of light (3×10^8 meters per second) gives us a *time* of 9 meters. Conversely, a distance of 2 billion miles divided by the speed of light (671 million miles an hour) gives us a *distance* of 3 hours. Source: Ibid.

17. Hoffman, Banesh. *Relativity and Its Roots* (Mineola, NY: Dover-pbk, 1983), p. 126.

18. Poincaré was the first to propose an invariant interval, in 1905; "the quantity ($L^2 - c^2\, T^2$) where L represents the space interval and T the time interval." In 1908, Minkowski presented it in its 4-dimensional differential form: $c^2 dt^2 - dx^2 - dy^2 - dz^2 = c^2\, ds^2$. (Source: Marchal, C., Henri Poincaré: A Decisive Contribution to Relativity, General Scientific Direction, ONERA, 5.) http://www.annales. org/archives/x/Relativity.doc. Last accessed August 2013.

19. See: physicspages.com, "space-time intervals: invariance," Apr. 11, 2011. http://physicspages.com/2011/04/07/space-time-intervals-invariance/. Last accessed Aug. 2013.

20. The *velocity* of an object traveling through space and time or through spacetime is expressed in four dimensions. It is called the 4-velocity. Particles and collections of particles travel at various speeds through space, but always travel at the speed of light through *spacetime*. In other words, the magnitude of the 4-velocity vector always equals c. This is shown mathematically in Greene, Brian. *The Elegant Universe, Superstrings, Hidden Dimensions, and the Quest for the Ultimate Theory* (New York: Vintage Books-pbk, 2000), Chap. 2, Note 6, p. 392.

21. The planet in the story is real. Gliese 581 g has been identified in *Scientific American* as the exoplanet most likely to host life. It is one of 5 to 6 planets which orbit the star Gliese 581, a red dwarf some 20 light-years from Earth in the constellation Libra. Scientist estimate planet Gliese 581 g is two to three times the mass of the Earth and has surface temperatures which allow liquid water. It is very close to its star, completing an orbit in about 30 days. (Source: Wall, Mike and SPACE.com, "Gliese 581 g Tops List of 5 Potentially Habitable Exoplanets," scientificamerican.com. July 25, 2012. http://www.scientific-american.com/article.cfm?id=gliese-581g-tops-list-of-5-potentially-habitable-exoplanets. Last accessed June 2013.

22. As noted, the spacetime diagram in the text is presented in Steve's (Earth) frame of reference. There are two other frames of interest here; Arianna's outgoing frame and her incoming frame. Wristwatch times and resultant aging experienced by Steve and Arianna is the same in all three reference frames.

For an example of this. See EINSTEINLIGHT, "The twin paradox: Is the symmetry of time dilation paradoxical?" www.phys.unsw.edu.au/einsteinlight/jw/module4_twin_paradox.htm. Last accessed June 2013.

23. Taylor, Edwin F. and Wheeler, John Archibald. *Spacetime Physics: Introduction to Special Relativity — Second Edition* (New York: W. H. Freeman and Company, 1992), p. 128.

24. Calder, Nigel. *Einstein's Universe: A Guide to the Theory of Relativity* (London: Penguin Books, 1982), p. 156.

25. *Special relativity* can explain the Twins Paradox with time dilation and the Doppler effect. Due to the finite speed of light, it takes time for stay-at-home Steve to receive information on Arianna's *turn-around* at Terra. This asymmetry is the key to Arianna's time running slower than Steve's. For a detailed explanation, go to my website, marksmodernphysics.com and click on "Its Relative", "Archives", and "The Twins Paradox". http://www.marksmodernphysics.com/. Last accessed June 2013.

    General relativity can explain the Twins Paradox using the Equivalence Principle (EP): Acceleration and gravity produce the same physical effects (see Chap. 10). During the turn-around at Terra, Arianna experiences a *change* in speed and direction, in other words acceleration. Per the EP, this is equivalent to a gravitational field. Arianna is pressed *forward* against her seat harness when her rocket slows down before the turn-around at Terra. She is pressed *back* against her seat when the rocket speeds up again on its return to Earth. In both cases, her body is pushed towards Terra and away from Earth. This is equivalent to her being *lower* in a gravitational field as compared to Steve's location on Earth. Per general relativity, clocks which are lower in a gravitational field run slower than higher clocks (again see Chap. 10). Thus time runs slower for Arianna during her slow-down and speed-up, so she ages slower than Steve, the stay-at-home twin. For a more detailed explanation, see Styer, Daniel F. *Relativity for the Questioning Mind* (Baltimore: The Johns Hopkins University Press, 2011), p. 156.

26. Kaku, Michio. *Einstein's Cosmos: How Albert Einstein's Vision Transformed our Understanding of Space and Time* (London: Phoenix, 2005-pbk), p. 48.

27. Ibid.

28. Ibid, p. 49.

Notes to Chap 9

1. Einstein, Albert. *The World As I See It* (New York: Philosophical Library, 1949). (Based on *Mein Weltbild*, edited by Carl Seelig.), p. 8–11.

2. NIST, "NIST Pair of Aluminum Atomic Clocks Reveal Einstein's Relativity at a Personal Scale," September 23, 2010. The NIST tests also verified time

dilation predictions of special relativity at relative speeds of about 20 miles an hour. http://www.nist.gov/public_affairs/releases/aluminum-atomic-clock_092310.cfm. Last accessed June 2013.

3. Pais, Abraham. *Subtle is the Lord: The Science and Life of Albert Einstein* (Oxford University Press, New York, 1982), p. 239.

4. "Über das_Relativitätsprinzip und die aus demselben gezogenen Folgerungen," *Jahrbuch der Radioaktivität und Elektronik 4*, Translation: "On the Relativity Principle and conclusions drawn from it," *Yearbook of Radio and Electronics* (1907): p. 411–462; reprinted in CPAE, vol. 2: *The Swiss Years: Writings 1900–1909*, p. 433–488. As cited in Stachel, John. *Einstein from 'B' to 'Z'* (Boston: Birkhäuser, 2001), p. 264.

5. Einstein in a letter to Arnold Sommerfeld on October 29, 1912; as cited in Damour, Thibault. *Once Upon Einstein.* (Oxfordshire, UK: A. K. Peters, Ltd., 2006), p. 79.

6. Brody, D. E. and Brody, A.R. *The Science Class You Wish You Had...: The Seven Greatest Scientific Discoveries in History and the People Who Made Them* (New York: Perigee Trade, 1997), p. 47.

7. Newton assumed gravity is transmitted instantaneously because instantaneous gravity is required to maintain his third law of motion: For every action there is an equal and opposite reaction. Consider a massive object like the Sun transmitting the force of gravity to a significantly less massive object like the Earth. The force weakens with the square of the distance between them. But if gravity takes a finite amount of time to get from the Sun to the Earth, the Earth will have moved during that time. So the distance and as a result the force of gravity is changed. This leads to an imbalance between the action and reaction forces. Source: Schutz, Bernard. *Gravity from the Ground Up* (Cambridge, England: Cambridge University Press, 2003), p. 13–14.

8. Thorne, Kip. *Black Holes & Time Warps: Einstein's Outrageous Legacy* (New York: W. W. Norton, 1994), p. 96.

9. Brody, D. E. and Brody, A.R. *The Science Class You Wish You Had...: The Seven Greatest Scientific Discoveries in History and the People Who Made Them* (New York: Perigee Trade, 1997), p. 45. The transmission of electromagnetism (EM) from place to place is *not* action at a distance. Particle physics tells us *photons*, the EM messenger particles, are constantly being exchanged between any two matter particles with EM charge. Similarly, gluons and weak bosons particles transmit the strong and weak forces between responding particles, respectively.

10. Rosenblum, B. and Kuttner, F. *Quantum Enigma: Physics Encounters Consciousness* (New York: Oxford University Press, 2006), p. 36.

11. Newton actually said it in Latin. Newton, *Princip*, (*Philosophiae Naturalis Principia Mathematica*) ca. 1846, 1.c., 676.

12. Newton, 1692, 3rd letter to Richard Bentley.
13. Fölsing, Albrecht, Ewald Osers trans. *Albert Einstein: A Biography* (New York: Viking, 1997), p. 274. As cited in Ohanian, Hans C. *Einstein's Mistakes: The Human Failings of Genius* (New York: Norton, 2008), p. 4.
14. Kaku, Michio. *Einstein's Cosmos: How Albert Einstein's Vision Transformed our Understanding of Space and Time* (London: Phoenix, 2005-pbk), p. 51.
15. Sparknotes.com, "Albert Einstein, Professor Einstein," 2012.
16. Pais, Abraham. *Subtle is the Lord: The Science and Life of Albert Einstein* (Oxford University Press, New York, 1982), p. 186.
17. Einstein letter to Jacob Laub, Bern, 19 May 1909. http://www.astro.physik. uni-potsdam.de/~afeld/einstein/einstein.html. Last accessed June 2013.
18. Bodanis, David. *E = mc²: A Biography of the World's Most Famous Equation* (New York: Walker and Company, 2000), p. 90.
19. Einstein timeline, einsteinyear.org, Institute of Physics, 2007. http://www. einsteinyear.org/facts/timeline/.
20. Pais, Abraham. *Subtle is the Lord: The Science and Life of Albert Einstein* (Oxford University Press, New York, 1982), p. 505.
21. Einstein timeline, einsteinyear.org, Institute of Physics, 2007. http://www. einsteinyear.org/facts/timeline/.
22. Ohanian, Hans C. *Einstein's Mistakes: The Human Failings of Genius* (New York: Norton, 2008), p. 181.
23. Pais, Abraham. *Subtle is the Lord: The Science and Life of Albert Einstein* (Oxford University Press, New York, 1982), p. 192.
24. Sparknotes.com, "Albert Einstein, Professor Einstein," 2012.
25. Fölsing, Albrecht, Ewald Osers trans. *Albert Einstein: A Biography* (New York: Viking, 1997), p. 27. As cited in Ohanian, Hans C. *Einstein's Mistakes: The Human Failings of Genius* (New York: Norton, 2008), p. 181.
26. Stachel, John. *Einstein from 'B' to 'Z'* (Boston: Birkhäuser, 2001), p. 267.
27. Ibid., p. 237.
28. Preface to Czech edition of Einstein, Albert. *Relativity, The Special and General Theory: A Popular Exposition* (New York: Crown, 1956). 1956a. As cited in Stachel, John. *Einstein from 'B' to 'Z'* (Boston: Birkhäuser, 2001), p. 237.
29. Moring, Gary. *The Complete Idiot's Guide to Understanding Einstein* (Royersford, PA: Alpha, 1998), p. 185.
30. Einstein timeline, Einsteinyear.org, Institute of Physics, 2007. http://www. einsteinyear.org/facts/timeline/.
31. Sparknotes.com, "Albert Einstein, Professor Einstein," 2012.
32. Ibid.
33. Ohanian, Hans C. *Einstein's Mistakes: The Human Failings of Genius* (New York: Norton, 2008), p. 191.

Notes to Chap 10

1. Hoffman, Banesh. *Relativity and Its Roots* (Mineola, NY: Dover-pbk, 1983), p. 131.
2. Einstein, Albert and Harris, Allan. *Einstein's Essays in Science* (New York: Dover, 2009). Reprint of *Essays in Science*, (New York: The Wisdom Library, A Division of Philosophical Library, 1934), p. 80.
3. Williams, David R., "The Apollo 15 Hammer-Feather Drop." NASA, last updated February 12, 2008. http://nssdc.gsfc.nasa.gov/planetary/lunar/apollo_15_feather_drop.html. Last accessed June 2013.
4. The Moon is about 1/80ᵗʰ the mass of the Earth. So we would expect its surface gravity to be much less than Earth's. There is, however, a countering effect. The Moon's radius is ¼ that of the Earth. This means the *surface* of the Moon is 4 times closer to its center than the surface of Earth to its center. By Newton's inverse square law, this is a 4 x 4 or 16 times greater effect. In other words, the Moon's mass makes its gravity less, but the closeness of its surface to its center makes its surface gravity greater. However, the Moon's lower mass more than offsets its smaller radius. The net result is the Moon's surface gravity is about one-sixth the Earth's surface gravity. Source: Hey, Anthony J. G. and Walters, Patrick. *Einstein's Mirror* (Cambridge, UK: Cambridge University Press, 1997), pp. 167, 168.

   It is a combination of weaker gravity at its surface and solar irradiation which results in the Moon's very thin atmosphere. Source: Goddard, Andy, "Re: Why doesn't the Moon have an atmosphere like the Earth?" Astronomy, madsci.org, February 24, 2002. http://www.madsci.org/posts/archives/2002–02/1014639434.As.r.html. Last accessed June 2013.
5. Compton, William David, "Where No Man Has Gone Before: A History of Apollo Lunar Exploration Missions." NASA, 1989. http://history.nasa.gov/SP-4214/contents.html. Last accessed June 2013.
6. Brody, D. E. and Brody, A. R. *The Science Class You Wish You Had...: The Seven Greatest Scientific Discoveries in History and the People Who Made Them* (New York: Perigee Trade, 1997), p. 28. Mass plays two roles in Newtonian physics. *Inertial mass* is a measure of an object's resistance to its velocity being changed. The force needed to change the object's velocity (i.e., to make it accelerate) is given by Newton's second law of motion: force = mass times acceleration ($F = ma$). On the other hand, *gravitational mass* has to do with Newton's equation of gravity: the strength of the force of gravity between two objects is proportional to the product of their masses: $Fg = (G\, m_1\, m_2)/r^2$). The fact that objects of different mass fall at the same rate means inertial mass and gravitational mass are equivalent.
7. Hartle, James B. *Gravity: An Introduction to Einstein's General Relativity* (New York: Addison Wesley, 2003), p. 14. Update: Williams, James G. *et al.*, "Lunar laser ranging tests of the equivalence principle," *Class. Quantum Grav.* **29** (2012) 184004.

8. Ibid., Chap. 3.

9. "The Great Works II," The Center for History of Physics, American Institute of Physics, 2009. http://www.aip.org/history/einstein/great2.htm. Last accessed June 2013.

10. CPAE: The Collected Papers of Albert Einstein, Vol. 3. *The Swiss Years: Writings, 1909–1911*, p. 487–488 (Princeton: Princeton University Press, 1987–2006). As cited in Stachel, John. *Einstein from 'B' to 'Z'* (Boston: Birkhäuser, 2001), p. 264.

11. Hartle, James B. *Gravity: An Introduction to Einstein's General Relativity* (New York: Addison Wesley, 2003), p. 110–113.

12. Einstein, Albert. "Fundamental Ideas and Methods of the Theory of Relativity", 1920. As cited in Isaacson, Walter. *Einstein: His Life and Universe* (New York: Simon & Schuster, 2008-pbk), p. 145.

13. Ibid.

14. Randall, Lisa. *Warped Passages: Unraveling the Mysteries of the Universe's Hidden Dimensions* (New York: Harper Collins, 2005), p. 97.

15. More precisely (as viewed from a "stationary" frame): When the two objects are released, they continue to move upward but with *constant* velocity. (Their velocity is the instantaneous velocity at the instant they were released.) Since the velocity of the rocket ship continues to increase as it accelerates, the floor of the rocket ship catches up with the two objects and hits them from below. Source: Lieber, Lillian. *The Einstein Theory of Relativity* (Lieber Press, 2007), p. 102.

16. Stachel, John. *Einstein from 'B' to 'Z'* (Boston: Birkhäuser, 2001), p. 304.

17. Kaku, Michio. *Einstein's Cosmos: How Albert Einstein's Vision Transformed our Understanding of Space and Time* (London: Phoenix, 2005-pbk), p. 65.

18. Curie, Eve, *Madame Curie* (New York: Doubleday, 1937), p. 284; Fölsing, Albrecht, Ewald Osers trans. *Albert Einstein: A Biography* (New York: Viking, 1997), p. 325. As cited in Isaacson, Walter. *Einstein: His Life and Universe* (New York: Simon & Schuster, 2008-pbk), p. 181.

19. Frucci, Adam, "World's Tallest Outdoor Elevator Provides Great Views, Sheer Terror," http://gizmodo.com/306627/worlds-tallest-outdoor-glass-elevator-provides-great-views-sheer-terror. Last accessed July, 2013.

20. The Equivalence Principle has its limitations. Einstein's 1907 calculation on the bending of light was off by a factor of two. A light beam bends *twice as much* in a gravitational field than it does due to acceleration alone, which effectively includes the warping of time only. The 1915 field equations of general relativity, which contain both the warping of time and space, give the corrected amount. Source: Ohanian, Hans C. *Einstein's Mistakes: The Human Failings of Genius* (New York: Norton, 2008), p. 226. (See Appendix E for more details.)

21. Kaku, Michio. *Einstein's Cosmos: How Albert Einstein's Vision Transformed our Understanding of Space and Time* (London: Phoenix, 2005-pbk), p. 154.

22. Isaacson, Walter. *Einstein: His Life and Universe* (New York: Simon & Schuster, 2008-pbk), p. 148.

23. Born, Max. *Einstein's Theory of Relativity* (New York: Dover, 1965), p. 318.

24. Ehrenfest published his paper on the rotating disc on September 29, 1909. Einstein mentioned the rotating disc in a letter to Arnold Sommerfeld on September 28, 1909. So it appears Ehrenfest and Einstein considered the issue at about the same time. Source: Stachel, John. *Einstein from 'B' to 'Z'* (Boston: Birkhäuser, 2001), p. 246.

25. Length contraction in special relativity applies to *uniform* motion. So, strictly speaking, to measure the disc we must choose a ruler so small it's motion on the *rotating* disc can, for all practical purposes, be considered uniform.

    The idea is to set the disc spinning. Noah at rest above measures the circumference of the spinning disc with a very small ruler. He tosses the ruler to Sue riding on the spinning disc. She then measures the disc's circumference. From Noah's point of view at rest above, the ruler now on the spinning disc is contracted. Thus Sue has to lay it end-to-end *more times* to make it go around the entire circumference. So she measures a longer circumference than Noah did.

    Since a ruler placed on the radius travels perpendicular to the rotating motion, it is unaffected. So Sue measures the same radius as Noah did. Thus Sue's measured circumference divided by the radius is greater than 2π (two times Pi). Source: Greene, Brian. *The Elegant Universe, Superstrings, Hidden Dimensions, and the Quest for the Ultimate Theory* (New York: Vintage Books-pbk, 2000), p. 62–64. A detailed mathematical explanation is given in Max Born's *Einstein's Theory of Relativity* (New York: Dover, 1965), p. 321–327.

Notes to Chap 11

1. From a clip of a lecture included in a 1993 episode of the PBS science series NOVA, entitled *"The Best Mind Since Einstein."* http://www.youtube.com/watch?v=fQ9IBqj0HwE&feature=youtu.be. Last accessed July 2013.

2. Paraphrased from the song "In the Year 2525 (Exordium and Terminus)," written by Rick Evans in 1964.

3. Foley, Jonathan, "Boundaries for a Healthy Planet," *Sci. Am.* April (2010). http://www.scientificamerican.com/article.cfm?id=boundaries-for-a-healthy-planet. Last accessed July 2013.

4. "Physics First" is the education concept that physics — the mother of all sciences — be taught in the ninth or tenth grade, before biology and chemistry.

5. According to general relativity, time runs slower for lower clocks even in a *uniform* gravitational field. Note that the elevator thought experiment is in uniform acceleration, which per the EP is equivalent to a uniform gravitational field.

6. Davies, Paul. *About Time: Einstein's Unfinished Revolution* (New York: Simon & Schuster-pbk, 1996), p. 100–101. The original manuscript is: Pound and Rebka (*Phys. Rev. Lett.* **3** (1959) 439.

7. Ibid., p. 57.

8. For more details, see Hyperphysics, "Hafele and Keating Experiment," 2012. Original manuscript: J. C. Hafele and R. E. Keating, *Science* **177**, 166 (1972).

9. For a detailed description of the Vessot/Levine rocket clock experiment, see Will, Clifford M. *Was Einstein Right? Putting General Relativity to the Test* (New York: Basic Books, 1993), p. 57–63.

10. National Maritime Museum, "History of the Royal Observatory". http://www.rmg.co.uk/about/history/royal-observatory/. Last accessed June 2013.

11. Rindler, Wolfgang. *Essential Relativity: Special, General, and Cosmological* (London: Springer-Verlag, 1977), p. 2; Davies, Paul. *About Time: Einstein's Unfinished Revolution* (New York: Simon & Schuster-pbk, 1996), p. 99.

12. Pogge, Richard, "Real-World Relativity: The GPS Navigation System," April 27, 2009. http://www.astronomy.ohio-state.edu/~pogge/Ast162/Unit5/gps.html. Last accessed June 2013.

13. Cartlidge, Edwin, "Gravity's effect on time confirmed," physicsworld.com , Feb 17, 2010. http://physicsworld.com/cws/article/news/2010/feb/17/gravitys-effect-on-time-confirmed. Last accessed June 2013.

14. Some time after writing the Neutronium story, I came across an old science-fiction book on beings who live on a Neutron star; *Dragon's Egg* by Robert L. Forward, (Del Rey; 1 Reprint edition: 2000). It has significantly more physics detail and is a fun and educational read.

15. Einstein, Albert. "Autobiographical Notes." In Schilpp, Paul Arthur, ed. *Albert Einstein: Philosopher-Scientist* (La Salle, III: Open Court Press, 1949), p. 10; Pais, Abraham. *Subtle is the Lord: The Science and Life of Albert Einstein* (Oxford University Press, New York, 1982), p. 38.

16. Einstein, Albert. "On the Method of Theoretical Physics," Herbert Spencer lecture, Oxford, June 10, 1933, in Einstein, Albert, *Ideas and Opinions*, based on *Mein Weltbild*, edited by Carl Seelig (New York: Bonzana Books, 1954), p. 270. As cited in Isaacson, Walter. *Einstein: His Life and Universe* (New York: Simon & Schuster, 2008-pbk), p. 19.

17. Thorne, Kip. *Black Holes & Time Warps: Einstein's Outrageous Legacy* (New York: W. W. Norton, 1994), p. 130.

Notes to Chap 12

1. Born, Max. *Einstein's Theory of Relativity* (New York: Dover, 1965), p. 335.

2. In the more rigorous language of calculus, the Equivalence Principle holds only over an infinitesimally small region of spacetime.

3. Egdall, Mark, "Teaching General Relativity to the Layperson" *Phys. Teach.* **47** (November 2009) 522–527. An anonymous reviewer kindly pointed out that mathematically the invariant (Minkowskian) interval in a reference frame in uniform motion is given by $d\sigma^2 = \eta_{\mu\nu}dx^\mu dx^\nu$, where $\eta_{\mu\nu}$ = diag [1,-1,-1,-1]. However, in generalized co-ordinates, which can describe an accelerating frame (among others), the expression for the invariant interval is $d\sigma^2 = g_{\mu\nu}(x) dx^\mu dx^\nu$.

4. Those familiar with calculus will recognize, as the length of the straight lines approaches zero, the difference between the "stitched together" lines and the curved surface also approaches zero. In the limit when the line length equals zero, this difference equals zero. Similarly, Einstein invoked calculus to "stitch together" a set of local free-float frames to form a global geometry. In the limit where the spacetime region equals zero, this global geometry is exact.

Notes to Chap 13

1. Pais, Abraham. *Subtle is the Lord: The Science and Life of Albert Einstein* (Oxford University Press, New York, 1982), p. 188.
2. Born, Max. *Einstein's Theory of Relativity* (New York: Dover, 1965), p. 320.
3. Einstein to Sommerfeld, October 29, 1912, CPAE Vol. 5: *The Swiss Years: Correspondence, 1902–1914*, Doc. 421; Fölsing, Albrecht, Ewald Osers trans. *Albert Einstein: A Biography* (New York: Viking, 1997), p. 315; Greene, Brian. *The Elegant Universe, Superstrings, Hidden Dimensions, and the Quest for the Ultimate Theory* (New York: Vintage Books-pbk, 2000), p. 62; Kaku, Michio. *Einstein's Cosmos: How Albert Einstein's Vision Transformed our Understanding of Space and Time* (London: Phoenix, 2005-pbk), p. 70.
4. Stachel, John. *Einstein from 'B' to 'Z'* (Boston: Birkhäuser, 2001), p. 281 and 303. Einstein knew to represent the spacetime interval with Gaussian coefficients but, per Stachel, did not know how to develop "generally covariant tensors . . . While the analogy to Gaussian surface theory had occurred to Einstein before he consulted Grossman . . . the later line of development from Riemann to Ricci and Levi-Civita only became clear to Einstein after consulting Grossman."
5. Pais, Abraham. *Subtle is the Lord: The Science and Life of Albert Einstein* (Oxford University Press, New York, 1982), p. 212.
6. Isaacson, Walter. *Einstein: His Life and Universe* (New York: Simon & Schuster, 2008-pbk), p. 192.
7. Sugimoto, Kenji, *Albert Einstein: A Photographic Biography* (New York: Schocken Books, 1989) p. 19. As cited in Kaku, Michio. *Einstein's Cosmos: How Albert Einstein's Vision Transformed our Understanding of Space and Time* (London: Phoenix, 2005-pbk), p. 25.

8. Einstein in a letter to Marcel Grossman's widow. As cited in Aczel, Amir D. *God's Equation, Einstein, Relativity, and the Expanding Universe* (Surrey, UK: Delta, 2000), p. 61.

9. Isaacson, Walter. *Einstein: His Life and Universe* (New York: Simon & Schuster, 2008-pbk), p. 192.

10. Einstein letter to Mileva Marić on Dec. 28, 1901. CPAE, Vol. 1: *The Early Years, 1879–1902*, Doc, 131, p. 190.

11. Einstein, Albert. "Autobiographische Skizze." In Seelig, Carl. *Albert Einstein: A Documentary Biography.* Translated by Mervyn Savill. (London: Staples Press,1956, p. 15–16 (Translation of *Albert Einstein: Eine Dokumentarische Biographie,* a revision of *Albert Einstein und die Schweiz.* (Zurich: Europa-Verlag, 1952); Isaacson, Walter. *Einstein: His Life and Universe* (New York: Simon & Schuster, 2008-pbk), p. 193.

12. Thorne, Kip. *Black Holes & Time Warps: Einstein's Outrageous Legacy* (New York: W. W. Norton, 1994), p. 113.

13. wfu.edu, "Carl Friedrich Gauss", April 4, 1997; Asimov, Isaac. *Biographical Encyclopedia of Science and Technology: The Lives and Achievements of 1195 Great Scientists from Ancient Times to the Present, Chronologically Arranged.* (New York: Doubleday, 1972).

14. Bell, Eric Temple, *Men of Mathematics* (New York: Simon Schuster, 1937). As cited in Math Odyssey 2000, CARL FRIEDRICH GAUSS (1777–1855). www. sonoma.edu/Math/faculty/Falbo/gauss.html. Last accessed June 2013.

15. Mathpages.com, 8.6 "On Gauss's Mountain". http://mathpages.com/rr/s8-06/8-06.htm. Last accessed June 2013.

16. O'Connor, J. J. and Robertson, E. F. MacTutor History of Mathematics, "Non-Euclidean geometry." http://www-groups.dcs.st-and.ac.uk/history/Hist-Topics/Non-Euclidean_geometry.html. Last Accessed August 2013.

17. Letter from Gauss to Farkas Bolyai, 1832. As cited in Randall, Lisa. *Warped Passages: Unraveling the Mysteries of the Universe's Hidden Dimensions* (New York: Harper Collins, 2005), p. 105.

18. Ibid., "János Bolyai"; Mathpages.com, 8.6 "On Gauss's Mountain". http://mathpages.com/rr/s8-06/8-06.htm. Last accessed June 2013.

19. wfu.edu, "Carl Friedrich Gauss", April 4, 1997; Biographer Waldo Dunnington, a life-long student of Gauss, established in *Gauss, Titan of Science* that Gauss's work on non-Euclidean geometry had in fact preceded the published work of János by a number of years.

20. Cutrone, Joseph W., "On Riemann's 1859 Paper 'Über die Anzahl der Primzahlen unter einer gegebenen Grösse' and Its Consequences," Sept. 2005. http://www.math.northwestern.edu/~jcutrone/Work/J.%20Cutrone%20Master's%20Thesis.pdf. Last accessed June 2013.

21. Isaacson, Walter. *Einstein: His Life and Universe* (New York: Simon & Schuster, 2008-pbk), p. 194.

22. Answers.com, "Bernhard Riemann", 2012. http://www.answers.com/topic/bernhard-riemann. Last accessed June 2013.
23. O'Connor, J. J. and Robertson, E. F. MacTutor History of Mathematics, "Georg Friedrich Bernhard Riemann". http://www.gap-system.org/~history/Biographies/Riemann.html. Last accessed June 2013.
24. Gauss letter to Ferdinand Karl Schweikart, 1824. As cited in Wheeler, John Archibald. *A Journey into Gravity and Spacetime* (New York: Freeman, 1990), p. 5.
25. Answers.com, "Bernhard Riemann", 2012. http://www.answers.com/topic/bernhard-riemann. Last accessed June 2013.
26. Clark, Roland C. *Einstein: The Life and Times* (New York and Cleveland: The World Publishing Company, 1971), p. 202.
27. Mathpages.com, 8.6 "On Gauss's Mountain". http://mathpages.com/rr/s8-06/8-06.htm. Last accessed June 2013.
28. Hartle, James B. *Gravity: An Introduction to Einstein's General Relativity* (New York: Addison Wesley, 2003), p. 21.
29. Based on Born, Max. *Einstein's Theory of Relativity* (New York: Dover, 1965), p. 321–327, where a full mathematical derivation is given.
30. Wheeler, John Archibald. *A Journey into Gravity and Spacetime* (New York: Freeman, 1990), p. 84. More precisely, the trampoline represents spacetime curvature *inside* a stellar object such as the Sun (assuming a perfectly spherical, uniform density object for simplicity). In this case, spacetime curvature is *contractile*. Per Wheeler, "it bends all non-approaching free-float world lines into approaching world-lines."
31. Ibid, p. 11–12.
32. Schutz, Bernard. *Gravity from the Ground Up* (Cambridge, England: Cambridge University Press, 2003), p. 222.
33. Russell, Bertrand, *ABC of Relativity* (Oxford, UK: Taylor & Francis, 2009), p. 79 (first published in 1925). As cited in Gardner, Martin. *Relativity Simply Explained* (Mineola, NY: Dover, 1997), p. 89.
34. Wheeler, John Archibald. *A Journey into Gravity and Spacetime* (New York: Freeman, 1990), p. 20.
35. Ibid.
36. Gardner, Martin. *Relativity Simply Explained* (Mineola, NY: Dover, 1997), p. 87.

Notes to Chap 14

1. Einstein, Albert and Harris, Alan. *Einstein's Essays in Science* (New York: Dover, 2009). Reprint of *Essays in Science*, (New York: The Wisdom Library, A Division of Philosophical Library, 1934), p. 84. As cited in Gaither, Carl C., *Gaither's Dictionary of Scientific Quotations* (New York: Springer, 2012); Hoffman, Banesh. *Relativity and Its Roots* (Mineola, NY: Dover-pbk, 1983), p. 158.

2. General relativity also had to agree with special *relativity* when there is no mass-energy present (flat spacetime) and when all motion is uniform (no acceleration). Source: Mook, Delo E., Vargish, Thomas, *Inside Relativity* (Princeton, NJ: Princeton University Press, 1987), p. 176.

   Other physicists at the time tried and ultimately failed to develop a new theory of gravity based on special relativity. Per Kip Thorne, they included "Gunnar Nordstrom in Finland, Gustav Mie in Germany, and Max Abraham in Italy." But none "adopted Einstein's spacetime curvature (approach). Instead they treated gravity, like electromagnetism, as due to a force field . . . in flat spacetime." Source: Thorne, Kip. *Black Holes & Time Warps: Einstein's Outrageous Legacy* (New York: W. W. Norton, 1994), p. 115.

3. Kopeikin, Sergei *et al.*, *Relativistic Celestial Mechanics of the Solar System* (New York: Wiley & Sons, 2011).

4. Will, Clifford M. *Was Einstein Right? Putting General Relativity to the Test* (New York: Basic Books, 1993), p. 91. The influence of other planets on the perihelion shift of Mercury is shown in Table N14.1 below. Ibid., p. 91.

5. Einstein to Arnold Sommerfeld, October 29, 1912. CPAE, Vol. 5: *The Swiss Years: Correspondence, 1902–1914*, Doc. 421; Calaprice, Alice, Ed. *The Ultimate Quotable Einstein* (Princeton: Princeton University Press, 2011), p. 359. As cited in Isaacson, Walter. *Einstein: His Life and Universe* (New York: Simon & Schuster, 2008-pbk), p. 193.

6. Isaacson, Walter. *Einstein: His Life and Universe* (New York: Simon & Schuster, 2008-pbk), p. 197.

7. Stachel, John. *Einstein from 'B' to 'Z'* (Boston: Birkhäuser, 2001), p. 240–241. Einstein also believed these gravitational field equations violated "Mach's principle", which states "the presence of matter and energy in the universe uniquely determines the gravitational field surrounding it." Source: Kaku, Michio. *Einstein's Cosmos: How Albert Einstein's Vision Transformed our Understanding of Space and Time* (London: Phoenix, 2005-pbk), p. 73.

8. Ibid.

9. CPAE, Vol. 4: *The Swiss Years: Writings, 1912–1914*," Doc. 13, Generalized Theory of Relativity.

10. Einstein to Arnold Sommerfeld, July 15, 1915. As cited in Isaacson, Walter. *Einstein: His Life and Universe* (New York: Simon & Schuster, 2008-pbk), p. 212.

11. Ibid., p. 213.

12. Einstein to Erwin Freundlich, Sept. 30, 1915. Ibid.

13. Ibid., p. 179. When he nominated Einstein for membership in the Prussian Academy of Sciences in 1913, Planck still believed Einstein's light quanta (particles) idea was wrong. Planck told the Academy: "One should not count it too heavily against him (Einstein) that in his speculations he occasionally might have missed the mark, as e.g., in his hypothesis of light quanta . . ." Source: CPAE, Vol. 5: *The Swiss Years: Correspondence, 1902–1914*, Doc. 527. As

Table N14.1. The Perihelion Shift of Mercury. *Newton's predictions disagrees with observations by 43 arc seconds.*

Newtonian Prediction	Mercury Perihelion Shift (per century)
Influence of:	
Venus	277 arc seconds
Jupiter	153 arc seconds
Earth	90 arc seconds
All others	10 arc seconds
Total Prediction (Newton)	*531 arc seconds*
Observations	*574 arc seconds*
Error	**43 arc seconds**

cited in Ohanian, Hans C. *Einstein's Mistakes: The Human Failings of Genius* (New York: Norton, 2008), p. 141.

14. Ibid., p. 200.
15. Ibid., p. 202.
16. Seelig, Carl. *Albert Einstein: A Documentary Biography.* Translated by Mervyn Savill. (London: Staples Press, 1956). (Translation of *Albert Einstein: Eine Dokumentarische Biographie*, a revision of *Albert Einstein und die Schweiz.* Zürich: Europa-Verlag, 1952), p. 148. As cited in Isaacson, Walter. *Einstein: His Life and Universe* (New York: Simon & Schuster, 2008-pbk), p. 180.
17. "WWI Timeline," The Great War and the Shaping of the 20th Century, 2004. Public Broadcasting Service. http://www.pbs.org/greatwar/timeline/time_1914.html. Last accessed June 2013.
18. Kaku, Michio. *Einstein's Cosmos: How Albert Einstein's Vision Transformed our Understanding of Space and Time* (London: Phoenix, 2005-pbk), p. 78.
19. Einstein in letter to Paul Ehrenfest. As cited in Charap, John M. *Explaining the Universe: The New Age of Physics* (Princeton: Princeton University Press, 2004) revised 9/23/08, p. 126; Moring, Gary. *The Complete Idiot's Guide to Understanding Einstein* (Royersford, PA: Alpha, 1998), p. 189; Clark, Roland C. *Einstein: The Life and Times* (New York and Cleveland: The World Publishing Company, 1971), p. 231.
20. Ohanian, Hans C. *Einstein's Mistakes: The Human Failings of Genius* (New York: Norton, 2008), p. 202.
21. Einstein to Elsa Einstein, after July 26, 1914. As cited in Isaacson, Walter. *Einstein: His Life and Universe* (New York: Simon & Schuster, 2008-pbk), p. 187.
22. Ibid.
23. Ibid., p. 214.

24. Kaku, Michio. *Einstein's Cosmos: How Albert Einstein's Vision Transformed our Understanding of Space and Time* (London: Phoenix, 2005-pbk), p. 77.
25. Ibid.
26. Einstein to Paul Ehrenfest, January 17, 1916. As cited in Isaacson, Walter. *Einstein: His Life and Universe* (New York: Simon & Schuster, 2008-pbk), p. 218.
27. Penrose, Roger. *The Road to Reality: A Complete Guide to the Physical Universe* (Kent, UK: BCA, 2004), p. 466.
28. Pais, Abraham. *Subtle is the Lord: The Science and Life of Albert Einstein* (Oxford University Press, New York, 1982), p. 256; Mathpages.com, "8.7 Strange Meetings". http://mathpages.com/rr/s8–07/8–07.htm. Last accessed June 2013.
29. Einstein, Albert. "The Foundations of the General Theory of Relativity," *Annalen der Physik* (March 20, 1916), CPAE, Vol. 6: *The Berlin Years: Writings, 1914–1917*, Doc. 30. As cited in Isaacson, Walter. *Einstein: His Life and Universe* (New York: Simon & Schuster, 2008-pbk), p. 220.
30. Einstein to Heinrich Zangger, Nov. 26, 1915. As cited in Isaacson, Walter. *Einstein: His Life and Universe* (New York: Simon & Schuster, 2008-pbk), p. 223; Kaku, Michio. *Einstein's Cosmos: How Albert Einstein's Vision Transformed our Understanding of Space and Time* (London: Phoenix, 2005-pbk), p. 76; Ohanian, Hans C. *Einstein's Mistakes: The Human Failings of Genius* (New York: Norton, 2008), p. 225.
31. Einstein to Hans Albert, Nov. 4, 1915. As cited in Isaacson, Walter. *Einstein: His Life and Universe* (New York: Simon & Schuster, 2008-pbk), p. 216.
32. Kaku, Michio. *Einstein's Cosmos: How Albert Einstein's Vision Transformed our Understanding of Space and Time* (London: Phoenix, 2005-pbk), p. 77. Per Kaku, in Einstein's Göttingen lectures he "still lacked certain mathematical tools called the 'Bianchi identities'". This prevented Einstein from "deriving his equations from a simple form, called the 'action'". Hilbert on the other hand used these identities to derive his final form of the gravitational field equations.
33. Isaacson, Walter. *Einstein: His Life and Universe* (New York: Simon & Schuster, 2008-pbk), p. 221.
34. Reid, Constance. *Hilbert-Courant* (New York: Springer-Verlag, 1986), 142. As cited in Isaacson, Walter. *Einstein: His Life and Universe* (New York: Simon & Schuster, 2008-pbk), p. 222. This is a secondary source. Isaacson notes that the original source for Hilbert's statement could not be found.
35. Kaku, Michio. *Einstein's Cosmos: How Albert Einstein's Vision Transformed our Understanding of Space and Time* (London: Phoenix, 2005-pbk), p. 77.
36. Wheeler, John Archibald. *A Journey into Gravity and Spacetime* (New York: Freeman, 1990), p. 11–12.
37. Schutz, Bernard. *Gravity from the Ground Up* (Cambridge, England: Cambridge University Press, 2003), p. 213.

38. Ohanian, Hans C. *Einstein's Mistakes: The Human Failings of Genius* (New York: Norton, 2008), p. 224.

39. Schutz, Bernard. *Gravity from the Ground Up* (Cambridge, England: Cambridge University Press, 2003), p. 1.

40. Curious.astro.cornell.edu, "Curious About Astronomy," Ask an Astronomer, Oct. 18, 2005. http://curious.astro.cornell.edu/question.php?number=542. Last accessed July 2013.

41. Pressure is defined as *force* per unit area, and force is the *flow of momentum*. For non-relativistic speeds, the momentum P is: $P = mV$ where m is mass and V is velocity. The force F, is: $F = ma = m\, dV/dt = dP/dt$. "The net force is the momentum flow from A to B minus the momentum flow from B to A." Source: Denker, John, "A Fluid has Pressure Everywhere," Physics Documents, 2003. http://www.av8n.com/physics/pressure-everywhere.htm. Last accessed July 2013. To see how pressure is represented in general relativity, see Baez, John, "The General Relativity Tutorial", 2006.

42. Thorne, Kip. *Black Holes & Time Warps: Einstein's Outrageous Legacy* (New York: W. W. Norton, 1994), p. 119.

43. Schutz, Bernard. *Gravity from the Ground Up* (Cambridge, England: Cambridge University Press, 2003), p. 241.

44. Bergmann, P.G. *The Riddle of Gravitation* (New York: Dover, 1993), p. 85.

45. Einstein was not the first to propose gravity travels at the speed of light. As Ohanian notes, the ever-prescient Poincaré took the first "tentative steps to extend . . . relativity to gravitational forces in 1905. He recognized that gravitational effects should propagate at the speed of light" and even speculated about gravity waves. Source: Ohanian, Hans C. *Einstein's Mistakes: The Human Failings of Genius* (New York: Norton, 2008), p. 84.

Notes to Chap 15

1. Workinghumor.com, "Humorous Quotes attributed to Yogi Berra 1925 — American Baseball Player." http://www.workinghumor.com/quotes/yogi_berra.shtml. Last accessed July 2013.

2. Fowler, Michael, "Measuring the Solar System," Physics Department, University of Virginia, 2007. In one of nature's great coincidences, the relatively small Moon is just close enough to Earth and the much larger Sun just far enough away so they both *appear* nearly the same size in our sky. During a full solar eclipse, when the Moon is between the Earth and Sun it almost blocks out the Sun entirely.

3. In his *Opticks* of 1704, Newton speculated that light might be bent by gravity. In 1784 English scientist Henry Cavendish calculated this deflection using Newton's theory of gravity. German astronomer Johann Soldner

made the same calculation independently in 1801. These calculations were rediscovered in the 1920's. (Eddington's calculation was actually 0.9 arc seconds.) Source: Schutz, Bernard. *Gravity from the Ground Up* (Cambridge, England: Cambridge University Press, 2003), p. 37; Ohanian, Hans C. *Einstein's Mistakes: The Human Failings of Genius* (New York: Norton, 2008), p. 241–242.

Based on his accelerating elevator thought experiment, in 1911 Einstein predicted starlight grazing the Sun would be deflected by 0.875 arc seconds. At Einstein's urging, German astronomer Erwin Freundlich led an expedition to the Crimea (then part of the Russian Empire) on the northern coast of the Black Sea for the solar eclipse of August 1914. A group from Lick Observatory in the United States also sent a team led by director William Wallace Campbell. The Russian army, who were at war with Germany, took Freundlich prisoner and confiscated his equipment. (He was soon released). The Americans were allowed to remain, but on the day of the eclipse, cloudy skies made photography impossible. This was most fortuitous for Einstein, as measurements would have shown him to be wrong. As noted, his 1915 field equations showed starlight grazing the Sun actually bends *twice as much* in a gravitational field or 1.75 arc seconds. Source: Ohanian, Hans C. *Einstein's Mistakes: The Human Failings of Genius* (New York: Norton, 2008), p. 226. (See Appendix E for more details.)

4. Bodanis, David. *E = mc²: A Biography of the World's Most Famous Equation* (New York: Walker and Company, 2000), p. 209.

5. Will, Clifford M. *Was Einstein Right? Putting General Relativity to the Test* (New York: Basic Books, 1993), p. 77–78.

6. Einstein to Pauline Einstein, Sept. 27, 1919. CPAE, Vol. 9: *The Berlin Years: Correspondence, January 1919 — April 1920*, Doc. 113; Calaprice, Alice, Ed. *The Ultimate Quotable Einstein* (Princeton: Princeton University Press, 2011), p. 365; Bolles, Edmund Blair. *Einstein Defiant: Genius versus Genius in the Quantum Revolution* (Washington, D.C.: Joseph Henry, 2004), p. 53. As cited in Isaacson, Walter. *Einstein: His Life and Universe* (New York: Simon & Schuster, 2008-pbk), p. 259.

7. Thomson, J. (1919). [Chair of] Joint Eclipse Meeting of the Royal Society and the Royal Astronomical Society. *The Observatory*, 42, 389. As cited in McCausland, Ian, "Anomalies in the History of Relativity," *Journal of Scientific Exploration*, Vol. 13, No. 2, 271–290, 1999; Bodanis, David. *E = mc²: A Biography of the World's Most Famous Equation* (New York: Walker and Company), 2000, p. 214; Ohanian, Hans C. *Einstein's Mistakes: The Human Failings of Genius* (New York: Norton, 2008), p. 239.

8. Isaacson, Walter. "Einstein's Creativity," J. Roderick Davis Lecture, Stanford University, Oct. 18, 2007. http://fora.tv/2007/07/04/Einstein_s_Creativity. Last accessed July 2013.

9. *The Times* of London archives, Nov. 7, 1919 issue, p. 12.

10. Einstein to Ludwig Hopf, February 2, 1920. As cited in Clark, Roland C. *Einstein: The Life and Times* (New York and Cleveland: The World Publishing Company, 1971), p. 305; Kaku, Michio. *Einstein's Cosmos: How Albert Einstein's Vision Transformed our Understanding of Space and Time* (London: Phoenix, 2005-pbk), p. 85.

11. Einstein to Heinrich Zangger, Dec. 24. 1919. CPAE, Vol. 9: *The Berlin Years: Correspondence, January 1919 — April 1920*, Doc. 233.

12. Crelinsten, Jeffery. *Einstein's Jury: The Race to Test Relativity* (Princeton: Princeton University Press, 2006), p. 206. Some later questioned whether Eddington's enthusiasm for fellow pacifist and internationalist Albert Einstein and his fondness for Einstein's new theory clouded his judgment. Modern examinations of the 1919 solar eclipse data support Eddington's integrity in this matter. Source: D. Kennefick, "Testing relativity from the 1919 eclipse — a question of bias," *Physics Today*, March 2009, p. 37–42. http://www.physicstoday.org/resource/1/phtoad/v62/i3/p37_s1?bypassSSO=1. Last accessed July 2013.

13. Ibid.

14. Ibid.

15. In a 1975 experiment, physicists . . . : Fomalont, E. B. and R. A. Sramek, R. A., "Measurements of the Solar Gravitational Deflection of Radio Waves in Agreement with General Relativity," *Phys. Rev. Lett.* **36** (1976) 1475. http://link.aps.org/doi/10.1103/PhysRevLett.36.1475. Last accessed July 2013.

16. Fomalont, E. B. *et al.*, "Progress in Measurements of the Gravitational Bending of Radio Waves Using the VLBA" *Astrophysical Journal* **699** (2) July 2009: 1395–1402. https://mospace.umsystem.edu/xmlui/bitstream/handle/10355/6818/ProgressMeasurementsGravitationalBending.pdf?sequence=1. Last accessed July 2013.

17. Greene, Brian. *The Fabric of the Cosmos: Space, Time, and the Texture of Reality* (New York: Vintage Books-pbk, 2005), p. 26–29, p. 416–418; Will, Clifford M. *Was Einstein Right? Putting General Relativity to the Test* (New York: Basic Books, 1993), p. 150–152.

18. Bernard Schutz tells us "the coefficients of the mixed (cross) terms between time and space coordinates in the spacetime interval (such as dxdt)" are the source of frame dragging from spinning sources in Einstein's field equations. The overall effect is dubbed *gravitomagnetism*. Source: Schutz, Bernard. *Gravity from the Ground Up* (Cambridge, England: Cambridge University Press, 2003), p. 250–251.

19. Per Brian Greene, frame dragging calculations for a huge hollow sphere were started by Einstein in 1912, "significantly extended by Dieter Brill and Jeffrey Cohen in 1965, and finally completed by Herbert Pfister and K. Braun in 1985." Source: Greene, Brian. *The Fabric of the Cosmos: Space, Time, and the Texture of Reality* (New York: Vintage Books-pbk, 2005), p. 417.

20. Schutz, Bernard. *Gravity from the Ground Up* (Cambridge, England: Cambridge University Press, 2003), p. 248.

21. Greene, Brian. *The Fabric of the Cosmos: Space, Time, and the Texture of Reality* (New York: Vintage Books-pbk, 2005), p. 417.

22. Will, Clifford M., "Viewpoint: Finally, results from Gravity Probe B," physics. aps.org, May 31, 2011. http://physics.aps.org/articles/v4/43. Last accessed July 2013.

23. Ohanian, Hans C. *Einstein's Mistakes: The Human Failings of Genius* (New York: Norton, 2008), p. 255.

24. ESA Bulletin 119, "Gravitational Waves and Massive Black Holes? — The LISA and LISA Pathfinder Missions," August 2004. http://www.esa.int/esapub/bulletin/bulletin119/bul119_chap1.pdf. Last accessed July 2013.

25. Gravity waves have been detected indirectly. General relativity predicts the distance between two stars orbiting a common point (binary stars) will decrease over time due to their emission of gravity waves and their subsequent loss of energy. American astrophysicist Joseph H. Taylor, then of the University of Massachusetts and research student Russell A. Hulse discovered the first "binary pulsar" in 1974. (Binary pulsars are a pair of "highly magnetized, rotating neutron stars".) With colleague Joel Weisberg, Taylor measured the distance between this pair of neutron stars over several decades. They found a steady decrease in distance between the two pulsars over time which matched general relativity gravity wave predictions to better than a third of a percent. Source: Hartle, James B. *Gravity: An Introduction to Einstein's General Relativity* (New York: Addison Wesley, 2003), p. 508.

26. "Gravitational Waves and Massive Black Holes? — The LISA and LISA Pathfinder Missions" ESA Bulletin 119, August 2004. http://www.esa.int/esapub/bulletin/bulletin119/bul119_chap1.pdf. Last accessed July 2013.

27. Stevenson, A. "Cosmic gravity wave background glimpses the early universe", arstechnica.com, August 19, 2009. http://arstechnica.com/science/news/2009/08/cosmic-gravity-wave-background-glimpses-the-early-universe.ars. Last accessed July 2013.

There are at least two advantages of gravity wave detection over EM waves. First if there is no other matter nearby, a binary system of black holes will emit no EM radiation, but still emits gravitational waves. Second, interstellar dust may block out EM radiation from distant stellar objects, but gravity waves pass through unhindered. Source: LIGO Scientific Collaboration, "The Potential of Gravitational Waves," 2013. http://www.ligo.org/science/GW-Potential.php. Last accessed July 2013.

28. Foreword to Thorne, Kip. *Black Holes & Time Warps: Einstein's Outrageous Legacy* (New York: W. W. Norton, 1994), p. 11.

29. Mathpages.com, Reflections on Relativity, "8.7 Strange Meetings". http://mathpages.com/rr/s8-07/8-07.htm. Last accessed July 2013.

30. Eisenstaedt, "The Early Interpretation of the Schwarzschild Solution," in Howard and Stachel, *Einstein and the History of General Relativity: Einstein Studies*, Vol. 1 (Boston: Birkhauser, 1989) p. 213–234.

31. Gribbin, John. *Unveiling the Edge of Time: Black Holes, White Holes, Wormholes* (New York: Three Rivers Press, 1994), p. 52.

32. Archive.ncsa.illinois.edu "Black Holes and Beyond," Einstein's Legacy, Nov. 16, 1995, http://archive.ncsa.illinois.edu/Cyberia/NumRel/BlackHoles. html. Last accessed July 2013; Kaku, Michio. *Einstein's Cosmos: How Albert Einstein's Vision Transformed our Understanding of Space and Time* (London: Phoenix, 2005-pbk), p. 103.

   Just three numbers fully describe a black hole: its mass, spin, and charge. "No other macroscopic object is so simple." Source: Schutz, Bernard. *Gravity from the Ground Up* (Cambridge, England: Cambridge University Press, 2003), p. 296.

33. As noted, real black holes are likely to rotate due to the spin of the stars and gases from which they are formed. Theoretically, a spinning black hole bulges at its equator, has a singularity shaped like an infinitely thin ring, and possesses an inner and outer event horizon. Source: Hubblesite.org, "How Big is a Black Hole?" Black Hole Encyclopedia. http://hubblesite.org/explore_astronomy/black_holes/encyc_mod3_q3.html. Last accessed July 2013.

34. Seidel, Edward, "A Black Hole is Born," Expo/Science & Industry/Spacetime Wrinkles, archives.nsca.illinois.edu. April 12, 2011. http://archive.ncsa.illinois.edu/Cyberia/NumRel/BlackHoleFormation.html. Last accessed July 2013.

35. Bodanis, David. $E = mc^2$: *A Biography of the World's Most Famous Equation* (New York: Walker and Company, 2000), p. 200.

36. Thorne, Kip. *Black Holes & Time Warps: Einstein's Outrageous Legacy* (New York: W. W. Norton, 1994), p. 46 and 347. Per Thorne, "the spin of a black hole produces *a swirl of space* around the hole". This frame-dragging effect in turn "holds the inner part of the accretion disc in the hole's equatorial plane." For a more detailed explanation of black hole jets, see Moskowitz, Clara, "Powerful Black Hole Jet Explained," space.com, 28 April 2008. http://www.space.com/5285-powerful-black-hole-jet-explained.html. Last accessed July 2013.

37. Mundin, P., "Bright Quasar 3C 273," *Encyclopedia of Astronomy and Astrophysics*, 2006. http://www.astro.caltech.edu/~george/ay21/eaa/eaa-3c273.pdf. Last accessed July 2013.

38. de Pastino, Blake. "Photo in the News: 1000 Black Holes Revealed in New Sky Survey," nationalgeographic.com, March 13, 2007. http://news.nationalgeographic.com/news/2007/03/070313-black-holes.html. Last accessed July 2013.

39. "How Many Black Holes Are There?", Journey to a Black Hole. hubblesite. org, http://hubblesite.org/explore_astronomy/black_holes/encyc_mod3_ q7.html. Last accessed July 2013.

40. Johnston, Wm. Robert, "Overview of general relativity," Last updated 3 November 2008. http://www.johnstonsarchive.net/relativity/einstein2. html. Last accessed July 2013.

41. Gribbin, John. *Unveiling the Edge of Time: Black Holes, White Holes, Wormholes* (New York: Three Rivers Press, 1994), p. 155.

42. Ibid. According to quantum mechanics, wormholes are extremely tiny, on the order of 10^{-33} centimeters in size. They exist for only around 10^{-45} seconds and flash into and out of existence "in a random, unpredictable manner." Source: Thorne, Kip. *Black Holes & Time Warps: Einstein's Outrageous Legacy* (New York: W. W. Norton, 1994), p. 56.

43. The Schwarzschild spacetime interval equation (Schwarzschild metric) has both positive and negative solutions (like the square root of 4 is either 2 or -2). Thus, per physicist Andrew Hamilton, the "complete Schwarzschild geometry consists of a black hole, a white hole, and two universes connected at their horizons by a wormhole". What is a white hole? It is the negative square root solution of Schwarzschild's geometry, or a "a black hole running backwards in time." This means that unlike a black hole which "swallows things irretrievably"; a white hole "spits them out". However, some physicist believe "white holes cannot exist since they violate the second law of thermodynamics." (2nd Law: The entropy or disorder of an isolated system will tend to increase over time.) Source: Hamilton, Andrew, "White Holes and Worm Holes," casa.colorado.edu, April 15, 2001. http://casa.colorado.edu/~ajsh/ schww.html. Last accessed July 2013.

44. Thorne, Kip. *Black Holes & Time Warps: Einstein's Outrageous Legacy* (New York: W. W. Norton, 1994), p. 474 and 524; Kaku, Michio. *Einstein's Cosmos: How Albert Einstein's Vision Transformed our Understanding of Space and Time* (London: Phoenix, 2005-pbk), p. 174–176. The quantum effects here are EM vacuum fluctuations (virtual particles). A wormhole model by Thorne suggests a *non-destructive* trip through the wormhole of a *rotating* black hole is theoretically possible. However, it requires enormous amounts of *exotic* matter possessing *negative* energy. Quantum mechanics does allow for such negative energy, e.g. in virtual particles, but whether scientists in the future could actually find and harness such huge amounts remains highly speculative. For an interesting take on the subject, go to: NASA, "Warp Drive, When?, Ideas Based on What We'd Like to Achieve," Glen Research Center, 2008. http:// www.nasa.gov/centers/glenn/technology/warp/ideachev.html. Last accessed July 2013.

Notes to Chap 16

1. Brown, Rich, "Magic Tails," 2012. http://magictails.com/creationlinks.html. Last accessed July 2013.
2. Allday, Jonathan. *Quarks, Leptons, and the Big Bang* (Bristol, UK: Institute of Physics Publishing, 2001), p. 224; Einstein, Albert "Cosmological Considerations Arising from the General Theory of Relativity." (Published as "Kosmologische Betrachtungen zur allgemeinen Relativitätstheorie," *Preussusche Akademei der Wissenschaften, Sitzungsberichte* (1917)), Pt. 1: 142–152.
3. Greene, Brian. *The Fabric of the Cosmos: Space, Time, and the Texture of Reality* (New York: Vintage Books-pbk, 2005), p. 230.
4. Baez, John, "The General Relativity Tutorial," 2006.
5. Einstein showed this repulsive gravity represented by the cosmological constant "becomes stronger and stronger over larger spatial separations." So the more space there is between galaxy clusters, the greater is the outward push of this negative gravity. It is "immeasurably tiny" on the scale of our solar system, but significant at cosmic scales. Thus Einstein's field equations with the cosmological constant added match Newton's predictions inside our solar system to a first approximation. Source: Greene, Brian. *The Fabric of the Cosmos: Space, Time, and the Texture of Reality* (New York: Vintage Books-pbk, 2005), p. 279.

 Einstein's cosmological constant possesses universal energy density and pressure which are, per Bernard Schutz, "constant in time and in space . . . (and) the *same* no matter which observer measures them." Einstein found this was "the only way to introduce negative pressure and still preserve the principle of relativity." His cosmological constant also possesses zero inertial mass. And since its pressure is uniform across the universe, it exerts no direct force. (Pressure forces are produced by pressure differences only.) Thus Einstein's cosmological constant is undetectable except for its gravitational effects. His ad-hoc cosmological constant is a very clever ether indeed. Source: Schutz, Bernard. *Gravity from the Ground Up* (Cambridge, England: Cambridge University Press, 2003), p. 254.
6. Nave, Carl R., "Cepheid Variable Stars", *Hyperphysics*, Georgia State University, 2013.
7. Bartusiak, Marcia, *The Day We Found the Universe* (New York: Vintage Books-pbk, 2009), p. 122–123. Hertzsprung's actual method was more complicated. For example, he invoked the Sun's motion through the galaxy. His calculated distances to Cepheids in the Small Magellanic Cloud, however, were too short by a factor of 2.65X. Several years later, American astronomer Harlow Shapley "improved and extended" Hertzsprung's method somewhat, using Cepheid's in the Milky Way and its globular clusters.

The Hertzsprung and Shapley papers are: Hertzsprung, E. (1914) "Über die räumliche Verteilung der Veränderlichen vom δ Cephei-Typus [On the Spatial Distribution of Variables of the δ Cephei Type]." *Atronomische Nachrichten* 196: 204; Shapley, H. (1918) "Studies Based on the Colors and Magnitudes in Stellar Clusters. Sixth Paper. On the Determination of the Distances to Globular Clusters." *Astrophysical Journal* 48: 108. As cited in Bartusiak, Marcia, *The Day We Found the Universe* (New York: Vintage Books-pbk, 2009), p. 286.

8. Osterbrock, Donald E., "Astronomer for All Seasons: Heber D. Curtis," Astronomical Society of the Pacific, June 2001; Bartusiak, Marcia, *The Day We Found the Universe* (New York: Vintage Books-pbk, 2009), p. 165. http://www. astrosociety.org/pubs/mercury/30_03/seasons.html. Last accessed July 2013.

9. Hubble had earlier found 11 Cepheid variables in NGC 6822 (now Barnard's Galaxy). He determined the distance to this barred irregular nebula to be greater than 700 million light years. Current estimates put it at 1.63 million light years away. Source: Bartusiak, Marcia, *The Day We Found the Universe* (New York: Vintage Books-pbk, 2009), p. 195; Hubble, Edwin P. (December 1925), "NGC 6822, a remote stellar system", *Astrophysics Journal* **62**: 409–433.

10. Belenkiy, Ari, "Alexander Friedmann and the Origins of Modern Cosmology," *Physics Today*. Vol. 65, no. 10, 38–43 (2012).

11. Ibid. Per Belenkiy, Einstein wrote this in a short note in the Zeitschrift für Physik (German Physics Journal) of September 1922. Friedmann immediately sent Einstein an extended letter detailing his work. Six months later, Einstein wrote in the journal: ". . . my criticism . . . was based on an error in my calculations. I consider that Mr. Friedmann's results are correct and shed new light." Still unable to accept the possibility of a dynamic universe, Einstein also wrote "the solution has no physical meaning." But, Belenkiy tells us, Einstein deleted this remark from the galley proofs at the last minute.

12. Egdall, Ira Mark, *Unsung Heroes of the Universe* (Decoded Science-eBook, 2012), Chap. 1.

13. Lemaître's paper: Lemaître, Georges, "A Homogeneous Universe of Constant Mass and Increasing Radius Accounting for the Radial Velocities of Extra-Galactic Nebulae," *Annales de la Société scientifique de Bruxelles* (Annals of the Brussels Scientific Society) Se`rie A 47: 49, 1927. Lemaître calculated a rate of cosmic expansion of 625 kilometers per second per megaparsec. Hubble's later estimate of recession velocity was 500. Both values are too high, due to observational errors and approximations at the time. Current calculations put the expansion rate at some 70 kilometers per second per megaparsec. As cited in Bartusiak, Marcia, *The Day We Found the Universe* (New York: Vintage Books-pbk, 2009), p. 240 and 244.

14. Einstein to Lemaître on October 1927 in Leopold Park, Brussels. Einstein was attending the Fifth Solvay Congress in Brussels at the time. Source: Smith, R. W. "Edwin Hubble and the Transformation of Cosmology." *Physics Today* (April

1990): 52–58. As cited in Bartusiak, Marcia, *The Day We Found the Universe* (New York: Vintage Books-pbk, 2009), p. 244.

15. Hubble met Dutch physicist Willem deSitter on a trip to Holland in 1928. There he learned of deSitter's "empty universe" solution to Einstein's cosmological field equations. In deSitter's model, the spacetime metric predicted "lines in the spectra of very distant stars or nebulae (are) systematically displaced toward the red, giving rise to a spurious positive radial velocity." DeSitter did not think this "spurious" velocity was real. Like Einstein's, his solution modeled a static universe. Encouraged by DeSitter, Hubble returned to Mt. Wilson and examined the recorded red shift of galaxies he had observed versus their estimated distance. The correlation held up. Nonetheless, whether it was because of DeSitter's "spurious" velocity interpretation or his own discomfort with theoretical physics, Hubble never fully accepted the idea of an expanding universe. Source: Kragh, Helge. *Cosmology and Controversy: The Historical Development of Two Theories of the Universe* (Princeton: Princeton University Press, 1999), p. 11–12; Kaku, Michio. *Einstein's Cosmos: How Albert Einstein's Vision Transformed our Understanding of Space and Time* (London: Phoenix, 2005-pbk), p. 100; Bartusiak, Marcia, *The Day We Found the Universe* (New York: Vintage Books-pbk, 2009), p. 225–238.

16. Einstein in a chat with George Gamow. Source: Gamow, G., *My World Line* (New York: Viking Press, 1970), p. 44. As cited in Bartusiak, Marcia, *The Day We Found the Universe* (New York: Vintage Books-pbk, 2009), p. 254.

17. Lemonick, Michael D., "Astronomer Edwin Hubble," The TIME 100, *TIME*, March 29, 1999. http://www.time.com/time/time100/scientist/profile/hubble.html. Last accessed July 2013.

18. Webb, James R., "The Origin and Evolution of the Universe," Lecture at Florida International University, Miami, Florida, September 2009.

19. Hawley, John F., Holcomb, Katherine A., *Foundations of Modern Cosmology* (New York: USA, Oxford University Press — 2nd Edition, 2005), Chap. 10 Question.

20. Lineweaver, C. H., Davis and T. M., "Misconceptions about the Big Bang," *Sci. Am.*, March 2005.

21. Hawley, John F., Holcomb, Katherine A., *Foundations of Modern Cosmology* (New York: USA, Oxford University Press — 2nd Edition, 2005), Chap. 10 Question.

22. Greene, Brian. *The Fabric of the Cosmos: Space, Time, and the Texture of Reality* (New York: Vintage Books-pbk, 2005), p. 237.

23. Egdall, Ira Mark, *Unsung Heroes of the Universe* (Decoded Science-eBook, 2012), Chap. 1.

24. Lemaître, Georges, "The Beginning of the World from the Point of View of Quantum Theory," *Nature* (1931), 127, 706. As cited in Bartusiak, Marcia, *The Day We Found the Universe* (New York: Vintage Books-pbk, 2009), p. 257.

25. Lemaître's address to the Eleventh Solvay Conference on Physics in Brussels in 1958. Source: Soter, Steven and Tyson, Neil deGrasse eds., "Cosmic Horizons: Astronomy at the Cutting Edge," New Press, American Museum of Natural History, 2000. http://www.amnh.org/education/resources/rfl/web/essaybooks/cosmic/p_lemaitre.html. Last accessed July 2013.

26. Einstein to Lemaître at joint seminar in California, January 1933. Source: Aikman, Duncan, *New York Times Magazine*, February 19, 1933. As cited in Midbon, Mark. "'A Day Without Yesterday': Georges Lemaitre & the Big Bang," Commonweal, March 24, 2000: 18–19. http://www.catholiceducation.org/articles/science/sc0022.html. Last accessed July 2013.

27. Bartusiak, Marcia, *The Day We Found the Universe* (New York: Vintage Books-pbk, 2009), p. 269.

28. English astronomer Fred Hoyle had his own explanation for the evolution of the universe which he called the "Steady State" theory. He coined the competing hypothesis the "Big Bang" theory as a derisive term and it stuck. Source: NASA, "Hoyle Scoffs at 'Big Bang' Cosmic Times 1955, Universe Theory," February 16, 2010. http://cosmictimes.gsfc.nasa.gov/online_edition/1955Cosmic/hoyle.html. Last accessed July 2013.

29. Lineweaver, C. H. and Davis and T. M., "Misconceptions about the Big Bang," *Sci. Am.*, March 2005.

30. Ibid.

31. During this era, the universe had expanded and cooled sufficiently to allow free protons and neutrons to undergo nuclear fusion. This produced mostly helium nuclei, plus traces of deuterium (a hydrogen nucleus with a proton and neutron), lithium and beryllium nuclei. The density and temperature of the universe dropped so quickly with expansion that there wasn't enough time to form the nuclei of heavier elements. Heavier elements up to iron are formed by nuclear fusion inside the cores of stars. Elements beyond iron are formed during the end-of-life explosions of massive stars called supernovae. As physicist Carl Sagan liked to say, "we are indeed made of star stuff". Source: Feuerbacher, B. and Scranton, R., "Evidence for the Big Bang", The TalkOrigins Archive, January 2006; Allday, Jonathan. *Quarks, Leptons, and the Big Bang* (Bristol, UK: Institute of Physics Publishing, 2001), p. 240.

32. Halpern. P. and Wesson, P. S. *Brave New Universe: Illuminating the Darkest Secrets of the Cosmos* (Washington: Joseph Henry Press, 2006), p. 10.

33. Durrani, Matin, "Ralph Alpher: 1921–2007," physicsworld.com, Aug 23, 2007. http://physicsworld.com/cws/article/news/2007/aug/23/ralph-alpher-1921-to-2007. Last accessed July 2013.

34. "People and Discoveries," A Science Odyssey, Public Broadcasting Service. http://www.pbs.org/wgbh/aso/databank/entries/dp65co.html. Last accessed July 2013.

35. Schoenstein, Ralph, "The Big Bang's Echo," All Things Considered, NPR, May 17, 2005. As cited in Levine, Alaina G., "The Large Horn Antenna and the Discovery of Cosmic Background Radiation," aps.org, 2009.

36. "People and Discoveries," A Science Odyssey, Public Broadcasting Service. Other scientists had seen the CMB before Penzias and Wilson but didn't realize its connection with the big bang. Canadian astronomer Andrew McKellar studied interstellar absorption lines in 1941 and observed an "average bolometric temperature of 2.3 K." In 1955, French radio astronomer Emile Le Roux reported a background radiation of 3 degrees K ± 2 degrees in a "sky survey at a wavelength of 33 cm." In 1957, Russian physicist Tigran Shmaonov reported that "the absolute effective temperature of the radio emission background is 4 ± 3K". Source: McKellar, A. (1941), "Molecular Lines from the Lowest States of Diatomic Molecules Composed of Atoms Probably Present in Interstellar Space" *Publications of the Dominion Astrophysical Observatory* (*Victoria, BC*) 7: 251–272; Kragh, Helge. *Cosmology and Controversy: The Historical Development of Two Theories of the Universe* (Princeton: Princeton University Press, 1999), p. 135; Shmaonov, T. A. (1957) Pribory i Teknika Eksperienta (Experimental Devices and Methods) Moscow.

37. oneminuteastronomer.com, "The Afterglow of the Big Bang," June 12, 2012. http://www.oneminuteastronomer.com/5922/cosmic-microwave-background/. Last accessed July 2013.

38. Measurements of the CMB by the Wilkinson Microwave Anisotropy Probe (WMAP) indicate a CMB temperature of 2.782 degrees Kelvin. Source: Halpern. P. *Edge of the Universe: A Voyage to the Cosmic Horizon and Beyond* (New York: John Wiley & Sons, 2012), p. 129.

39. bell-labs.com, "Penzias and Wilson's Discovery is One of the Century's Key Advances," 1998. http://www.bell-labs.com/history/laser/invention/cosmology.html. Last accessed July 2013.

40. Per astrophysicist James Webb, the big bang singularity extended through *all space* at a single point in time. A black hole singularity, on the other hand, "extends through *all time* at a single point (in space)." Source: Webb, James R., "The Origin and Evolution of the Universe," lecture at Florida International University, Miami, Florida, September 2009.

41. Feuerbacher, B. and Scranton, R., "Evidence for the Big Bang", The TalkOrigins Archive, January 2006.

42. The abundance of matter and extreme rarity of anti-matter is also a major unresolved issue with the current big bang theory.

43. Egdall, Mark, "A Universe from Nothing? Lawrence Krauss' Theories Explained," DecodedScience.com, March 12, 2012. http://www.decoded-science.com/a-universe-from-nothing-lawrence-krauss-theories-explained/11450. Last accessed July 2013.

44. Wheeler, John Archibald. *A Journey into Gravity and Spacetime* (New York: Freeman, 1990), p. 2.

45. Ibid, p. 99. The cosmological models of Albert Einstein, Willem deSitter, Alexander Friedman, and Georges Lemaitre assumed mass energy/density is uniformly distributed (homogeneous) on the scale of the universe. They also assumed the universe looks the same in every direction (isotropic). With these key assumptions, models were able to show that the overall configuration of the universe must be open, flat, or closed.

46. In the three spatial dimensions of real space, the possible geometries of our universe are flat, hyperspherical, and hyperboloid. These are three-dimensional equivalents of a plane, sphere, and hyperbola, respectively. Mathematically, each has an impossible to visualize three-dimensional exterior. Source: Halpern. P. *Edge of the Universe: A Voyage to the Cosmic Horizon and Beyond* (New York: John Wiley & Sons, 2012), p. 18–19.

47. Yost and Daunt, "The Geometry of the Universe," Astronomy 162, Stars, Galaxies, and Cosmology, Department of Physics, University of Tennessee. http://csep10.phys.utk.edu/astr162/lect/cosmology/geometry.html. Last accessed July 2013.

48. Greene, Brian. *The Fabric of the Cosmos: Space, Time, and the Texture of Reality* (New York: Vintage Books-pbk, 2005), p. 242.

49. Halpern, Paul , "How large is the observable universe?" NOVA, The Nature of Reality, October 10 2012. http://www.pbs.org/wgbh/nova/physics/blog/2012/10/how-large-is-the-observable-universe/. Last accessed July 2013.

50. The expansion of the universe magnifies things. Thus for the universe to be flat today, one second after the big bang it had to be flat to one part in one quadrillion (one plus 15 zeros). Source: Halpern. P. and Wesson, P. S. *Brave New Universe: Illuminating the Darkest Secrets of the Cosmos* (Washington: Joseph Henry Press, 2006), p. 96.

51. Allday, Jonathan. *Quarks, Leptons, and the Big Bang* (Bristol, UK: Institute of Physics Publishing, 2001), p. 262; Greene, Brian. *The Fabric of the Cosmos: Space, Time, and the Texture of Reality* (New York: Vintage Books-pbk, 2005), p. 284; web.mit.edu, "Alan Guth, Victor F. Weisskopf Professor of Physics," MIT Department of Physics, 2012. http://web.mit.edu/physics/people/faculty/guth_alan.html. Last accessed Aug. 2013.

52. Halpern, P. *Edge of the Universe: A Voyage to the Cosmic Horizon and Beyond* (New York: John Wiley & Sons, 2012), p. 58.

53. Kaku, Michio. *Einstein's Cosmos: How Albert Einstein's Vision Transformed our Understanding of Space and Time* (London: Phoenix, 2005-pbk), p. 172. Inflation theory also tells us why the CMB is so extremely uniform all across the sky (the so-called "Horizon" problem). In the very beginning of the universe prior to inflation, space expanded slowly enough for a "uniform temperature to be broadly established." Through the intense burst of rapid expansion we

call inflation, this high uniformity was suddenly dispersed across the universe. Source: Greene, Brian. *The Fabric of the Cosmos: Space, Time, and the Texture of Reality* (New York: Vintage Books-pbk, 2005), p. 290.

Inflation theory is still very much a work in progress. The "specific mechanism that led to an inflationary era," how inflation came to end, and whether it has or will happen again remain among the open questions. Source: Halpern, P. *Edge of the Universe: A Voyage to the Cosmic Horizon and Beyond* (New York: John Wiley & Sons, 2012) p. 59 and 109.

54. "Five Year Results on the Oldest Light in the Universe," WMAP 5-year Results Released, March 7, 2008. Updated Nov. 11, 2011. gsfs.nasa.gov, http://map.gsfc.nasa.gov/news/5yr_release.html. Last accessed July 2013.

"Planck Reveals an Almost Perfect Universe," Planck Space Telescope, European Space Agency, Mar. 21, 2013. esa.int, http://www.esa.int?Our_Activities/Space_Science/Planck/Planck_reveals_an_almost_perfect_Universe. Last accessed Aug. 2013.

55. Greene, Brian. *The Fabric of the Cosmos: Space, Time, and the Texture of Reality* (New York: Vintage Books-pbk, 2005), p. 294.

56. Ibid, p. 295.

57. "The Journey Continues, New Answers and New Puzzles," Ideas of Cosmology, Center for History of Physics, 2013. aip.org, http://www.aip.org/history/cosmology/ideas/journey.htm. Last accessed July 2013.

58. Lincoln, Don, "Dark Matter," *Phys. Teach.* **51** (March, 2013) 134–138. Based on the big bang theory and observations, physicists are generally convinced the preponderance of dark matter is not a form of ordinary matter that no longer gives off EM radiation we can detect. In other words, dark matter is *not* made of quarks or leptons, the fundamental classes of particles which make up atoms and molecules.

Some physicists support an alternative to dark matter called Modified Newtonian Dynamics, or MOND. This theory is based on a modification to Newton's second law, F=ma. MOND has had some predictive success, particularly in explaining the observed rotation of galaxies. Nonetheless, the theory remains controversial in its current form. For one thing, it still needs "some residual dark matter to explain the dynamics of clusters of galaxies," as Lincoln points out.

59. Penrose, Roger, *Cycles of Time, an Extraordinary New View of the Universe* (UK: The Bodley Head, 2010). As cited in Kaiser, David, "Going Supernova," London Review of Books, Vol. 33 No. 4, February 17, 2011.)

60. Caldwell, Robert R., "Dark Energy," physicsworld.com, May 30, 2004. http://physicsworld.com/cws/article/print/2004/may/30/dark-energy. Last accessed July 2013.

61. Evidence from a number of space borne instruments support the dark energy hypothesis, including the WMAP (Wilkinson Anisotropic Probe) as well as

the 2DF (Two-Degree Field) and SDSS (Sloan Digital Sky Survey). Our universe has regions of matter which are less dense and more dense. Using data from several of these instruments, four independent groups of researchers found, "dark energy has *slowed down* the collapse of overdense regions". Source: Ibid.

62. Turner, Michael, "Explained in 60 Seconds," *CAP Journal* 2, No. 2 (February 2008): 8. As cited in Halpern, P. *Edge of the Universe: A Voyage to the Cosmic Horizon and Beyond* (New York: John Wiley & Sons, 2012), p. 45.

63. Halpern, P. *Edge of the Universe: A Voyage to the Cosmic Horizon and Beyond* (New York: John Wiley & Sons, 2012), p. 20 and 80.

64. Greene, Brian. *The Fabric of the Cosmos: Space, Time, and the Texture of Reality* (New York: Vintage Books-pbk, 2005), p. 301.

65. Freedman, R. A. and Kaufmann III, W. J. *Universe*, 6th Edition (New York: W. H. Freeman, 2002), p. 661. Future of universe projections in text based primarily on this book.

Notes to Epilogue

1. Einstein aphorism for a friend, September 18, 1930. Quoted in Hoffman, Banesh and Dukas, Helen. *Albert Einstein: Creator and Rebel* (New York: Plume, 1995), p. 24. AEA 36–598.

2. Einstein timeline, Einsteinyear.org, Institute of Physics, 2007; Kaku, Michio. *Einstein's Cosmos: How Albert Einstein's Vision Transformed our Understanding of Space and Time* (London: Phoenix, 2005-pbk), p. 80.

3. Einstein timeline, Einsteinyear.org, Institute of Physics, 2007. In one particularly disturbing episode, before he married Elsa, Einstein reportedly "made a pass" at her oldest daughter and expressed his "preference for the daughter over the mother." He apparently relented after an emotional scene from Elsa and the cold shoulder from her daughter and married Elsa. Source: Ohanian, Hans C. *Einstein's Mistakes: The Human Failings of Genius* (New York: Norton, 2008), p. 237.

4. From 1912 to 1915, Robert Millikan worked to prove Einstein's Photoelectric Effect predictions wrong. After four years of meticulous testing, Millikan was forced to concede. Einstein's formula "represents very accurately the (observed) behavior," Millikan reported, "in spite of its unreasonableness since it seems to violate everything we knew about the interference of light." Millikan confirmed Einstein's mathematical predictions, but remained unconvinced regarding Einstein's *interpretation* that light is made of energy particles. Source: Millikan, R. A., "Einstein's Photoelectric Equation and Contact Electromotive Force," *Phys. Rev.* (1916) VII, I, 18, submitted Sept. 15 (1915). http://www.ffn.ub.es/luisnavarro/nuevo_maletin/Millikan_1916_1.pdf.

Last accessed July 2013; Pais, Abraham. *Subtle Is the Lord: The Science and Life of Albert Einstein* (Oxford University Press, New York, 1982), p. 357; Rosenblum, B. and Kuttner, F. *Quantum Enigma: Physics Encounters Consciousness* (New York: Oxford University Press, 2006), p. 60; Einstein time-line, Einsteinyear.org, Institute of Physics, 2007.

It was not until 1923 that physicists began to accept the idea of Einstein's photons. In the famous Compton Effect, light was shown to change frequency after it bounced off electrons. But the data did not agree with a light wave, a moving electron, and the resultant Doppler Effect. When "Compton assumed that light was a stream of *particles*, each with the energy of an Einstein photon," his calculations precisely matched the experimental data. Source: Rosenblum, B. and Kuttner, F. *Quantum Enigma: Physics Encounters Consciousness* (New York: Oxford University Press, 2006), p. 70.

5. Pais, Abraham. *Subtle Is the Lord: The Science and Life of Albert Einstein* (Oxford University Press, New York, 1982), p. 503.

6. Hughes, Virginia. "Einstein vs. the Nobel Prize, Why the Nobel Committee repeatedly dissed this 'world-bluffing Jewish physicist'," *Discover* magazine, Sept. 28, 2006. http://discovermagazine.com/2006/sep/einstein-nobel-prize#.UdJt_zu7JWI. Last accessed July 2013.

7. Einstein in postcard to Bose in 1925. James, Ioan. *Remarkable Physicists: From Galileo to Yukawa* (New York: Cambridge University Press, 2004), p. 317.

8. Goldman *et al.*, "BEC — What is it and where did the idea come from?," Physics 2000, University of Colorado, Boulder. (This website has an excellent lay explanation of Bose-Einstein condensates — http://www.colorado.edu/physics/2000/bec/what_is_it.html. Last accessed July 2013.)

What Einstein did not realize was that Bose-Einstein condensation applies only to atoms which are *bosons*. Fermions are particles with half-integer spin, such as electrons and other matter particles. (As noted, spin is a measure of the angular momentum of a particle.) Bosons, on the other hand, have integer spin, such as photons which have a spin of 1. All force-carrier particles are bosons. Composite particles, atomic nuclei, and atoms are bosons if they contain an even number of fermion particles.

9. In these Bose-Einstein condensates "all wave functions overlap . . . and quantum effects become apparent on a macroscopic scale." Source: Ibid, "bec/how it is made"; "Press Release: The 2001 Nobel Prize in Physics". Nobelprize.org. Oct. 9, 2001. http://www.nobelprize.org/nobel_prizes/physics/laureates/2001/popular.html. Last accessed July 2013.

10. Isaacson, Walter. *Einstein: His Life and Universe* (New York: Simon & Schuster, 2008-pbk), p. 231.

11. Ibid, p. 364.

12. Albert Einstein to Elsa Einstein, July 12 and 17, 1919. Ibid, p. 246.

13. Einstein timeline, Einsteinyear.org, Institute of Physics, 2007.

14. Schreiber, Georges, *Portraits and Self-Portraits* (Boston: Houghton Mifflin, 1936). Reprinted in *Out of My Later Years*, p. 13, AEA 28–332.

15. Stachel, John. *Einstein from 'B' to 'Z'* (Boston: Birkhäuser, 2001), p. 4 and 8.

16. Greene, Brian. *The Fabric of the Cosmos: Space, Time, and the Texture of Reality* (New York: Vintage Books-pbk, 2005), p. 77–123. For a detailed discussion of quantum entanglement, I highly recommend Chap. 4 of Greene's book. It is the clearest explanation on this tricky subject I have found to date.

17. Ibid., p. 114.

18. David Bohm's so-called Causal Interpretation of quantum mechanics is the most famous non-local *hidden variable* theory. (There are a number of others.) Bohm's theory reproduces the predictions of quantum mechanics without resorting to probabilities. In Bohm's clever but convoluted construct, a particle's attributes are pre-programmed, i.e., known *before* measurement. Based on an idea from Louis de Broglie, a hidden superluminal "guiding wave" governs the motion of a particle. However, the theory remains non-local. Source: Goldstein, Sheldon, "Bohmian Mechanics", *The Stanford Encyclopedia of Philosophy (Fall 2012 Edition)*, Edward N. Zalta (ed.). http://plato.stanford.edu/entries/qm-bohm/. Last accessed July 2013.

19. Isaacson, Walter. *Einstein: His Life and Universe* (New York: Simon & Schuster, 2008-pbk), p. 471–472.

20. Weart, Spencer, and Gertrud Weiss Szilard, eds. *Leo Szilard: His Version of the Facts* (Cambridge, MA: MIT Press, 1979) p. 83–96. Ibid., p. 472.

21. Einstein in first letter to Roosevelt, dated Aug. 2, 1939. Ibid., p. 474.

22. Sachs told the story to a U.S. Senate special committee hearing on atomic energy in Nov. 27, 1945. Ibid., p. 476.

23. Ohanian, Hans C. *Einstein's Mistakes: The Human Failings of Genius* (New York: Norton, 2008), p. 166.

24. Investigations after the war revealed the Germans were not anywhere near developing an atomic bomb. Werner Heisenberg, father of the Uncertainty Principle, led the unsuccessful German nuclear energy research project. For a detailed history of the Manhattan Project, see: "The Manhattan Project, An Interactive History," Office of History and Heritage Resources, U.S. Department of Energy. http://energy.gov/sites/prod/files/Manhattan_Project_2010.pdf. Last accessed Aug. 2013.

25. Rhodes, Richard. *The Making of the Atomic Bomb* (New York: Simon & Schuster, 2012), p. 377+ ; mphpa.org, "Manhattan Project History, Early Government Support, The MAUD Report," August 2003, 2005. http://www.mphpa.org/classic/HISTORY/H-04e.htm. Last accessed July 2013.

26. Kaku, Michio. *Einstein's Cosmos: How Albert Einstein's Vision Transformed our Understanding of Space and Time* (London: Phoenix, 2005-pbk), p. 147.

27. "Einstein Deplores Use of Atom Bomb," *New York Times*, Aug 19, 1946, 1; *Newsweek*, March 10, 1947. As cited in Isaacson, Walter. *Einstein: His Life and Universe* (New York: Simon & Schuster, 2008-pbk), p. 485.

28. Einstein, Albert. "This is My America," unpublished, summer 1944, AEA 72–758. Ibid., p. 475–476.

29. Ibid. As cited in Isaacson, Walter. *Einstein: His Life and Universe* (New York: Simon & Schuster, 2008-pbk), p. 479.

30. Stachel, John. *Einstein from 'B' to 'Z'* (Boston: Birkhäuser, 2001), p. 4.

31. Schreiber, Georges, *Portraits and Self-Portraits* (Boston: Houghton Mifflin, 1936). Reprinted in *Out of My Later Years*, 13. AEA 28–332.

32. Gonzalez, Antonio M. "Albert Einstein," Donostia International Physics Center, San Sebastian, Spain. http://dipc.ehu.es/. Last accessed July 2013.

33. Einstein to assistant Johanna Fantova, as recorded in her diary. As cited in Glaister, Dan, "When Einstein was left as sick as a parrot," *The Guardian*, April 26, 2004. http://www.guardian.co.uk/world/2004/apr/26/science.germany. Last accessed July 2013.

34. AEA 3–12; Isaacson, Walter. *Einstein: His Life and Universe* (New York: Simon & Schuster, 2008-pbk), p. 543.

35. Tributes by Niels Bohr and I. I. Rabi, "Albert Einstein: 1879–1955," *Sci. Am.* **192** No. 6, June 1955, p. 32.

36. In addition to string theory, researchers are working on a number of other approaches to the unification of quantum mechanics and general relativity. They include Loop Quantum Gravity, Non-commutative Geometry, Causal Dynamical Triangulations, Group Field Theory, Twistor Theory, Causal Set theory, and others. Source: Anderson, Mark, "Moving Beyond String Theory," Wired, Sept. 26, 2006. http://www.wired.com/science/discoveries/news/2006/09/71828. Last accessed July 2013.

37. Thorne, Kip. *Black Holes & Time Warps: Einstein's Outrageous Legacy* (New York: W. W. Norton, 1994), p. 525. String theory or some other quantum gravity theory may shed light on other open issues in modern physics, including: (1) the physics behind inflation, or some other explanation for the uniformity and flatness of the universe, (2) why there is so much matter and so little antimatter in the current universe, (3) what gives neutrinos their particular masses, (4) why the 18 or 19 fundamental parameters of the Standard Model are the values they are, and why there are three families of fundamental particles with their particular masses, (5) why the strong interaction parameter is so small, (6) why gravity is so weak compared to the other forces, and (7) why the cosmological constant has its particular value (predictions based on vacuum energy are at least 55 orders of magnitude higher than the observed value.) Source: Michael Dine, "String Theory in the Era of the Large Hadron Collider," *Physics Today*, December 2007.

38. A number of possible tests of string theory have been suggested. See for example: Pavlak, A. and McDonald, K. "Physicists Develop Test for 'String Theory'," physorg.com, January 2007, http://phys.org/news88786651.html. Last accessed July 2013; Atkinson, N., "Method to Test String Theory Proposed", *Universe Today*, January 2008, http://www.universetoday.com/12615/method-to-test-string-theory-proposed/. Last accessed July 2013; Borland, J., "Physics Prof Proposes String Theory Test (But It'll Cost Us)," Wired Science, January 2008. http://www.wired.com/wiredscience/2008/01/physics-prof-pr/. Last accessed July 2013.

   Recent Planck Space Telescope observations show "unexplained features" in the Cosmic Microwave Background "at large angular scales which do not match" the standard model of cosmology. These include asymmetry in average temperatures in opposite hemispheres, and a large cold spot. Some astrophysicists propose this is evidence for multiple universes predicted by string theory. Source: "Planck Reveals an Almost Perfect Universe," Planck Space Telescope, European Space Agency, Mar. 21, 2013. esa.int, http://www.esa.int?Our_Activities/Space_Science/Planck/Planck_reveals_an_al most_perfect _Universe. Last accessed Aug. 2013; Math.columbia.edu, "Not Even Wrong, A Tale of Two Oxford Talks." http://www.math.columbia.edu/~woit/wordpress/?p=5966. Last accessed Aug. 2013.

   Based on the Planck data, other physicists suggest the geometry of the universe may be slightly open rather than flat. Source: Cowen, Ron. "Universe may be curved, not flat," Nature.com, Sept. 20, 2013. http://www.nature.com/news/universe-may-be-curved-not-flat-1.13776. Last accessed October, 2013.

Notes to Appendix A

1. Leighton, R., *Principles of Modern Physics* (New York: McGraw-Hill Education, 1959), p. 9. For a derivation of the Lorentz transform from the light postulate, see Leighton, p. 7–9.

2. Time dilation, length contraction and combining velocities formulas are given in Einstein, Albert *Relativity, The Special and General Theory: A Popular Exposition* (New York: Crown, 1956), p. 39, 85–87; McFarland, Ernie. *Einstein's Special Relativity: Discover it for yourself* (Toronto: Trifolium Books, 1997), p. 3, 67–68.

Notes to Appendix B

1. Taylor, Edwin F. and Wheeler, John Archibald. *Spacetime Physics: Introduction to Special Relativity — Second Edition* (New York: W. H. Freeman and Company, 1992), p. 11–12.

Notes to Appendix C

1. Here mass, energy, and momentum are all given in "mass" units, e.g. kilograms. The speed of light, c is a constant; so is used as a conversion factor. For example; momentum, p in kilogram-meters per second divided by c in meters per second gives p in kilograms. Similarly, energy, E in joules (kilogram — meters^2 per second^2) divided by c^2 in meters^2 per second^2 gives E in kilograms. Source: Taylor, Edwin F. and Wheeler, John Archibald. *Spacetime Physics: Introduction to Special Relativity — Second Edition* (New York: W. H. Freeman and Company, 1992), p. 203.

Notes to Appendix E

1. Kaku, Michio. *Einstein's Cosmos: How Albert Einstein's Vision Transformed our Understanding of Space and Time* (London: Phoenix, 2005-pbk), p. 72.
2. At the time, Einstein was still considering the curvature due to time warp only. He mistakenly thought the inclusion of space warp would result in "particles with different velocities falling with different accelerations", so he excluded it. This omission led to incorrect predictions for the perihelion shift of Mercury and the bending of light in a gravitational field. In addition, Einstein had yet to realize the Metric Tensor cannot be defined *before* the Energy Tensor is established; thus the multiple solutions issue. He resolved these problems over the next several months and produced his final field equations in December, 1915. Source: Ohanian, Hans C. *Einstein's Mistakes: The Human Failings of Genius* (New York: Norton, 2008), p. 197–198.
3. Ibid., p. 216.
4. Stachel, John. *Einstein from 'B' to 'Z'* (Boston: Birkhäuser, 2001), p. 231.
5. Based on Schutz, Bernard. *Gravity from the Ground Up* (Cambridge, England: Cambridge University Press, 2003), p. 231–237.
6. Ohanian, Hans C. *Einstein's Mistakes: The Human Failings of Genius* (New York: Norton, 2008), p. 226.
7. Derivations for these equations can be found in Schutz, Bernard. *Gravity from the Ground Up* (Cambridge, England: Cambridge University Press, 2003), p. 235.
8. Ibid.

Figure Credits

Figure	Credit	Page
A. Einstein	In Public Domain. Use of Einstein images with permission of Greenlight LLC	Cover
Figure 1.1	Image courtesy of ETH-Bibliothek Zurich, Image Archive	7
Figure 1.2	Image courtesy of ETH-Bibliothek Zurich, Image Archive	8
Figure 1.3	The three images in Public Domain	10
Figure 1.4	Image courtesy of Sophia Rare Books (http://www.sophiararebooks.com/). Copyright © 2009–2013 Sophia Rare Books. All rights reserved	13
Figure 2.1	Alien cartoons courtesy of Microsoft PowerPoint® Clip Art	19
Figure 2.3	From Universe, 6/e by Freedman and Kaufmann ©2002 by W.H. Freeman and Company. Used with permission	27
Figure 2.4	Based on figure courtesy of NASA	28
Figure 3.1	Image courtesy of AIP Emilio Segre Visual Archives	35
Figure 3.3	Rocket cartoon courtesy of Microsoft PowerPoint® Clip Art	40

Figure	Credit	Page
Figure 5.1	Image courtesy of ETH-Bibliothek Zurich, Image Archive	58
Figure 6.4	Truck cab cartoon courtesy of Microsoft PowerPoint® Clip Art	71
Figure 6.7	Based on image in Public Domain	78
Figure 6.8	Based on image in Public Domain	79
Figure 6.9	Image courtesy of ETH-Bibliothek Zurich, Image Archive	81
A. Einstein	Cartoon courtesy of Sidney Harris	93
Quarks	Cartoon courtesy of Microsoft PowerPoint® Clip Art	102
Figure 7.7	Image courtesy of Archives Curie et Joliot Curie, Paris. ©Musée Curie (Coll. ACJC)	104
Doc. Brown	Image and quote with permission of Universal Studios, UniversalClips.com	109
Figure 8.1	Image courtesy of ©Bettman/CORBIS	112
Figure 8.4	Clocks, rulers cartoons courtesy of Microsoft PowerPoint® Clip Art	115
Figure 8.6	Image in Public Domain	123
Figure 8.7	Tree cartoon courtesy of Microsoft PowerPoint® Clip Art	124
Cruise Flyer	Cartoons courtesy of Microsoft PowerPoint® Clip Art	135
A. Einstein	Image courtesy of ETH-Bibliothek Zurich, Image Archive	147
Figure 10.1	Cannon cartoon courtesy of Microsoft PowerPoint® Clip Art	152
Figure 10.2	Image courtesy of NASA	153
Figure 10.3	House cartoon courtesy of Microsoft PowerPoint® Clip Art	155
Figure 10.4	Alien cartoons courtesy of Microsoft PowerPoint® Clip Art	158
Figure 11.2	High rise cartoon courtesy of Microsoft PowerPoint® Clip Art	175

Figure	Credit	Page
Figure 11.3	Tower image in Public Domain, photographed by Lubos Motl	177
Figure 11.4	— Hydrogen Maser Clock image courtesy of Finmeccanica Inc. — Rocket launch image courtesy of Brian Lockett, Air-and-Space.com	178
Figure 11.6	Euclid image in Public Domain	184
Figure 13.2	Image courtesy of AIP Emilio Segre Visual Archives	200
Figure 13.3	Gauss and Riemann images in Public Domain	201
Figure 13.4	Potato image courtesy of Designs By Rain	203
Figure 13.5	Potato image courtesy of Designs By Rain	204
Figure 13.6	Trampoline and bowling ball cartoons courtesy of Microsoft PowerPoint® Clip Art	209
A. Einstein	Image in Public Domain	215
Figure 14.3	Image courtesy of AIP Emilio Segre Visual Archives	222
P. Einstein	Pauline Koch Einstein image courtesy of The Granger Collection, New York	233
Figure 15.2	Inspired by Figure 8.1 in *Was Einstein Right?* by Clifford M. Will. Available from Basic Books, an imprint of the Perseus Books Group. Copyright © 1986	236
Figure 15.3	— Quasar-galaxy illustration from *The Riddle of Gravitation* by P. G. Bergmann by Dover Publications, 1993 — Einstein Ring courtesy of L. J. King (U. Manchester), NICMOS, HST, and NASA — Einstein Cross courtesy of NASA, ESA, and STScI	240
Figure 15.4	Based on image in Public Domain	241
Figure 15.7	Image courtesy of ESO New Technology Telescope, La Silla, Chile	245
Figure 15.9	Basic figure from *Unveiling the Edge of Time: Black Holes, White Holes, Wormholes* by John Gribbin by Three Rivers Press, 1994. With permission of David Higham Associates, London	247

Figure	Credit	Page
Figure 15.10	Figure from *Unveiling the Edge of Time: Black Holes, White Holes, Wormholes* by John Gribbin by Three Rivers Press, 1994. With permission of David Higham Associates, London	248
Figure 16.1	— Galaxy images courtesy of NASA — Hubble image is reproduced by permission of The Huntington Library, San Marino, California	253
Figure 16.2	Courtesy of the Archives, California Institute of Technology	254
Figure 16.4	Image courtesy of NASA/JPL	262
F. Zwicky, V. Rubin	Images courtesy of AIP Emilio Segre Visual Archives	264
A. Einstein	Image courtesy of AIP Emilio Segre Visual Archives	276

ALSO BY IRA MARK EGDALL

UNSUNG HEROES
of the UNIVERSE

The story of six individuals who — despite extraordinary achievements in quantum mechanics, general relativity, astronomy, cosmology, and space exploration — remain for the most part unknown to the general public:

- *Georges Lemaître* — A Catholic priest who discovered the expansion of the universe two years before Edwin Hubble, Monsignor Lemaître also proposed our universe began with a "primal atom" — what we now call the big bang.
- *Fritz Zwicky* — This cantankerous astronomer discovered dark matter, supernovae, neutron stars, galactic cosmic rays, and galaxy clusters.
- *Henrietta Swan Leavitt* — Hired as an unpaid volunteer to catalogue star images at Harvard Observatory, her ground-breaking discovery was the stepping stone to the 20th century cosmology revolution.
- *Pascual Jordan* — This unheralded physicist invented quantum field theory, the most accurate and strangest theory in the history of science.
- *Alexander Friedmann* — The brilliant Russian mathematician showed our cosmos could have begun in a singularity — an infinitesimally small point containing the entire universe.
- *Joseph Kittinger* — In an act of courage beyond all sanity, "try any-thing" Joe became the first human in space.

Unsung Heroes of the Universe is an eBook available on Amazon.com and Smashwords.com.

Further Reading
In order of easier to more difficult

Walter Isaacson, *Einstein, His Life and Universe* (New York: Simon & Schuster-pbk, 2008).
— A complete and excellent biography of Albert Einstein. A fascinating read.

Brian Greene, The *Elegant Universe, Superstrings, Hidden Dimensions, and the Quest for the Ultimate Theory* (New York: Vintage Books-pbk, 2000).
— A brief chapter on special relativity and one on general relativity from the master of popular science writing. Both are excellent. Detailed explanation of string theory.

Brain Greene, *The Fabric of the Cosmos: Space, Time, and the Texture of Reality* (NewYork: Vintage Books-pbk, 2005).
— A wonderful presentation of our latest understanding on the nature of time, quantum theory, relativity, and the cosmos.

Richard Wolfson, *Simply Einstein: Relativity Demystified* (New York: Norton, 2003).
— One of the best expositions on special relativity for the lay reader. One chapter on general relativity. Entertaining, lucid, and well-organized.

Lewis Carroll Epstein, *Relativity Visualized* (San Francisco: Insight Press, 1997).
— Thought-provoking visual presentation of spacetime and general relativity. Fun diagrams and paper exercises clarify basic principles.

Michio Kaku, *Einstein's Cosmos: How Albert Einstein's Vision Transformed Our Understanding of Space and Time* (London: Phoenix-pbk, 2005).
— Well-written presentation on the development of special and general relativity, including interesting biographical information on Einstein.

Banesh Hoffman, *Relativity and Its Roots* (Mineola, NY: Dover-pbk, 1983).
— Primarily a book on special relativity, but does provide key insights into the development of general relativity. Includes the simplest explanation of the metric tensor I have found.

Edwin F. Taylor and John Archibald Wheeler, *Spacetime Physics: Introduction to Special Relativity* (New York: W. H. Freeman and Company, 1992).
— Modern view of special relativity starting from the unity of spacetime. This superb text has become a standard for introductory physics courses (some mathematics).

John Archibald Wheeler, *A Journey into Gravity and Spacetime* (New York: Freeman, 1990).
— A wonderful non-mathematical explanation of gravity as curved spacetime. Clear explanations of free float frames and the local nature of gravity. A joy to read.

Albert Einstein, *Relativity, the Special and General Theory: A Popular Exposition* (New York: Crown, 1956).
— Step-by-step explanation of special relativity by the master himself. Somewhat old-fashioned, but one gets the thrill of reading about relativity in Einstein's own words.

Bernard Schutz, *Gravity from the Ground Up* (Cambridge, England: Cambridge University Press, 2003).
— A great book. Takes a middle course between a popular science book and a text. Explains general relativity with mathematics at the basic algebra level. Includes some astronomy.

Lillian Lieber, *The Einstein Theory of Relativity* (Lieber Press, 2007).
— A charming and informative exposition on the application of tensors to Einstein's theory of general relativity. Lots of math, but practically explained.

James B. Hartle, *Gravity: An Introduction to Einstein's General Relativity* (New York: Addison Wesley, 2003).
— Excellent text on general relativity for advanced undergraduate physics majors. Introduces tensor mathematics.

Wolfgang Rindler, *Essential Relativity: Special, General, and Cosmological* (London: Springer-Verlag, 1977).
— Classic special relativity, general relativity, and cosmology text for advanced undergraduate physics majors. Introduces tensor mathematics.

Index

absolute rest frame 32, 38–9
absolute space 81, 118, 134, 236–7
    and rotating bucket 237
absolute time 71, 81
accelerating rocket ship 159, 161,
    188–90
acceleration:
    definition of 21, 141–2, 147, 151
    and twins paradox 133–4
    in zero gravity 154–62, 165–70,
        189–93
    1-g 155, 158–9, 161, 188
accelerators. *See* particle accelerators
accretion disk. *See* black holes,
    accretion disk
action at a distance 24, 146, 229, 272
adding speeds. *See* speeds, combining
aether. *See* ether
alien abduction test 157–62
alpha magnetic spectrometer 264
Alpher, Ralph 257–9
altitude:
    and warping of space 196–7
    and warping of time 139–40,
        175–83, 196
Ampère, André-Marie 25
Andromeda galaxy 17, 252, 258
angular momentum 244
Annalen der Physik (Annals of
    Physics) ix, 9, 12–3, 83, 110, 231
anomalies 11, 142, 146, 231

antimatter 101, 128
antiparticles 100
any reference frame will do 204–5,
    223, 236
Apollo 15 152
Aristotle 152
Arkani-Hamed, Nima 95
Aspect, Alain 272
Atkinson, Robert 105
atomic bomb 95, 274
atomic clocks. *See* clock, atomic
atomic energy 98
atoms 12, 24, 26, 43, 63, 103, 105–6,
    110, 185, 258, 261, 270–1
    nuclei 61, 95, 103–4, 106, 258
Aurivillius, Christopher 270
Australian National University 264

Bailong elevators 162–3
barn-pole paradox. *See* pole-barn
    paradox
basketball and geodesic. *See* geodesic,
    and basketball
BEC (Bose-Einstein condensates)
    270
Becquerel, Henri 11
Belenkiy, Ari 253
bending of light:
    in a gravitational field 169,
        232–35
    See also gravitational, lensing

Berlin   ix, 220–1, 273
   University of   220
Berne   3, 9, 11, 110–1
big bang theory   x, 249, 257, 259,
   262
   cosmic microwave background
   and. *See* CMB
big crunch   260
binary pulsars (X-ray pulsars)   42
binary stars   40–2
black holes   x, 101, 140, 229, 241,
   243–5, 266–7
   accretion disc   244
   event horizon   242–3
   evidence for   244
   formation of   101
   jets   245
   mass of   242–4
   singularity   242–4
   supermassive   244–5
   and time   x, 140, 241–2
blue-shift   167, 182
Bodanis, David   95, 106
Bohr, Neils   100, 275
BOOMERANG   262
Born, Max   112, 169, 187
Bose-Einstein condensates. *See* BEC
Boylai, Farkas   201
Boylai, Janos   201
braking distance   91–2
Brecher, Kenneth   42
Brownian motion   12–3
bucket of spinning water.
   See Newton's bucket

Campbell, William Wallace   235
cannon ball, falling   152
Cartesian coordinates. *See* coordinates,
   Cartesian
causality   183
Cepheid variable stars   251–2
CERN   42, 63, 90, 133

chain reaction. *See* nuclear chain
   reaction
Christoffel, Elwin   218
Chu, Steven   178
circumference of circle
   in rotating disc   247
   surrounding Sun   247
classical physics   10–1, 36, 92
clock:
   atomic   5, 63, 134, 139–40, 168,
      173, 177–8
   light. *See* light clock
   in rockets   5, 63, 134, 139
   in satellites   5, 134, 139
   in space   57, 59, 61, 66
   universal   71
   See also warping, of time
CMB (cosmic microwave
   background)   17, 257, 259, 261–2
Cockcroft, John Douglas   104
CoGent   264
Colorado State University   63
Columbia University   273
combining speeds. *See* speeds,
   combining
compass   6
   and magnetic field   22–3
concave water surface   236, 238
conflict:
   between Newton's law of gravity
      and special relativity. *See*
      special relativity, Newton's
      theory of gravity vs.
   between Newton's laws of
      motion and Maxwell's
      theory   11, 32–3, 45
conservation of   25, 88–9, 99, 215–6,
   224, 227, 229
   energy   99, 215–6, 224, 227, 229
   mass-energy   99, 215–6, 224,
      227
   momenergy   227, 229

momentum   88–9, 215–6, 224,
    227, 229
constant light speed   31
constant velocity motion. *See* motion,
    uniform
continuum, spacetime. *See* spacetime,
    continuum
conversion, matter/energy   95,
    98–101, 104, 106
coordinates:
    Cartesian (equally-spaced)   196,
        209
    continuously-changing
        (Gaussian)   197, 203
    and principle of general
        covariance   205, 215–6, 219,
        222, 224, 229
    spacetime   124, 198, 227
Copernicus, Nicolaus   18, 141, 234,
    253
cosmic gravity wave
    background   241
cosmic microwave background.
    See CMB
cosmic rays   61, 89
cosmological constant   250–1, 255,
    265–6
    and dark energy   265
Coulomb, Charles Augustin de   25
covariant, covariance   205, 215–6,
    219, 222–4, 229, 235–8
critical density   261, 263–5
Crommelin, Andrew   232
Curie, Marie   104, 149–50, 162
Curtis, Heber   252–3
curvature:
    Einstein equation and. *See* general
        relativity, Einstein equation
    of space   140, 195, 207–8, 211–2,
        227–30, 246, 261–2
    See also geometry of universe;
        spacetime curvature

curvature tensor   219, 226–7, 229,
    250
curve of least effort   210
curved spacetime   211, 226
curved surface geometry.
    See geometry, curved surface

DAMA (dark matter
    experiment)   264
Daredevil Dave   76, 78
dark energy   248, 265–7, 276
dark matter   248, 263–5, 267, 276
    evidence for   263
    possible make-up of   264
de Sitter, Willem   40–2
    star experiment   41–2
density, mass/energy/
    momentum   226–8
Descartes, René   21
diameter   133, 184–5, 198, 202, 247
    of circle surrounding Sun   185,
        246–7
Dicke, Robert   259
dictum, Galileo's. *See* Galileo's dictum
differential geometry. *See* geometry,
    differential
dimensions:
    in space   112, 114, 197
    in spacetime. *See* spacetime, four-
        dimensional
Dirac, Paul   100, 102
disc, spinning. *See* spinning disc
distance:
    braking   91–2
    contraction of, in special
        relativity. *See* length contraction
    and time   51, 82, 96, 115–6, 119,
        139, 190–1, 195–6
    warping of, in general relativity.
        See space, warping of
Doppler effect   64, 166
double star system. *See* binary stars

dynamic universe. *See* universe, dynamic

Earth:
    equatorial bulge of   142
    tides of   142
    warping of time due to   139–40, 168–9, 175–6, 183, 207–8
    warping of space due to   140, 196–7, 207–8, 247
eclipse, solar. *See* solar eclipse
$E = mc^2$ ix, 1, 82–4, 92, 95, 98–9, 100–6, 273
    applies to all forms of energy   98–9
    as $E = m$ 95–6
    evidence for   104–5
    1905 paper   92–5
    and Sun   105–7
Ehrenfest Paradox   169–71
Einstein Cross   240
Einstein equation/field equations   226–8, 250. *See also* general relativity, Einstein equation
Einstein Ring   239–40
Einstein, Albert:
    birth   6
    college years   7–8
    and empiricism   30, 38, 80–1, 153–4
    and EPR paradox. *See* EPR paradox
    "greatest blunder".
        See cosmological constant
    in gymnasium   6–7, 35, 221
    in Italy   35–6
    1905 papers   12, 38–40, 42–5, 66–7, 83, 92, 110, 112
    1916 paper   223–4
    Nobel Prize   148, 269, 270
    and nuclear weapons   273–4
    at patent office   3, 8–9, 11, 32, 43, 58, 80, 83, 110, 147–8, 154, 199
    and unified field theory   270, 275
    See also general relativity; photoelectric effect; special relativity
Einstein, Eduard   148, 222, 271
Einstein, Elsa Löwenthal   221, 271
Einstein, Hans Albert   9, 11, 222, 224, 271, 273
Einstein, Hermann   6, 9
Einstein, Maja   6–7, 9, 273
Einstein, Mileva Marić   148, 221, 269, 271
Einstein's epiphany   154–5, 176
Einstein-Grossmann approach.
    See Entwurf theory
Einstein-Szilárd letter   274
electric:
    charge   24–6, 61, 100
    current   22–3
    field   22–3, 26–7
electricity:
    and magnetism   7, 10, 22, 24–6
    static   24
electromagnetic (EM) 26, 28, 37, 103
    field   26
    radiation   26, 28
    theory   10, 27, 83
    waves   10, 26–7, 32, 37, 47, 168
electrons   24, 26, 61, 89, 102–3, 105–6, 228, 258
elevator falling to Earth   165, 167
elevator light experiment   162–9
ellipse   217, 223
EM radiation   26–8, 99, 101, 247
embedding diagrams   245–8
energy:
    chemical   99, 105
    conservation of   99, 215–6, 224, 227, 229

conversion of. *See* conversion,
  matter/energy
density   183, 225–6, 228, 242,
  250, 260–5
  frozen   96, 139
  kinetic   84, 90–4, 103
  and matter   266
  and momentum   215, 224, 227–9
  Newtonian   216
  non-material   96, 98–9, 101, 103,
    146, 185, 225, 227–8
  relativistic   90–1, 94, 97–8, 215,
    224, 227
  total   97, 99
energy of motion   90, 92. *See also*
  energy, kinetic
entanglement, quantum   272–3, 276
Entwurf theory   219–20, 222–3
EP. *See* equivalence principle
EPR paradox   272
equations of general relativity   216,
  238, 240, 248, 259. *See also* general
  relativity, Einstein equation
equivalence principle (EP)   162
escape velocity   216–17, 228
ETH. *See* Zurich Poly
ether   11, 30–3, 38–9, 43, 46–7
Euclid   183–4, 204
Euclidean geometry   60, 169–70,
  183–4, 187, 198–203, 205, 209–10, 218
event horizon   242–3
events:
  simultaneous   66, 67–74
  in spacetime   114, 116, 119, 122,
    205
everyday speeds   5, 50–1, 64, 72, 75
expansion of space. *See* universe,
  expansion of
experimental evidence for:
  bending of light (in gravitational
    field)   232–4
  big bang   258–9

black holes   244–5
Bose-Einstein condensates   271
dark energy   248, 264–7, 276
dark matter   248, 263–4, 267, 276
$E = mc^2$ 82–4, 92–5, 98–106,
  273
expansion of universe. *See*
  universe, expansion of   253–5
flat universe. *See* universe, flat
frame-dragging   238–9
Galileo's principle (of falling
  bodies)   153
gravitational lensing   239–40
gravitational redshift/time
  dilation   176–9
light postulate   40–2
quantum entanglement
  (non-local)   272–3
space warp   185
time dilation   60–3

falling cannon ball. *See* cannon ball,
  falling
falling objects   151–3, 189
Faraday, Michael   23, 25
Father of Spacetime   111–2
Fermi, Enrico   274
Feynman, Richard   173
field:
  electric   22–3, 26–7
  gravitational   153–9, 166–76,
    189–99, 205–9, 218–30
  magnetic   22–4, 26–7, 112
field equations of general relativity.
  See general relativity
fishnet over potato   203–4
Fitzgerald, George   43, 80
Fomalont, Edward   235
Ford, W. K.   263
forgive us, Sir Isaac   232
four-dimensional spacetime   123,
  187, 211

frame dragging   140, 237–8
frame of reference. *See* reference
   frame.
free-fall   154–7, 162, 164–6, 192, 197,
   211–2
free-float   155–6, 164–5, 167, 188, 193,
   197–8, 211, 230
free-float frames, local   193, 197–8, 230
frequency of light   27–8, 166–8,
   176–7, 243
Friedmann, Alexander   253, 256
frozen energy. *See* energy, frozen
fusion. *See* nuclear fusion
future of universe. *See* universe, future of

galaxy   134, 185, 207, 240, 244–5,
   252–3, 255–6, 259, 263, 266
   distance measurements   254
   redshift observations   254
galaxy clusters   134, 255–6
Galilean transform   22, 29, 42, 45
Galileo Galilei   9–10
Galileo's dictum (on uniform
   motion)   18, 21–2, 29, 32, 36, 42,
   44–7
Galileo's principle (of falling
   bodies)   151, 153, 155, 159, 161–2
gamma rays   28
Gamow, George   257–8
Gauss, Karl Friedrich   200–5, 212,
   218, 220
Gaussian coordinates. *See* coordinates,
   continuously changing
Gaussian metrical coefficients   204,
   206
general covariance, principle of. *See*
   principle, of general covariance
general relativity:
   conservation of mass-energy
      and   224
   conservation of momentum
      and   87, 89, 216

einstein equation   226–8, 250
equivalence principle and.
   See equivalence principle
   evidence for   147, 152, 157,
      159–63, 166, 169–71, 174–6, 187,
      189, 192, 196, 224
   field equations of   224, 230, 246
   goals of   215, 229
   manuscript of   231
   Newton's theory of gravity
      and   142–3, 185, 217, 232
   predictions of   140, 177, 237, 241
   spacetime curvature and   134,
      140, 194–5, 199, 201, 203, 205,
      207–13, 215, 218–9, 222, 225–35,
      238–9, 242–4, 250–1, 260–4
   and time travel. *See* time travel
   warping of spacetime and.
      See warping, of spacetime
GEO   240
geodesic   184, 210–11, 226
   and basketball (free-fall
      path)   211–12, 226
geometry:
   curved surface   201, 204–5, 210, 212
   differential   200, 202, 218, 222
   Euclidean   60, 169–70, 183–5,
      187, 198–203, 205, 209–10, 218
   Non-Euclidean   198–200, 202,
      205, 210, 218
   plane   60, 183, 185, 204
   of universe   260–5
global positioning satellites
   (GPS)   178
global region of spacetime   187, 192,
   198
gluons   102
Gonzales, Antonio   275
Göttingen, University of   202, 219
Gravesande, Willem 's   91
gravitational:
   collapse   229

constant   153, 226, 250, 265
lensing   140, 239–40, 263
red-shift   167, 177, 180–1, 242,
   255
time dilation   166, 169, 176–80,
   183
waves   140, 239–40, 266
gravitational disturbances   143,
   145–6, 217
gravitational field:
   global   198, 230
   inverse square law and   144
   mass and   94, 96
   uniform   156
gravitational field equations   218,
   222, 224
gravitational lensing   140, 239–40,
   263
gravitational time dilation   166, 169,
   176–80, 183
gravitational waves   240, 266
gravity:
   as illusion   212
   instantaneous   151, 230
   relativistic theory of   147, 150–1,
      202, 215, 222, 230
   sources of   96, 185, 215, 227–8
   speed of   143–6, 230, 240–1
   strength of   146, 190
   transmission of   146, 230
   weak   152, 183, 215–7, 224
Gravity Probe B satellite   239
gravity waves   140, 239–41
Greenwich Observatory   178
Grossman, Marcel   150, 199–200, 219

Habicht, Conrad   80–1, 105, 275
Hafele, Joseph   177
Hahn, Otto   273
half-life   61–2
Hall, David   60–2
Haller, Friedrich   148

hammer and feather (Moon drop)
   152–3
hand-clap events   119
Hartle, James   203
Harvard College Observatory   251
Harvard Tower Test   176
Harvard University   177
Hawking radiation   266
Hawking, Stephen   241, 266
helium, nuclei   106, 258
Herman, Robert   258
Hertzsprung, Ejnar   251
Hilbert, David   219–20, 224
Hobson, Art   96, 103
Hooker Telescope   252
Hubble, Edwin   253–5
Hubble's Law   255–6
Humason, Milton   255
Hume, David   81
hydrogen:
   nuclei   106, 258
hyperspace, dimension of   246

inertia   20–1, 83, 85, 92, 94–6
   law of   21
inertial balance scale   85–6
infinity. See universe, infinite
inflation theory   262–3, 267
instantaneous gravity   151, 230
Institute of Theoretical Physics
   (Princeton, NJ)   149
interior angles of triangle   198
invariance, invariant   43, 118, 153–4
inverse square law. See gravitational
   field
Italy   35–6, 221, 240, 251, 264

javelin   52–4
jets, black hole. See black holes, jets
Johns Hopkins University   265
Judaism   7
Jupiter   66, 114, 135, 142

Kaivola, Matti   63
Kaku, Michio   83
Keating, Richard   177
Kelvin, Lord   10
kinetic energy   84, 90–4, 103

laboratories, two identical   44–5, 141
large hadron collider (LHC)   90
Larmor, Joseph   32
laser, beam   52–3, 163–8
Laub, Jakob   148
Laue, Max von   111
law of inertia   21
Lawrence Berkeley National
   Laboratory   264
laws of motion (Newton)   20, 45
laws of physics:
   for uniform motion   3–4, 11,
      15–22, 24, 29, 30, 32, 37–8, 42–7,
      59, 65, 67, 71, 75, 118–9, 122–4,
      130, 139, 141, 144, 155, 162,
      191–2, 195–6, 204–5, 227, 235
   for non-uniform motion   4, 192
Leavitt, Henrietta Swan   251
Leavitt's Law   251–2
Leibniz, Gottfried   82, 91–2
Lemaître, Georges   253–7
length contraction:
   and special relativity   ix, 49–51,
      65–6, 74–6, 115, 121, 126
   and general relativity (space
      warp)   169–70, 195, 230
Lick Observatory   235
light:
   bending of, in gravitational
      field   169, 232, 235
   energy of   90, 93–4, 97, 102, 167
   ether and   31
   frequency of   28, 166–8, 176–7,
      180, 242–3, 258
   and gravity   162, 239, 270, 276
   high-energy   258

   nature of   95, 269
   as particle   12, 96, 100–1, 148
   spectrum   28, 167, 254
   speed of. See speed of light
   transmission of   11, 38, 46
   visible   27, 101–2
   as wave   30, 37
   See also electromagnetic (EM)
light clock   57–60, 166
light postulate   38–40, 42, 46, 59
light quanta   148–9
light wave. See electromagnetic (EM),
   waves
light year   96, 118, 127, 129–31, 157,
   207, 240, 251–2, 260, 262, 272
LIGO (laser interferometer
   gravitational wave
   observatory)   240
Little Miss Muffet   236
Lobachevsky, Nikolai   202
local spacetime region   187
Lorentz, Hendrik   43–4, 46–7, 80, 233
Lorentz contraction. See length
   contraction
Lorentz factor   50–1, 57, 64–5, 75–6,
   89–90, 97, 126, 128, 131
Lorentz transform   43–51, 53–4, 60,
   118, 120–2
   equations of   60, 121–2
   and Maxwell's equations   43–4
Löwenthal, Elsa. See Einstein,
   Elsa Löwenthal
luminiferous ether. See ether
luminosity. See stars, luminosity of

Mach, Ernst   81
magnetic field   22–7, 112, 245
magnetism   7, 10, 22–7, 29, 46, 270
magnets   23–4, 26, 133
Manhattan Project   274
manifesto, counter-manifesto
   (WWI)   221

mapping spacetime. *See* spacetime, mapping
Mars, Marsmart 123, 126–7
mass:
of black hole 242–4
and energy equivalence 94–5, 107
as source of spacetime curvature 228
total body 103–4
mass density 228
mass threshold 102
Massachusetts Institute of Technology (MIT) 105
mass-energy:
conservation of 99, 215–16, 224, 227
equivalence 83, 94–6, 113, 107, 228
inclusion in momenergy 226–7
spacetime grips 225
mass-energy density 183, 225, 242, 250, 260–2, 265
critical 261, 263–5
infinite 242
of universe 250–1, 257, 260–2, 265
mass-energy relationship 84, 92–104
massive stars, very 229
matter:
invisible. *See* dark matter
movement of 225, 228
ordinary 263–5
matter particles 96, 100–2, 104
MAUD Report 274
Max Planck Institute for Nuclear Physics 63
Maxwell, James Clerk 9–10, 13, 25–7, 29–30, 32–3, 37, 44
Maxwell's equations 7, 10, 26, 29, 31–2, 37, 42–5, 47, 93
Maxwell's theory of electromagnetism 10, 25, 27, 30

mechanics, science of 9–10, 21–2, 38, 45, 89
Mercury's orbit, perihelion 147, 217–18
metric:
in general relativity 204, 206–7, 227, 250, 256
in Newtonian physics 115
in special relativity 116, 119–20, 134
metric tensor 227, 250
Michelson-Morley experiment 11, 32, 38, 43
microwave background radiation. *See* CMB
microwaves 28, 258
Mileva Marić. *See* Einstein, Mileva Marić
Milky Way galaxy 17, 30, 32, 250, 252–3, 255
Minkowski diagram. *See* spacetime diagram
Minkowski spacetime interval equation 118
Minkowski, Hermann 82, 110–4, 116–23, 125–6, 134, 175, 185, 187, 198
Miss Muffet. *See* Little Miss Muffet
molecules 12, 24, 61, 103, 185, 228
momenergy 226–9, 250
momenergy tensor 226–9, 250
momentum:
angular 244
conservation of 89, 216
density 228
inclusion in momenergy 226–9
Newtonian 88–9, 216
relativistic 89–90, 97, 215, 224, 227
as source of spacetime curvature 227–9, 238

Moon   74, 84–7, 142, 152–3
motion:
    accelerated   85
    disc's   169
    laws of (Newton)   21, 24, 146
    moving clock's   59
    moving laboratory's   141
    non-uniform   4, 192
    in principle of relativity.
      See relativity postulate
    quark   103–4
    uniform   3–4, 15–22, 24, 29–30,
      37–8, 42–7, 59, 65, 118–19, 122–
      4, 139, 141, 191–2, 195–6, 204–5
Mount Neutron   179–83
Mount Washington   61–2
Mount Wilson   252, 255
muons   60–3, 101, 133–4

NASA   153, 245, 262
    Jet Propulsion Laboratory
      (JPL)   153
National Bureau of Standards
    (US)   178
natural path. *See* geodesic
nebulae   252–3
Neptune   142
neutron star   228, 243–4
Neutronium   179–80, 183
neutrons   103–4, 106, 228, 258, 273
New York Times   234
Newton, Isaac   9–11, 13, 20–1, 25,
    229–31
    absolute space and   46, 81, 115,
      195, 236–7
    absolute time and   46, 53, 64, 71,
      81, 115, 143, 168, 195
    inverse square law and   146
Newton's bucket   236–38
Newton's law of universal
    gravitation. *See* Newton's theory of
    gravity

Newton's laws of motion   21–2, 24,
    45, 50
Newton's theory of gravity   142–4,
    146, 153, 185, 215–7, 229–34
    issues with   142–147, 229–30
Newton's universe   168, 226, 228
Newtonian Limit   216
Nobel Prize   148, 269–70
Non-Euclidean geometry.
    See geometry, Non-Euclidean
non-material energy   96, 98–9, 101,
    103, 146, 185, 225, 227
now, relativity of   73–4
nuclear chain reaction   273–4
nuclear fission   273–4
nuclear forces, fields   103, 244
nuclear fusion   106
nucleus, atomic. *See* atoms, nuclei

observable universe   245, 253, 261–3,
    265
    flat   261–5
Olympia Academy   81, 105, 202, 275
orbit:
    elliptical   17, 217–8, 223
Ørsted, Hans Christian   22–3, 25
oscillation, period of   86–7
outer space, zero gravity of   154–7,
    159, 168, 189, 193, 228

painter falling from a roof   154
paradox:
    Ehrenfest. *See* Ehrenfest paradox
    twins. *See* twins paradox
    pole-barn. *See* pole-barn
      paradox
parallax and star distance   251
parallel lines meet on sphere   183–4
parallel universes   260–1
parallelogram   203–4
Parker, Candace   211, 226
particle accelerators   63, 89, 101

particle decay 61
particles:
    and antiparticles 100
    electric charge of 61
    of light. *See* photons
    mass of 102, 104
    massless 65
    transformation of. *See* particle
        decay
    as waves 26
patent office 3, 8–9, 11, 32, 43, 58, 80,
    83, 110, 147–8, 154, 199
path:
    curved 164–5, 210–2
    geodesic 184, 210–1, 226
    shortest 183–4, 210
Peierls, Rudolf 274
pen:
    and length contraction 5
    and stretching due to
        gravity 140
Penrose, Roger 247, 264
Penzias, Arno 258–9
perihelion of Mercury 217, 223, 231
period of oscillation 86–7, 252
Perlmutter, Saul 264–5
personal reference frame. *See*
    reference frame, personal
Peters, Achim 178
photoelectric effect 11–3, 111, 148,
    270
photons ix, 58–60, 65–6, 96, 100–2,
    104, 106, 114, 143, 164–5, 258–9, 270,
    272
    energy of 100–2, 106, 258
    in light clock 59
    and zero mass 96
    and photoelectric effect.
        See photoelectric effect
    See also light
physics in 1900 8–10, 32, 46
picturing spacetime 113

picturing spacetime curvature 209
Planck, Max ix, 10, 12, 28, 111, 141,
    149, 220–1, 232, 234
Planck's constant 28, 232
plane geometry. *See* geometry, plane
Pluto 142
Podolsky, Boris 272
Poincaré, Henri 46, 80, 149, 187
polarization 112, 272
pole-barn paradox 75–80
positron 100–1
postulates 35, 46, 67, 71, 83, 265
potato surface 203–4
Pound, Robert 176–7
Prague 149–50, 221
precession:
    of Mercury 142, 217–8. *See also*
        perihelion of Mercury
    of planetary orbits 140, 142
present, relativity of 57, 73
pressure 228–9, 243, 250
Principe, Gulf of Guinea 232–3
Principia (Newton) 10, 146
principle:
    of equivalence. *See* equivalence
        principle
    of falling objects. *See* Galileo's
        principle
    of general covariance 205,
        215–16, 219, 222, 224, 229, 235
    of relativity 46, 141–2, 150, 235
privatdozent 147–8
proper time 125, 129, 211, 226
proton-proton chain 106
protons 61, 90, 100, 103–4, 106, 228,
    258
Prussian Academy of Sciences 220,
    223–4
pulsars 42
Pythagorean theorem 60, 118

quantization of light 111, 270

quantum:
  entanglement   272–3, 276
  gravity   149, 244, 270, 276–7
  mechanics/physics   10–12, 100,
    149, 244, 267, 270–2, 276–7
quarks   102–4
quasar   239–40, 244–5

race car:
  and length contraction   51
  and time dilation   47–51
radiation:
  electromagnetic   26, 28, 95
  primordial. *See* CMB
radio interferometry   235
radioactive   94–5, 105, 176
  decay   95, 105
  iron   176
radioactivity   11, 94, 169
radius:
  of rotating disc   169–70
ratio of circumference to diameter:
  on sphere   184
  of Sun   185, 246–7
Rebka, Jr., G. A.   176
Reciprocal Lorentz Factor   64–5, 90
red-shift. *See* gravitational, red-shift
reference frame:
  definition   20
  personal   124–6, 157, 238
  and principle of general
    covariance   205, 215–6, 229,
    235–7, 258
region, local   206, 230
relativistic:
  energy   90–1, 94, 97–8, 215, 224,
    227
  mass   89–91, 97–8, 100, 215, 224,
    227
  momentum   89–90, 97, 215, 224,
    227
  quantum mechanics   100

speed   5, 49, 53, 65, 74–5, 89, 91,
    97–8, 127, 133–5, 151, 228, 230,
    232
velocity combining   52–6
relativity:
  of motion   3, 5, 20, 22, 45, 116,
    141, 144, 169, 224, 235
  of now   73–4
  of simultaneity   66–73, 79–80
  of space   12–13, 67, 74, 82, 84,
    107, 112, 116, 140, 170, 185, 191,
    197, 229–30, 247
  of time   3, 12, 57, 60, 63, 66, 72–3,
    81–2, 95, 110, 134–5, 139–40,
    168, 178, 196
  See also special relativity; general
    relativity
relativity papers. *See* Einstein, Albert,
    1905 papers, 1916 paper
relativity postulate   44–6, 65, 69, 162,
    204
relativity theory. *See* special relativity;
    general relativity
rest energy   96–8, 228
rest frame, absolute   16, 20, 30, 32,
    38–9, 46, 236
Ricci curvature tensor   219
Ricci scalar   227
Ricci-Curbastro, Gregorio   218–19
Riemann tensor   219
Riemann, Georg Bernhard   200–3,
    205, 212, 218, 220
Riess, Adam G.   264–5
Rocket Clocks   177–8
rocket length   75
rocket time   63, 65, 135
Roosevelt, Franklin Delano   x, 273–4
Rosen, Nathan   272
Rossi, Bruno   60, 62
rotation:
  and bucket. *See* Newton's bucket
  frame dragging and   237–9

Royal Greenwich Observatory   178
Royal Society, London   234
Rubin, Vera   263–4
Rumi, Jalal ad Din   15
Russell, Bertrand   211
Rutherford, Ernest   105, 149
RV (recreation vehicle)   29

's Gravesande, Willem.
    See Gravesande, Willem 's
Sammy surface   179–83
satellite   5, 28, 134, 139, 178, 239
    GPS   178
Schmidt, Brian   264–5
Schutz, Bernard   226
Schwarzschild solution   242–4, 246–7
Schwarzschild, Karl   241–4, 247
shape of universe. See universe,
    geometry of
shortest path   183–4, 210
shrinking of space. See length
    contraction
signing ceremony   68–74, 80
simultaneity, relativity of   66–74, 79
simultaneous events   66
singularity   242–4, 253, 259–60
    in big bang   253, 259–60
    in black hole   242–4
Sitter Star experiment   41–2
Sitter. See de Sitter, Willem
Slipher, Vesto   252–4
Sloan Digital Sky Survey   266
Smith, James H.   60–2
Smithsonian Astrophysical
    Observatory   177–8
Sobral, Brazil   232–3
solar eclipse   140, 185, 232–3, 235
Solovine, Maurice   80–1, 105, 275
Solvay Conference (1927)   149, 254
space:
    absolute   46, 81, 115, 195, 198,
        236–7

concept of   3, 81, 107, 109–10
curvature of   208, 212, 227, 246,
    261
effect of motion on. See length
    contraction
expansion of   140, 253–6, 257–9,
    261–2, 264–6
flat   183, 193, 209–10, 246, 261–3
infinite   250, 258, 261
meaning of   81–2
relativity of. See length
    contraction; warping, of space
rest frame, absolute   32, 38–9
rotating object drags   238
shape of. See universe, geometry of
stretching of   140, 171, 208, 247,
    256
travel through   125, 143, 210, 240
warping of   170–1, 185, 208, 232
space interval   82, 116–26, 129, 139,
    191–2, 197–8, 205–7
Space Telescope Science
    Institute   264–5
spaceship, alien   19–20, 157–8
spacetime   107, 109–34, 139–40,
    185, 187–8, 190–8, 205–12, 218–19,
    225–30, 238–40, 242–4, 247–8, 250–1,
    260–4
    continuum   109, 112, 187, 206
    coordinates   114, 124, 195, 198,
        227
    four-dimensional   123, 187, 206,
        211
    geometry   118, 139, 187, 198,
        205–6, 210–12, 218, 222, 260–1
    local region of   187–8, 193, 206,
        210
    mapping   205–6
    mass-energy grips   225
    mathematics of   112, 134
    warping of   185, 187, 192, 197–8,
        207–8, 212

spacetime coordinates   114, 124, 195,
  198, 227
  continuously-changing   198
spacetime curvature   134, 140, 193–5,
  207–13, 215, 218–19, 222, 225–30,
  235, 238–9, 242–4, 250–1, 260–4
  as gravity   134, 140, 195, 207–8,
    209–12, 215, 225, 227–30, 238–9,
    244, 251.
  infinite   242
  intervening galaxy's   239–40
  picture   209
  source of   228–9, 238
  universal   261
  zero   261–2
  See also general relativity,
    spacetime curvature and
spacetime curvature distorts
  spacetime   230
spacetime diagram   113–4, 118–9,
  125, 128, 196
spacetime event   242
spacetime as fabric   109–10, 195,
  209–10, 230, 240
spacetime interval:
  absolute   118, 134
  and acceleration   191
  calculated   117
  changing   207
  in general relativity   205
  generalized   206–7
  global change in   192–4, 198,
    206–8, 212, 219, 227
  local   198, 206, 227
  mathematics of   123, 134, 185,
    198
  timelike   118
  warping of   185, 192, 198, 207–8,
    212
spacetime interval equation   118–9,
  122, 125, 129–30, 191
  generalized   206–7, 227

spacetime, propagation of   210,
  229–30, 240
spatial dimensions. See dimensions,
  in space
special relativity:
  and absolute spacetime.
    See spacetime interval
  combining speeds in. See speeds,
    combining
  and $E = mc^2$. See $E = mc^2$
  and length contraction. See length
    contraction
  and light speed. See speed of light
  and Lorentz factor. See Lorentz
    factor
  and Lorentz transform. See
    Lorentz transform
  manuscripts   13
  Newton's theory of gravity
    vs.   142–7, 151, 153, 168, 183,
      185, 195–6, 207, 212, 215–18,
      223–4, 226, 228–42
  and quantum mechanics   11,
    100, 179
  and spacetime. See spacetime
  and spacetime interval. See
    spacetime interval
  and time dilation. See time
    dilation
  and time travel. See time travel
  and twins paradox. See twins
    paradox
speed of light:
  absolute nature of   26–32, 36–42,
    47, 65, 72, 96, 118
  accurate value of   37
  equal to one   95–6
  evidence for its constant
    velocity   40–2
  and general relativity   143–5,
    151, 154, 210, 216–7, 230,
    255–6

and light postulate. *See* light
postulate
as maximum speed through
space 36–42, 52–5, 65, 89–90,
97–8
and Maxwell's electromagnetic
theory 10–1, 26–32, 36–42
and relativity principle.
See relativity postulate
and speed of gravity (spacetime
curvature) 143–5, 230, 240
as universal speed limit 55, 97–8
speeds, combining 52–6
formula 55
sphere:
and non-Euclidean
geometry 183–4
hollow, in frame-dragging 238
pinch-off. *See* event horizon
spinning bucket. *See* Newton's bucket
spinning disc 169–70
starlight, bending of 223, 232–3, 239
stars:
binary. *See* binary stars
brightness of 245, 251–2
Cepheid variable 251–2
collapsing 228–9, 244, 247
luminosity of 245
nuclear processes in core of 101
See also supernovae
static electricity 24
static universe. *See* universe, static
stitching spacetime 187–94, 195, 204,
227, 230
string theory 276–7
strong nuclear force 276
Sun:
and bending of starlight.
See starlight, bending of
curves spacetime 210
and $E = mc^2$ 105–7
gravity of 149, 232–3

mass-energy of 208, 210, 247
scattering of photons from core
of 106
statistics of 105–6
time on surface of 228
superCDMS 264
supernovae 101, 114, 179, 241
and black hole formation 244
and dark energy discovery 265
and neutron star formation 244
surface of Earth analogy 193
Surface Sammy 179–83
Swiss Federal Polytechnical Institute.
See Zurich Poly
Szilárd, Leó 273–4

Talmud, Max 7, 183
Taylor, Edwin 115, 132
Teller, Edward 273
tense 73–4
tensor 219, 226–9, 250
test of. *See* experimental evidence for
theory of relativity:
special. *See* special relativity
general. *See* general relativity
Thirring, Hans 238
Thomson, J. J. 234
Thorne, Kip 80
thought-experiment 75
time:
absolute. *See* absolute time
and black holes 241
concept of 3, 81, 107, 109–10
dilation. *See* time dilation
effect of motion on. *See* time
dilation
everyday experience and 5,
139–40
as fourth dimension 112–14, 123
in general relativity 109, 205
and light clocks. *See* light clock
Newtonian 45, 64, 68, 115, 195, 212

as proper time. *See* proper time and slowing of with relative motion. *See* time dilation and space unification. *See* spacetime in special relativity. *See* time dilation warping of, in general relativity. *See* time dilation, gravitational travel through   125, 143, 247
time dilation   ix, 48, 51, 57–66, 115–6, 126–135, 166, 169, 174, 176–183
   gravitational   166, 169, 176–80, 183
time interval   48–51, 63–5, 82, 87, 115–27, 129, 139, 182, 191–2, 205–7, 227
Time magazine   xii
time travel   109, 132, 179–80, 182–3
   with altitude   179–80
   into future (special relativity)   109, 131–2
   into past and future (general relativity)   181–3
   See also wormholes
time zero, of big bang   259
Times of London   12, 234
Tina Top   180–3
Tom Thumb   236–7
Toronto, University of   235
trampoline   209–10, 230
transform   61–2, 100–1
   Galilean. *See* Galilean transform
   Lorentz. *See* Lorentz transform
transmission of gravity. *See* gravity, transmission of
triangle   118–9, 183–4, 198, 202
   interior angles of   183–4
Turner, Michael   265
twins paradox   127–34
Tyson, Neil deGrasse   102

Ullmo, Jean   57
ultraviolet light   11
unequally spaced coordinates. *See* coordinates, continually changing
unification:
   of electromagnetism and gravity. *See* unified field theory
   of quantum mechanics and general relativity. *See* quantum, gravity
   of space and time   112–3
unified field theory   270, 275
uniform motion. *See* motion, uniform
uniformly moving ship   18, 45
universal speed limit. *See* speed of light, as universal speed limit
universe:
   accelerated expansion of   265–6
   critical density of   261–5
   dynamic   253–6
   evolution of   140, 225, 249, 259
   expansion of   x, 140, 253–6, 259–62, 264–6
   finite   248, 257–8, 261–2
   flat   261–2
   future of   248, 249–50, 260–7
   geometry of   139, 259–65
   infinite   250, 258, 261
   mass-energy density of   250, 261, 265
   multiple universes   276
   origin of   140, 225, 249, 259. *See also* big bang theory
   static   250–1, 253
   visible   245, 263–5
University of Berlin   111, 220
University of Chicago   60, 265, 274
University of Colorado   247, 271
University of Göttingen. *See* Göttingen, University of
University of Zurich   110, 148
uranium   11, 95, 273–4

vacuum 28, 30, 37–40, 42, 146, 152, 195
velocity 4, 37, 50–1, 53, 88–92, 174,
192, 251, 255
relative 50, 93, 97, 120–1
Venus 223
verification of. *See* experimental
evidence for
Verrier, Urbain Le 142
very long baseline array 235
VIRGO 240
visible universe 245, 263–4
visualizing spacetime diagrams 113,
119
Vulcan 142

Wallal, Australia 235
warping:
of space 170–1, 173, 183, 185,
187, 191, 197, 232
of spacetime 134, 192–3, 196–8,
207–8, 210, 212, 223, 238. *See
also* spacetime curvature
of time 168, 173–4, 178–9, 182,
185, 187, 191, 232, 246. *See also*
gravitational, time dilation
wave:
electromagnetic 28, 32, 47.
See also electromagnetic (EM),
radiation
frequency of 27–8, 101, 163,
166–8, 176–7, 180, 242–3, 254,
258
sound 30
wave, light. *See* electromagnetic (EM),
waves
wavelength 27, 166–7, 258
weak gravity 216–17, 224, 229
Weber, Heinrich 8
weight:
vs. mass 84–7
as mostly energy 102–4

weightless 154–6, 158, 164, 166
Wheeler, John Archibald 115, 132,
209–12, 225, 242, 260
wherewhen 113–4
white holes 267
Wieman, Carl 271
Wigner, Eugene 273
Wilczek, Frank 102
Williams, J. G. 153
Wilson, Robert 258–9
WIMPs (weakly interactive massive
particles) 264
WMAP (Wilkinson microwave
anisotropy probe) 263
world-line 125–6, 128–9
World War I x, 221, 241, 269
World War II 274–5
wormholes x, 140, 245, 247–8
wristwatch time 123–5, 129–31,
211, 226

X-rays 28, 102

Year of Einstein 12–3
Young Albert Einstein 8, 36, 183

Zaslaw twins 84, 127
zero curvature 260
zero gravity 84, 154, 156, 159, 165,
167, 170, 190, 243
Zurich 7, 11, 113, 149–50, 218, 221–2,
271
University of. *See* University of
Zurich
Zurich Poly (Swiss Federal
Polytechnic Institute) 7–8, 80, 107,
111, 150, 195, 199, 220
Zwicky, Fritz 263–4